The Urban Context

Ethnicity, Social Networks and Situational Analysis

Edited by
Alisdair Rogers and Steven Vertovec

BERG PUBLISHERS

Oxford/Washington D.C., USA

First published in 1995 by
Berg Publishers Limited
Editorial offices:
150 Cowley Road, Oxford, OX4 1JJ, UK
13590 Park Center Road, Herndon, VA22071, USA

Library of Congress Cataloging-in-Publication Data
A catalogue record for this book is available from the Library of
Congress.

British Library Cataloguing in Publication Data
A catalogue record for this book is available from the British
Library.

ISBN 0 85496 317 0 (Cloth)
      1 85973 072 8 (Paper)

Printed in the United Kingdom by WBC Book Manufacturers,
Bridgend, Mid-Glamorgan.

Contents

List of Figures

List of Tables

List of Contributors

Muhammad Anwar is Professor at the Centre for Research in Ethnic Relations, University of Warwick and formerly Senior Research Officer, Commission for Racial Equality. He is the author of *The Myth of Return: Pakistanis in Britain* (Heinemann, 1979) and *Race and Politics* (Tavistock, 1986), as well as co-editor (with P. Werbner) of *Black and Ethnic Leaderships in Britain* (Routledge, 1991).

David Boswell is Senior Lecturer in Sociology, Faculty of Social Science, The Open University. He has done extensive fieldwork in South Central Africa and Malta, and is co-editor (with J. Clarke) of *Social Policy and Social Welfare: A Reader* (Open University Press, 1983).

Gary Bridge is a lecturer at the School for Advanced Urban Studies, University of Bristol. He has researched gentrification and class in London and acts as a consultant on matters of urban policy.

Margaret Grieco is Professor of Sociology, University of Ghana, Accra, and has held visiting fellowships in Oxford, Finland and Amsterdam, among other places. She is author of *Keeping it in the Family: Social Networks and Employment Chance* (Tavistock, 1987) and *Workers' Dilemmas: Recruitment, Reliability and Repeated Exchange* (Routledge, 1992), co-editor (with L. Pickup and R. Whipp) of *Gender, Transport and Employment* (Avebury, 1989) and has published widely on transport, employment and related policy issues.

Kayleen Hazlehurst is a Senior Lecturer in the Faculty of Arts, Queensland University of Technology, Brisbane, and was formerly a Senior Criminologist with the Australian Institute of Criminology, Canberra. She has researched in Canada, New Zealand and Australia, and is the author of *Political Expression and Ethnicity: Statecraft and Mobilisation in the Maori World* (Praeger, 1992) and *Racial Conflict and Resolution in New Zealand* (Australian National University, 1988) and the editor of *Ivory Scales: Black Australia and the Law* (University of New South Wales, 1987).

Peter Jackson is Professor of Geography, University of Sheffield. He is author of *Maps of Meaning: an Introduction to Cultural Geography* (Unwin Hyman, 1989), co-author (with S.J. Smith) of *Exploring Social Geography*, editor of *Race and Racism* (Allen & Unwin, 1987) and has written numerous articles on social and cultural geography in the UK, the USA and Canada.

Bruce Kapferer is Professor and Chair of Anthropology, University College, London. He is the author of *Celebration of Demons: Exorcism and the Aesthetics of Healing in Sri Lanka* (Indiana University Press, 1983, republished by Berg, 1991), *Legends of People, Myths of State: Violence, Intolerance and Political Culture in Sri Lanka and Australia* (Smithsonian, 1988) and *Strategy and Transaction in an African Factory* (Manchester University Press, 1972).

J. Clyde Mitchell is Emeritus Fellow of Nuffield College, Oxford University, and formerly Professor of Sociology at Manchester University, as well as Director of the Rhodes-Livingstone Institute, Salisbury (now Harare), Southern Rhodesia (now Zimbabwe). He is the author of *Cities, Society and Social Perception* (Clarendon, 1987), editor of *Social Networks in Urban Situations* (Manchester University Press, 1969) and co-editor (with J. Boissevain) of *Network Analysis: Studies in Human Interaction* (Mouton, 1973).

Chris Pickvance is a Professor and Director of the Urban and Regional Studies Unit, University of Kent, Canterbury. He is the editor of *Urban Sociology: Critical Essays* (Tavistock, 1976), and co-editor (with M. Gottdiener) of *Urban Life in Transition* (Sage, 1991), and (with E. Preteceille) of *State Restructuring and Local Power* (Pinter, 1991). He is also an editor of *The International Journal of Urban and Regional Research*.

Alisdair Rogers is a College Lecturer in Geography at Keble and St Catherine's Colleges, Oxford University. He is co-editor (with M. Keith) of *Hollow Promises: Rhetoric and Reality in the Inner City* (Mansell, 1991).

Susan Smith is Ogilvie Professor of Geography, Edinburgh University. She is the author of *The Politics of 'Race' and Residence* (Polity, 1989) and *Crime, Space and Society* (Cambridge University Press, 1986), as well as co-author (with P. Jackson) of *Exploring Social Geography* (George Allen & Unwin, 1984) and (with D. Clapham and P. Kemp) of *Housing and Social Policy* (Macmillan, 1990).

Steven Vertovec is Principal Research Officer at the Centre for Research in Ethnic Relations, University of Warwick. He is author of *Hindu Trinidad: Religion, Ethnicity and Socio-economic Change* (Macmillan, 1992), editor of *Aspects of the South Asian Diaspora* (Oxford University Press, 1991) and co-editor (with C. Clarke and C. Peach) of *South Asians Overseas: Migration and Ethnicity* (Cambridge University Press, 1990).

Pnina Werbner is Senior Lecturer at the Department of Sociology and Social Antrhopology, Keele University. She is author of *The Migration Process: Capital, Gifts and Offerings Among Pakistanis in Britain* (Berg, 1990) and co-editor (with H. Donnan) of *Economy and Culture in Pakistan: Migrants and Cities in Muslim Society* (Macmillan, 1991) and (with M. Anwar) of *Black and Ethnic Leaderships in Britain* (Routledge, 1991).

Introduction

Alisdair Rogers and Steven Vertovec

The essays in this volume contribute to current debates in social and cultural studies of urban environments by combining insights from a range of disciplinary perspectives. Since the 1970s, many of the most important contributions within the field of urban studies have been the result of such interdisciplinary efforts. Yet such approaches have developed with the growing awareness that attempts to establish single-discipline-based, universal definitions of 'the city' and 'urban social behaviour' are misplaced. This is partly due to the fact that analysts from various disciplines are likely to 'select from the total set of diacritical features of the city those which are theoretically pertinent for analysis in terms of a specific discipline,' (Mitchell, 1987, p.20). Mitchell goes on to observe that:

> The most we can do is to establish types of cities with similar basic demographic, geographic, and economic characteristics ... and then specify the urban contexts implied by these characteristics. Having specified the context, the task of interactional urban sociology is to state explicitly the assumptions about the way in which these characteristics are likely to bear upon the social behaviour of the inhabitants of these towns. When this is done we may then try to verify and elaborate these assumptions by analysing social behaviour in specific situations. (1987, p.21)

This contextual and situational approach advocated by J. Clyde Mitchell represents an analytical, middle-ground mode of inquiry which is flexible enough to accommodate the interests of anthropologists, geographers, sociologists and others. It is an approach which informs the contributions to this volume, which are made by researchers from several disciplinary backgrounds.[1]

1. All the contributors were at one time colleagues or students of J. Clyde Mitchell in either Africa or the UK. Some of the essays in this volume were first presented at a symposium held in honour of Mitchell's retirement at Nuffield College, Oxford University in July 1986. The editors wish to acknowledge the College's assistance and encouragement in holding this event. They also acknowledge the contribution of Peter Hayward to the redrafting and improving of maps and diagrams.

The chapters' geographical settings range from New Zealand and
Australia to Los Angeles and New York, the Scottish borders to
Malta, and the hop-fields of Kent to the UK inner city. Most share
Mitchell's own concern with ethnicity, which he interpreted as a
particularly urban phenomenon. Yet his techniques and ideas are
also amenable to the analysis of class and gender, interests pursued by several chapters, sometimes in combination with ethnicity. Others focus on forms and processes of urbanisation and the
cultural construction of the built environment itself. In methodological terms, they include ethnographic and mathematical
analyses, often together. What connects these diverse interests is
a family of methodologies and insights – comparative analysis,
case study, situational analysis and social networks – each of
which was developed and extended by Mitchell and his colleagues in South Central Africa and beyond. The essays both
draw from and add to a contextual and situational perspective on
urban phenomena. Together, the authors attest to the continuing
fascination with the 'urban' despite the many intellectual obituar-
ies pronounced over it.

Anthropology, Geography and Urban Studies

If there is a common origin to urban studies then it must be the
Chicago School, whose influence is acknowledged by anthropology, geography and sociology. Setting aside antecedents in
Durkheim, Weber and Marx, it was the writers associated with
Park, Burgess and Wirth who provided both the intellectual
grounds for a distinctive urban enquiry and the associated methods. Thus, while Peach (1975) can identify Park's essay on 'The
urban community as a spatial pattern and moral order' as the
'fountainhead' of a spatial sociology-cum-social geography,
Jackson and Smith (1984) find inspiration in both the ethnographies of Chicago and the pragmatic philosophy of Dewey, James
and others for their revisionist social geography. Both approaches showed a concern for the intra-urban relationships between
social relations and spatial forms.

     The intellectual innovations of the Chicago School also pro-
foundly influenced the broad area of study which came to be
called urban anthropology (Hannerz, 1980; Howe, 1990). Its models of human ecology and equilibrium representing urban spatial

and social relationships were drawn upon and elaborated by anthropologists with respect to a variety of intensive field studies in non-Western settings. Urban anthropology's early concerns and debates, which especially surrounded the so-called rural–urban continuum, drew centrally upon such models to outline and describe the kinds, sources, and manifestations of discontinuity between village and city environments (a field of inquiry epitomised by Redfield, 1941, and shared in sociology by Pahl, 1968).

Akin to, and growing out of, the debates over rural–urban criteria in anthropological analysis, the quest for adequate comparative typologies of cities came to exercise anthropologists for decades (see especially Fox, 1977; Redfield and Singer, 1954; Sjoberg, 1960). Not far removed from these typological inquiries, commencing mainly in the 1950s there was an increasing interest in processes of urbanisation. This topic was understood to be initiated by the migration of peoples from rural to urban areas, or by larger structural changes taking place throughout the whole of a society. Studies of urbanisation included examination of many kinds of change surrounding social structures and social institutions, interpersonal ties, ethnic or tribal identities, and the roles of formal associations (e.g. Forde, 1956).

Yet many anthropologists gradually withdrew their attention from questions of what constituted the nature of different kinds of cities and how previously rural people adapted to them, to questions surrounding what kind of social phenomena lay within cities. Hence urban anthropology came to be more 'in the city' than 'of' it, with the city itself becoming 'the locus rather than the focus' of study (Hannerz, 1980, p.3; Mitchell, 1987, pp.22–3). Urban anthropology thus evolved into a multifarious set of ethnographies about subjects such as ethnic migrants, ghetto populations, urban subcultures, and poverty-induced socio-cultural adaptations (e.g., respectively, Mayer, 1961; Hannerz, 1969; Spradley, 1970; Lewis, 1966). Although some anthropologists were highly critical of such a disparate range of studies characterising the field (Fox, 1972), others saw such a development as logical – in that anthropology's traditional methods of intensive small-scale study were being maintained in more complex and encompassing settings – and as good – in that anthropology's long-time obsession with non-literate, rural or tribal non-Western peoples was being displaced in favour of studies concerning peoples and places of virtually limitless scope. Similar developments happened in geography, where, for example, Herbert and Smith (1979) downplayed the specifically urban in their review of social problems in cities. In the same vein, Saunders (1985a; 1985b) confidently announced the death of urban sociology following its failure to discover a social process which corresponded absolutely with a spatial form. Freed from the shackles of defining the 'urban', sociology and geography could address pressing social problems or even advance a new field: the sociology of consumption (Saunders, 1985a). A notable exception was the attempt by Harvey (1985) and other Marxists to revive the urban process under the rubric of a spatialised political economy.

Nevertheless, through the 1980s, urban anthropology remained no less disparate and wide-ranging, while many of its key focuses were expanded yet further. In that decade:

> an urban anthropology broader than that of the 1950s–1970s [made]
> headway with issues of grassroots politics, evolving ethnic ideolo-
> gies, religious ferment, women's situations, the changing organiza-
> tion of work, youth and popular cultures, and the effects of world
> economic dynamics on migration and urban efflorescence and disin-
> vestment. (Sanjek, 1990, p.173)

In sociology and geography also, the fascination with the urban has not diminished and is indeed subject to a re-enchantment. This involves a proliferation of themes and theories which mark a renewed, though more nuanced, attention to the relationship between urban settings, social behaviour and cultural meaning. These include an interest in contemporary processes such as globalisation, creolisation, empowerment and the transformation wrought by new information technologies (Castells, 1989; Cohen and Fukui, 1993). The connections between modernity and the city are being re-examined and the genesis of urban theory is being pushed backwards into the mid-nineteenth century (Berman, 1983). This involves for example, a reappraisal of Simmel, Benjamin and Freud on the one hand (e.g. M.P. Smith, 1980) and Baudelaire and the French Impressionists on the other (Clark, 1985). There is also a critical feminist angle on modernity which has revealed the gender-related assumptions implicit in both definitions of modernity and the city (Wilson, 1991) The 'postmodern turn' attracts advocates and critics alike back to the past and forward towards the future of the city and the need to discover new 'cognitive maps' of social life (Jameson, 1984; see also Harvey, 1989). Others have revived earlier debates on urban life, social justice and the cultural differentiation of the public sphere in search of guidelines to changed times (e.g. Young, 1990). What is perhaps worth noting about many of these interventions is that they are concerned with finding a place for culture alongside the established tenets of political economy, spatial analysis and sociology. A *rapprochement* of anthropology with its cognate disciplines is surely apparent here. Altogether, the urban stubbornly refuses to acknowledge reports of its demise and, if anything, finds itself thrust towards the centre of end-of-century debates on global–local relations, citizenship, new economic regimes and cultural experience.

Amidst this revival, part of the discussion has moved towards means of operationalising new insights. The clearest illustration of this is the debate surrounding the various localities programmes which engaged UK social scientists in the 1980s (Cooke, 1989; see also exchanges in the journals *Antipode*, 1987 onwards, and *Environment and Planning A*, 1991). Locality, generally urban, was the proving ground of epistemological exchanges over realism, structuration and postmodernism, but it also raised fundamental questions of method. Notwithstanding considerable developments in theory, method and areas of study, within anthropology and geography serious problems of conceptualisation, abstraction, scale and inference remain. Often such problems have precluded the possibility of interdisciplinary exchange and analysis. While we cannot address all these issues, we can hope to indicate how a situational approach, after Mitchell, represents a resolution of at least some of them. Further, although it was conceived and developed in socio-economic and intellectual circumstances which differ from those extant today, the situational approach continues to have considerable methodological value with respect to new and changing areas of anthropological and geographical study. The contributions to this volume demonstrate such.

Situational Analysis

The situational approach to urban social behaviour emerged out of the Rhodes-Livingstone Institute and what is known as the Manchester School of anthropology, under the tutelage of Max

Gluckman (Werbner, 1984; see also Chapter 2 in this volume). Central to their concerns was the analysis of social problems in 'a total society' or overarching 'social field': in the period of its most influential work (1940s–1960s), this was operationalised particularly in studies of tribal peoples adapting to conditions of migration, industrialisation, urbanisation, and colonial domination (e.g. Epstein, 1958; Mitchell, 1956; Southall, 1961). Yet the scholars of this emergent social scientific tradition recognised that no single researcher could account in depth for the entire range of phenomena encompassing the issue under study. Hence, much thought went into methodological questions involving the isolation or 'circumscription' of research topics and units of analysis, modes of interconnection between 'domains' of human activity, and orders or levels of theoretical abstraction.[2]

In keeping with these methodological concerns, situational analysis *per se* has been codified by Mitchell (1966; 1983; 1987), but its origins can be traced to Gluckman's account of the opening ceremony for a bridge in Zululand (1958, originally published in 1940). Using this event as a starting point he unpacks the nature of African social and cultural life within the context of white colonial domination, showing how elements in the wider social order are expressed by way of those in the situation. In addition to Mitchell, other anthropologists of the Manchester School extended and refined the method (Garbett, 1970; Van Velsen, 1967). Victor Turner's *Schism and Continuity in an African Society* (1957), which examines through the concept of 'social drama' the ways in which social realities are manifested in times of crisis, is perhaps the foremost example of such extension and refinement.

In brief, situational analysis can be defined as: '[T]he intellectual isolation of a set of events from the wider social context in which they occur in order to facilitate a logically coherent analysis of these events' (Mitchell, 1987, p.7). The aim is therefore to isolate a small set of social actions for intensive analysis, and to achieve this circumscription in a logically meaningful manner which makes possible an understanding of the larger context (see Chapter 2). To do so requires that the analyst identifies and specifies several different levels of abstraction which are not reducible

---

2. These subjects, among others, were outlined in the famous 'Salisbury seminars' and discussed in the groundbreaking volume entitled *Closed Systems and Open Minds* edited by Gluckman (1964). See also Southall (1961) and Mitchell (1966).

to each other but which stand in a logical and reflexive relation to one another. Each level is given its own analytical space, so to speak, and the strength of situational analysis lies in their combination as opposed to their reduction to a single order of reality.

There are three epistemologically distinct components of the social structure to be specified (Mitchell, 1987, p.9). The first is a *set of events*, activities, or behaviour which the analyst has some theoretical justification for regarding as both a problem and logically interconnected in some way. The second component or *situation*, which distinguishes situational analysis from Gluckman's original formulation, consists of the meanings which the actors themselves attribute to the event or activities. These may be specific to the occasion, subject to negotiation or contestation among the actors and may include the study of symbolic construction. Lastly, there is the *setting* or the structural context within which behaviour occurs, and this is an analytical construct not necessarily shared by or known to the actors themselves. Mitchell (1987, p.17) summarises the procedure as follows:

> The setting and situation, therefore, stand in a reflexive relationship to one another. I mean by this that an analyst wishing to interpret a specified type of behaviour in a town needs to work with two different referents simultaneously. The first of these is an appreciation of the set of circumstances in which the actors are placed and which determine the arena within which the analyst postulates the behaviour must take place. The second is an appreciation of the set of meanings the actors themselves attribute to the behaviour. The analysis then consists of an interpretation in general theoretical terms of the behaviour as articulated both with the setting and with the actors' cognitive definition of the situation.

He goes on to argue that there is no universal set of contextual parameters which are apposite to every situation, but that they must be re-specified on each occasion.

What then constitutes the urban context relevant to situational analysis? It is generally accepted that there can be no universal definition of the urban across all cultures and economies such as those postulated by Wirth and the modernist theorists. This does not mean, however, that there is no value in identifying specifically urban conditions as part of a set of contextual parameters. Even size, density and heterogeneity may be appropriate to the context, although they are highly unlikely to exhaust it. Other content definitions of the urban may also be relevant, such as collective consumption, local-level political processes and spatial proximity (Pickvance, 1985). In the case of South Central Africa, which Mitchell describes, they may include geographical mobility, the economic foundations of the town and the mode of production, and the political and administrative framework.

Contextual parameters are elements of an account which the analyst may take as given, usually described by phenomena of a different order to social behaviour itself. They are external, but only in an analytical sense. There is no implication that contextual features are somehow insulated from social action, impervious to change. In his discussion of urban movements, for example, Pickvance (1985; 1986a) notes that the national political context itself may be partly shaped by movements in the past. Their conceptual separation is an analytical necessity rather than a statement about the nature of reality.

There is, however, a problem regarding the exact status and method of specifying context. Mitchell suggests that it may be respecified on each occasion, but for certain purposes this may be counter-productive. The point is well illustrated by an exchange between Pickvance (1985; 1986a) and Castells (1985) over social movements. Castells argues that in *The City and the Grassroots* (1983), contrary to Pickvance's criticism, he did take context into account when judging the relative success of movements, but only those elements of context which had observed effects at the level of the movement itself. By contrast, Pickvance demonstrates that, for the purposes of comparative analysis, the same contextual features must be specified each time on the basis of theoretical judgement rather than observation. The features are not just background, but vital elements of an experimental procedure which require specification so that generalisations about movements can be made. The specification of contextual parameters is therefore an important step in comparative analysis, which is one method of extending the situational perspective. To appreciate the method it is helpful to consider first the related question of making sustainable generalisations or causal statements from limited instances. This is the matter of inference from case studies.

Mitchell (1983; 1987) has examined the method of case study analysis, which Susan Smith (1984a) has recommended as a means of practising humanistic geography. One method of drawing generalisations from limited sets of data is based upon the assumptions of statistical representativeness. This means that the data are selected in such a way that the analyst has good grounds for believing that they are representative of a target population within the assumptions of sampling theory. Such procedures commonly require large data sets such as questionnaire surveys, about which descriptive generalisations may be made.

Florian Znaniecki (1934), however, pointed out that this is only one way of making generalisations, albeit the most pervasive in social science then as now. An alternative procedure is analytical induction or logical inference, in which the sustainability of the conclusions depends not upon the data but upon the logical consistency of the inference or analysis. The success of the method depends upon whether the analyst is able to adduce the necessary linkages among the theoretically significant features in the data (Mitchell, 1987, p.31). The intensive or logical method is relevant to situational analysis. The event or behaviour selected does not have to be typical or recurrent. As Kapferer explains in Chapter 2, it is not a microcosm of a wider social reality, but vital to the construction and reconstruction of embracing realities themselves. Gluckman chose an untypical occasion which had not happened before, for example. The method does, however, place the burden of analysis upon the researcher, in that the data cannot be allowed to just 'speak for themselves'.

The question arises nonetheless, as Chris Pickvance notes in Chapter 1, that it is quite possible to make incorrect inferences from case studies. Mitchell argues that the validity of the results depends upon corroboration rather than replication. They are tested either in different situations or by judgement by the academic community of which the analyst is a member. In this volume, Pickvance and Peter Jackson (Chapter 6) both advocate the former practice – codified as comparative analysis – which, as the former stresses, is much more than a mere juxtaposition of cases. Mitchell (1987, p.244) makes the case for comparative analysis as follows:

> In order to be able to appreciate the regularities in behaviour that may arise in urbanism we need to separate both the city from the social order and the perception from the situation. Recourse to comparison is obviously an aid in achieving this. In principle what is being achieved in comparative analysis is that the manifestation of certain regular relationships among selected theoretically significant

features in two [or more] instances is being demonstrated by showing
how the operation of contextual variations enhances or suppresses
the expected pattern.

In fact, as Pickvance (1986b, p.166) suggests, there are two distinct aims of the method:

[T]o discover whether a theoretically-derived model holds in empirical cases and to see whether an empirically-based relationship
derived from the study of one society holds in another.

It is rare to discover two situations which share the same contextual parameters. It is for this reason that Pickvance (1986b)
outlines three models of comparison, namely single model,
linked sub-model and diverse model approaches. They are each
underpinned by different conceptions of causality and context. In
Chapter 1 Pickvance extends his discussion by drawing on Mill's
distinction between plural causation and the more restrictive universal causation to identify two kinds of comparative analysis.
He suggests that urban theorists have often failed to understand
the difference between them, and therefore have incorrectly used
comparison as a means of adjudicating between rival epistemological claims. The looser form, that based on plural causation,
enables him to explore the causes of UK local government's often
reckless financial dealings with the private sector by reference to
comparable situations in socialist Eastern Europe. The analysis is
based on his participation in the Thanet locality research project.
    Elsewhere, Jackson (1991) has called for a locality research
which is more sensitive to cultural differences and the 'maps of
meaning' constructed around particular places. Although less
explicit in his comparative methodology, in Chapter 6 he deploys
the comparison between arts-related investment in New York
and historic preservation in Minneapolis-Saint Paul to tease out
such place-specific relations between cultural and economic
processes. By engaging in studies of two cases which are similar
in many respects but differ on a few key factors, he is able to pin-
point the role of specific groups and local institutions in the 'manufacture' of meaning-laden landscapes. In doing so, he avoids the
reduction of the cultural to the economic, while remaining
attuned to the peculiarities of place.
    Situational, case and comparative analyses are therefore com-
plementary methods. They each require theoretical judgements

about causality, necessary connections and abstraction. Consequently they are not a rationale for naive empiricism and make great demands of analytical rigour. Several essays in this volume make reference to these methods.

New Contexts and Situations

Gluckman, Mitchell and their co-workers developed situational analysis in a particular context, that of colonial South Central Africa. The salient contextual features included rural-to-urban migration, the incorporation of peasants into capitalist work environments, 'exogenous' urbanisation and the administrative processes of a colonial (and later, independent) state. In the intervening decades the world has turned, although many of these older features survive in combination with newer ones. International migration from colonial periphery to core, such as that of Pakistani migrant workers examined by Anwar (Chapter 9) and Werbner (Chapter 8), has become commonplace. Indeed, with the rise of diasporas, refugees, business elites, expatriate communities and other so-called global cultures (Featherstone, 1990) the very distinction between rural periphery and urban core is being dissolved. As James Clifford remarked (1988, p.22), ethnographies are now written on a moving earth. Such novel cultural and social juxtapositions maintain the need for an urban inquiry sensitive to changing contexts, while also generating new kinds of situation. Both Anwar and Werbner are interested in the transportation of a 'traditional' gift economy into the heart of 'modern' urban industrial social relations, for example.

None the less, Margaret Grieco in Chapter 7 reminds us that the process of labour migration described by Mitchell in Africa was not unknown in the core economies themselves. She outlines a practice which was commonplace in South East England before the Second World War, the annual movement of urban labour to the hop-fields of Kent for the seasonal harvest. Not only were the social networks of streets and neighbourhoods relocated for the season, but urban traders accompanied what she terms 'a moveable community'. This regular translation meant that sections of the urban working class continued to possess, and transmit from one generation to the next, important rural skills. Elements of the urban context were consciously reproduced in rural settings and, being such a regular event, maintained an active interaction between two sides of a dualism usually considered in terms of a linear progression.

A more common theme among the chapters in this volume is the legacy of this initial phase of urbanisation, particularly as it concerns the second generation and beyond. Chapters 8 and 9 on Pakistani migrants both identify the role of family reunification and the birth of children in the adopted country as key moments in the formation of social networks. However, as Anwar (Chapter 9), Hazlehurst (Chapter 3) and Rogers (Chapter 4) note in their contributions, a significant element of this changed context is economic decline and/or restructuring. In her discussion of the urbanised Maori youth, Kayleen Hazlehurst mentions the impact of economic downturn on their radicalisation and the creation of urban gangs which challenged traditional rural-based leadership. Competition for jobs in the restructured urban economy of Los Angeles affects relations between African-Americans and Latinos in Alisdair Rogers's analysis. The fact that there is an ethnic division of labour, and that certain sectors (e.g. public employment) are in retreat while others (e.g. low-wage manufacturing) are advancing, affects the relative employment chances of the two groups. The latter draws in immigrant labour which, in turn, transforms the social geography of urban neighbourhoods and brings the two groups into common social space.

The colonial legacy is never far away. Kayleen Hazlehurst's ethnography of an investiture in New Zealand shows how the granting of honours from a foreign Queen at a ceremony held in a place associated by some with the betrayal of Maoris by the self-same imperial state and its failure to uphold the land rights treaty can cause conflict. In this instance, the actors' different interpretation of events hinges partly on the time-frame in which they are placed. The land rights treaty, the Treaty of Waitangi, took place in 1840. For some the action remains, in a sense, immediate, while for others it belongs to the past and cannot be held to blame for the subsequent ills of the Maori people. The land rights issue is also prominent in questions of Aborigine identity in Australia, as Kapferer's chapter shows. He is also able to find continuities between the bureaucratic orders of colonial Zambia and late twentieth-century Australia. In both cases, the identity of particular groups is highly determined by the state. Susan Smith describes an annual ceremony held in the Scottish border town of Peebles.

Here too, the colonial legacy as revealed in ceremonial objects and the continuation of a racist language which was established in imperial times causes division. The choice of a 'golliwog' as a theme suitable for children's dressing up and the subsequent controversy enables Smith to address the 'common-sense' or taken-for-granted racism present in a local event.

Alongside economic change there has been a restructuring of urban space itself. Western cities are not only the sites of the formation of new immigrant communities, but also of a changed geography of class, gender and culture. Gary Bridge (Chapter 10) addresses the social consequences of one such development, gentrification, by which formerly working-class districts are 'invaded' by the middle classes. Susan Smith (Chapter 5) points out that rural gentrification is also a significant new development. Peter Jackson (Chapter 6) deals with such gentrification in an expanded definition, to include the recycling of the past in new cultural practices and buildings. Such 'invention of tradition', to use the phrase coined by Hobsbawm and Ranger (1983), is in many ways the latter-day equivalent of the *kalela* dance. Urban and rural communities continue to express themselves in parades, carnivals, events and architecture. Thus, Kapferer's Aborigine dance performance, Smith's Beltane festival, Rogers's Cinco de Mayo parade, and Hazlehurst's investiture all contain elements of the past reworked to current interests, thereby raising questions of whose past and whose interests? Both Jackson and Smith suggest the connection of such activities to the changed times of the postmodern, in which a search for authenticity, sense of place, right of belonging and such elements of 'cognitive mapping' (Jameson, 1984) become important. And, as Smith's discussion of the difference between popular carnival and state spectacle demonstrates, it is often difficult to know where to draw the line between cultural practices of resistance and practices geared to perpetuating inequalities in political power. This same distinction between resistance and complicity is also apparent in Kapferer's comparision of two rival dance companies in a small Queensland town, Kuranda. As in Peebles, the question of who can lay the most legitimate claim to authentic identity – in this instance Tjapukai – arises, as does the tension between tradition and innovation. Kapferer is willing to argue that performances and art directed towards tourist audiences may not be a debasement of culture, but rather creative in their own right.

In Mitchell's analysis of the *kalela* dance (1956) he points out
that where the dance takes place is significant to its interpretation. This attention to place, or the geography of the setting, is
also apparent in the essays collected here. The fact that the
investiture ceremony described by Hazlehurst occurs not in
Government House but on a Maori *marae* makes a lot of difference to both the actors present and her own analysis. When
police come onto the *marae* they represent an intrusion of the state
into the sacred space of the Maori nation. The 'mismatch'
between both the Cinco de Mayo parade and the ceremony to
open a park in honour of Martin Luther King and their surrounding neighbourhoods in Los Angeles is a paradox which Rogers
makes central to his interpretation. Why, he asks, does a Mexican
national parade take on the cultural styles of African-Americans?
The route taken by the Beltane riding, as described by Smith,
forms a central element in the event. In both these cases – an area
of Los Angeles undergoing residential succession and therefore
on the social 'borders' of two ethnically-defined territories, and a
border region of Scotland which is at once regarded by its residents as typically Scottish and particularly border-region – there
is more than one level to the geography of the setting. Such a
hierarchy of scale as a component of the context is most evident
in Hazlehurst's chapter, where empire, nation, tribe, urban–rural,
the sacred space of the *marae* and even the placing of the seats and
participants form a nested series of salient geographical facts to
be included in the interpretation. A situational analysis which
attends to the detailed geography of place and to the hierarchy of
scale is therefore a vital ingredient in urban analysis.

As well as literal spaces, two authors discuss space and place
in more metaphorical terms. Kapferer points out that the unstructured situations in which African tribespeople constructed and
reconstructed categorical forms of identity were marginal places
in urban life. Such spaces of leisure find their analogy in the
spaces of tourism of the Queensland town, of which the
Aborigine dance companies make use. Tourist space allows what
would otherwise be marginal to the social and political order to
enter its midst, because the boundaries of the order are relaxed.
Smith's concern with 'places on the margin' is somewhat different. She suggests that in the postmodern world the organisation
of social life may best be grasped by concentrating on what happens at the periphery rather than the core. What Kapferer's con-

tribution indicates is that centrality and peripherality may themselves be contingent. The dance performance, for example, carries added weight because it is part of an Australian National Folk Festival held in the town. Kuranda, like Peebles and Adams-Vermont, becomes a particularly contested region.

Despite their wide range, therefore, certain common themes are evident in the chapters. New rounds of economic, social and spatial restructuring create new sets of contextual features, and the geographical juxtaposition of new communities establishes the context for new situations which are subject to often divergent and contested interpretations by actors. Situational analysis is required not only to unravel such situations, but also to bring into focus the views of both insiders and outsiders.

Social Network Analysis

The second methodological theme integrating these essays is that of social network analysis, in which Mitchell has also been a pioneer (1969; 1973). The chapters by Anwar, Werbner, Bridge and Grieco explore the use of this method in the UK urban context. Hannerz (1980, p.181) has suggested that social network analysis 'probably constitutes the most extensive and widely applicable framework we have for the study of social relations'. It is particularly suited to a situational perspective, since it abstracts those aspects of interpersonal relations which cut across institutions and the boundaries of aggregated concepts such as neighbourhood, workplace, kinship or class. Furthermore, it makes no *a priori* assumptions about the type of relationships an individual is involved with, although, as we shall suggest, it does enable hypotheses about the qualitative nature of urban social relations to be empirically tested.

The use of social network analysis in anthropology has been extensively reviewed elsewhere (Hannerz, 1980; Mitchell, 1974a). As a method of abstraction and analysis it envisages each person as a node linked with others to form a network. The analyst may choose to quantify both the interactional attributes of the linkages and the overall morphological attributes of a network. Mitchell (1969) has codified the language of network terminology and distinguished between its metaphorical and analytical uses. He argues elsewhere (1987) that there now exist sufficient formal analytical principles, drawn particularly from graph theory, to extend its usage beyond metaphorical levels and to assuage critics of the vagueness of its early formulations. There would seem to be at least four reasons for advocating a wider use of network analysis in urban studies.

The first of these reasons concerns the classical views of urbanism put forward by modernist theorists such as Wirth, Park, Tonnies, Redfield and Simmel. One of the legacies of their thinking was the distinction between two kinds of society, variously termed urban and rural, modern and traditional or *Gesellschaft* and *Gemeinschaft* (Pahl, 1968). Although these forms of society were more ideal types than concrete expressions, they tended to resonate with geographical spaces. The city and the countryside were conceived as two different types of society. Wirth and Park went further, and attempted to root particular kinds of social relations in the material or ecological conditions of the city. Yet, as Mitchell points out and as Gans and Pahl, for example, demonstrated, the Chicago School theorists consistently failed to find the behaviour expected of the city, and indeed discovered much that was incompatible with their expectations.

We have already suggested that the urban diacritica of Wirth and others might be specified among a set of contextual parameters. Using social network analysis one may go a step further and rewrite the Chicagoans' expectations in the form of empirically testable hypotheses. It enables us to establish in a quantitative fashion whether or not the type of relationships they predicted for urban dwellers – namely a high level of secondary contacts – in fact exist.

Mitchell (1987) proposes three network concepts which underpin the classic theses of urbanism: reachability, multiplexity and intensity. Reachability, or mesh, measures 'the extent to which links radiating out from some given starting person through other persons eventually return to that same person' (p.304); in other words, how true is it that everyone knows everything about everyone else, and are urban meshes larger than rural? Measures of reachability or compactness are used in three of the chapters in this volume. Both Werbner and Anwar explore the density of Pakistani migrant workers' social networks in UK cities following the initial period of rural-to-urban migration. Anwar is able to show that, for a sample of sixteen cases questioned over a decade, the reachability of their network has increased over time.

This might be considered to contradict expectations of a loosening of social ties consequent upon urbanisation. Pnina Werbner regards the high density and reachability of migrant networks as the foundations of an elaborate gift economy embedded in an urban setting, and also at odds with any assumption of the anomic dissolution of the social relations of community.

Along slightly different lines, Bridge shows that there are no significant differences of network density between social classes in a gentrified part of London. As such his analysis focuses on the 'other end' of the urbanisation process, as working-class communities formed around industrial locations are supposedly broken up by incoming middle-class home-buyers. Although careful to qualify his findings given the small size of his sample, Bridge at least points to the use of social networks in distinguishing among class-based community types in urban areas.

The second concept, multiplexity, indicates the extent to which two persons are linked in more than one way, for example as kin and employer/employee. It might be thought that in rural or small-scale societies, relations are more multiplex rather than single-stranded, and that the reverse is true of urban situations. Among the migrants in Werbner's study, such multiplex ties were common, particularly as friends assumed the roles and obligations normally associated with kin in the context of urban-based gifting systems. She describes a hierarchy of both exchanges and relations, though notes that multiplex ties are not always socially 'near' relations. The inclusion of non-kin into the *biraderi* which comes about as a result of the changed circumstances of migrants' lives abroad is also a theme explored by Anwar.

The final concept, intensity, is defined as 'the degree to which individuals are prepared to honour obligations, or feel free to exercise the rights implied in their link to some other person' (Mitchell, 1969, p.27). Wirth and Park expect urban relations to be of low intensity, displaying cynicism, anomic attitudes or lack of attachment. Werbner discusses the question of intensity regarding exchanges in the gift economy of Pakistanis in Manchester. The complex obligations involved in the making of loans and the giving of sweets on ritual occasions involve intricate relations between kin and friends, which require from the participants careful calculations of the likelihood of reciprocation. The use of the mathematics of network analysis enables her to explore one of anthropology's core concerns – gifts and exchange – without reducing such transactions to depersonalised exchanges of neo-classical theory. In each of the three cases network analysis provides the formal mathematical procedures for testing these assumptions, although of course it cannot identify their causation.

The second major reason for extending social network analysis is one which addresses a perennial problem for geography in particular: that of spatial formalism or spatial fetishism. By this is meant the representation of social relations as relations between spaces, for example rural and urban or core and periphery. The fetishism comes in attributing to spaces the power to act, interact or dominate, and Richards (1984) is critical of anthropology's adoption of such over-simplified spatial concepts from geography. In this regard, it is significant that Barnes's (1954) original formulation of the network concept arose from the realisation that there were analytically separate social fields occupying the same territory. Also, such networks extended beyond the territory in question. This conceptual displacement of the social by the spatial has characterised studies of rural–urban migration in the past. The idea that such movement consists of a single transfer of individuals from one situation to another resulting in fundamental changes in their social relationships persisted for a long time. As Mitchell demonstrated in Central Africa however, and as many writers have accepted for contemporary migration, the movement is often likely to be circulatory rather than irreversible. This might be expected of periods or forms of industrial capitalism which cannot or will not provide a social wage, requiring a separation of the worker from his or her longer-term basis of social reproduction. Grieco's chapter here demonstrates how relatively recent such processes were even in the UK.

The spaces 'urban' and 'rural' cannot therefore be used as surrogates of social change. It was this observation that Mayer (1961) made so clearly in his analysis of Xhosa migration to East London. By contrasting the two adaptations of the 'School' and 'Red' Xhosa to urban conditions and their use of networks as a resource, Mayer showed how urban residence did not act deterministically on African migrants. Two of the chapters here, by Bridge and Rogers, also argue that attitudes and behaviour cannot be read off space and spatial change as readily as some ecological analyses would seem to imply. Bridge questions whether there is a clear or distinctive working-class response to gentrification, and whether this response necessarily takes the form of hostility or resistance, as much of the literature assumes. His evidence, based on network analysis and questionnaire survey, suggests that response to gentrification is mediated by a person's 'immediate social environment' and does not take such unambiguous forms. In a similar way (though not based on network analysis), Rogers criticises the assumption that the sharing of space by different ethnic groups in the process of residential succession must always lead to ethnic conflict.

A social network perspective therefore challenges the ready equation of spatial proximity with social interaction, which is an axiom of social geography (Peach, 1975). While this equation can be tested empirically through such things as inter-marriage rates, social network analysis permits the fuller consideration of a person's 'immediate social environment' (Bott, 1971). Bridge adds a dimension of space to his network analysis by using a measure of geographical range. He finds that there is no significant correlation between social class and the geographical spread of social networks among the residents of the gentrified area. Indeed, since most networks are metropolitan-wide for all social classes, the idea that gentrification necessarily destroys close-knit working-class communities must be thrown into doubt. Although space is still important in the formation and maintenance of social networks, its exact significance needs to be established empirically. Social network analysis facilitates the tracing of the connections between locality and wider contexts, between 'here' and 'there' (Massey, 1993).

What is apparent from Bridge's analysis is that dependence on one's social network may vary according to stage in the lifecycle. Social networks may also be regarded as resources, and this perspective is the third major reason for extending their use. Grieco discusses how East End women rely on social networks to not only obtain employment in the hop-fields, but also to arrange transport to the fields. The migrant workers in Werbner's study make use of their networks in obtaining start-up loans for businesses. While the individuals in both cases may be considered in some sense marginal to the core economy, the current round of economic and political restructuring is likely to mean that more and more people are required to make use of informal modes of provisioning and employment. This not only relates to the widespread observations on the growing informalisation of core capitalist economies (Portes and Sassen-Koob, 1987), but also the erosion of state modes of collective provision through social and welfare services. Women, in particular, are being obliged to create new networks of child-care and mutual assistance in the absence of formal provision, although men rendered surplus to the needs of the economy may be joining them (Mackenzie, 1989). The breakup of old Fordist and Keynesian hierarchies is creating new spaces for both networking and networks. Wherever access to information becomes important, social network analysis will become a key research tool.

The fourth and final advantage of social network analysis is expressed by Hannerz (1980, p.175):

> [N]etwork notions seem particularly useful as we concern ourselves with individuals using social roles rather than with roles using individuals, and with the crossing and manipulation rather than the acceptance of institutional boundaries.

Urban anthropology has commonly relied upon institutional analysis, but this is only one form of abstraction. In the course of a day, an individual has many encounters of varying types in many situations (cf., for instance, Epstein, 1969). Network analysis permits a generalisation towards the individual or the group rather than towards the institution (Mitchell, 1969). Locality research appeared to concentrate on institutions such as union membership, and social aggregations such as occupation, gender and ethnicity. The localness of a place is given by establishing their particular combination using aggregated data. As such it is a structural form of analysis. An intensive research strategy could use social networks to either verify such observations or point towards new hypotheses. Pahl's (1984) work in the Isle of Sheppey contains something of an alternative, focusing on the biographies of a small number of families to reveal the significance of the household in managing resources or structuring life chances. A mathematical analysis focused on individuals in their daily round as they encounter various institutions would seem also to fit the calls for a more practice-oriented social theory (see below).

Aside from these four points there are other potential uses of network analysis, some of which are discussed at the end of Bridge's chapter. There are certain limitations of network analysis. It is time-consuming even for small networks and can encourage an undue mathematisation of social relations. There is a requirement to select individuals or groups according to good theoretical grounds which one believes to be appropriate for one's purposes. The problem of relating network data to the wider social context through abstraction and analysis is not in principle insurmountable, though it may be difficult in practice. Therefore, while the metaphorical usage of the method will undoubtedly increase, analytical usage is likely to be restricted to a small range of carefully chosen problems. Mitchell himself (1993) stresses the need to combine such quantitative analyses with more established ethnographic research, and this would seem to be a realistic and manageable goal.

Ethnicity and Social Perception

If social network analysis abstracts the personal order of social relationships, then ethnicity belongs to the categorical order in which behaviour is related to the perception of social types (Mitchell, 1956; 1974b; 1987). In his introduction to *Urban Ethnicity*, A. Cohen (1974) noted that there are many confusing definitions of the term 'ethnicity' (indeed, these have multiplied considerably since the time he made this observation – see Bacal, 1991). Much of the confusion surrounding the concept of ethnicity results from its overloaded nature, serving too many purposes. Once more drawing upon the concerns of the Manchester School in Africa (Werbner, 1984), Mitchell (1987) proposes that some of this muddle may be disposed of by distinguishing the notion of ethnicity at different analytical levels. Situational analysis facilitates such a clarification.

To begin with, one must distinguish between 'folk' and 'academic' definitions. The former includes two kinds of processes, identified variously as either: (1) communal and categorical, (2) internal and external, or self-identification and the categorisation of others (see also Barth, 1969; R. Cohen, 1978). As Mitchell (1987, p.182) observes:

> We need to distinguish between ethnicity construed as the way in which a set of actors make use of and display their particular common cultural characteristics in some social situation and ethnicity as the way in which observed or presumed differences in culture become an element in inter-group relationships in some social setting.

The second of these processes is one of social perception involving categorical distinctions, in which an individual allocates some other individual to an ethnic category so as to 'provide some rationale for adopting attitudes and adjusting behaviour toward that person' (p.183). This process is not likely to be idiosyncratic, but based upon shared presumptions which are social in their origin.

The necessity of making such categorisations is likely to be greater in urban conditions, particularly where recently-arrived migrants are concerned. The very density and heterogeneity of urban populations, interacting in a range of public places, demands some ordering on the part of the individual. A recurring theme in the modernists' vision of urban life was, as Baudelaire described it, *'le transitoire, le fugitif, le contingent'* (the transitory, the fleeting, the contingent) (in Berman, 1983). The streets were a moving chaos in which the occupational categories of the workplace no longer served to allocate status. In these spaces an alternative and independent system of public identification operates, managing traffic relationships and forming the basis of social avoidance and territorialisation (S. Smith, 1984b). In uncertain conditions where it is not possible for each individual to know every other, then ethnicity provides a common-sense set of expectations and cues to appropriate behaviour. It is likely to draw upon visual diacritica, such as skin colour or dress. It may also act to protect the individual from dangers such as crime (S. Smith, 1984b), or to provide the basis for structuring encounters such as joking relationships between co-workers of different ethnic background (Handelman and Kapferer, 1972). Ethnicity therefore involves, in Mitchell's formulation, principally a practice relating to the everyday behaviour of people in urban contexts. As Kapferer (1988, p.233) sees it:

> Mitchell's point was that in the modern urban industrial setting ethnic categories were culturally creative innovations entirely relevant to, and formed within, modern capitalist conditions. He also argued that the ethnic idea, which stressed the cultural homogeneity of an internally undifferentiated category of persons, gained force as constitutive of social relations through the structure of the urban setting.

The second definition of ethnicity is quite distinct from the first, though it is related to it in a non-arbitrary and theoretically consistent manner. The academic definition is 'an abstract analytical category postulated by an observer to order and structure empirical data' (Mitchell, 1987, p.237). As such it is an emergent property of observational data, a construction for analytical purposes which is not necessarily shared by or known to the subjects themselves. Mitchell argues (p.238):

> In analyses of this kind the regularities in the behaviour of categories of people are interpreted in the light of the analyst's identification of the people concerned as members of ethnic groups, and of the command and control of the groups over the disposition of scarce resources.

These folk and academic definitions of ethnicity deal with different aspects of the same phenomenon and there is no necessity for them to be identical. However, he goes on to suggest that:

> [O]ur insights and understandings are extended if we are able to juxtapose the findings from structural analyses of manifestations of ethnicity against those based on cognitive data, since it is only by this procedure that *apparent* contradictions may be resolved. (p.248) [emphasis in the original]

These distinctions correspond to the division made in situational analysis between situation and setting. According to Mitchell, 'ethnicity is not a pervasive element in social relationships but one which emerges in particular social situations' (p.241). This point is brilliantly demonstrated by Mitchell in *The Kalela Dance* (1956), where he evinces processes and factors according to which a person is self-categorised, or categorised by others, depending upon 'different types of social relationships in different situations' (p.32). Criteria of ethnic (in this case, 'tribal') category membership and modes of behaviour are shown to be fluid and changeable. In *The Kalela Dance*, Mitchell shows us that 'the set of relationships among a group of tribesmen in their rural home is something very different from the set of relationships among the same group when they are transposed to an urban area' (p.44). Any regularities in ethnic identification, behaviour and social relations are not therefore an intrinsic or primordial property of persons, but a property of the consistency of situational definitions. Consequently ethnic identity is both situational and negotiated by actors amongst each other, and any continuity is possible in principle but not guaranteed. However, Kapferer (1987, p.xiv) importantly points out that Mitchell's situational approach does not deny the 'reality' of ethnic sentiments and ethnic relations; rather, it helps us understand how:

> Ethnicity is a construction because it takes its form, is constituted as primordial, in a common-sense, taken-for-granted world, in particular structural contexts. Ethnicity in the world which Mitchell explores becomes the *sine qua non* of personhood, of self. It is the force which generates common-sense views of the kind that ethnic identity *is* primordial and 'natural' to the person which contributes to the emotional power of ethnic identity, and creates it as a potent political force in both a positive and negative sense.

To Mitchell's two analytically distinct definitions a third may perhaps be added. It is implicit in *The Kalela Dance*, but made more apparent by Kapferer in Chapter 2. Alongside the Wirthian focus on money and economy as urban features, he notes the significance of the bureaucratic order of the colonial state. Just as towns in colonial situations may be legal or juridical entities (through pass laws and controls over labour circulation, for example), so categorical identity is propagated by the state's administrative apparatus. Here Kapferer refers to Foucault's treatment of the relationship between modern state formation and the production of new identities through the techno-rational order. Australia's multicultural policies also embody and extend this 'categorical imperative' which, as he has discussed elsewhere (1988), retains rather than overturns the egalitarian-individualism of earlier assimilationist discourses. Kapferer sees in the carnivalesque aspects of the *kalela* dance a challenge to this order, through its mocking of authority figures, plays on sexuality, and ridiculing of colonial tribal categories and their supposed traditional elements.

Mitchell's use of ethnicity tends towards a form – rather than a content-definition such as that described in the *Harvard Encyclopaedia of American Ethnic Groups* (Thernstrom, Orlov and Handlin, 1980). The encyclopaedia lists fifteen different definitions according to content. Of course some attention to content is necessary to distinguish ethnicity from other types of social categorisation. Kapferer, for example, indicates how such forms may be 'filled' with meaningful content by dance performers. In practice, folk definitions of ethnicity may be inseparable from other factors such as regionalism or class. Mitchell's own analysis of ethnic categorisation in the African Copperbelt indicates a convergence of perceptions surrounding geographical distance or provenance, social and cultural distance, and ethnic group categories. 'The more distant a group of peoples is from another, both socially and geographically,' Mitchell (1956, p.28) importantly demonstrates, 'the greater the tendency to regard them as an undifferentiated category and to place them under a general rubric'. In this volume, David Boswell's essay on social space and perceptual categories in Malta (Chapter 11) adds analytical weight to Mitchell's original observation. He employs the same methods of multidimensional and cluster analysis that Mitchell used on occupational prestige to explore the ways in which Maltese people accord social prestige to residential areas. This examination of social perception is appropriate to this city-state, where an unusually high degree of locality-based classification and reputation is found. In the event, he discovers that the status hierarchy of places is less unilinear than that of occupations among Maltese residents. Boswell's use of mathematical techniques points to ways in which the complex determinations of class, ethnicity and place may be unravelled.

However, it is in the analysis of ethnicity that the real strengths of the situational approach become apparent. Social actors are regarded as constructing their own world, and their perceptions are given full analytical weight. Yet the actors' definitions do not exhaust the explanation, since the analyst may also make abstractions which have an analytical status quite separate from the actors' own. Kapferer (1987, p.viii) makes a strong case for the approach:

> Mitchell's situational method locates the analysis at the level of practice. It is at this level that social actors 'speak', and it is their 'speech' or their interpretations upon their own actions and the actions of others that Mitchell subjects to analysis. For Mitchell the situation has a logic of its own. It is both a 'practice of structure' and a 'structure of practice'.

Practice is not reduced to structure, nor structure to practice, but a clear distinction is drawn between them and each is given its epistemological space. There is of course more than a passing similarity between this method and that of the so-called 'structurationist school', namely Giddens, and of 'practice theory', particularly as advanced by Bourdieu. Yet Mitchell's approach is arguably more amenable to ethnographic research, while in a complementary manner he has also been able to call upon network analysis and the powers of mathematics to reveal the 'generalities of the principles which are constitutive within the logics of situations' (Kapferer, 1987, p.ix):

> Above all, what is apparent is that Mitchell has been successful in conducting empirical research in a structurationist and practice-oriented vein, something which has yet to emerge elsewhere from contemporary urban studies. Above all, Mitchell has shown that a recognition of levels of analysis need not mean the abandonment of a belief in the ontologically inter-related nature of reality, nor the capacity of subjective agencies to devise strategies to change objective structures. In fact, it is the recognition of this very principle which demands the analytical clarity and theoretical justification of the situational approach.

The Chapters

Although we have discussed various themes found in the chapters in our discussion above it is helpful to reprise their contents and methods.

Chris Pickvance discusses problems found in comparative analysis by returning to key distinctions made by J.S. Mill, specifically that between universal and plural causation. After establishing that comparative analysis is therefore unsuitable for deciding between the claims of Weberians and Marxists in urban and regional studies he provides an instance of where such analysis is appropriate. He attempts to explain the actions of local councillors in Thanet, Kent, during the 1980s, showing how political corruption can be explained by the context in which they find themselves. This explanation is tested by comparison between Western and Eastern European models of local government.

Four chapters provide case studies of contested events using ethnographic observation, three of which take their cue from *The Kalela Dance*. Bruce Kapferer returns to *The Kalela Dance* in order to draw out its aspects of resistance and play, which challenge the categorising practices of the colonial bureaucratic order. After isolating the specific ways in which politico-administrative practices of identity formation and alienation operated alongside processes of monetisation and industrialism in the African urban context, he turns to a situational analysis of another dance, one performed by Aborigines in a small Queensland town. The context is comparable, as the actors are confronted with similar questions of the place of tradition, the status of a colonial audience (this time, mainly tourists), and the fact that resistance to a dominant ideology is still influenced by – if not pursued within – that ideology. Thus, tradition itself is not external to the bureaucratic-rational realities of the Australian state, nor was it to the African colonial state. Situational analysis, for Kapferer, provides the analytical means to examine such contradictions

Kayleen Hazlehurst develops a situational analysis of Maori identity in New Zealand. Two prominent Maori figures are called to account by radicals from urban areas for their acceptance of imperial honours from the Queen. The award ceremony takes place not at Government House but at a Maori meeting house, and on Waitangi Day, the national holiday marking the signing of the treaty by which the UK Crown took suzerainty over the islands. The investiture and the outbreak of crowd unrest which accompanied it reveal the complex and conflicting loyalties within the Maori political world. Hazlehurst's privileged access to informants puts an interesting twist on the interpretation of these events. Along the way she explores how ethnic associations are conditioned by ideology, relative status and kinship, and reveals the significance of rural and urban contexts for the negotiation of 'Maoriness'.

Also influenced by Mitchell's account of the *kalela* dance, Alisdair Rogers reveals the structure of African-American/Latino relations in Los Angeles from a comparison of two public events. The Cinco de Mayo parade and the dedication of a park to the memory of Martin Luther King Jr both demonstrate paradoxes. The former is a Mexican holiday which takes on African-American cultural styles as well as participants, while the latter is an attempt to claim symbolic space for African-Americans in a neighbourhood which is increasingly Latino. Rogers explains these cases with reference to their contextual features, and together they demonstrate the significance of setting in shaping and explaining ethnic relations in an urban context. Finally, these events are reviewed in light of the 1992 riots which took place in the same streets.

The contrast between social strategies of inclusion and exclusion which Rogers finds in the two separate events is found in a single event by Susan Smith. She questions much current, post-modernist theory in which social and geographic boundaries are regularly downplayed or discounted in favour of concepts surrounding globalisation, flexible and fluid social relationships, and multiple identities. While not denying the usefulness of such theory and the importance of such concepts, Smith advocates the need for a continuing recognition of aspects of social and physical 'boundedness' as expressed in key public acts. Using complementary anthropological and geographical approaches, her study of annual celebrations in a Scottish Borders town demonstrates ways in which boundaries of space, identity and role are re-articulated within encompassing and changing contexts. A single episode may reveal both positive aspects of the celebration of local identity and negative aspects of gender subordination and 'common-sense' or taken-for-granted racism. Academics must learn 'where to draw the line' in the interpretation of such events. As with the investiture, the parade and park ceremony, this event struggles to contain and resolve all the factors present in the setting, and so generates varying interpretations among those present.

Peter Jackson also addresses the changed circumstances often labelled 'postmodern'. In a comparison of New York's loft-living and urban renewal in Minneapolis-Saint Paul he demonstrates that arts-related investment and historic preservation are not universal trends among US cities, but are historically and geographically specific. His discussion relates to the interaction between capital and culture and the manufacture of meaning which has become prominent in accounts of gentrification and urban economic strategies. His comparison of urban change in the two cities also contributes to the contemporary debate on architecture, the aesthetics and making of the built environment and the post-modernisation of the city.

Four essays in this volume employ network methodology or ideas. Margaret Grieco adopts Mitchell's themes of labour circulation and networks as resources to examine the informal organising capabilities of labour and the role of women in this process. She uses documentary and anecdotal sources to reconstruct the seasonal migration of women and children from London's East End to the hop-fields of Kent, a practice which persisted until the 1940s. She characterises this process as a 'moveable feast, a moveable community', in that important elements of the urban social environment were brought with the labourers and reconstructed in the fields.

Pnina Werbner uses the notion of a gift economy among Pakistani migrants in Manchester to critique neo-classical economic interpretations of networking and to reveal the cultural value of transactions. Using the networks of specific individuals, loans, and the exchange of sweets she demonstrates the extension of the gift economy beyond kin to friends in shared contexts, the factory, neighbourhood and place of origin. Social network analysis is usually restricted to synchronic studies.

Muhammed Anwar's essay is a useful example of the diachronic value of the method by way of a repeat survey of the same group of individuals. In this case examining networks of Pakistani workers in Rochdale (first presented in *The Myth of Return*, Anwar, 1979), Anwar demonstrates how, over the intervening years, the nature of these has, in important ways, both changed and remained the same.

Gary Bridge employs network analysis and case biography to unravel the relations between class and community in the context of gentrification. His investigation of the networks of a group of residents in Fulham, London, is aimed at questioning the widespread assumptions that structures of patriarchy and class can be mapped into the motivations and behaviour of individuals without taking into account their immediate social environments. He seeks to establish empirically whether, in fact, the networks of working-class and middle-class residents do differ. This information is then used to explain why there is often an inconsistency between individuals' objective class position and their attitude to social change in their neighbourhoods.

Finally, David Boswell combines the themes of the social grading of occupations from UK sociology and Mitchell's own concern for prestige, occupation and ethnicity in an original investigation of people's perception of occupation and residential area statuses in Malta. The unique geography of Malta's city-state and the history of internal migration which Boswell is able to reconstruct provide the context for a detailed mathematical analysis of these issues. He finds that residents do indeed make consistent valuations of places, but that the dimensions along which they do so, although analytically identifiable, are more complex than those deployed for occupation alone.

Bibliography

Anwar, M., *The Myth of Return: Pakistanis in Britain*, London: Heinemann, 1979

Bacal, A., 'Ethnicity in the Social Sciences: A View and a Review of the Literature on Ethnicity', *Reprint Paper in Ethnic Relations*, no.3, Coventry: Centre for Research in Ethnic Relations, University of Warwick, 1991

Barnes, J.A., 'Class and Committees in a Norwegian Island Parish', *Human Relations*, vol.7, 1954, pp.39–58

Barth, F., 'Introduction', in *Ethnic Groups and Boundaries*, F. Barth (ed.), Oslo: Universitetsforlaget, 1969

Berman, M., *All That is Solid Melts Into Air*, London: Verso, 1983

Bott, E., *Family and Social Network*, 2nd edn, London: Tavistock, 1971

Castells, M., *The City and the Grassroots: A Cross-Cultural Theory of Urban Social Movements*, London: Edward Arnold, 1983

_____, 'Commentary on C.G. Pickvance's "The Rise and Fall of Social Movements"', *Environment and Planning D: Society and Space*, vol.3, 1985, pp.55–61

_____, *The Informational City: Information Technology, Economic Restructuring and the Urban-Regional Process*, Oxford: Basil Blackwell, 1989

Clark, T.J., *The Painting of Modern Life: Paris in the Art of Manet and His Followers*, London: Thames & Hudson, 1985

Clifford, J. *The Predicament of Culture: Twentieth Century Ethnography, Literature and Art*, Cambridge, Mass.: Harvard University Press, 1988

Cohen, A., 'Introduction', in *Urban Ethnicity*, A. Cohen (ed.), London: Tavistock, 1974

Cohen, R., 'Ethnicity: Problem and Focus in Anthropology', *Annual Review of Anthropology*, vol.7, 1978, pp.379–403

Cohen, A.P. and Fukui, K. (eds), *Humanising the City? Social Contexts of Urban Life at the Turn of the Millennium*, Edinburgh: Edinburgh University Press, 1993

Cooke, P. (ed.), *Localities: the Changing Face of Urban Britain*, London: Unwin Hyman, 1989

Epstein, A.L., *Politics in an Urban African Community*, Manchester: Manchester University Press, 1958

_____, 'The Network and Urban Social Organization', in *Social Networks in Urban Situations*, J.C. Mitchell (ed.), Manchester: Manchester University Press, 1969

Featherstone, M. (ed.), *Global Culture: Nationalism, Globalization and Modernity*, London: Sage, 1990

Forde, D. (ed.), *Social Implications of Industrialization and Urbanization in Africa South of the Sahara*, Paris: UNESCO, 1956

Fox, R.G., 'Rationale and Romance in Urban Anthropology', *Urban Anthropology*, vol.1, 1972, pp.105–33

_____, *Urban Anthropology: Cities in Their Cultural Settings*, Englewood Cliffs, N.J.: Prentice-Hall, 1977

Garbett, G.K., 'The Analysis of Social Situations', *Man*, vol.5, 1970, pp.214–17

Gluckman, M., *Analysis of a Social Situation in Modern Zululand*, Rhodes-Livingstone Papers, no.28, Manchester: Manchester University Press, 1958

_____ (ed.), *Closed Systems and Open Minds: The Limits of Naivety in Social Anthropology*, Edinburgh: Oliver & Boyd, 1964

Handelman, D. and Kapferer, B., 'Forms of Joking Activity: A Comparative Approach', *American Anthropologist*, vol.74, 1972, pp.484–517

Hannerz, U., *Soulside: Inquiries into Ghetto Culture and Community*, New York: Columbia University Press, 1969

_____, *Exploring the City: Inquiries Toward an Urban Anthropology*, New York: Columbia University Press, 1980

Harvey, D., *The Urbanization of Capital*, Oxford: Basil Blackwell, 1985

_____, *The Condition of Postmodernity: An Enquiry into the Origins of Cultural Change*, Oxford: Basil Blackwell, 1989

Herbert, D. and Smith, D.M. (eds), *Social Problems and the City*, Oxford: Oxford University Press, 1979

Hobsbawm, E. and Ranger, T. (eds), *The Invention of Tradition*, Cambridge: Cambridge University Press, 1983

Howe, L., 'Urban Anthropology: Trends in Its Development since 1920', *Cambridge Anthropology*, vol.14, 1990, pp.37–66

Jackson, P., 'Mapping Meanings: A Cultural Critique of Locality Studies', *Environment and Planning A*, vol.23, 1991, pp.215–28

_____, and Smith, S.J., *Exploring Social Geography*, London: George Allen & Unwin, 1984

Jameson, F., 'Postmodernism, or the Cultural Logic of Late Capitalism', *New Left Review*, no.146, 1984, pp.53–93

Kapferer, B., 'Foreword', in *Cities, Society and Social Perception: A Central African Perspective*, J.C. Mitchell, Oxford: Clarendon, 1987

_____, *Legends of People, Myths of State: Violence, Intolerance and Political Culture in Sri Lanka and Australia*, Washington, D.C.: Smithsonian Institution Press, 1988

Lewis, O., *La Vida: A Puerto Rican Family in the Culture of Poverty – San Juan and New York*, New York: Random House, 1966

Mackenzie, S., 'Women in the City', in *New Models in Human Geography II*, R. Peet and N. Thrift (eds), London: Unwin Hyman, 1989

Massey D., 'Power-geometry and a progressive sense of place', in *Mapping the Futures: Local Cultures, Global Change*, J. Bird, B. Curtis, T. Putnam, G. Robertson and L. Tickner (eds), London: Routledge, 1993

Mayer, P., *Townsmen or Tribesmen: Conservatism and the Process of Urbanization in a South African City*, Cape Town: Oxford University

Press, 1961

Mitchell, J.C., *The Kalela Dance: Aspects of Social Relationships Among Urban Africans in Northern Rhodesia*, Rhodes-Livingstone Papers, no.27, Manchester: Manchester University Press, 1956

_____, 'Theoretical Orientations in African Urban Studies', in *The Anthropological Study of Complex Societies*, M. Banton (ed.), London: Tavistock, 1966

_____, 'The Concept and Use of Social Networks', in *Social Networks in Urban Situations*, J.C. Mitchell (ed.), Manchester: Manchester University Press, 1969

_____, 'Networks, Norms and Institutions', in *Network Analysis: Studies in Human Interaction*, J. Boissevain and J.C. Mitchell (eds), The Hague: Mouton, 1973

_____, 'Social Networks', *Annual Review of Anthropology*, vol.3, 1974a, pp.279–99

_____, 'Perceptions of Ethnicity and Ethnic Behaviour: An Empirical Exploration', in *Urban Ethnicity*, A. Cohen (ed.), London: Tavistock, 1974b

_____, 'Case and Situational Analysis', *The Sociological Review (N.S.)*, vol.31, 1983, pp.187–211

_____, *Cities, Society and Social Perception: A Central African Perspective*, Oxford: Clarendon, 1987

_____, 'Situational Analysis and Social Networks', paper delivered at the Third European Conference on Social Network Analysis, Munich, 10–14 June 1993

Pahl, R., 'The Rural–Urban Continuum', in *Readings in Urban Sociology*, R. Pahl. (ed.), Oxford: Pergamon, 1968

_____, *Divisons of Labour*, Oxford: Basil Blackwell, 1984

Peach, C., 'Introduction: The Spatial Analysis of Ethnicity and Class', in *Urban Social Segregation*, C. Peach (ed.), London: Longman, 1975

Pickvance, C., 'The Rise and Fall of Urban Movements and the Role of Comparative Analysis', *Environment and Planning D: Society and Space*, vol.3, 1985, pp.31–53

_____, 'Concepts, Contexts and Comparison in the Study of Urban Movements: A Reply to M. Castells', *Environment and Planning D: Society and Space*, vol.4, 1986a, pp.221–31

_____, 'Comparative Urban Analysis and Assumptions About Causality', *International Journal of Urban and Regional Research*, vol.10, 1986b, pp.162–84

Portes, A. and Sassen-Koob, S., 'Making it Underground: Comparative Material on the Informal Sector in Western Market Economies', *American Journal of Sociology*, vol.93, 1987, pp.30–61

Redfield, R., *The Folk Culture of Yucatan*, Chicago: University of Chicago Press, 1941

_____, and Singer, M., 'The Cultural Role of Cities', *Economic Development and Cultural Change*, vol.3, 1954, pp.53–73

Richards, P., 'Spatial Organization as a Theme in African Studies', *Progress in Human Geography*, vol.8, 1984, pp.551–61

Sanjek, R., 'Urban Anthropology in the 1980s: A World View' *Annual Review of Anthropology*, vol.19, 1990, pp.151–86

Saunders, P., *Social Theory and the Urban Question*, 2nd edn, London: Hutchinson, 1985a

_____, 'Space, the City and Urban Sociology', in *Social Relations and Spatial Structures*, D. Gregory and J. Urry (eds), Basingstoke: Macmillan, 1985b

Sjoberg, G., *The Preindustrial City*, New York: The Free Press, 1960

Smith, M.P., *The City and Social Theory*, Oxford: Basil Blackwell, 1980

Smith, S., 'Practising Humanistic Geography', *Annals of the American Association of Geographers*, vol.74, 1984a, pp.353–74

_____, 'Negotiating Ethnicity in an Uncertain Environment', *Ethnic and Racial Studies*, vol.7, 1984b, pp.360–73

Southall, A. (ed.), *Social Change in Modern Africa*, London: Oxford University Press, 1961

Spradley, J.P., *You Owe Yourself a Drunk: An Ethnography of Urban Nomads*, Boston: Little, Brown, 1970

Thernstrom, S., Orlov, A. and Handlin, O. (eds), *Harvard Encyclopaedia of American Ethnic Groups*, Cambridge, Mass.: Harvard University Press, 1980

Turner, V., *Schism and Continuity in an African Society*, Manchester: Manchester University Press, 1957

Van Velsen, J., 'The Extended-case Method and Situational Analysis', in *The Craft of Social Anthropology*, A.L. Epstein (ed.), London: Tavistock, 1967

Werbner, R.P., 'The Manchester School in South-Central Africa', *Annual Review of Anthropology*, vol.13, 1984, pp.157–85

Wilson, E., *The Sphinx in the City: Urban Life, the Control of Disorder and Women*, London: Virago, 1991

Young, I.M., *Justice and the Politics of Difference*, Princeton: Princeton University Press, 1990

Znaniecki, F., *The Method of Sociology*, New York: Rinehart, 1934

Chapter 1

Comparative Analysis, Causality and Case Studies in Urban Studies

Chris Pickvance

This chapter addresses three questions: the role of comparative analysis in social science, the debate between theoretical perspectives in urban and regional studies, and the nature of the theoretical inferences that can be made from case studies. I shall argue that, as conventionally practised, comparative analysis is inadequate because it makes a restrictive assumption about the patterns of causation operating in the social world, and that a second type of comparative analysis which does not make this restrictive assumption needs to be given equal importance. I then go on to show how the hopes placed on comparative analysis in urban studies have been too high, and in particular that it cannot be used as a way of resolving conflicts between Marxist and Weberian perspectives on urban and regional phenomena. Finally I address the question of theoretical inference in case studies and, taking some current research as an example, show how earlier arguments about comparative analysis lead one to question the 'obvious' theoretical interpretation of the case study.

Two Types of Comparative Analysis

In one sense all analysis, i.e. any attempt to find causes, is comparative – even when the data concern a single case. This is because it involves a comparison between the observed situation and an imagined situation in which the suspected case is absent (Zelditch, 1971). More usually, however, comparative analysis refers to the analysis of data collected on two or more cases (whether they are groups, organisations, towns or societies). But research into two or more cases does not in itself amount to comparative analysis since data on these cases may simply be juxtaposed or presented sequentially without any attempt to explain the similarities and differences appearing. Hence the term comparative *research* is mistaken. Comparative analysis is best defined as the collection of data on two or more situations, followed by an attempt to make sense of them by use of one or more explanatory models. In the present chapter we shall only be concerned with cross-national comparative analysis and will use the term 'comparative analysis' as a shorthand for this – but the argument developed applies whatever the unit of comparison.

Since comparative analysis makes use of the same logic as all causal analysis, J.S. Mill deserves credit as its founding father. Without going into Mill's Canons of Scientific Inquiry in detail we can summarise them by saying that they were means of discovering which phenomena were constantly conjoined, and hence (in his view) causally related. A would be taken as a cause of B if B always followed A, or A was one of a set of causes which were jointly sufficient to produce B. The three key points about Mill's analysis for our purposes are: that it assumes that all potential causes can be identified, and hence underestimates the practical problems of causal analysis; that it involves seeing cause as constant conjunction, and that it gives no role to theory in causal inference. The first of these is a real and important practical difficulty, but I wish to concentrate on the second and the third, which are more fundamental.

The fact that Mill is associated with the idea of cause as constant conjunction is ironic since immediately after discussing his Canons (in *A System of Logic*, Chapters 8 and 9), he introduces a radically different idea of causation in Chapter 10. Whereas the earlier discussion had assumed that single causes were connected with single effects – both in the sense that given causes had unique and thus distinct effects, and that given effects had unique and thus distinct causes – he goes on to state that, '[this] supposition does not hold in either of its parts ... it is not true that the same phenomenon is always produced by the same cause; the effect a may sometimes arise from A, sometimes from B' (1906, p.285). He then points out that this 'renders uncertain' his Method of

Agreement since if conditions *ABC* are associated with *a* in one case, and *ADE* in another, it would be assumed that *A* is the cause of *a*. 'The moment, however we let in the possibility of a plurality of causes, the conclusion fails' (1906, p.286). This is because *a* may have been produced by *C* in the first case, and *D* in the second. Mill argues that, whereas in natural science plural causation might seem bizarre, in social science it may even be the norm.

The neglect of Mill's remarks on plural causation has been discussed elsewhere (Pickvance, 1986, p.177). What is clear is that by disregarding plural causation, social scientists have been able to avoid its radical implications for causal analysis of all sorts.

It is important to be clear about what Mill means by the 'plurality of causes', or 'plural causation' as I call it. Plural causation and multiple causation are quite distinct ideas. The latter refers to the presence of two or more causes acting on the phenomenon of interest; the former refers to the fact that on different occasions (places and times) different causes act. (By different causes I mean different variables, or the same variables but with different values.) Plural causation, in other words, contrasts with universal causation; it has nothing to do with the number of causes involved. Universal causation is the idea that (as in natural science) causal processes are the same wherever and whenever a phenomenon is produced, e.g. there are no physical or biological laws which apply only in capitalist societies. Plural causation is a wide category since it refers to a continuum (Figure 1.1). At one end might be the idea that all industrial societies have common causal processes. At the other is the idea that different instances of the same phenomenon at the same time but in different places

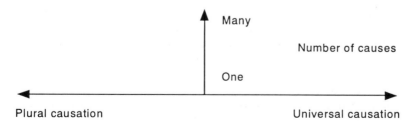

Figure 1.1 The Difference Between Plural and Universal Causation

have different causes, for example the achievement of low unemployment rates after 1974 could have been the product of strong labour movements acting on governments (Sweden) or of a bourgeois concern for social stability (Switzerland or Japan), (Therborn, 1986, pp.110–11).

Present-day comparative analysis generally relies on Mill's ideas of cause as constant conjunction, and in particular on his Joint Method of Agreement and Difference: that *A* and *B* are causally related if two or more instances of *A* have in common only *B*, and *A* never occurs in the absence of *B*. It is not my claim that this method should be jettisoned, but rather that it is only valid in so far as the restrictive assumption of universal causation is correct. Conversely, in so far as plural causation exists, a different type of comparative analysis is necessary. Since we cannot know which of these assumptions about causality should be made, the only reasonable approach is to keep open the possibility of both types of comparative analysis.[1]

The second major problem with Mill's approach to causality is that by insisting on constant conjunction as the essence of causation he gives no role to theory. Today we would argue that there is a radical distinction between constant conjunction (perfect correlation) and causation, and that it is only if a correlation can be given theoretical meaning (i.e. we can imagine a process which accounts for it and can give a causal order to the variables) that we would entertain the idea of a causal relationship. Failing that, the correlation would be treated as spurious. Mill may have neglected theory because of his faith in the possibility of enumerating all potential causes. The use of theory to eliminate certain variables as causes is in effect a short-cut alternative given the impossibility of this, though, as our theoretical knowledge develops, new classes of variables may need to be brought in or taken out of the list of potential causes.

Theory, then, has a vastly more important role in causal analysis than Mill thought, and the existence of plural as well as universal causation means that comparative analysis as usually practised is insufficient.

1. Since writing this chapter I have become aware that C. Ragin (1987) was simultaneously developing the same line of argument. He uses the concept 'multiple conjunctural causation' rather than plural causation, and goes on to develop a combination of quantitative and qualitative comparative analysis to deal with it. See also the special issue of the *International Journal of Comparative Sociology* (vol.32, 1991) which he introduces. (N.B. Ragin, wrongly in my view, asserts that Mill equated plural causation with multiple causation (Ragin, 1987, p.37).

Comparative Analysis in Urban and Regional Studies

I now turn to the urban and regional studies field, where there has been a call for more comparative analysis for at least the last ten years. I shall argue that conflict between theoretical perspectives in this field cannot be resolved by comparative analysis, as some have claimed, because of some fundamental differences between these perspectives which prevent them being compared.

To explain the emergence of the interest in comparative analysis in urban and regional studies it is necessary to go back a little in time. Around 1970 a new paradigm emerged in this field: inspired by Marx's analysis of capitalism, it sought to redefine 'urban' and 'regional' phenomena, and demonstrate that they could be successfully understood by a deployment of updated Marxian concepts and theories (Castells, 1977). In the first flush of enthusiasm for this approach, highly abstract models were applied to existing societies without regard to their historical evolution and specific character. If the models did not quite fit, as was often the case, this was no problem: since Marxian analysis uncovered real structures concealed from the actors, actors' views of the truth could be dismissed as irrelevant. Alternatively, the urban and regional experience of particular societies was more closely examined, but then erected into an ideal type to which other societies would eventually converge. Differences among capitalist societies were thus either ignored, or inadequately treated.

Theoretical battle was joined, and a methodological dispute ensued. Weberians such as Pahl (1977) argued that many of the urban and regional phenomena of interest to Marxists, such as stratification of housing by occupation and regional inequalities, could be found in state socialist societies too, and hence could not be the result of the capitalist mode of production. Instead, Weberians claimed that if a phenomenon was found in two societies then this must be due to features common to the two societies. Industrial technology, a high level of economic development, or bureaucratic organisation, for example, were seen as common features imposing imperatives which produced convergent urban and regional phenomena. In other words, socio-economic system type was not as significant as Marxists claimed; Marxists had committed the error of spurious correlation. The only way forward, according to Weberians, was to carry out cross-national comparative analysis. They therefore urged the comparison of capitalist and state socialist societies to check the causal importance of broad features of industrialism, level of economic development and bureaucratic organisation.

The strength of this position was twofold: it appealed to a widely-held theory and a widely-shared methodology. Weberian theory emphasises the societal trends towards rationalisation and the emergence of complex organisations staffed by officials operating on the basis of legal-rational authority. This is consistent with a prediction that ideological differences between capitalist and state socialist societies would gradually be submerged by technological and organisational imperatives. The methodology of this position is also widely shared. As we saw earlier, the notion that common effects have common causes underlies comparative analysis as traditionally practised.

Meanwhile, those applying Marxist models of explanation were encountering the law of diminishing returns. Highly abstract models of a capitalist mode of production could at best set out certain limits within which existing societies and the interrelations of their institutions (e.g. state and economy) would fall. They could not come close to understanding their character since the weight of the past gave rise to all sorts of specificities. As a result Marxists then started to take an interest in differences between capitalist societies and in their historical development: is the split between banking and industrial capital in the UK responsible for its feeble growth rate? Why do some capitalist countries (France and Japan) pursue much more active industrial policies than others (the USA, the UK since 1979)? Once again, cross-national comparative analysis was seen as advancing knowledge.

However, Marxists did not agree with Weberians on the type of comparative analysis to be carried out. Marxists were only interested in explaining differences among capitalist societies, since their model was adapted to this. It was believed that by making the basic model more complex (while retaining its Marxist character), differences between UK, French or US development could be accounted for. By contrast they were insistent that the analysis of state socialist societies had no bearing on that of capitalist societies: analyses of the latter were claimed to be self-validating because of the close fit between the theory and the facts of a capitalist society.[2] As Castells (1975, p.18) wrote:

2. Or to be more precise, the selection of facts addressed by Marxist research questions – see p.42.

In order to study a process in a capitalist society one might suggest, as Pahl seemed to, that one should compare the process under capital- ism and socialism. But one can look at capitalism without considering socialism, indeed the comparison between them can be misleading or impossible. Capitalism is a social system which functions according to specific rules, not just a historical situation. If we can understand these rules and show how they generate the contradictions which exist within capitalism we have an analysis of capitalism which is valid without the need for any comparison with socialist systems.

Despite the agreement between Marxists and Weberians on the need for comparative analysis of some sort, they did not agree on what form it should take, suggesting that the dispute had reached an impasse. But, one might ask, is this not a false impasse? Is not comparative analysis after all a way of manipu- lating data on different countries so as to identify causal antecedents? Or was Mill wrong?

To answer these questions we return to our earlier arguments: firstly, that Mill did not appreciate the role of theory in causal analysis; secondly, that his Canons of Scientific Inquiry were only valid if universal causation was assumed to be present. This sec- ond argument will be developed later by means of an example (see pp.43–47). Here I develop the first point only.

The limited potential of comparative analysis to adjudicate between Weberian and Marxist explanations primarily arises because Weberian and Marxist perspectives differ in other ways than their substantive explanations. Theoretical perspectives are distinctive in: the concepts they hold to be most useful in under- standing the world and the rationale that links them, e.g. ratio- nalisation or capital accumulation; the research questions they favour; the substantive explanations (sometimes called theories) they advance for the research questions posed, and their tacit assumptions about how to deal with evidence which is missing or whose interpretation is ambiguous (Pickvance, 1984, p.33). The first two of these features deserve special attention.

For some writers it is the distinctiveness of the concepts of dif- ferent theoretical perspectives which is the source of the difficul- ties in comparing their explanations. Different perspectives are seen as self-contained conceptual worlds, with no possibility of translation or communication between them. But this view of the radical non-comparability of theories has a fatal flaw: it fails to explain how people can 'think themselves' into and out of one or

other theoretical universe and have a sense that they are address-
ing a world 'out there' through differing concepts.[3] The fact that
they can do this suggests that the incommensurability of theories
is not a major problem.

A second possibility is that it is the difference in research questions which causes the major difficulties in comparing Marxist
and Weberian explanations. In my view this is the central source
of problems. In general the research questions favoured by different theoretical perspectives differ in three ways: in their substantive content (focus on the economic, political, etc.), their scale
(from interpersonal relations to world-wide economic linkages)
and their level of abstraction (highly abstract v. highly concrete).
Each perspective has a set of questions which it is well adapted to
tackling – Alford and Friedland (1985) call this its 'home domain'.
Outside this set the power of the perspective rapidly falls off.[4] It
follows that perspectives can only really be compared when they
have the same 'home domain' in terms of substantive content,
scale and level of abstraction of research questions.

It is patently clear that Marxist and Weberian theories differ in
the 'scope' of their research questions (Willer, 1967). Marxist theories of capitalist society make no claim to understand state
socialist societies, whereas theories of industrial society are
applicable to both types. The fact that their scope is different is no
reason for preferring the perspective with the larger scope. The
choice should rather be based on their respective power to
explain aspects of the same kind of society (i.e. capitalist). But
what this means is not entirely clear since, while both perspectives address 'aspects of capitalist society', there are major differences in the substantive content, scale and level of abstraction of
research questions they pose within this heading. The Marxist
perspective contains a highly abstract economic theory with
world-level implications which is absent from the Weberian,
while the latter takes a far more detailed interest in the functioning of organisations and in social interaction than the former.

3. This theoretical relativism would also undermine any notion of critique, since, if theories cannot be compared, intelligible claims of superiority cannot be made (Pickvance, 1984).
4. In arguing this I am of course rejecting the claims of certain perspectives to explain
everything. When examined, such claims involve either (a) an unjustified restriction of questions, e.g. a declaration that questions outside the home domain are unimportant and not
worth asking, or (b) a reductionist attitude which regards phenomena outside the home
domain as 'really' something else (and familiar), as in some Marxist attempts to explain gender or ethnic phenomena as class or economic phenomena.

Both, however, advance theories of stratification and of political institutions. In my view it is the non-overlap of home domain research questions which is the major obstacle to the use of comparative analysis in adjudicating between Weberian and Marxist explanations.[5]

Hence, the hope that comparative analysis (of any kind) can resolve the conflict between Marxist and Weberian analyses in urban and regional studies seems misplaced. However, a somewhat less ambitious but no less important role for comparative analysis does exist, and in the next section I shall show how the two types of comparative analysis identified earlier can be combined to refine theoretical inferences arising from case studies.

The Use of Comparative Analysis in Making Theoretical Inferences from Case Studies: An Example

Theoretical Inference from Case Studies: Understanding Council Economic Policy in Thanet

The obvious starting point for a discussion about theoretical inferences from case studies is J. Clyde Mitchell's article 'Case and Situation Analysis' (1983). He distinguishes between several usages of the term 'case study' before defining it as a 'detailed examination of an event (or series of related events) which the analyst believes exhibits (or exhibit) the operation of some identified general theoretical principle' (1983, p.292). He points out that it is the identification of the general theoretical principle which separates the case study from a simple account of events.

Mitchell's aim is to restore the case study to its true position in sociology, a position from which it has been dislodged by the influence of statistical approaches. His essential distinction is between two types of inference: statistical inference on the one hand, and logical, scientific, or theoretical inference on the other. Statistical inference concerns the confidence with which we can assert that a correlation observed in a sample will occur in the

5. An additional obstacle is that explanatory concepts like the rate of profit, industrial technology and bureaucratic organisation are either so abstract or so omnipresent that it is difficult to attribute causal power to them. By definition, causation is never observable and is always a matter of inference, but when the entities believed to have causal power resemble 'conditions' rather than 'active forces' (such as interest groups), causal inference is all the more difficult.

population from which the sample is drawn. Issues of representativeness and typicality thus arise here. In scientific inference the
question is whether the theoretical connection which we believe
accounts for a correlation between observed data is indeed a true
one. The essence of Mitchell's argument is that case studies are
often dismissed on the grounds that they do not allow confident
statistical inferences to be made, when in fact their strength lies in
the making of scientific inferences.

I agree with Mitchell's distinction between scientific inference
and statistical inference, but want to question the impression
(and it may be only an impression) one gains from his article that
scientific inferences developed from case studies are likely to be
true. He gives some striking examples where this is so, but none
where it is not! Whereas Mitchell argues that the case study is
capable of uncovering 'theoretically necessary linkages' (1983,
p.207), the question I want to raise is: given the plurality of theories, how do we know that a linkage which makes theoretical
sense of a case study finding is not mistaken? I shall argue that it
is possible to make mistaken causal inferences from case studies,
and that comparative analysis can help demonstrate this.

In research undertaken in the mid-1980s, a team at the Urban
and Regional Studies Unit, University of Kent at Canterbury of
which I was a part studied the economy of Thanet and the role of
the local council in it.[6] Thanet is a declining resort area with high
unemployment (21 per cent according to official figures in 1986)
and a labour force of low-paid and poorly unionised workers, in
small- to medium-sized firms. It has a high proportion of retired
people and relatively few professionals and managers. The council continues to promote Thanet as a tourist area and spends at a
high level compared with the rest of Kent to maintain tourist
attractions and leisure facilities such as the Margate Winter
Gardens. It has also responded to Thanet's decline as a tourist
resort by seeking to attract new sources of employment, e.g. manufacturing industry, the expansion of the port at Ramsgate, and
(with more mixed feelings) former geriatric and mental hospital
patients to fill the former tourist hotels as the government's '

6. This project, 'Restructuring the Service Sector in Thanet', was undertaken between 1985
and 1987, and was financed by the Economic and Social Research Council under its Changing
Urban and Regional Systems Initiative. The analysis presented here refers to the situation at
this time. For further information see Buck, Gordon, Pickvance and Taylor-Gooby (1989) and
Pickvance (1990).

community care' policy leads to the transfer of geriatric and psychiatric patients into 'the community'.

There is a widespread feeling that the council has a responsibility to intervene in the local economy. But this is combined with a lack of confidence in the local council and local politicians. In the decade up to 1987 the reputation of the local council and local politicians was strikingly low. This arose from three sources. The first was a series of scandals involving local councillors (some of which were reported in the national press, e.g. a councillor who got a friend to pose as an Arab sheikh interested in the port facilities at Ramsgate to persuade the Sally Line ferry company into signing a contract with the council; a councillor and Chair of the Finance Committee who were jailed for counterfeiting £20 notes; and another who resigned after being accused of being a prostitute). The second was a series of generous or 'unwise' deals in which the council was involved in its efforts to attract investment to the area, e.g. interest-free loans and purchase of shares to help fund a hotel development company; free dredging of a harbour channel to allow Port Ramsgate to stay open, and acceptance by councillors and council officers of a free cruise and presents from the Sally Line. The third was more a suspicion of financial mismanagement – the Winter Gardens absorbed some £250,000 per year in losses, i.e. 2 per cent of all the council's spending – and led to calls for the resignation of those involved.

One could multiply the examples. The argument which I wish to make is that the economic situation facing the council, its policies, and to some extent the public reaction to them, were not simply coincidentally related, but that there is a causal linkage, or what Mitchell would call 'a theoretical principle'. In other words, Thanet council faced structural constraints which meant that it had little alternative but to offer generous inducements in its dealings with potential investors. The structural constraints were economic and political. The level of unemployment was perceived as a situation needing action by both the council and local population. However, the council was aware that it was in a competitive bidding situation with other councils who could also offer sites, attractive environments and financial inducements.[7] The overall position of councils is weaker still in periods of eco-

---

7. In the USA Goodman (1979) has used the term 'the last entrepreneurs' to describe the new role of state governments in trying to attract employers.

nomic crisis when the level of private investment taking place is
low. I would thus argue that Thanet council's policies and the
perception of them as unwise and excessive in cost were not simply the result of inadequacies of the councillors (though these
also may have existed). Rather, given even the most competitive
councillors, the council would have faced the same constraints.
Hence I would argue that it was in the logic of the situation that
the council acted in this way. I would call this a theoretical or logical inference of the type Mitchell refers to.

The empirical basis of this theoretical inference in the Thanet
case is clear enough, but what is its theoretical basis? What
broader framework of ideas leads us to expect that councils faced
with local economic decline will be particularly likely to enter
into generous deals with private firms? One such answer is: an
understanding of how capitalist firms operate, and the scope this
leaves for public action. Capitalist firms do not operate in pursuit
of social goals, but of private profit. A council wishing to alter
their behaviour (e.g. get them to locate in its area rather than elsewhere) cannot therefore rely on moral persuasion. It must change
the profitability of the firm's operations by cutting its costs or
increasing its income. This much is common to both Marxist and
non-Marxist understandings of how public bodies act in capitalist economies. Marxists would argue further that there are structural limits to the action of local councils: that councils in
capitalist societies have neither the power to compel firms to act
in certain ways nor the power to set up municipal enterprises in
competition with private firms. For these reasons they are obliged to rely on financial incentives.

Hence there are ample theoretical reasons for thinking that
council inducements to local private firms are a comprehensible
pattern of activity. The question which arises out of Mitchell's
discussion is whether we can be confident that we have correctly
identified the theoretical nexus. We have advanced a rationale
which centres on public–private relationships within a capitalist
society. A sceptic might, however, suggest that what we are wit-
nessing is not limited to capitalist societies, but an instance of a
more general incapacity of the state to manage social problems,
and that this could be shown by studying state socialist societies;
the implication is that if similar relations between local councils
and (state) firms can be found there, we would be in the presence
of processes general to industrial societies – at least under condi-

tions of economic crisis in which a squeeze on public spending was being applied.

Alternative Explanations of Council Behaviour

In the remainder of this chapter I want to suggest that a case study such as that of council economic intervention in Thanet does not enable us to distinguish between theoretical principles which interpret council behaviour as occurring for different reasons in different societies, or for the same reason in all societies, whether capitalist or state socialist.

To start with I shall advance some evidence in support of the idea that in state socialist societies (as they existed until 1989) councils were also in a weak situation and hence were likely to be highly dependent on (state) enterprise. I shall then discuss the implications of this argument for the validity of the influences from the Thanet case study.

Four general points can be made about the relations between local councils and state enterprises in state socialist societies. Firstly, despite the existence of central economic planning (to varying extents according to the country), the spatial aspects of economic planning were treated as of secondary importance (Andrusz, 1984, p.252). This means that there was no co-ordination of the spatial effects of decisions of different ministries (energy, different manufacturing sectors, roads, etc.) and local councils were in the position of 'picking up the pieces' of central decisions, rather than being the lowest level of a territorial planning hierarchy which has had a major input into decision-making. One reason for the weakness of councils and territorial collectivities generally in the planning process is that they had little bargaining power. By contrast, large firms could exert great influence over central attempts at economic planning and territorial planning due to their sheer importance to the national economy and their political connections (Hamilton, 1970). Kornai's (1980) argument that they were subject to only a 'soft budget constraint' draws attention to this: the bargaining power of large firms meant that central planning bodies could not exert strict budgetary control. In brief, there were good reasons why councils were in a weak position *vis-à-vis* state firms.

Secondly, firms were important sources of welfare and social services and were thus responsible for a range of activities which in capitalist societies would devolve onto local councils (Sik,

1988). For example they had direct or indirect control over a considerable amount of the housing stock, since it was used as a means of attracting and retaining labour. In the Soviet Union this led to an enduring conflict between firms and councils, with the latter able to make few inroads into the position of the former (Andrusz, 1984). Firms may also have been significant in providing access to health care, holidays, and even food.

Thirdly, in the 1980s, as councils were starved of funds they increasingly relied on large firms (which were better funded) and which had thus become even more important sources of social provision (Misztal and Misztal, 1987). Finally, another feature of state socialist societies, at least until 1980, which affected the position of councils *vis-à-vis* firms was the policy of economising on infrastructural investment (Ofer, 1977). In order to give top priority to industrial investment, a relatively small percentage of investment was devoted to infrastructure such as transport, housing, health, education and telecommunications. One calculation shows that between 1965 and 1978 state socialist countries devoted 28–46 per cent of their investment to infrastructure, compared with 45–65 per cent for Western European capitalist and Southern European capitalist countries (Csizmadia, Ehrlich and Partos, 1984). The result was that urban growth lagged behind industrial growth, and many industrial workers were forced to commute from the under-equipped urban periphery and rural areas.[8] For councils the policy of under-investing in infrastructure translated into a structural shortage of funds.

There is therefore evidence that councils in Eastern Europe and the Soviet Union faced a parallel type of situation regarding state firms to that encountered by councils in the UK and the West with respect to private firms. Large (state) enterprises had tremendous muscle because of their importance to the national economy, and a bidding process by councils would have been quite plausible as councils competed to get them to locate in their area.

For the sake of argument let us assume that this is true, and consider the various theoretical arguments which can be made to account for this parallel. According to traditional comparative analysis, the common fact of council weakness relative to enter-

8. For an analysis of this 'under-urbanisation' pattern, see Konrad and Szelenyi (1977) and Szelenyi (1983).

prises must be explained by a common feature of capitalist and state socialist societies. Weberians would suggest that the most obvious is industrialism: the argument would be that in both capitalist and state socialist societies, economic enterprises (despite their different legal status – private v. state-owned) are vital to the nation's welfare and they exert power over territorial institutions such as councils (Model A, Figure 1.2). This explanation has the virtue of economy but seems to have been 'imposed' almost by the comparative analysis based on universal causation.

In contrast, comparative analysis based on plural causation would suggest that the subordinate relation of councils to firms may occur for different reasons in different societies. In capitalist societies, the argument would go, local councils are in a weak position with respect to firms because initiative for development lies with private enterprise, and structural constraints prevent councils from exercising compulsion over private firms or setting up municipal enterprises (Model B, Figure 1.3).

In state socialist societies, the argument would go, local councils (we speculate) are in a similarly weak position because they lack the power to compel (state) firms due to the councils' weak role in the planning system and their limited resources due to the

Figure 1.2 Weberian Model (Model A)

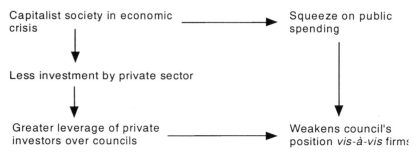

Figure 1.3 Initial Model Based on Thanet Case Study (Model B)

policy of economising on infrastructure and the greater role of firms in social welfare (Model C, Figure 1.4).[9]

To summarise, both the 'capitalist logic' model (B) and the 'industrial logic' model (A) fit the facts of the Thanet case, and both the 'socialist logic' (C) and the 'industrial logic' model (A) fit the constructed state socialist case. This means that case studies, despite their 'depth', do not lead unequivocally to particular theoretical principles. The principle one initially selects with great confidence may turn out to be only one of a plurality which 'fit the facts'.

What is interesting in the light of the argument of the first part of this chapter is that reliance on the conventional logic of comparative analysis (i.e. universal causation) would lead only to the 'industrial logic' model (A). Consideration of plural causation widens the range of models considered to include the capitalist and socialist models (B and C). The question remains, however, whether the different explanations expressed in these models are in conflict or are complementary. In this particular case, at least, it will be argued that the two explanations are complementary. Whether this is a general conclusion about explanations reached by the two types of comparative analysis is not clear.

The idea of different types of comparative analysis leading to complementary explanations is compatible with the work of

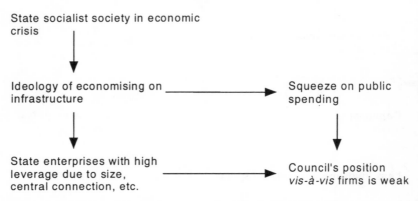

Figure 1.4 Speculative Model for Councils in State Socialist Societies (Model C)

9. For another example of the use of plural causation in East–West comparisons see my discussion of Szelenyi's study of occupational stratification of housing as due to a distinctively state socialist mode of redistribution (Pickvance, 1986; 1988).

Tilly. Tilly (1984) distinguished between 'universalising' and 'variation-seeking' comparative analysis.[10] In universalising comparative analysis, the aim is to show that the surface variety among different cases conceals a deeper common process. The drive is towards the discovery of similarities. An example is Marcuse's (1982) analysis of West German and US housing policy. His thesis is that in both countries housing policy since the Second World War has had the same character, that of facilitating market processes, and has been driven by the same force, the 'housing industry' (i.e. housing finance institutions and building firms). He makes an exception for West Germany between 1945 and 1956 (reconstruction) and 1967 and 1973 (response to social tension) when the market-supporting character of housing policy was checked.

The virtue of this analysis is its extreme simplicity. However, this is achieved at considerable cost. The 'common feature' explained, i.e. market-supporting housing policy, involves abstracting from the particular way in which market processes have been facilitated, and moreover the analysis ignores half of the post-war period when West Germany had a more anti-market policy.

Tilly's second type of comparative analysis is variation-seeking. Its aim is to seize on differences and explain them.[11] In Marcuse's study the differences in question could have been the specific forms of pro-market housing policy (e.g. support for landlords or support for owner-occupation), and the 1945–56 and 1967–73 periods of anti-market housing policy in West Germany compared with the periods of pro-market policy. The interesting possibility is that universalising and variation-seeking comparative analysis could be used in tandem, with the former seeking to explain abstract similarities in terms of abstract concepts, and the latter explaining differences (at a lower level of abstraction) in terms of less abstract concepts. The two types could thus be complementary.

10. Tilly also distinguishes two other types of comparative analysis: 'individualising', which seeks to grasp the particularity of an individual case, but does not in my mind involve comparative analysis as defined here, and 'encompasing', which appears to be a specific type of variation-seeking analysis in which variation is explained by reference to a country's position within the world system.

11. Tilly's two types of comparative analysis are not the same as the types distinguished earlier, based on the two types of causation. His 'universalising' type presupposes universal causation, but his 'variation -seeking' type is compatible with either universal or plural causation.

The relevance of universalising and variation-seeking comparative analysis to our example can now be established. In the first case, universalising comparative analysis searches for common causes of the subordinate relations of councils to firms in East and West. When combined with Weberian theories it finds a possible explanation in industrialism. The price it pays is that the concept of industrialism abstracts from the specific socio-economic system and ideology of each society. In the second case, variation-seeking comparative analysis addresses the same question but seeks more specific explanations than industrialism. A focus on specific ideologies and the functioning of capitalist and state socialist socio-economic systems puts flesh on the abstract idea of industrialism and therefore complements it. (In other cases, variation-seeking comparative analysis will address more specific questions, as suggested in the housing policy example.)

Conclusion

In conclusion, I hope to have demonstrated three arguments. Firstly, I have shown that there are two types of comparative analysis, based on universal causation and plural causation, and that these have major implications for the substantive conclusions drawn from comparative analysis. Secondly, I have shown that the debate in urban sociology between advocates of Marxist and Weberian approaches cannot be resolved by comparative analysis. This is partly because of the above-mentioned division in comparative analysis – with Marxists opting for a pattern of causation common to capitalist societies, and Weberians opting for a pattern common to industrial societies – and partly because of the non-overlap of research questions posed by each approach.

Finally, I have supported Mitchell's defence of theoretical inference in the case study as distinct from statistical inference, but argued that the theoretical principles used to make sense of case studies are themselves more open to debate than he suggests. By using the (actual) case study of Thanet and by creating a parallel for Eastern Europe and the Soviet Union, I have shown that the two approaches to comparative analysis lead to very different conclusions. If universal causation is assumed, then the state socialist evidence requires a reformulation of the initial theoretical inference based on the Thanet case study. If, on the other hand, universal causation is rejected, then the evidence on council behaviour in state socialist societies is irrelevant to inferences from the Thanet case study. In addition, the possible complementarity between models based on the logic of industrialism and those based on the logic of capitalism and state socialism was pointed out.

In sum, neither comparative analysis nor the case study is quite what it seems.

Bibliography

Alford, R.R. and Friedland, R., *Powers of Theory*, Cambridge: Cambridge University Press, 1985

Andrusz, G.D., *Housing and Urban Development in the Soviet Union*, London: Macmillan, 1984

Buck, N.H., Gordon, I., Pickvance, C.G. and Taylor-Gooby, P., 'The Isle of Thanet: Restructuring and Municipal Conservatism', in *Localities: The Changing Face of Urban Britain*, P. Cooke (ed.), London: Unwin Hyman, 1989

Castells, M., 'Contribution to Discussion', in *Proceedings of the Conference on Urban Change and Conflict*, M. Harloe (ed.), London: Centre for Environmental Studies, 1975

_____, *The Urban Question*, London: Edward Arnold, 1977

Csizmadia, M., Ehrlich, E. and Partos, G., 'The Effects of Recession on Infrastructure', *Acta Oeconomica*, vol.32, 1984, pp.317–42

Goodman, R., *The Last Entrepreneurs*, Boston: South End Press, 1979

Hamilton, F.E.I., 'Aspects of Spatial Behaviour in Planned Economies', *Papers of the Regional Science Association*, vol.25, 1970, pp.86–104

Konrad, G. and Szelenyi, I., 'Social Conflicts of Under-urbanization', in *Captive Cities*, M. Harloe (ed.), Chichester: John Wiley, 1977

Kornai, J., *The Economics of Shortage*, Amsterdam: North-Holland, 1980

Marcuse, P., 'Determinants of Housing Policies: West Germany and the United States', in *Urban Policy Under Capitalism*, N. Fainstein and S. Fainstein (eds), Beverly Hills: Sage, 1982

Mill, J.S., *A System of Logic*, 8th edn (1st edn 1843), London: Longman, 1906

Misztal, B. and Misztal, B., 'Scarce State Resources and Unrestrained Processes in the Socialist City: The Case of Housing', in *Housing Markets and Policies Under Fiscal Austerity*, W. van Vliet (ed.), Homewood, Ill.: Greenwood, 1987

Mitchell. J.C., 'Case and Situation Analysis', *Sociological Review (N.S.)*, vol.31, 1983, pp.187–211

Ofer, G., 'Economizing on Urbanization in Socialist Countries', in

Internal Migration, A.A. Brown and E. Neuberger (eds), New York: Academic Press, 1977

Pahl, R.E, 'Managers, Technical Experts and the State: Forms of Mediation, Manipulation and Dominance in Urban and Regional Development', in *Captive Cities*, M. Harloe (ed.), Chichester: John Wiley, 1977

Pickvance, C.G., 'The Structuralist Critique in Urban Studies' in *Cities in Transformation*, M. P. Smith (ed.), Beverly Hills: Sage, 1984

_____, 'Comparative Urban Analysis and Assumptions About Causality', *International Journal of Urban and Regional Research*, vol.10, 1986, pp.162–84

_____, 'Employers, Labour Markets, and Redistribution Under State Socialism: An Interpretation of Housing Policy in Hungary 1960–1983', *Sociology*, vol.22, 1988, pp. 193–214

_____, 'Council Economic Intervention and Political Conflict in a Declining Resort: The Isle of Thanet', in *Place, Policy and Politics: Do Localities Matter?*, M. Harloe, C.G. Pickvance and J. Urry (eds), London: Unwin Hyman, 1990

Ragin, C.C., *The Comparative Method*, Berkeley: University of California Press, 1987

Sik, E., 'The Welfare System and its Future in Hungary: Towards "Self-Welfarisation"?', in *Shifts in the Welfare Mix*, A. Evers and H. Wintersberger (eds), Frankfurt: Campus Verlag, 1988

Szelenyi, I., *Urban Inequalities Under State Socialism*, Oxford: Oxford University Press, 1983

Therborn, G., *Why Some Peoples are More Unemployed than Others*, London: Verso, 1986

Tilly, C., *Big Structures, Large Processes and Huge Comparisons*, New York: Russell Sage Foundation, 1984

Willer, D., *Scientific Sociology*, Englewood Cliffs: Prentice-Hall, 1967

Zelditch, M., 'Intelligible Comparisons', in *Comparative Methods in Sociology*, I. Vallier (ed.), Berkeley: University of California Press, 1971

Chapter 2

The Performance of Categories: Plays of Identity in Africa and Australia

Bruce Kapferer

In *The Kalela Dance* (1956) J. Clyde Mitchell explored the role of ethnic (or tribal) categories or terms in the framing of social action. The study was grounded in his extensive anthropological fieldwork knowledge of Central and Southern African societies. *The Kalela Dance* was significant within the methodological developments of Gluckman's 'Manchester School', important for Gluckman's own general statements on urban change and for the elaboration of the 'situational' approach which stressed the analysis of social practice (see Gluckman, 1958; Kapferer, 1987; Mitchell, 1983; 1987; Werbner, 1984). More generally, *The Kalela Dance* is a landmark in the anthropological understanding of processes of change and the examination of forms of life in urban/industrial Africa which has significance beyond the colonial setting of the study. Thus, Mitchell's argument is of long-lasting influence for sociological studies of ethnicity which have received a recent renewal of interest with the current upsurge in a world-wide nationalism in which ethnic identity appears to play a major role (see Kapferer, 1988).

My interest is to examine further some of the arguments set out by Mitchell. I will start with a consideration of some of his main points in *The Kalela Dance*, concentrating in re-analysis on some of its resistant aspects. An argument I develop is that the play of the *kalela* is related to the bureaucratic order of the colonial system. The discussion then turns to the different context of Aboriginal identity in Australia. Aborigines, perhaps more than the Zambians of Mitchell's study, were extremely determined by the bureaucratic orders of the colonial and post-colonial state. I apply some of Mitchell's insights and extensions from them to performances of identity among Aborigines in a small town in northern Queensland. A broad point uniting the colonial Zambian and contemporary Australian materials is that the dynamics of identity and what Mitchell terms 'categorical relations' flow from the ideological and institutional orders of the bureaucratic state.

Mitchell's study of the *kalela* shows how the dancers exposed contradictions within the urban/industrial context of their performance. These contradictions, I suggest, were not merely those born of colonial realities but integral within the historical ideological and institutional worlds which spawned colonialism and other diverse transmuted manifestations of widespread contemporary realities. This is certainly implicit in Mitchell's argument and in the broader statements made by Gluckman (1961). I think that further implications can be drawn, ones related to ideological forces engaged in the practices which Mitchell explored and, most specifically, those connected with the dynamics of ethnic identity.

Identity and Resistance: A Perspective from Colonial Central Africa

Mitchell is in many ways the pioneer of current anthropological approaches to ethnicity, as was also Epstein (1958), who worked in co-operation with Mitchell and in the same urban context. Other well-known work, for example that of Barth (1969), makes very similar points, although he tends to universalise principles that Mitchell takes as more germane to urban/industrial contexts. Mitchell's perspective, as with Gluckman's, is ultimately a development from the Nuer studies of Evans-Pritchard. Barth's own work was influenced in a similar UK social anthropological tradition, though more powerfully affected by the pragmatic individualism of Malinowski, to which Gluckman, Mitchell and others in the Manchester anthropological tradition of the time were opposed (see Gluckman, 1949).

In *The Kalela Dance*, Mitchell (see also Mitchell, 1987) is directed to stress the situated meaning of ethnic terms or, in the Central African urban context of his study, tribal markers. He concentrates on their categorical nature: that is, they are broad homogenising terms which describe collectivities of human beings with reference to those characteristics of tribal identity they are presumed to have in common. Such marked categorisation of people included and excluded persons according to criteria of no relevance or meaning in the local village contexts of origin of those who used these markers. In other words, the tribal categories used in urban discourse were innovative constructions born of the urban context itself. This observation gave rise to Gluckman's (1961) famous statement that an urban African is 'a townsman, a tribesman is a tribesman'.

The description by Mitchell, Epstein and Gluckman of urban African ethnicity as 'tribalism' was to mark it as being through and through a modern phenomenon. It was *not* a resurgence of pre-colonial or pre-industrial 'traditional' tribal forms. The point, although very simple, had to be emphatically stressed and, possibly, the continued reference to 'tribe' confused and weakened the point. A major reason for the emphasis was the context of anthropology itself, which then was committed to so-called 'acculturation approaches' to social change, a conservative gradualism to which Gluckman, Mitchell and others in the Manchester School were opposed both intellectually and politically.

Gluckman was criticised for overdrawing the distinction between urban and rural life and failing to note the continuities between them. This was a kind of criticism that ignored the whole orientation of the Manchester Central African studies and their direction from the Rhodes-Livingstone Institute of which Mitchell, for a period, was the Director. I should add that Gluckman and Mitchell were not concerned with opposing a dynamic modern urban context to a static, traditional, rural one. Urban and rural contexts in Africa, they stressed, were part of an overall dynamic social field.[1] The 'tribal' worlds of Central Africa

1. The distinction between urban and rural African forms was strongly influenced by well-known sociological concepts stemming from Durkheim (mechanical/organic solidarity), Maine (status/contract), and Tönnies (community/association). Durkheim and Maine were thoroughly explored in Gluckman's research classes. Mitchell, in his lectures to students, would stress the misapplication of Durkheimian distinctions in the work of such famous studies as that of Robert Redfield's *The Folk Cultures of Yucatan* (1941). The Durkheimianism of the 'Manchester School' notwithstanding, Gluckman, Mitchell, Epstein and Victor Turner (among many others brought together in the setting of Manchester anthropology in the late 1940s through to the early 1960s) were concerned to break away from bounded and system-integrated notions of cultural or social totality. This direction was indicated in the development of concepts like social field (by Gluckman, Turner, Bailey and Kapferer) which stressed the dynamic and processual nature of social worlds, their inner discordancies and ruptures, their lack of boundedness, and articulation into more embracing realities. For example, Gluckman, Mitchell and Epstein stressed the importance of global political and economic developments in the comprehension of social processes at the local level.

were also in transformation and not to be seen in timeless and static terms. They were interested, for example, in the emergence and restructuring of African institutions of power under colonial conditions (Gluckman, Mitchell and Barnes, 1949), in the monetisation of non-capitalist economies and their corresponding social transformation, and so on.

The work of Gluckman and of Mitchell in particular was largely opposed to that kind of anthropology which fetishised tradition or which romanticised 'culture', placing them in some kind of suspended animation set apart from the heat of dramatic social and political changes. A major target of their criticism was that school of anthropology which conceived of innovative or original forms of cultural and social action as 'survivals' or 'debased' or signs of social breakdown – thus Gluckman's well-aimed attack on Malinowski's functionalist view of social change in Africa. Gluckman not only pointed to the numerous theoretical failings in Malinowski's perspective (failings of which a conservative social anthropology in the UK took relatively little note until the late 1960s and 1970s) but indicated that it was part of a legitimising ideology of colonialism.

This broader political point is implicit in Mitchell's *The Kalela Dance*, in which he dispels a colonialist reasoning which underpinned much anthropological understanding of social change. Thus he was critical of Godfrey Wilson's (1940) use of the term 'detribalisation' in an important study of the small mining town of Kabwe (then Broken Hill) in Zambia. The term, in retrospect, was in accordance with the ruling analytical metaphors – those of 'assimilation', 'Westernisation', 'modernisation', 'development' – of anthropological and sociological modernist theorising concerned with the 'adjustment' of hitherto 'tribal' worlds within 'advanced' capitalist and technological realities. Such terms – in the colonial context self-justifying and full of implicit prejudice – deflected attention from the contradictions and dehumanisations of a rational/bureaucratic and exploitative political system serving Western interests. It encouraged a kind of sociological psychologism of a type that considered the reasons for the difficulties confronting Africans as ones of personal adjustment to situations never before experienced; their problems were not born of the external world but of inappropriate psychologies in the process of adjustment. Mitchell's (and Gluckman's) radical (at that time) point was that the forms of action of Africans in town were *not* so much manifestations of the problems of personal adjustment or of the personal disorders of change; they were forms of action entirely relevant to the urban industrial worlds in which they found themselves as migrants. Forms of action described as disordered or instances of detribalisation were structurally relevant to the situation and displayed dimensions of the 'logic' of the situation in which Africans found themselves. A broader implication of Mitchell's situational argument was that human beings can quickly adjust their action to most contexts. As soon as they were in town, Africans responded to its particular circumstances and their social and political position within it and developed and constructed their action accordingly.

I have underlined the critical context of Mitchell's work. It sometimes appears to have been missed. One critic, for example, saw *The Kalela Dance* in itself as promoting colonial attitudes rather than contesting them. Thus Magubane (1971) viewed Mitchell as contributing to a colonial interest and accused him of furthering tribal division by trying to elucidate the dynamics of urban tribal or ethnic categories. By so doing, it was suggested, Mitchell was promulgating attitudes which impeded the formation of the rational unity of the post-colonial independent African state. Magubane sadly missed the point and betrayed his own commitment to a rationalism indeed at the heart of the colonial order and of its self-proclaimed legitimacy. It is to aspects of this rationalism to which I now attend.

The concluding paragraphs of Mitchell's *kalela* study powerfully condense the fundamental structure of his argument. The last, in which he cites Louis Wirth at length, underlines the conditioning of the urban *kalela* within the terms of the colonial state and its bureaucratic/capitalist order.

In towns the pattern of the social system is determined largely by the industrial system which forms the basis of their existence, and by the laws which government has enacted to regulate the life of the towndwellers. As cities have developed on the basis of industrial production, 'the pecuniary nexus which implies the purchasability of services and things has displaced personal relations as the basis of associations. Individuality under these circumstances must be replaced by categories' (Wirth, 1938). 'Tribe' on the Copperbelt has become one of these categories, and it is in this sense only that *kalela* is a 'tribal dance' (Mitchell, 1956, p.44).

Mitchell understands the political and economic order of the colonial towns as contexts of radical anonymity. However, this is *not* a natural or essential dimension of urban life in Mitchell's analysis, as it is in the work of so many students of urban life such as Louis Wirth. It is so for Africans as a direct product of UK Colonial policy. Regulations limited the permanent settlement of Africans in the towns, constituting them as largely centres of wage labour only. This encouraged the maintenance of rural ties among Africans and the phenomenon of circulatory migration, whereby African migrants returned to their villages at the end of their employment lives and broke stays in urban employment with periods of extended returns to their rural homes. The instability of urban residence and the fact that, at the time of Mitchell's work, few could settle permanently in town, militated against the establishment of long-term social ties. A system of tied housing existed in the towns – Africans received their housing from employers. They did not have a choice over accommodation which might have facilitated the recreation of social ties in accordance with principles not directly linked to the administrative and industrial order of towns. There was relatively little opportunity for persons of similar ethnic or linguistic backgrounds to live together. Most of those who came to the towns were already strangers, drawn as they were from diverse cultural backgrounds and from a large geographical region.

The construction and engagement of tribal categories in Mitchell's analysis constituted an effort by Africans to generate social relations where there were none. These categories operated to enable the creation of social ties in accordance with principles of similarity and difference. For example, those people who recognised some similarity in customs and language despite the fact that they were from different tribes (e.g. Bemba, Bisa, Lala) operated such broader category membership as the basis of social association: they would refer to themselves as 'Bemba' when in actuality they might not be. Further, these kinds of categorical relations (ones based on perceived similarity, or perceived closeness or distance in terms of language and custom) could also be used to develop a wider net of relational possibilities, but founded in difference.

Mitchell notes the development of tribal joking relationships as an urban phenomenon. Thus, members of different tribal categories, on the basis of perceived differences in customary tradition or history of pre-colonial antagonism, would make such differences the basis of social association. In some ways it was an innovation upon well-established village practice where there were institutions of inter-clan joking, which took the form of the ritual exchange of insults and involved prescribed assistance often at times of life crisis, particularly at death. The institution of tribal joking as it developed under urban conditions assumed the form of the routine exchange of liberties. It was a means for establishing social relations and demonstrated how, in town, broad stereotypical categories of similarity and difference were engaged to structure interpersonal relations.

Mitchell argued that the structuring of social relations along tribal category lines was most apparent in what he called 'unstructured situations'. By and large he meant by this non-work situations where there was not a determinant organisational structure which defined and provided the terms for social interaction. In other words, where Africans had the greatest autonomy or freedom to direct their own action then the distinctly modern urban/industrial character of ethnicity or tribalism became a major form for the organisation of social relations.

What I want to underline is the potentially subversive relation of the phenomenon of tribalism to the administrative and political order in which it was spawned. Mitchell does not stress the critical and subversive potentiality of African discourse centring around tribalism. Well after he completed his researches, tribalism became a feature of national politics resistant to the colonial regime. In the period leading to Zambian independence, for example, the core of major African political parties in contest for power had some basis in the mobilisation of supporters along the tribal categorical lines discussed by Mitchell. But here I am confining discussion to notions of ethnicity or tribalism as a resource for political mobilisation. Rather, I wish to emphasise the tribalism of practices such as the *kalela* as being implicitly, if not explicitly, critical of the techno-rational and bureaucratic world in which it was performed.

Mitchell makes special point of the play and humour of the *kalela*. This achieves some of its impetus, I suggest, in the contradictions which Africans in town at that time lived. The fun of the *kalela* songs, their absurd play with tribal identity, and in many cases their obscene explosion of cultural stereotypes, was an 'attack' on the alienating and oppressive dimension of urban realities.

The urban *kalela* dancers are predominantly men and formed into teams who compete against each other. During my own fieldwork in Kabwe, Zambia (see Kapferer, 1972), in the mid-1960s *kalela* dancing took place on weekends in the housing areas controlled by the town municipal authorities and not in the townships controlled by the mining company. The dancing competitions were sponsored by the municipal council. The manner of the performances was the same as described by Mitchell, with the dancers moving in short, shuffling steps in a circle around a large 44 gallon oil-drum covered in cow hide which was beaten deafeningly. The team described by Mitchell was presided over by an elected leader, referred to as a 'king'. He had multiple responsibilities as the team organiser, treasurer and general administrator. The 'king' did not dance, but would act like a celebrity attending a public function such as a sporting event. Dressed in a dark suit, collar and tie, hat and white-rimmed sunglasses the 'king' would interrupt the proceedings to shake hands with the performers. Other roles of significance in the *kalela* team were the leader (who led the dancing and composed the songs), a 'doctor' and a 'nursing sister' played by the only woman that Mitchell saw performing. Emphasis was laid on cleanliness, neatness and presentation of attire.

Such *kalela* performances built their enjoyment, fun and humour around a diversity of contraries experienced as part of urban African life. Thus the play on smart dress pointed up the signifance of class and status in urban life which belied the humble – in the main low-status – tasks of most of the *kalela* participants. The *kalela* songs developed their humour around tribal stereotypes, themselves largely constructions of urban life, and the paradoxical qualities of urban living.

Mitchell is primarily concerned with the general sociological import of *kalela* as thoroughly constructed in terms of the structural principles conditioning urban existence. He is well aware of the political context of *kalela*, and that it could be seen as an institution of African political resistance. He refers to the political role of dances such as the *mbeni*, suggested by some to be a historical antecedent of the *kalela*, and banned by colonial authorities because of its antagonistic content. Other dances, for example the *malipenga*, made great fun of the stiffness of the military officialdom of colonial powers, perhaps of the constraint and rigidity of its authority. Politically resistant commentary of this nature was not absent from some *kalela* performances I have witnessed. One I saw performed by Unga dancers from Chief Matipa's district at the village of Paramount Chief Kopa (both Matipa and Kopa are Bisa chieftaincies within which the Unga lived)[2] made much of the point that Kopa was a colonial appointment, and that the claims of a rival, Kapumfi Mfwembe, had been ignored. Kapumfi represented some opposition to colonial rule and was a lineal descendant of Naseba, a Bisa heroine, a kind of Joan of Arc figure who had rallied Bisa opposition to Ngoni conquerors in pre-colonial times.[3] Broadly, however, the *kalela*, from Mitchell's evidence and my own observations over ten years later, was not an overt act of political resistance.

None the less, the play of the *kalela* manifests, in my view, contradictions at the heart of bureaucratic/industrial orders anywhere, but which achieve particular intensity in the context of the colonial towns of Central Africa. Mitchell argues that categorical relations – the tribalism of the towns – is a feature of mass industrial societies; thus Africans are behaving like human beings everywhere in the urban centres of mass industrial society. Tribal categories, dependent on type of urban situation, are simply the most efficient, and cast the widest net of possibilities in the work of developing social relations in largely anonymous settings.

But I note a further factor. The construction of relations and the formation of significant categories of identity are not merely a 'natural' function of the development of mass industrial societies. They may be integral in their formation, but certain modes of institutional or organisational ordering are systematic with certain kinds of political ordering regardless of such factors as scale (mass society or small community) or anonymity. For example,

2. The Unga generally live within the Bangweulu Swamp region. They are predominantly fishers (see Brelsford, 1946). At the time of my fieldwork they were subjects of much Bisa derogatory diatribe. Bisa, for example, would make fun of their living conditions, commenting that the Unga were different from everyone else for they were born with webbed feet! A joking relation, in fact, existed between Unga and Bisa. The Unga *kalela* dancers brought to the surface political conflicts within the Bisa chieftaincies. Chief Matipa was in political disagreement with Kopa.

3. Paramount Chief Kopa, at the time of my fieldwork in Bisaland in 1963 (Kapferer, 1967), was politically opposed by villages closely connected to Kapumfi Mfwembe, located at the fringe of the Lake Bangweulu swamps. Just prior to my fieldwork there had been minor anti-colonial skirmishes. It was a politically transitional time for Zambia, which was then on the verge of full national political independence. I should note the difference in the rural *kalela* dances I observed from those Mitchell describes in the urban context. The dance I saw at Kopa's village consisted of two lines of dancers, one of young men the other of young women. The men were dressed in their finest town clothes and the women in fine dresses. In some ways, the dance communicated the wealth of returning migrant workers.

dominant forms of organisational structure determine or produce appropriate forms of social action. This is an underlying
part of the tribalism argument developed by Mitchell. It is specifically the argument when Mitchell accounts for the relative
insignificance of tribal categorical relations in the highly organised mining company areas of the Copperbelt towns. These areas
were virtually 'total institutional', the mining companies defining
most areas of African life. Mitchell argues that the mine structure
provided the key frame for the development of social interactional relations and rendered others, such as those of tribal identity,
irrelevant or redundant. Tribalism, in Mitchell's view, is a kind of
'free' form emergent in the conditions of an urban world but
developed by Africans in settings relatively undetermined by
urban and economic organisational orders or in those interstitial
structural zones, or, in Victor Turner's sense, marginal locales of
urban life (Turner, 1957; 1974). Places of 'leisure' were those areas
where the operation of tribal identity and category were most in
evidence.

Let me pursue Mitchell in the direction his argument suggests,
but which, to a degree, lies hidden or subordinated in his more
general sociological concerns. Mitchell's analysis of the *The Kalela
Dance* indicates resistance. This is a resistance not of an overtly
political kind (of the expressly anti-colonial sort) but a resistance
to certain determinations of the urban system of which Africans
are a part. To put it another way, the *kalela* is the anti-structural,
in a Turnerian sense, thrown up by the structural process of
urban formation.

It is possible to see the plays in the *kalela* around the role types
of 'doctor', 'nurse', and 'king' as 'attacks' on positions of routine
authority over Africans in their urban world established through
the agency of colonial power. Medical positions are not merely
high in status, but critical points through which Africans encountered the authority and power of colonial state realities – a phenomenon, of course, by no means limited to colonial Africa.
Similarly, there is some suggestion that the role of 'king' and the
play around it has some reference to the 'tribal elder system': a
system established by the colonial authorities in town to assist
with the administration of Africans.

Following the point a little further, the tribalism that Mitchell
describes, a social form developed by Africans in the marginal
areas of town life (i.e. outside structurally determining orders), is

antagonistic to the categories established by the authorities and through which they strove to control Africans. This is the full implication of Mitchell's own argument and evidence; I am simply making it more apparent. The colonial authorities saw Africans as tribespeople bound in traditional custom. The *kalela* dancers make scurrilous, obscene statements about the customs of other tribes. Mitchell stresses this as a manifestation of the emergence of joking relations functional in the establishment of urban social relations. But the fun and humour centred about others' customs can also be seen as an immanent critique of a colonial order which saw urban people as tradition-bound, and even an implicit criticism of the stereotypes of Africans which those connected to the command of the colonial system (colonial officials, missionaries and anthropologists) were assiduously constructing in the interests of control.[4] If the *kalela* was an instance of the formation of urban identities and relations, it was critical of those imposed by the colonial authorities.

It is also possible to see an implicit resistance more positively. The play on tribal value, the praise of one's own tribal customs relative to that of others – a marked feature of the *kalela* songs – can be seen as a response to the alienating conditions of urban life. I do not refer to that form of alienation which is a common assumption in urban studies, the notion of the individual isolated and estranged in the circumstances of mass society; rather, I refer to that alienation created through the bureaucratic order of the modern state. Colonial contexts such as colonial Zambia are extreme examples of the bureaucratic orders of contemporary states. There the bureaucracy is in naked control without modification in an electoral or democratic process.

The properties of modern bureaucratic orders, their foundation in a scientific and techno-rationalism, is documented by numerous scholars, Weber and more recently Foucault being among the most influential. Foucault's (1970) discussion stresses the taxonomic schemes of modern bureaucratic systems in which the 'person' is effectively disembodied and reconceived as so many attributes or component parts to be variously arranged

4. The Bisa in the area where I first did fieldwork were amused by the fascination which the White Father Catholic priests (the White Fathers were the main missionary organisation in Zambia's Northern Province) showed in Bisa (and Bemba) sexual practices. To the Bisa this seemed to be the main thing that concerned them. Indeed, the White Fathers had compiled a large work centring around Bisa sexual customs and written in Latin.

according to the techo-rationalism of the operations of the bureaucratic system itself. Contemporary notions of 'identity' can be demonstrated as very much linked to the processes of modern state formation and their bureaucratic orders – from the sixteenth and seveneteenth centuries on. Such conceptions of identity which involve the characterisation of individuals as clusters of identities arranged (and rearrangeable) hierarchically are systematic with bureaucratic operation. The person is separated from a structure of social relations, further internally individuated, and then made existent or non-existent as a property of an abstract system of bureaucratic operations. Elsewhere (Kapferer, 1993) I have referred to this process as the 'categorial imperative'.

My implication in the context of this discussion is that issues of identity and processes of the formation of categories of association on the basis of identity attributes are stimulated by the operation of bureaucratic systems, as in colonial Zambia. The production of identity categories and the formation of social relations through them is not merely a 'natural' sociological response to anonymous urban worlds. The urban world of Zambia, by the fact of the supreme control of the colonial bureaucracy, was constituted, *made into*, a field of identity and identity categories the significances of which were commanded within the bureaucratic system.

The *kalela*, its focus on identity, and its concern for self-definition through identity stereotypes, gains impetus in the frame of the bureaucratic orders of the Zambian towns. This was the dominant logic of the urban situation. Simultaneously, the *kalela* was a reaction to the disembodied character of the operation of the bureaucratic order, an implicit resistance to its alienation.

Dance, perhaps above all, is a technique of the body, the expression of the body as the experiential centre of the lived-in world. This is why dance is so often engaged as a medium of resistant expression in contexts of radical alienation. Dancers also – and the *kalela* dancers are no exception – engage the sexual body, the vital source of metaphors which not only insist on the body as the centre of experience and the heart of the reconstitution of experience but also on the body as the locus of power and of its reappropriation. The *kalela* songs are full of sexual play which, in my view, achieve added significance in the political context of colonial Zambia. The sexual body as the centre of the generation of social relations, as distinct from the abstract

bureaucratic order, is also a feature of the urban tribal joking relationships described by Mitchell.

The elaboration, some recent analysts might say the 'invention', of cultural and customary characteristics in the urban discourse of tribalism might also be seen as a reaction to
bureaucratic alienation.[5] A frequently observed phenomenon of
bureaucratic taxonomies is their relative lack of subjective content or, as I indicated above, the construction into them of a content by bureaucratic agents rather than by the living human
beings to which the content refers. The creativity and imaginative
elaborations of the songs, as well as, perhaps, an implicit joke
against the stereotyping activities of the colonially dominant, is
an active constitution of the meaning of identity in the concrete
contexts of everyday experience. The *kalela* songs are replete with
the humour of everyday events.

I have stressed 'tribalism', certain dynamics of identity and the
play of categories and stereotypes as both constituted in the
structural contexts of urban life and, simultaneously, as a reaction to the alienation produced by the political orders of the
towns. I stress a point to some extent congruent with that
expressed by Mitchell, Gluckman and their colleagues and followers (of whom I am one). The tribalism of Africans in town was
through and through a contemporary urban phenomenon and
not a mere continuation of old tribal ways, as many colonial officials and social scientists insisted. Moreover, the colonisers and
the colonised were given to constitute and construct the import of
tribal identity, to engage the logic of the category, in similar
ways. This led to a paradox (exacerbated perhaps by African
resistance to colonial definitions and their alienation within colonial bureaucratic worlds) whereby the African mirroring of colonial practice was conceived by the colonisers as the persistence of
tribal practice and sentiments.

A theme I have been developing is that the construction of
identity is powerfully influenced through the bureaucratic order
of the contemporary state. The impetus to and the process of its

5. In the 1960s Mitchell became fascinated with the East London studies (Mayer, 1961)
and the Xhosa distinction between 'Red' and 'School'. The Red Xhosa, the traditionally oriented, were to a large extent involved in constructions of tribal identity and custom in
response to the extreme bureaucratic policies along apartheid exclusionary lines of the white
South African government. Mitchell recognised that this response fitted his earlier observations made north of the Zambezi. The Red Xhosa responses underlines the point I am making
about extending the implications of Mitchell's work.

construction and the significances attached to identity cannot be separated from this fact. This does not mean that the phenomenon of identity is limited to the historical circumstances of contemporary states, only that the bureaucratic character of modern states creates a particular stress on identity, and is active in the construction of identity and in the way people come to see themselves as possessing identities of particular form and content.

Aboriginality and Ideologies of Identity and Resistance in Australia

The contemporary situation of Australian Aborigines extends the point. Australian Aborigines are highly determined within the bureaucratic orders of the modern Australian state. Their identity as such, and what constitutes its significant dimensions – especially regarding administrative control, access to diverse resources, human rights, etc. – has long been of bureaucratic concern, but in this last thirty or so years has increasingly become central in public debate throughout Australia. This is particularly so with regard to land rights legislation and decisions. A recent High Court ruling that native lands were unlawfully alienated in the course of discovery and exploration is the latest event in widespread political discussion which has issues of Aboriginal identity at its centre.

Before I go any further, it should be emphasised that Australian Aborigines are integral in wider debates within the Australian population as a whole concerning issues of identity. Multiculturalism, the importance of protecting the cultural rights of ethnic 'communities', is a key ideological pillar of the state, important in popular nationalism and vital in asserting the distinction of Australia and its egalitarian image in the contemporary global context (see Kapferer, 1988). Aborigines have been able to open space, increasingly in the last thirty years or so, in these ideological discourses of state and people, and to pursue political and social interests long denied them. The shift to a state policy of multiculturalism (from the 1970s) and away from previous policies of assimilationism enabled a great diversity of populations with Aboriginal ancestry to assert such identity and to win political and economic rights in relation to their identity as Aborigines.

In many ways, the multicultural ideology of the state is a dimension of what Mitchell refers to as 'categorical relations'. Basically, the ethnic 'communities' of multiculturalism are conceived by the agents of the state and also, often by those who would identify with such communities, as relatively undifferentiated internally, and adhering to common cultural/linguistic characteristics. These 'imagined communities' are abstractions: that is they gloss situated differences and internal structural variations and process. Furthermore, they subdue other significant forms of social association (e.g. class) which cross-cut communal boundaries and may render such boundaries relatively unimportant in practice.

Elsewhere I (Kapferer, 1988) have argued that an ideology or discourse of multiculturalism is consistent with the notion of egalitarian-individualism which is a logic of discourse in many contemporary democratic states, and which is integral within multiculturalism as it was in state (and popular) assimilationist orientations. Egalitarian-individualism, marked in diverse contemporary nationalist pronouncements, asserts the individual to be the embodiment of community, the community being an expanded individual. Such an orientation is central in state-bureaucratic modes of organisation and control (especially visible in the management of immigration) and also in resistance to state-bureaucratic measures. Thus abstract bureaucratic assertions concerning the definition of community will be contested at the level of individual experience, the definition of the category, the stereotype, always being at risk in its individually specific manifestation – part of the humour, I have suggested, of the *kalela*.

A concern to achieve agreement between the abstract and the concrete is part of the impetus for cultural performances, public presentations of customary activity, culture as spectacle, whereby the abstract is both experienced and the 'community' made manifest in its internal uniformity to audiences. The movement to the spectacle of culture is usually related to transformations in capitalism, the commodification of culture, tourism, the development of systems of mass communication – all connected with the formation of mass society and the institutional complexes of the nation-state. I do not debate this, but indicate that the contemporary phenomenon of culture as spectacle is motivated in contemporary ideological processes which, while they may refract

processes of alienation, also promote it (a problematic of the
capacity of abstract categories to encompass the existentially concrete). This is so with regard to the bureaucratic institutions of the
state which are concerned to define and to discover the substantive through the abstract (they infer and manipulate persons
through the assumptions carried in the abstract category).

The tropical rainforest town of Kuranda, perched on the high
bluffs overlooking the city of Cairns in northern Queensland,
contextualises some of the general aspects I have been discussing
in relation to Aboriginals and identity. Kuranda, once a logging
town, is now a major tourist centre. It has long been a place for
white Australians seeking an alternative lifestyle, and was a
well-known centre of the counter-cultural movement of the
1960s. The Cairns region is one of contest, where the conflicts of
modernity (and post-modernity) find sharp expression. Thus the
proponents and antagonists of the ecology movement, of
Aboriginal rights, of development planning, etc. find the cause
and the reason for the pursuit of their political interests.
Their assertions refract paradoxes of a Hobbesian kind at the
ideological heart of contemporary democratic states – Australia
especially.

Ecology and Aborigines, two of the most frequently addressed
issues, expose anxieties concerning individual rights in the face
of government and bureaucratic controls and the problems of
local community autonomy in the face of alien business and
industrial interests (these days often Japanese). The virtues of a
'natural' individual common sense and of ordinary practicality,
so often at the centre of egalitarian-individualist discourse in
Australia regardless of political position, features extensively in
discussions and protests relating to ecology and to Aborigines. In
Kuranda, ecology and Aboriginal identity have become matters
of some entrepreneurial endeavour and directed to the business
of attracting tourists.

The explicit use of ecology and Aboriginality in monetary pursuit underlines the fact that they are issues vitally part of capitalist and contemporary technological realities, integral to such
realities: they are expressive of the contradictions within the
structures of these realities despite their frequent representation
as somehow external and sometimes furiously opposed to them.
This observation in no way reduces the commitment of the persons involved in such issues or the significance of the point of

their arguments, although the parties to such issues will use the extent of the commercialism involved to question the authenticity or legitimacy of particular groups or persons engaged.

In Kuranda there were two Aboriginal groups engaged in the organisation of dance/song performances. Both claimed to represent the 'culture' of the traditional Tjapukai (Djabagi) rainforest Aborigines. The most professional performances were those organised twice a day at the Tjapukai Dance Theatre explicitly for tourists. This had been established in 1987 out of the co-operation of a North American immigrant to Australia, Jeff Rappaport (who had professional training in a New York theatre production), and an Aboriginal, Dave Gardiner (married into the Tjapukai community), who has considerable theatrical flair. (He is also a well-known performer in a local rock band, which, like many other Aboriginal rock groups, makes excellent use of the didgeridoo.) The members of the Tjapukai Theatre performance group are drawn from a variety of Aboriginal communities, and one is a Torres Strait Islander. They have been selected for their performance skills, not on the basis of identity. Moreover, the material they present has little to do with what might have been Tjapukai cultural knowledge. What is presented is a bricolage of a diversity of Aboriginal cultural themes, imaginatively interpreted and tuned to fit non-Aboriginal conceptions, usually romantic, of Aboriginality.

The performance plays on white/black stereotypes in a way well-rehearsed and designed not to offend white audiences. Rappaport and Gardiner have won a series of tourist industry awards and regularly go on international tours presenting Aboriginal culture. For all the commercialism of the project, Gardiner is committed to the presentation of Aboriginal identity in a way that builds local Aboriginal self-pride. He notes the new respect accorded Aborigines in Kuranda achieved by his enterprise. (It is, perhaps, the most successful economic venture in the town.)

The performance of the Tjapukai Theatre is a perfect example of an invented tradition. Some of the humour of the performance is a self-conscious awareness of this fact. In a sense, the audiences collude in the construction. None the less, my impression is that most who witness the performance accept it as a presentation of traditional Aboriginal worlds. The performance is appropriate to the category 'aborigine' as this is imagined in white-dominated realities. In effect, a specific tribal group, Tjapukai, is culturally defined at the most inclusive level of Aboriginal identity, which subsumes specific Tjapukai identity.

There is considerable anger in Kuranda towards the Tjapukai Theatre, and this reaches beyond envy at the success of its sheer commercialism. Aborigines and non-Aborigines throughout Australia are cashing in on the entrepreneurial possibilities of Aboriginal identity. Aborigines and non-Aboriginal sympathisers quickly dispel that romanticism which would see something inappropriate or wrong with the commercialisation of 'tradition'. As one highly active white interlocutor for local Tjapukai interests declared to me, '[t]heir culture kept them alive in the past and through tourism it can keep them alive today!' The opposition to the Tjapukai Theatre derives from its claim to represent the Tjapukai. Those in Kuranda who have stronger genealogical claim to Tjapukai ancestry in effect have had its use appropriated by outsiders.

This appropriation was the undercurrent in a cultural performance (held in the local church hall) of Tjapukai community members in Kuranda in 1990. The occasioning of the performance was stimulated by the choice of Kuranda as the site for the Australian National Folk Festival. The Tjapukai Theatre was performing as a programmed event in the festival, and the use of its splendid modern theatre had been granted the festival organisers. The festival placed local conflict over the legitimate 'ownership' of the Tjapukai name on the national stage. The performance I witnessed was complicated by other factors. Much assistance and stimulation for the organisation of the performance came from non-Aboriginals who were concerned to give back aspects of their 'tradition' lost as a function of the depradations of white settlement and missionary activity. These people were conscious of the fact that the distinctiveness of Tjapukai forms of life had been smashed in the colonial process.

The return of tradition to the Tjapukai (and to other tribal communities) is receiving federal government funding. Aboriginal museums are being created exhibiting aspects of local traditional pasts. In Kuranda (for the Tjakupai), and for other groups elsewhere, language reconstruction programmes are underway, and positive attempts are being made to introduce local Aboriginal languages at secondary schools.

A widespread non-Aboriginal and Aboriginal view is that the parlous state of Aboriginal communities, the chronic alcoholism and violence, is a consequence of the loss of traditional values. The reconstruction and assertion of these values is considered to be crucial to the rehabilitation of Aborigines. This attitude receives force in a wider Australian ideological climate which stresses the virtues of autonomy linked with tradition (also, in a contemporary political climate of privatisation and the winding down of social services, the economic retreat of the state expressed in an increased emphasis on the virtues of self-help). I note that the kind of colonialist argument against which Gluckman and Mitchell reacted in Zambia is being reproduced in the different historical context of contemporary Australia. This is not merely, I suggest, because in distinct ways they are colonial contexts, but is connected to the rationalism of contemporary bureaucratic systems and of the encompassing worlds of which they are a part. The rationalism of bureaucracy encourages a counter-rationalism of tradition.

I underline the notion of tradition as a powerful value within white Australia and integral to an egalitarian/individualist discourse revolving around the relation of state to society. It is particularly relevant in the north Queensland context I am discussing, and especially Kuranda, which can be described as a life-world whose non-Aboriginal inhabitants make an express point of the practice of self-reliance, who have explored technologies constructed and worked by the persons who depend on them, and who emphasise moralities (often rationalist and explicitly non-religious) of the person or of the individual, free of the dictates of conventions established by superordinate institutions which deny autonomy. That Kuranda represents such values more widely in Australia has contributed to its being a place of tourist pilgrimage, and influenced its choice as the venue of the national folk festival. Kuranda is a centre for the reason of the individual as against the reason of the state.

Driven by genuine concern for the plight of the Tjapukai community, the participation of non-Aboriginals in the organisation of the Tjapukai performance is also an engagement in the practice of their own value and an attempt to realise its self-regenerating force. Moreover, for some of the whites participating in the event (mainly behind the scenes), Aborigines, as icons of tradition – of egalitarian autonomy, of a technology and morality commanded

by the individual – constituted a white ideal and their reconstruction of it is a kind of realisation of the ideal. White and Tjapukai
community interests in the retrieval of tradition coincided. The
reconstruction of a Tjapukai tradition enables the Tjapukai to
reappropriate a distinct identity. This is demanded not merely
because such an identity is a marketable commodity, but because
a possession of a distinct identity is vital as a means of access to
various state-controlled resources, one being land.

The Tjapukai community performance contained many of the
same elements as the Tjapukai Theatre. It drew humour from
white/black stereotypic contrasts: jokes about snakes as 'bush
tucker', puns using Aboriginal English (e.g. Djama roll, conflation of 'bama' or food with the English 'jam'), etc. Other linguistic
expressions (e.g. 'G'day') were engaged, stressing the unity of
performers and audience as Australians – significant in a recent
political past of Aboriginal exclusion from the ordinary rights of
citizenship. The performance progressed through a series of set
piece representations of their situation, often commenting on
aspects of modern life and the loss of traditional knowledge. The
performance ended, as at the Tjapukai Theatre, with the song
'Proud to be an Aborigine'.

A centrepiece of the performance was a song about 'Queen
Maggie'. Maggie is an old Tjapukai, not present on the occasion,
who is a resource of traditional knowledge – important to the
community as a link to the shattered past. The story of Maggie
was sung in Tjapukai (transliterated by one of the white
helpers).[6] None of the performers knew the language, but cue
cards were held in front of them as they sang, the woman leader
of the group 'translating' the words of the song back to the audience.

A major point of this event was to demonstrate before the
audience (composed of Tjapukai, other Aborigines and whites)
the legitimate claim of the performers to Tjapukai identity. The
song created around Maggie had other import. The performance
group was largely comprised of women, a fact which communi-
cates the centrality of Aboriginal women in local community
organisation which, as others have pointed out, is not necessarily
a continuity from a traditional past, but rather of state welfare
policies which targeted women as the foci for the distribution of

6. This person had written a Tjapukai grammar. He had been trained in anthropology.

resources and, to some extent, as the means whereby control over Aboriginal communities could be exerted (Collmann, 1988). In the changed circumstances of Aboriginal rights, Aboriginal women are often at the forefront of securing greater benefits for their communities.

I have noted one of Mitchell's general observations on the basis of his African materials: that identity categories and stereotypes become vital in the generation of social relations within relatively unstructured situations. He adds to this that a phenomenon of such categories in the anonymous settings of mass-urban societies is that they become integral in the forming of social and political relations. The Australian Aboriginal data, even the limited Tjapukai materials I have presented, demonstrate these points – dramatically so, for it is in areas of leisure, in the domains of 'play', *par excellence* the zone of tourism in contemporary societies, that the discourse of identity comes into the most visible force. Perhaps, as sociologists suggest, the increased capitalisation of leisure and the huge development of tourist enterprise has contributed in no small way to the intensity of a modern politics of culture and identity. Following Mitchell's insight, however, it is in the 'open' space of tourism, where Aboriginals are relatively free of the social and political controls which have determined and subordinated them, that they can construct alternative definitions of their identity or, indeed, bring into the open dimensions of their identity which have been suppressed and insist on crucial revaluations. Here, too, Aboriginals can exploit ideological understandings, integral to dominating worlds, of individual freedom, personal autonomy, equality, etc. It is in the fields of leisure that the ideals of social and political order can come into open expression without necessarily being contradicted by harsh realities – in the everyday experience of Aborigines, heavy unemployment and a continuing social and political marginalisation.

Mitchell implied that in relatively unstructured contexts new structures could come into operation. In this Australian context, categories of Aboriginality come into performance play, and new structures are created through the category. The degree of this process in Australia cannot be understressed. People who once suppressed aspects of their Aboriginalness, or had it denied them, are not only asserting it but developing new relations and repositioning themselves in social structures in terms of their

Aboriginality. The tourist situation is one area in which such a process is facilitated.

The situation of play established in tourist contexts enables a discourse of categories. It enables processes of destructuring and restructuring – a vital aspect of play in any context. But, of course, no situation can be understood as unstructured, hence my use of the term 'relatively'. As far as the Aboriginal context I have referred to is concerned, the leisure/tourist situation enables those cast to the margins of the political and social order to enter into its midst, for no other reason than that the boundaries of that order are relaxed. Tourists escape the boundaries of their everyday confinement and, indeed, are oriented to the marginal. In the situation of tourism, Aborigines, for example, take a central position, and in such a position begin to have some control over their context and to contest or develop their own identity constructs.

Not only do Aborigines enter structure through their play into tourist worlds but they may also reveal patterns of relation which have hitherto been obscured. The Tjapukai Theatre performances were creative in their constructions of Aboriginality, but also in generating a specific Tjapukai identity present prior to the assertions of the theatre. The Tjapukai Theatre structured relations through abstract categories which pointed to a concreteness (localness) that these categories did not have. Thus the Tjapukai Theatre performance informed the audience of the traditional geographical boundaries of the Tjapukai and conveyed a sense that they were representatives of the Tjapukai. A world of actual Tjapukai social relations was revealed and brought into a contested relation to the broader category representations of the Tjapukai Theatre.

An obvious feature of the Tjapukai materials is the role non-Aboriginals play in Aboriginal constructions. It is a mark of the destruction that occurred of their worlds and of the still-continuing dependence upon persons who are from the world which crushed them. In contrast, Zambians had far greater autonomy in their constructions of themselves. However, such clear difference aside, this Aboriginal material reveals what I consider is common to the two contexts: the identities constructed are formed in the institutional conditions of dominance and powerfully influenced by the ideologies – even in resistance to such conditions – which underpin such institutions.

Conclusions

Mitchell's study of the *kalela* dancers was an exercise in situational analysis, the exploration of the dynamics of an event of social practice to explore dimensions of embracing realities. The event was not a mere or apt illustration – an ethnographic example of wider processes – but important in its internal dynamics. To put the point in more recently fashionable terms, a concentration on the process of the event itself gave authority to the practitioners and less to the impositions of an alien observer. The participants, in their expressive action and in the diverse conundrums they themselves explored concerning the world of their existence, revealed what their existence was *for them*. Gluckman, Mitchell, and Victor Turner (who probably turned the approach to the greatest effect in his analyses of ritual) effectively realised that the world of lived realities was the proper anthropological focus and that this involved attention to verbal and non-verbal action. Moreover, this action was productive of what anthropologists abstractly called 'structure'. Situated events did not simply represent the wider reality; they were, through their participants, 'structurating' processes, vital in the construction and reconstruction of lived realities.

I have attempted to extend this approach of Mitchell in his *kalela* study; thus my concentration on its resistant aspects which involved attention to the content of the songs and of other aspects of the action. My argument reinforces Mitchell's position concerning the distinctive and innovative urban qualities of the *kalela* performances; their demonstration of the absurdities and discordancies in experience of colonial bureaucratic impositions, and the expressions by Zambians of how an urban world may be comprehended, defined and acted within.

There is no lament in Mitchell at the loss of tradition, as there is in the despairing romanticism of much anthropology. He is fascinated, and positively, with the upsurge of new forms. This is the excitement of the *kalela*. As Mitchell describes it, the *kalela* plays havoc with the conceptions of tradition prevalent among colonial administrators and, too often, anthropologists. What I suggest, in extension of Mitchell, is that the views of tradition of colonialists – and more recently, among those non-Aboriginals in Australia, for example, who wish to restore tradition – are constructions within contemporary bureaucratic-rational realities.

Tradition among Aborigines is not only being invented but its impetus is integral to modern ideologies, a mode of resistance internal to contemporary ideological discourse.

Furthermore, the assertion of traditional value can fail to note the import of innovative forms. Tourist art, for example, is often seen as a debasement of traditional forms – this is particularly so in the context of Aboriginal Australia. Without getting into any discussion regarding aesthetic merits, I have noted that it can have positive political force. It is in the play space of tourist practices that Aborigines are able to engage with dominating ideologies and to work new definitions of their situation.

Much of my discussion concentrated around Mitchell's analysis of categorical relations and its general import for the understanding of ethnic identity. My specific development is that the emergence of such relations is a function of the formation of the modern state and its bureaucratic order. The colonial state was a bureaucratic system *par excellence* and its power was to form the worlds of its control to the terms of its abstract scientific-rational categories. The formation of categorical relations was not only a response to natural situations of anonymity, for instance, created in the development of mass industrial and urban society, but emergent through the anonymisation of existential realities in the establishment of the contemporary state and its bureaucratic system. This was remarkably so in the case of Aborigines. The structures of their worlds were actively destroyed in the orders of the colonial and post-colonial state. Aboriginal constructions of self-identity and the relations established through such constructions must be understood in such a historical context: the categories of Aboriginality are simultaneously motivated in the bureaucratic world of the state and resistant to its determinations.

Bibliography

Barth, F. (ed.), *Ethnic Groups and Boundaries*, London: Allen and Unwin, 1969

Brelsford, W.V., *Fishermen of the Bangweulu Swamps*, Rhodes-Livingstone Papers, no.12, Manchester: Manchester University Press, 1946

Collmann, J., *Fringe-Dwellers and Welfare: The Aboriginal Response to Bureaucracy*, St Lucia: University of Queensland Press, 1988

Epstein, A.L., *Politics in an Urban African Community*, Manchester: Manchester University Press, 1958

Foucault, M., *The Order of Things*, London: Tavistock, 1970
Gluckman, M., *Malinowski's Sociological Theories*, Rhodes-Livingstone Papers, no.16, Manchester: Manchester University Press, 1949
_____, *Analysis of a Social Situation in Modern Zululand*, Rhodes-Livingstone Paper no.28, Manchester; Manchester University Press, 1958
_____, 'Anthropological Problems Arising From the African Industrial Revolution', in *Social Change in Modern Africa*, A. Southall (ed.), London: Oxford University Press, 1961
Gluckman, M., Mitchell, J.C. and Barnes, J.A., 'The Village Headman in British Central Africa', *Africa*, vol.19, 1949, pp.89–106
Kapferer, B., *Cooperation, Leadership and Village Structure*, Zambian Papers 1, Manchester: Manchester University Press, 1967
_____, *Strategy and Transaction in an African Factory*, Manchester: Manchester University Press, 1972
_____, 'The Anthropology of Max Gluckman', in *Power, Process and Transformation: Essays in Memory of Max Gluckman*, B. Kapferer (ed.), *Social Analysis*, no.22, 1987
_____, *Legends of People, Myths of State*, Washington: Smithsonian Institution Press, 1988
_____, 'Bureaucratic Erasure: Identity, Resistance and Violence: Aborigines and a Discourse of Autonomy in a North Queensland Town', paper presented to Decennial Conference of the Association of Social Anthropologists, Oxford, 1993
Magubane, B., 'A Critical Look at Indices Used in the Study of Social Change in Colonial Africa', *Current Anthropology*, vol.12, 1971, pp.419–45
Mayer, P., *Townsmen or Tribesmen: Conservatism and the Process of Urbanization in a South African City*, Cape Town: Oxford University Press, 1961
Mitchell, J.C., *The Kalela Dance: Aspects of Social Relationships Among Urban Africans in Northern Rhodesia*, Rhodes-Livingstone Papers, no.27, Manchester: Manchester University Press, 1956
_____, 'Case and Situational Analysis', *The Sociological Review (N.S.)*, vol.38, 1983, pp.187–211
_____, *Cities, Society, and Social Perception: A Central African Perspective*, Oxford: Clarendon Press, 1987
Redfield, R., *The Folk Culture of Yucatan*, Chicago: University of Chicago Press, 1941
Turner, V.W., *Schism and Continuity in an African Society*, Manchester: Manchester University Press, 1957
_____, *Dramas, Fields, and Metaphors*, Ithaca, NY: Cornell University Press, 1974
Werbner, R.P., 'The Manchester School in South-Central Africa', *Annual Review of Anthropology*, vol.13, 1984, pp.157–85

Wilson, G., *The Economics of Detribalization*, Rhodes-Livingstone Papers, nos 1 & 2, Oxford: Oxford University Press, 1940/42

Wirth, L., 'Urbanism as a Way of Life', *American Journal of Sociology*, vol.44, 1938, pp.1–24

Chapter 3

Ethnicity, Ideology and Social Drama: The Waitangi Day Incident 1981

Kayleen M. Hazlehurst

The Significance of Waitangi Day

For the modern *Pakeha*,[1] Waitangi Day, on 6 February, commemorates not only a compact between two founding peoples under the 1840 Treaty of Waitangi but, perhaps more importantly, the establishment of UK dominion in New Zealand. From 1973, when Waitangi Day was made a national public holiday, it was marked by a large-scale celebration held on the Treaty House grounds at Waitangi, near the Northland township of Paihia. This well-kept historic area has been a centre for much official ceremony and is a major tourist attraction.

To those Maori who would 'honour the Treaty in their hearts', the official Waitangi Day celebration is the time to acknowledge and reaffirm the sacredness of the pact. The Maori academic, Auckland District Maori Council administrator and political commentator, Dr Ranginui Walker, recognised in 1974 that the pageantry of Waitangi Day was an exercise in myth-making. But he was encouraged at the time by the representation of New Zealand as 'a plural society, a multi-cultural nation' (Walker, 1974, p.73).

To others, especially of the younger generation of Maori, the public holiday exhibited an artificially and hypocritically arranged blend of Maori and *Pakeha* symbols, as calculatedly ambiguous as the treaty itself. For radicals, the annual Waitangi

---

1. *Pakeha* – 'fair skinned' or 'foreign'. Throughout this chapter the term *Pakeha* refers to European settlers and later immigrants and their descendants (white New Zealanders).

Day ceremony came to be seen as a *Pakeha* fabrication, garishly ornamented with uniformed parades, naval displays, and Maori concert parties, which paid homage to European values and conquest. As the New Zealand historian Keith Sinclair put it, '6 February provided annual occasions for lamentation' (Sinclair, 1986, p.263).[2]

The Waitangi National *Marae*[3] (*Titiri o Waitangi Marae*) or lower *marae* (which lies out of sight about a mile downhill from the Treaty House, upper *marae*), belongs to the Northern tribes of that region, but holds special significance to all Maori as the site where the great chiefs discussed the covenant they were to make with the UK. This less manicured domain has the feel of homeliness and belonging characteristic of tribal meeting houses.

Waitangi Day was from its inception a symbolically contested event. Intended as an occasion to affirm a desired national unity, it offered a matchless opportunity to express the grievances which stood as fundamental impediments to unity. Deculturated urban Maori youth – those who experienced the worst of unemployment, educational and housing inequities, and other disadvantages which afflicted their people – took an aggressive stance towards Waitangi Day celebrations. So too did some of a growing minority of articulate higher-educated young Maori.

While the elders said they 'wait patiently for the *Pakeha* to honour the treaty', the more assertive young people – who remain within the embrace of the traditional Maori world – could not share their elders' faith. Waitangi Day celebrations were punctuated by incidents of protest. In the first decade of the protest movement to the late 1970s, demonstrations took mostly symbolic forms: threats to cut down the Waitangi flag-staff, the heckling of speakers, the declaration of Waitangi Day as 'a day of mourning', and harsh public criticism. But increasingly the incidents included throwing of missiles and jostling of government officials. It was not only the liberal and radical sectors of the Maori world which demanded the righting of nineteenth- and twentieth-century wrongs. Conservative leaders, and their organisations, also made representations about these grievances. Maori land-holding, it was pointed out, had continued to decline, even

---

2. The history of the treaty and relevant recent developments may be studied in Claudia Orange, *The Treaty of Waitangi* (1987).

3. *Marae* – ceremonial gathering place, place for political debate, associated with a large meeting house, other buildings, and surrounding grounds.

during recent years of apparent heightened responsiveness. Chronic land loss, the stripping of traditional shell-fish beds, the pollution of fishing grounds, and significant local and national legislation, all were in direct breach of the second article of the treaty: that the Maori people would be guaranteed the 'full, exclusive and undisturbed possession of their lands and estates, forests, fisheries and other properties'.[4]

In 1979 a small group of urban activists formed a new organisation called the Waitangi Action Committee, with the determined aim of halting the Waitangi Day celebrations until such time as the 'treaty had been honoured'. The leadership and core membership of this group consisted of a vocal and strong-willed matriarch, Titewhai Harawira, her adult children, and their young Maori and *Pakeha* friends. The majority of this group ranged in age from their late teens to early thirties. They shared a common sense of deprivation through unemployment or underemployment, through the dislocation and impact of urbanisation, and the loss of Maori culture. They were suspicious of what they perceived to be the '*Pakeha* system' (which they felt did not receive them as equals), but uncomfortable as well with traditional Maori social mores. Their identity was closely bound to a passionate adoption of an emerging and progressively defined Maori cause. Most of them had participated in protest activity over some years. Some had experienced short terms of imprisonment. The anger and commitment of all had been fuelled by frequent confrontations with the police.

It became a common complaint of the elders that the youth no longer listened to them, that they 'trampled upon the *mana* of their people' by their non-observance of Maori customs and courtesies.[5] Some protest tactics and more expansive demands rang of separatism – an ill-defined objective which could be maliciously caricatured by their opponents as 'apartheid'. Many middle-aged

4. The Treaty of Waitangi is the treaty made between Her Majesty Victoria, Queen of the United Kingdom of Great Britain and Ireland with the Native Chiefs and Tribes of New Zealand, and was signed at Waitangi, 6 February 1840. This reference is from the English version of the treaty. The Maori version, when translated back into English, varies from the English version (Orange, 1987). Points of controversy regarding the treaty prior to 1981 are identified in 'The Treaty of Waitangi, and parts of the Current Statutory Law in Contravention Thereof' (New Zealand Maori Council Report, presented to the Minister of Maori Affairs, Hon. D. MacIntyre, and the Minister of Justice, Hon. D. Riddiford, 4 October 1971), and Ngata, 'Land Grievances and the Treaty' (*Te Maori*, July/August, 1971).

5. *Mana* – personal authority, spiritual and secular power, spiritual significance or potency of an event, place, person, or tribe.

conservative leaders found this demand, and the public reaction
to it, disturbing. Among those most concerned about the implications of radical protest politics was the president of the New
Zealand Maori Council, Graham Latimer. Throughout his life
Latimer had followed closely the conciliatory style of Maori leadership. He had achieved considerable influence in the conservative National Party and was widely seen as the embodiment of a
political style which fostered collaboration between Maori and
Pakeha.

With care and patience, Latimer pointed out early in 1980,
much ground had been won by the New Zealand Maori Council
(Fleras, 1986; Hazlehurst, 1988a). Since the 1960s this national
organisation had made these advances through constructive dia-
logue and regular submissions to government. The establishment
of a tried and trusted process of consultation through the formal
channels and appointed spokesmen of the council had done more
for the Maori goal of self-determination than the clamour of
youthful protest, Latimer believed. Protest, said Latimer, could
be destructive to race relations. It threatened to undermine the
hard-won recognition of the Maori in the New Zealand national
political arena. He concluded that the government must take
some responsibility for the emergence of 'extremist activities'
because of its failure to vest the New Zealand Maori Council with
sufficient funds to carry out its functions effectively (*Te Maori*,
Feb./Mar. 1980, p.25).

While frequently disagreeing with Latimer's conservatism, the
prominent Maori academic, Dr Patrick Hohepa, shared some of
Latimer's concerns. In spite of his public image as a forthright
commentator and radical sympathiser, Hohepa had emphasised
that there was merit in both conciliatory and confrontationist politics. The formal organisations of the New Zealand Maori Council
and the Maori Women's Welfare League were successful pressure groups. Ultimately the fight for reform had been on similar
political fronts – whether it was conducted in the 'respectable'
way through national Maori organisations, or in the radical way
through public demonstrations.

But, as the 1970s drew to a close, Hohepa was among those
who had deep misgivings about the adequacy of the existing
political structure to meet the needs of the Maori people.
Although long active in Labour Party politics, close to senior
Maori political figures in the brief Kirk Labour administration of

1972–5 and, in 1981, an ardent supporter of the new Maori political party, Mana Motuhake (Hazlehurst, 1993), Hohepa doubted the ability of conventional approaches to induce the long-overdue reforms. Like other radical critics, he sensed the enormous positive potential inherent in the Treaty of Waitangi. But, to the extent that any institutions or practices were grounded in the treaty, they were vulnerable to the vagaries of interpretation. One of the central issues of the Maori protest movement was the validity of the treaty itself. By a simple process of deduction this view concluded that as 'the treaty has never been honoured it is therefore not a legal document'. If the New Zealand nation-state was said to be founded upon the Treaty of Waitangi, and the treaty was not a legal document, all agencies of the nation-state (police, courts and government) were equally illegal and not to be recognised.

Prelude to Waitangi Day – 1981

As chairman of the Tai Tokerau District Maori Council representing the Northland tribes, and president of its powerful national body, the New Zealand Maori Council, Graham Latimer had been proposed by his Northland supporters for the 'highest possible honour'. Though initially unwilling, he eventually yielded to the insistence of his people that his name be put forward for a knighthood.

Latimer's career as a conservative Maori leader had undoubtedly been remarkable. Although his schooling was cut short at the age of fourteen, he became a man of great accomplishment and energy. He was well known to Maori and *Pakeha* alike for his years of voluntary service on Maori organisations and related government bodies in the interests of Maori people. At the pinnacle of his career in 1981, Latimer had many a ministerial door open to him at Parliament House, and had been a long-time favourite and confidant of Maori Affairs Minister, Ben Couch, and Prime Minister Rob Muldoon. Through the New Zealand Maori Council, and upon the strength of his personal *mana*, Latimer attempted to use the trust he had won with the National Party government to stimulate legislation and programmes favourable to Maori people.

Royal honours had been incorporated into the Maori status

system since the early twentieth century. They had always been more popular with the loyalist and conservative Maori sectors than with either the strongly traditional or the emergent liberal and radical sectors. When Latimer accepted a Knighthood in the Order of the British Empire he made a special request. He asked that his investiture be held not, as was customary, at the Governor-General's official residence (Government House) in the capital city of Wellington, but in the Northern Maori heartland on the Waitangi National *Marae*. It was clear that the purpose of holding the ceremony on the lower *marae* was to ensure that the investiture received the blessings of the Maori people. The request, however, opened a Pandora's box.

Also chosen to be honoured by the Queen as a Dame Commander of the Order of the British Empire was the elderly Maori land rights campaigner, Mrs Whina Cooper. The 86-year-old dowager was fondly regarded throughout New Zealand for her gentleness, elder-wisdom, and unusual courage. She was recognised for her community and administrative service on both Maori and non-Maori voluntary organisations. In the 1950s she had been the founding president of the New Zealand Maori Women's Welfare League and, later in life, a leading Maori land rights campaigner. She wished to join Graham Latimer at Waitangi for her investiture.

Many Maori liberals and protesters, and a few elders as well, saw the acceptance of honours from the Crown – the same Crown which in their minds had 'usurped Maori sovereignty' and 'failed to uphold the treaty' – as an act of betrayal. Conservative Maori saw no contradiction at all in their leaders receiving such an accolade. Many among the major Northland tribes (Ngapuhi, Te Aupouri, Te Rarawa and others), were keen that the investitures should be held at a *marae* imbued with *mana*, and were planning a big Waitangi Day turnout.

Latimer did not, however, have the unanimous support of his Tai Tokerau District Maori Council to hold his investiture on the Waitangi *marae*. When it was finally decided to proceed with the investiture plans, several Auckland members of the Waitangi Action Committee journeyed to the next Tai Tokerau council meeting, held at Mangamuka *marae* on 17 January, to challenge this decision. The meeting broke up following confrontation and bitterness. The protesters felt they had not been allowed to speak their minds to the council. The Tai Tokerau people felt that the protesters' bullying tactics demonstrated a lack of respect for tribal etiquette and integrity.

A leaflet entitled 'The Treaty of Waitangi is a Fraud' was distributed by the Waitangi Action Committee. In language that reflected contemporary feminist and socialist aspirations, the protest was summarised by the leaflet as 'only part of the greater struggle' against the 'exploitations of this corrupt system'. Maori people need to fight for 'total change', it said. To achieve this, 'we must ally ourselves to the most powerful sectors of the New Zealand population – women and the working class.' Grievances listed by the leaflet included Maori imprisonment statistics, unemployment, land loss, forestry and fisheries. Readers were informed that there would be a march from the northern city of Whangarei to Waitangi (about 100 km in distance). 'If you cannot join the march, join us at Waitangi,' supporters were encouraged.

The Evening Debates – 5 February 1981

The protesters – about twenty-six adults, and a few young children – were welcomed to the Waitangi National *Marae* by waiting local elders on the evening before the investitures. Behind a banner, emblazoned 'Waitangi: A Day Off or a Rip Off?', the sixteen members of the protest group who had marched from Whangarei had been joined at Paihia by other sympathisers, including seven *Pakeha*.

For *Pakeha* New Zealanders, Waitangi Day occurs on 6 February. For the Maori it begins the day before. One of the most important aspects of any Maori gathering is the evening debates, where opinions are shared and grievances aired. The evening debates on 5 February 1981 were held in the dining hall – away from the sleeping quarters of the meeting house. They began after dinner at 8.30 p.m. and continued into the night, as was customary, until about 4 a.m. the following morning. About 150 local and visiting Maori attended.

While their language was controlled, local elders expressed with some fervour their concern about the plans for the following day. From the tone and emphasis of their speeches it was apparent that people were fearful of clashes between the protesters and the police. The importance of peaceful behaviour and co-operation was emphasised through the reiteration of historical happen-

ings at Waitangi, of Maori verse and proverbs, and of the deeds
of great chiefs of the past who had signed the treaty or who had
given their lives as peace-makers. The youth were exhorted
to: 'Go in peace and do not bring dissension as you did a year
ago.'

The local people were also disturbed at the discovery that the
Waitangi Board of Trustees – while approving the holding of the
investitures on their *marae* – were no longer responsible for the
organisation of that day. Instead the Tai Tokerau council had
'rented' the *marae* for the occasion from the board and had taken
over this responsibility.[6] Having acquired the organising function, an event unusual in itself, the Tai Tokerau council took
another unusual decision. In order to provide protection for its
chairman, and other visiting dignitaries, the council had asked
the police to provide extra security during the investitures. In
normal circumstances, Maori wardens – volunteers entrusted by
local Maori committees with statutory authority and the task of
preserving order in the community – would have had sole
authority on such an occasion (Fleras, 1980). It was a major departure from custom to compromise the autonomy of the *marae* by
soliciting police intervention.

When Dr Patrick Hohepa took the floor he said he spoke from
three positions. His age and views placed him between the youth
and the elders in both sentiment and status, but today he spoke
on the protesters' behalf. He also spoke as a senior member of the
Northland Ngapuhi tribe, stating his connections with the
Waitangi National *Marae* through his grandmother. In addition,
he spoke as a resident of Auckland. Hohepa delivered the greetings of the protesters to the elders, assuring them that the 'party
which walked from Whangarei' had no wish to 'trample on the
ways of this *marae*'. Hohepa said what most worried him was
newspaper accounts that police had been invited to enter the
marae. He was fearful, he said, that the Maori people would lose
their freedom of speech if the authorities were allowed to infringe
on Maori custom and meeting places. The Maori people, Hohepa
reminded his hearers, held the treaty covenant as holy
and sacred. But in his mind the covenant had been broken. He
said:

6. The Waitangi Board of Trustees is a body of representatives appointed by the New
Zealand District Maori Councils and Northern tribes to administer the affairs of the Waitangi
National *Marae*.

We have honoured our side. Let them honour theirs ... One hundred and forty-one years have passed. Do we support the young people who have come down to say today the treaty was a fraud? ... I am part of the old world, I still believe that there is *mana* in the treaty. But, let them honour it!

A tea break was called at about 10.30 p.m. The protesters had been advised to listen quietly to their elders and were promised an opportunity to speak after tea. When the people reassembled, Latimer, Cooper and some of the Tai Tokerau elders had left the dining hall for their beds. The young people felt deceived by this exodus. The tone of the protesters' address was at first angry, then suddenly abusive and taunting. Fearful shouting broke out when a youth employed blasphemies in his speech. Some members were shocked and indignant. Others were barely restrained from physical retaliation. The youth's speech was submerged in an exchange of barbed accusations between the two groups. The youths were blamed for their own unemployment. They were accused of atheism and idleness: 'Without Jesus you'd be dead!'; 'You just don't want to work!'; 'We pay for your wages on the dole!'

Contrary to *marae* etiquette, the young speaker, Hone Harawira, would not submit to pressures from the gathering to sit down. His supporters screamed 'He's got the floor! He's got the floor!' Harawira turned his attack upon Latimer and Cooper, purposely mispronouncing Cooper's name:[7]

> Tomorrow Graham Latimer and 'Whiner' Cooper are going to be knighted. Now, for the last few weeks we've been hearing from Graham Latimer that we are going to make a fool of Maoridom ... Now Graham Latimer, on the other hand, and Whina Cooper are going to accept a decoration from the same state that ensures that we can't even get a job, that we can't even build homes on our own land, that we can't even speak our language in our own schools. And you say that we're making fools of Maoridom ... [They] are going to bring police on to the *marae* ... 'Snakes in the grass!'

The reference to 'Whiner' Cooper was doubly contemptuous. It first attacked her personal *mana*. Secondly, by pronouncing her name in a way which only the most ignorant Anglocentric *Pakeha*

7. The 'wh' in the spelling of Maori words represents a sound like an 'f'. Thus Whina Cooper's forename should sound like 'Finner'.

might do, Harawira implied that this revered figure was no better – deserving of an honour from reactionary enemies rather than from her own people. This was a severe insult to Whina Cooper, who had spearheaded many Maori emancipation enterprises, including the Great Land March of 1975.[8]

A relative of the old lady rushed at Hone Harawira, telling him to sit down. A fight broke out between the two men. After intervention by the wardens, order was restored and the debates continued, but to a dwindling audience. Finally the determined remnants of the meeting, consisting mainly of the protesters and about forty others, resolved about 4.00 a.m. that the 'people did not want the knighting ceremony to proceed on their *marae*'. Dr Hohepa was 'unanimously' elected to put this view to the dignitaries the following morning.[9]

The Investitures – 6 February 1981

In spite of the generally expressed dismay of the local people and their elders over Tai Tokerau's security plans, and dark warnings of violence on the Waitangi National *Marae* being voiced by the press, Sir Graham and Dame Whina resolved not to select another time or location for their investitures. They were reassured by the ambition of their Northland supporters that they should receive these honours 'on behalf of all Maori people', and by their own convictions that they should not submit to the bullying of a few urban radicals who were opposed to it.

It was to be a grand day. A special police escort was to accompany distinguished representatives of the government and the Crown to the *Titiri o Waitangi Marae*. The official party included the Governor-General, Sir David Beattie and Lady Beattie; the Prime Minister and Mrs Muldoon; Ben Couch, Minister of Police and of Maori Affairs; Venn Young, Minister of Lands; Rear Admiral K.M. Saull, Chief of the Naval Staff; a handful of other officials, Opposition representatives and their wives; and the dis-

8. In mid-September 1975 the Te Roopu o te Matakite Land March set out from Te Hapua, a community at the northern tip of the North Island, and arrived at its southern tip on the steps of Parliament House, Wellington, one month later. The marchers, who had swollen to an estimated 30,000 in number, demanded that 'Not One More Acre of Maori Land' be alienated (Walker, 1990, pp.213–15).

9. This account of events on the evening of 5 February 1981 is based on the author's contemporary fieldnotes.

tinguished Waitangi National Trust Board member, Tureti Pomare, and his wife. The Maori gathering represented a cross-section of ideology, opinion, and political interest among the Maori public and leadership. Northland elders and other members of the welcoming party sat, with quiet dignity, in front of the meeting house. As a senior member of the *marae*, Hohepa took an active part in the *mihi* (speeches and rituals of welcome). A determined cluster of Latimer's conservative supporters gathered to the northern side of the ceremonial dais erected in the *marae* courtyard, flanked by a costumed concert party ready to perform.

The veranda of the meeting house to the west was crowded with spectators and news reporters in cotton shirts, summer dresses and other casual attire. At the front of the meeting house about thirty protesters sat on the grass before the row of chairs occupied by local elders and visiting Maori dignitaries – a number of whom wore the distinguishing yellow and black badge of the new Maori political movement, Mana Motuhake. The official party seating was arranged at the opposite end of the *marae* grounds, to the east. Positioned thus, near the entrance gates, it provided easy access to the road where large black limousines would wait to reclaim their official charges.

A gathering of about four hundred people rested on the grass or stood shoulder-to-shoulder to watch the proceedings. They lined six deep behind the roped off exterior boundary of the *marae* grounds and filled the *marae* courtyard, leaving only a small grassed opening for the ceremonial activities. Sir Graham and Dame Whina were the first of the official party to arrive. The *mihi* included speeches of praise and the presentation of gifts on behalf of the Tai Tokerau district. Dame Whina was given a woven flax *kit* (Maori carrying bag), and Sir Graham, a *tewhatewha* (carved wooden fighting axe) in symbolic recognition of the many 'battles' he had fought on behalf of the Maori people.

After the *mihi*, Hohepa made his address. Using the customary elder speech-making mode (assertive intonation, exaggerated gesturing, pacing back and forth) he appealed to Latimer and Cooper not to continue with their investitures. The wheels of the ceremony, however, were already in motion. The *Pakeha* leaders were arriving, cutting short his speech. It was agreed between the local elders that a representative of the dissident youth should be allowed to present their grievances in the presence of the Governor-General, Sir David Beattie, and Prime Minister Muldoon.

The people accepted the patrolling of their own uniformed Maori wardens, about forty in number, within the *marae* grounds. But they were obviously discomforted by the presence of about thirty police officers who had quietly formed a line on the far side of the road beside the *marae* entrance. Minutes before the arrival of the official cars, the police detachment crossed the road and formed a tight funnel from the cars to the *marae* entrance. Others dotted the outer perimeter of the grounds. Although the police did not enter the *marae* grounds, there was a noticeable shift in the crowd's mood – an increase in tension and apprehension – as the police neared the *marae* entrance and switched to the alert: 'Watch out for anything that might be thrown', the Chief Inspector in command was overheard to warn his officers.

Radio-equipped wardens and police milled, watched, and spoke in low tones to each other. Two lone protesters, one in army surplus trousers, another in jeans, T-shirt, and a red, yellow and black Rastafarian hat, roved through the crowd shouting sporadic slogans – particularly within earshot of the police – 'What's wrong with our wardens? Can't they do their job?'; 'Do we have to bring the state goons in here?', and 'The treaty is a fraud'.

More police arrived with the official cars, bringing their numbers to over forty. They joined the others at their post. Although few of the visitors would have known, all of the police were under strict instructions not to enter the *marae* grounds unless dire circumstances warranted it. The official party were seated without incident beside the dais. The *marae* welcome to the European officials, delivered by several Maori elders, included gifts to the Governor-General and his wife of carved wooden and flax woven handiwork. The welcoming song and dance, performed by the cultural group, was greeted with boisterous clapping and cheering from the conservative sector of the crowd. Following these formalities, a representative of the protesters, Arthur Harawira, was allowed to address the party:

> Once more you walk into these gates empty-handed ... As a young Maori affected by the Treaty of Waitangi, I say to you, you're not welcome here. This is my marae and you're not welcome. You should go out of that gate and never come back until you have something decent that Maori people can get a grip on, sink their teeth into. Not sold-out promises. We have nothing to celebrate here. What do we have to celebrate? The treaty is a fraud. It was signed at a time when

the *Pakeha* were a minority. And it was designed for their protection and benefit, not ours. You have never kept your side of the bargain, and now you come to give us medals. We don't want your medals. What value are those medals to us? We want back our land.

At the end of the presentation a group of the protesters stood to deliver a few verses of a protest song.

Hey Maori people,
Get up, get up and fight for your rights.
Don't let the system suppress you,
No more, no more, no more.

Some members of the crowd booed at the protesters, a few clapped. Having made their presentation and aroused little support, the protesters seemed helpless to stop the investitures proceeding. They withdrew into their group. A white-haired elder arose to respond. he scolded the youth for their manner and accusations, telling them to listen to their elders. Much of his address was in Maori, thereby rendering it inaccessible to most of the protesters. The youth sat quietly, detached from his admonitions.

The Minister of Police and Maori Affairs, Ben Couch, was the first speaker for the visitors. Of Maori descent himself, his speech was described by the press as 'humorous, biting, ironic'. Using a very casual form of address, '*E hoa*', not normal in a formal speech, Couch's rather rude and off-hand manner ridiculed the former speaker, Arthur Harawira:

E hoa Harawira, thank you. Thank you for what you said ... But *e hoa* Harawira, I'm asking you to bear in mind that you have got the right to demonstrate, and the freedom to do so, but remember this – your freedom stops where Ben Couch's nose and everyone else's nose begins ... We were told that we came on to this *marae* with nothing. *E hoa*, every time a Minister of the Crown has come onto this place, there had always been a *koha* [parting gift, donation]. And you're gonna get another one now. In fact, you're gonna get two! One is for the Maori Language Board of Tai Tokerau, which is set up for us to teach our own Maori. You know, besides singing the *Pakeha* song that you sang!

Couch's stinging reference to the deculturated state of the urban youth struck home. Among some of the audience and guests his words caused mocking amusement. The more mirth he aroused, the more he appeared to enjoy himself at the expense of the youth. He himself, was 'glad that the treaty had been signed', he said. 'The Ngapuhi tribe were the ones with the guns and they had been exterminating the other tribes.' This reference to the nineteenth-century conflicts between the tribes brought jeering laughter from the protesters.

When Couch reiterated his well-publicised motto, that he was 'a New Zealander first and a Maori second', someone in the crowd suggested that he be made an 'honorary *Pakeha*'. On one hand he talked of things 'Kiwi',[10] while taunting the youth for 'using *Pakeha* methods' and for singing '*Pakeha* songs'. The visible humiliation of the youth was heightened by the jubilation of the conservative element in the crowd.

The Governor-General, the Queen's personal representative at the investiture, replied to his hosts with a few opening words in Maori. Some of the protesters ridiculed his pronunciation with a taunting applause. Sir David Beattie's speech, however, was delivered in the gentle style for which he was well regarded. His words were received by the gathering relatively without interruption:

> February the sixth is the day we focus on our beginnings; it marks the start of our nationhood ... Indeed, some Maori elders have referred to the Treaty of Waitangi as New Zealand's 'Magna Carta'.

Observing the many symbolic aspects of Waitangi Day, Sir David noted that 'the presence of the Maori items' in the ceremonies proved that Maori culture was still 'vibrant and alive' today. 'Its future, in the hands and voices of the young people, is assured.' Associating the investitures of Sir Graham Latimer and Dame Whina Cooper with the Waitangi Day celebrations and with the Waitangi National *Marae*, said the Governor-General, 'is not only a fitting tribute to these distinguished persons, it is an action which symbolises the very spirit of Waitangi'.

It could be argued, he said, that racial equality between the signatories of the treaty had not yet been achieved,

> But if equality has not been achieved, the fault does not lie in the treaty itself. However cynically some people may regard the events of

10. *Kiwi* – derived from the native Kiwi bird. It is a term referring to all New Zealanders, to emphasise national unity.

1840, there can be no mistaking the instructions given to Hobson. They were unequivocal. He was instructed that any agreement negotiated had to be absolutely fair and that is the essence, the spirit, of the treaty. Any shortcomings in the achievement of equality in this country are our shortcomings; they are not inherent in the treaty. The spirit of the treaty cannot be faulted. It will live on.

Concluding with a question, the Governor-General asked:

> If we did not focus attention on this day, if we do not celebrate Waitangi Day, what other day or event could we celebrate? The treaty has been called 'The spirit and conscience of a young nation'. Is there any other document in our heritage that comes close to it?

The visitors' addresses were closed by Tureti Pomare. Pomare reinforced Sir David's speech with the conservative Maori view of the treaty:

> The Treaty of Waitangi, with all its imperfections, has been the one instrument which has enabled the Maori people to come a long way. The future of our nation lies in the hands of those, both spiritual and temporal, who realising their responsibilities, attempt to do away with every cause of misunderstanding, friction, and intolerance.

The treaty, Pomare stressed, had been signed as a 'solemn act of faith' between Maori, Crown and Church representatives. 'Let us use our vast resources and energies,' he said, 'towards a better way of life for future generations'.

The investiture ceremony began with a blessing, given by the Maori Anglican Archbishop, Paul Reeves. The Governor-General, in formal attire, waited quietly on the dais. His wife stood on his left, in a white suit, white hat, and gloves. A uniformed aide was on his right. On a small table covered by a blue cloth, a red velvet cushion rested, bearing the ribboned medals. Dame Whina Cooper stood in front of the meeting house, waiting to cross the few metres of grass to the steps of the dais. She was chaperoned by her tall, youthful, nephew, Tau Henare Cooper. An ancestral feathered cloak fell gracefully from her shoulders over a long hand-printed skirt. She bore an elder's *tokotoko* (carved walking stick)[11] in her left hand. A single feather decked her thick white hair. She carried the dignity and authority of

---

11. *Tokotoko* – walking stick, carried as a sign of elderhood, used by striking through the air to emphasise points during elder speeches.

elderhood with a queenly bearing. Tau Henare also wore a single feather in his hair. His feathered cloak (of more modern vintage) – tied in the style of men, under one arm and over the opposite shoulder – was worn over a dark suit. He supported his aunt's arm and carried her flax *kit* for her. Sir Graham Latimer, who stood directly behind Dame Whina, was accompanied by a male relative and was followed by Archbishop Reeves. Sir Graham also carried a *tokotoko* and was wrapped in a 'cloak of honour'. The purple vestments and waist sash of the Archbishop were in prominent contrast to Latimer's beige suit and antique cloak.

Suddenly a protester – a hand on his hip – stood to challenge Cooper and Latimer one last time to reconsider accepting the royal decorations:

> This is your last chance to stop shaming your people ... How can you accept that medal, Whina, when you know your Maori people are losing their land?

'Don't get on your knees,' shouted another youth, 'they will steal your wallet.' The investiture party stood silent and still, their eyes fixed forward, ignoring the entreaties, waiting to be summoned to the platform by Sir David. The composed bearing of the party belied their inner conflict. Tension etched furrows on their brows. Their bodies seemed to sink and lean a little more upon their canes. Dame Whina gripped the hand of Tau Henare for support.

There were a few 'boos' at the protesters from the crowd. Some of the gathering tried to ignore the youth by turning their backs slightly and looking towards the procession. As the party began to walk across the courtyard towards the dais several Maori wardens formed a line between them and the offending youth. The protesters broke into an angry chant of 'Shame! Shame! Shame!' The concert party struck up a Maori song in an effort to drown out the protesters' heckling and to give moral support to their leaders. Dame Whina and her nephew ascended the steps and reached the Queen's representative.

Without warning, a youth sprang from the protesters' ranks, sprinted across the grass and leaped on to the dais. In an instant he was thrown to the ground by the Governor-General's bodyguard. It was unclear what the youth, Mangu Awarau, intended when he reached the dais. Some say it was to grab the Queen's medal before it could be presented; others suggest it was to pull off Dame Whina's cloak, to emphasise her dishonour. Though protected by her nephew, who pushed the protester away, Dame Whina was knocked almost to the floor in the scuffle. As Sir David and Lady Beattie helped the old lady to recover herself, four Maori wardens fell upon the struggling protester on the ground. Other protesters sprang to their feet shouting 'Shame! Shame! Shame!' and 'Get off him!'

Police poured onto the sacred *marae* grounds. Within seconds their helmets had woven a long, white snake, insulating the official party from the astonished crowd. In an eruption of angry cursing, one protester after another was picked up bodily, or arm-wrestled out of the *marae* gates and into two waiting police vans. Nine protesters were dragged away shouting and screaming 'Shame, Shame!'; 'Look what you're doing to your young people!' and 'Where has our *mana* gone now? – With the *Pakeha*!'

In the uproar an elderly Maori woman pummelled two of the youths. Some of the bystanders were struck in retaliation or by accident by the thrashing protesters as they were carried away. 'This is a peaceful protest' objected another bystander. 'Stop the violence!' The conservative sector of the crowd, distressed and linking arms for mutual support, began singing the Christian sacred song 'How Great Thou Art'. 'Those people who just got arrested were fighting for your rights, whether you believe it or not', screamed one of the remaining protesters for the ears of anyone who would listen.

The Maori wardens had formed a protective circle around Sir Graham and the dais. Sir David, steadfastly ignoring the struggling and shouting bodies only metres away from his platform, calmly proceeded with the investitures. Ben Couch called for three cheers for Sir Graham and Dame Whina. 'Three cheers for the young Maori arrested in defence of their land', a *Pakeha* supporter responded.

Within a matter of minutes – the protesters removed, the honours presented – the visitors were evacuated and swept away to the safety of their waiting limousines. As quickly as they had come, the police disappeared with both their official and deviant charges – abandoning the crowd to the care of the wardens once more. People chattered and argued bewilderedly among themselves. A deeply saddened Dame Whina and Sir Graham seemed not to be consoled by the embraces and hand-clasping of their clustering friends and family. After a polite appearance at the dining hall they too soon left the *marae*, leaving the hosts and other guests to consume alone the luncheon which had been specially prepared for the visitors. There was a pervasive sense of anti-climax as two groups sought to rekindle the fading attention of the dispersing crowd. A handful of committed speakers shouted a defence of the protesters in an attempt to explain the morning's events. But even the noisy preaching and song of a prepared-for-any-event evangelical Christian troupe, bearing a large placard, 'Turn Back To God', was in vain. A few listeners and converts milled close by; others stood at a safer distance to observe and debate. A group of senior women, still visibly shaken, gathered to weep and console each other. Others moved off in resignation to talk among themselves and to attend to the business of lunch.

New Zealand's race relations conciliator, Hiwi Tauroa, told the press that his 'heart was weeping for the elders' who had attempted to include the young people in the official welcome, and then saw the disturbance develop. 'We are just standing around in a circle hanging our heads with shame', one elder told Archbishop Reeves. Some of the local elders said 'this thing would never have happened if the police had not been invited by Tai Tokerau and the right protocol had been observed.' Sir Graham Latimer said he was 'disgusted' by the incident. He criticised the elders for departing from their programme by allowing the protesters to speak. It was a 'deliberate ploy' of the protesters, he said, to gain access to the ground and to get past the wardens. The young people have no consideration or respect.'

Prime Minister Muldoon deplored the incident, describing the protesters who disrupted the investitures as 'young hooligans'. 'It's very clear they're not seeking Maori rights', he told the press. 'They're seeking *Pakeha*-style disruption.' They were offered, and they accepted, the courtesy and opportunity to state their case on the *marae* according to Maori custom, Muldoon said. But they misused this privilege. The Prime Minister concluded that, in his belief, the protesters would become 'outcasts' from Maoridom. Front page headlines of 'Waitangi Marae in Uproar' and 'Violence Disrupts Investiture' were accompanied by dramatic photographs of shouting protesters being led or carried bodily from the *marae*. Nine protesters were charged with rioting, carrying a maximum penalty of two years' imprisonment, and some also with using obscene language, carrying a maximum fine of NZ$500. The issue was hotly debated for some weeks after the event. Ten months later the riot charges were dismissed.[12]

The Urban Maori Community

To many observers the Waitangi Day fracas in 1981 was the unsurprising culmination of several decades of economic disloca-tion, social tension, and rising political consciousness among the younger generation of Maori. To others it was an aberration, the consequence of a series of miscalculations and errors of judge-ment which could easily have been avoided. But, however it was interpreted, it cannot be understood without examining how the Maori community had evolved in the recent past.

Essentially rural-based before the Second World War, Maori society underwent rapid urbanisation over the next forty years. By 1981 over 80 per cent of the Maori population were concen-trated in the cities and townships of the North Island in general, and in the central and southern suburbs of Auckland city in par-ticular. With the expansion of New Zealand's industrial economy the unskilled and semi-skilled labour market became increasing-ly accessible and attractive to the migrant during the 1950s and 1960s. Post-war New Zealand boasted of a proud record of race relations based on bicultural accommodation and equality. Surveys conducted by the Department of Maori Affairs in the early 1960s, however, revealed that there were significant dispar-ities between Maori and European standards of living, education-al attainment, housing and amenities, and opportunities for upward mobility. The sudden economic slump of the mid-1970s further restricted Maori employment opportunities. The increas-ingly insecure economic environment created a disturbing dis-continuity in New Zealand, and particularly Maori, social life.

---

12. In the mêlée and confusion after the eruption at the investiture, on 6 February 1981, it was difficult to get a clear view of the grounds. Several different versions circulated at the time in gossip and in the press. I was able to take a series of photographs from an elevated vantage point by standing on top of the hand rail of the meeting house veranda – above the heads of the spectators. This account of the sequence of events was based upon a later analy-sis of these photographs, reports and photographs recorded by journalists, and my own observations and discussions with spectators positioned at other points on the grounds immediately after the event and on later occasions. Senior police officers later explained to me their orders and expectations (see *New Zealand Listener*, 14 Mar. 1981; *New Zealand Herald*, *Auckland Star*, *Northern Advocate*, 7 Feb. 1981; Sir David Beattie, *Waitangi Day Speech Notes*, 6 Feb. 1981).

Meanwhile, the urban Maori community had adapted to its new
environment by introducing organisational structures which it
felt were 'traditionally Maori', or at least Maori by invention.
Identifiable urban communities began to appear, particularly in
the poorer neighbourhoods of the cities.

Still residing in some city areas were extended family clusters
of *tangata whenua* – people with traditional and land-based associations with the area before the metropolis enveloped them.
Some of these Maori had their own *marae*. As immigrants began
to outnumber the local descent groups they formed their own
associations, elected their own suburban Maori committees, and
struggled to raise sufficient money to build new community centres and *marae*. Where possible, *kaumatua* (traditional elders) of
the *tangata whenua* were invited to perform as guest speakers and
conductors of ceremony, but if none were available, immigrant
elders or younger leaders conducted these activities. Leadership
in the urban community of the late 1970s and early 1980s was
largely dominated by men in their forties and fifties. The presence of a *kaumatua* was extremely rare. Participation of youth,
women, and upcoming politicians in their thirties in community
debate was not only tolerated, but becoming increasingly the
norm. Status and position could also be acquired by virtue of
superior education and political astuteness. It was not uncom-
mon for the *kaumatua* to be replaced by a younger elite. Seniority
of descent was no longer a necessary qualification for *rangatira*
status, nor for influence in the urban setting.[13]

By the early 1980s urban social organisation and community
regulation had come to focus on the urban *marae* (or the community centre), the elected Maori committee, and many other voluntary Maori organisations and committees. These voluntary
associations included locally-based mutual-aid, life crisis or family clubs, and cultural and sporting groups similar to those in the
rural communities. There were also suburban branches of large
national organisations such as the Maori Women's Welfare
League, the Maori Wardens' Association, and the New Zealand
Maori Council. Maori people also affiliated with, and formed,
Maori sections of the major political parties and conventional
church groups, or maintained branches of their own churches –
the Ringatu and Ratana faiths.

13. *Rangatira* – traditional nobility, heads of families, recognised leadership by birth
and/or ascribed qualities.

The transplanting of rural organisational structures and patterns and the regular visiting of tribal homelands manifest a continuing bond between the rural and urban sectors of the Maori world. Where etiquette requires, due honour is still given to tribal commitments and custom. Local and regional leaders today are expected to attend all important functions and to show their respect at funerals of important Maori. Consequently the work of an active leader is vigorous, highly pressured, and shaped by a tiresome regime of travel between city, town, and country. Maori business is conducted within a labyrinth of actual and potential associations – the broadly-based 'Maori world' network. A single leader's politically functional network may consist of a dozen or more major subgroups (interest nets) and hundreds of minor ones. He or she will be aware of many other associations accessible through 'friends of friends' (see Hazlehurst, 1993).

Community-oriented Maori are not only tied by obligation and preference to a selection of these interest nets, they are also surrounded by a sea of Maori organisations which are themselves independently and interdependently connected. These organisations work on behalf of Maori individuals. They speak for them politically, mediate with government, and try to improve Maori standards of living and the educational opportunities of their children. They are available to help individuals solve practical daily problems, to guide them in times of crisis, celebrate their achievements, and provide comfort and support in times of need or personal loss. In the urban situation, away from the territorial soil of the tribe, formal and psychological association with the Maori world is based on social principles relevant to the contemporary setting. Although migratory patterns have resulted in some urban communities having distinct tribal affiliations, these principles are usually super-consanguinal, super-tribal, and super-regional, and revolve around a hub of urban Maori associations and affiliations.

From his anthropological study of a Maori committee in an Auckland suburb, Walker concluded in 1975 that 'voluntary association' is the 'key to the successful adjustment of the Maori to urban life.' The city, he said, is 'tribally neutral ground'. Unlike the tribal hinterland, it 'introduces a multi-tribal variable into social relations'. The Maori urban experience in this respect, said Walker, is not unlike that recorded in earlier African urban studies (in Kawharu, 1975, pp.167–86; see also Banton, 1957; Little, 1957; Lopata, 1964; Mayer, 1962; 1966; Mitchell, 1969; 1970).

The protective network of voluntary association, which provides so many options and avenues for support, to a much larger extent than in the *Pakeha* community, watches over and submerges the 'individual'. It commits the Maori to the more highly-valued concept of 'community'. As Maori society traditionally acknowledged differences of status and class, factors of education, occupation, residence and marital attachment, these do not in themselves determine ethnicity. Neither do physiological features conclusively define 'Maoriness'. The factors which determine the recognition and acceptance of an individual as 'a Maori' are predominantly social (see also Metge, 1967).

Ethnic affiliation is most powerfully judged by the philosophy and behaviour which confirms affiliation, loyalty, and understanding of 'the Maori way'. Ideally this is pervaded by the spirit of Maori *aroha* (love, sympathy), from which flows a caring and mutually supportive defence system which acts on the political as well as the personal level in protecting Maori interests.

Modern Maori Leadership

Modern Maori leadership has emerged, and has been shaped, in response to an identifiable role in inter-ethnic exchange. The increasing proliferation of modern Maori organisations has facilitated this exchange up to the highest levels of the nation's power structure. Maori politicians have been particularly occupied with relationships with *Pakeha*-dominated institutions, governmental agencies, and political parties. Much of the maintenance of peaceful race relations in New Zealand must be attributed to sixty years of the highly-polished brokerage of both Maori and *Pakeha* leaders (Bhagabati, 1967; Firth, 1951; Hazlehurst, 1988a; Metge, 1967; Schwimmer, 1968; Walker, 1975; 1987; 1990; Winiata, 1967).

A point not widely acknowledged, wrote Kernot, is the fact that 'the existence of persons and organisations with mediator roles' provides a clear indicator that Maori and *Pakeha* 'recognise each other as belonging to separate socio-political groups which may or may not be in conflict' (1964, pp.171–8).

Without enforcing segregation, either by statute or choice, both Maori and *Pakeha* display a determination to maintain their sense of ethnic distinctiveness. Although interaction is an everyday occurrence, and intermarriage common, distinguishable boundaries are present. A variety of strategies, courtesies, frames of reference and mythologies are nurtured which ensure the relative independence of the 'Maori world' and the '*Pakeha* world' – while not being so inflexibly institutionalised as to inhibit a generous degree of interdependence and exchange.

National Maori leaders fall into two main categories – based upon their ideologies, their political resources, and *modus operandi*. The first great Maori brokers of the 1920s and 1930s – James Carroll, Maui Pomare, Peter Buck and Apirana Ngata – were the advance guard of a specific style of leadership whose influence reached into the country's political and administrative halls of power. This style, which was characterised by cultural mediation, conciliation, and co-operation, is constantly referred to as 'conservative'. From the early 1970s several waves of political dissent occurred. Early confrontationist leaders became widely dubbed as 'liberals'. They also acted as cultural brokers but, unlike their conservative contemporaries, their crusading style of leadership included strategies of public criticism, vigorous lobbying, and open challenges to policy and practice. They acquired fame (or notoriety) in their attempts to 'awaken' the conscience of the nation and its governments.

As distinguished from the elderly *kaumatua*, who continued to see that *marae* and tribal etiquette was observed and passed on, the contemporary elite of the 1980s dealt, to a greater or lesser extent, with the modern economic and political world – the world of wider society as it affected the Maori people. Although there was division in their ranks over the method of performing this role, along conciliatory or confrontationist lines, these national figures followed a pattern of political and cultural brokerage set down some sixty years earlier. The urban Maori experience produced a third sphere of political activity – loosely referred to as 'radical'. The political rhetoric and methods employed from the mid-1970s by the younger, most urbanised, sector of the Maori world included a strong element of protest and activism, and communicated a growing sense of tension and unrest.

Issues and Grievances

As the New Zealand economy sank into recession, many urban families suffered serious breakdown. Parental unemployment, the burden of 'not having enough to make ends meet' and the temptations of city life have taken their toll. Unless parents made a conscious effort to hold on to their *Maoritanga*[14] they themselves began to reflect the social and economic environment in which they lived. Maori community leaders charged their people with irresponsible parenting, child neglect, and self-indulgence in the local pubs and 'housie' (bingo) halls. The education system was criticised for its suppression of Maori language and its failure to make curricula relevant. In 1971 Walker noted the corroding influence of urban life upon the Maori family's function of social-isation and transmission of culture to the next generation (*Te Maori*, Feb./Mar. 1971, p.43).

By the early 1970s dismay began to be expressed by communi-ty leaders and the media at the emergence of urban gangs. The gangs appeared to be composed of socially alienated youths, many of whom were from broken homes. Most notably it was believed that they harboured an uncertain self-identity and appeared to have little respect for, or access to, the guidance of their Maori elders or homelands. They grouped together for secu-rity and emotional support on the streets of their neighbour-hoods. Recruitment into the gangs occurred at school as young as ten years old. Younger children followed their older brothers into junior chapters of semi-criminal street gangs – the Mongrel Mob, Black Power, Headhunters, King Cobras, and others.

The numbers of angry, under-employed, and disaffected youths were also growing. The goal of these Maori youths was not to 'raise the consciousness' of the general public through scholastic achievement or administrative intervention, as the lib-eral leaders Walker and Hohepa had done some years earlier. Nor was it to seek input into the national political process – the pattern of leadership established and continued by conservative and liberal leaders. From the mid- to late 1970s, activist youths were able to unite and form *ad hoc* organisations which they used to mount public protest. Their methods ranged from peaceful sit-ins to aggressive demonstrations.

Maori activists found allies among a variety of intellectual and socialist quarters. They frequently held strong trade union affilia-tions, and drew their membership from sectors of the deculturat-ed urban youth and student leadership. Protest groups were typically small, sporadic and issue-oriented – assembling under a

14. *Maoritanga* – Maori culture, the Maori way of life.

specific grievance and dissolving once action had been taken. They were receptive to Marxist philosophy and often incorporated anti-capitalist slogans into their rhetoric. In displays of civil disobedience they challenged 'the system' over issues of Maori land rights, language and cultural preservation, and inequitable access to the country's wealth and resources. They asserted their identity in non-tribal terms and gave voice to contemporary Maori grievances. For a decade there was a gathering storm of public demonstrations, petitions, lobbying, land occupations, organised mass marches and increasingly effective permeation of the media. Minor confrontations with the law were followed by lengthy court hearings, demonstrations outside prisons, and heightened public debate (Hazlehurst, 1988b).

In the analysis of Walker and other liberal Maori thinkers, these youth were the heirs of the worst effects of assimilationist policy. Cultural identity had been denied to them by both societies. Instead of integrating the Maori and European races, it was claimed, the policy succeeded in throwing the younger Maori generation into a state of confusion which could only be remedied by renewed cultural pride and economic security. The activist groups, which grew out of the discontent of the 1970s, 'dramatised the new generation's deep sense of cultural loss by adopting the *Pakeha* tactics of demonstrations, protest and sit-ins' (Walker, private papers, May 1979).[15]

Less understanding, however, were the conservative spokesmen of both the Maori and *Pakeha* communities. Alarm at increasingly hostile demonstrations led to Maori protesters and their supporters being labelled by politicians, the public and the press as misguided youths, radicals and even communists. Protesters not only challenged political and economic inequities between Maori and *Pakeha*; they also challenged three generations of co-operation, peaceful cohabitation, and the common purpose and comradeship of two world wars (Hazlehurst, 1988a). Their attacks disrupted a carefully nurtured set of relations between conservative elements in both societies. There was a growing, if rarely articulated, fear that the violent street gangs might be politicised to the protesters' cause.

15. It was the representations made by an early protest group, Nga Tamatoa, which led the Ministry of Education to reverse its former policy on Maori language in 1974. Since this time there had been a significant revival of the Maori language in New Zealand secondary schools and university institutions.

The Waitangi Incident: An Analysis

As Gluckman's (1958) analysis of the opening of a bridge in
Zululand, and Mitchell's (1956) classic analysis of the *kalela* dance
portray, the influences of the recent history, structure and nature
of relations are reflected, often repeatedly, in different social situations. The investiture of Sir Graham Latimer and Dame Whina
Cooper in 1981, and the subsequent decisions and actions taken
by the actors involved, is only one of many possible examples of
continuing influences and associations at work in New Zealand.

Traditional Maori categories of tribe and sub-tribe were (and
are still) markers of social identity. But in recent decades they are
by no means the only organisational factors. Where there is an
absence of single tribal identity, urban Maori communities must
focus on inter-tribal values and interests of region. Other loyalties
of religion, party politics, ideology and generation all serve as
social coagulants, creating both cohesion and separation.

The capacity of the Maori political world to manage complex
cross-currents and conflicting loyalties was tested by the 1981
Waitangi investiture. In the reasoning of Sir Graham Latimer and
Dame Whina Cooper, the honours to be conferred upon them represented a gift from, and to, their people: 'An honour bestowed
upon one is an honour bestowed upon all' (Maori proverb). It was
their duty as well as their privilege to accept gracefully. Many
Northland supporters and relatives were immensely proud of
their Sir Graham and Dame Whina, and passionately wished these
honours for them. Shrewd politician that he was, Latimer was well
aware of the potential, and the history, of controversy which had
surrounded Maori acceptance of royal honours. He proposed that
the ceremony be conducted on the Waitangi National *Marae* to
ensure that it had the ultimate sanction of 'the Maori people'.

The disruption of the Latimer and Cooper investitures on 6
February 1981 was, in the prevailing climate, a wholly predictable gesture on the part of the Waitangi protesters. Latimer,
Cooper and their supporters were determined to pursue their
plans. The protesters were equally determined to disrupt them.
The ensuing conflict, over several weeks before the event, erupt-
ed in a clash of wills and ideologies during *marae* debates the
evening prior to the investitures. By the morning of the appointed day no real consensus of opinion had been reached. Both were
to proceed with their intentions.

Hohepa's formal presentation of the protesters' objections to Sir Graham and Dame Whina the next day was cut short as the European dignitaries arrived. As a way of accommodating all sides, peacemakers among the local elders agreed to allow the protesters to have their say to the Governor-General, Prime Minister and other assembled guests, before proceeding with the ceremony. Many issues and emotions exacerbated the tensions into the resultant clash – not the least of which was a vague determination in these young people to voice their anger and to obstruct the investiture – though in what form and to what limits seemed not to have been decided. The lack of organised intent left room for the spontaneous display of defiance staged by the young man who leaped upon the dais.[16] The abundant presence of the police, in apparent disregard for the Maori wardens within the *marae* grounds, also caused resentment. The escalation of hostilities during the debates the evening before, the undisciplined behaviour and offensive rhetoric of the protesters, the ill-judged impulse of Minister Ben Couch to make a little political mileage out of the situation, and the later sensationalism of the press, all added to the impact of events.

In the days after the incident the ideological and political battle was taken up by powerful figures in both the Maori and *Pakeha* worlds. The Prime Minister, politicians, Church people, ministers of the Crown, lawyers and idealists were swept up into an exchange of verbal blows. The schism of opinion expressed was more along right/left, than brown/white lines. The Maori were no more united in their perceptions or aspirations than were the *Pakeha*.

Although over the previous four decades most Maori voters had made common cause politically with the Labour Party, the National Party had also been able to secure a small but staunch following, particularly in the rural regions. The newly-founded Mana Motuhake Party, contesting the four Maori seats in Parliament for the first time in 1981, drew strength away from Labour. With a pan-Maori appeal, Mana Motuhake attempted, with mixed success, to bridge the gaps between the politically active and the apathetic, between urban and rural communities, conservative and radical ideologies, and generational perceptions of ethno-political relations (Hazlehurst, 1993).

16. For another example of spontaneous action taken by Maori protesters and community reactions, see Hazlehurst (1988b).

But in dealing regularly with *Pakeha* power structures it was not surprising that conservative Maori leaders should see the advantage of accepting honours from the Crown. As well as consolidating their status among their supporters, they would also be acquiring status in the *Pakeha* world, and thus enhancing their positions in negotiations with these powers. In the context of their philosophy of cultural coexistence this presented no contradiction. As cultural brokers it was seen to make good sense. Liberal and radical thinkers, however, were less accommodating. With the development of pro-Maori and anti-assimilationist sentiments, more rigid expectations of Maori loyalties emerged. In this view Latimer was seen to be wanting to have his cake and to eat it too. To receive recognition from the Crown must mean a depreciation of Maori status – thus the 'shame' and 'betrayal'. Such a suggestion of betrayal of Maoridom by the acceptance of European recognition for service done to the Maori people was viewed by conservatives as an absurd twist of the imagination and politically self-serving. The protesters, they claimed, used whatever public event they could to grasp media attention.

The argument of the protesters, however, was not quite so shallow. They saw their cause as the latest episode in an old struggle – of hostilities, deceit, and disillusionment between the conflicting interests of the country's indigenous residents and the later, settled European population. Conservative Maori, well aware of this, had frequently made concessions for the behaviour of the deculturated youth. To the surprise of their *Pakeha* friends, traditional and conservative leaders often gave consideration to the protesters' grievances, and occasionally, when it seemed just, supported their cause and attended their court cases when they came into conflict with the law.

In 1981 the Maori world was far from ready to embrace a pan-Maori identification, transcending other political and social divisions. But unity in the face of *Pakeha* injustice or incomprehension was another matter. Paradoxically, events which exposed Maori political fragmentation could also give impetus to expressions of cultural solidarity. Since the advent of urbanisation, those who had participated in Maori social life have functioned within a multidimensional framework. Active politicians have had at their disposal a complex of affiliatory interest nets, ranging from local personal ties, to potent inter-tribal and inter-organisational associations across the country. No less effective or potentially operational in a self-professed 'bicultural society' such as New Zealand are the associations between Maori and *Pakeha*, their central figureheads and institutions.

In the aftermath of the investiture Sir Graham himself was rebuked by some of his own and some local elders for having insisted on the ceremonies being held at Waitangi. They had warned that it would not be wise, and that 'bad things' would happen by bringing Waitangi and Crown honours together. There seemed some doubt as to how much Sir Graham received the authority of the Tai Tokerau District Maori Council, and how much he acted on his own volition – under pressure from relatives and friends. Confusion was also apparent over who had given the police authority to enter the *marae* grounds. While legally the police could enter anywhere, a wide discretion is normally given to Maori sanctions and controls on their own *marae*. An invitation to send more police by a respected Maori leader or organisation would be given very serious attention by the authorities – if for no other reason than that such a request was extremely rare, if not unique. In this case, it was notable that once they had removed the protesters the police quickly retreated from the area, allowing the Maori wardens to take back responsibility for *marae* security.

It was later clarified that the invitation had been given by Latimer, purportedly acting on behalf of the Tai Tokerau district council. The intensity with which Robert Muldoon became involved in the defence of his minister, Ben Couch, suggests that some communication had occurred between the Prime Minister, the Minister of Police, and Latimer before the event. All were to be in attendance at the ceremony, and Sir Graham, for his part, felt he was acting responsibly by ensuring adequate protection for the visiting dignitaries and the general public.

In order to avert an even greater calamity, Latimer invoked his association with the most potent of state authorities, rather than rely exclusively on his extensive network of Maori affiliations to subdue any possible conflict. The police were under instruction to intervene in the event of a disturbance of the peace. Did the extent of the feared disturbance warrant the intrusion of unwelcome state officers on to the *marae* grounds? The Maori wardens seemed to have had the matter in hand. Why did the police fear serious violence or riot?

In a subsequent interview with the author in July 1981, Sir Graham Latimer made an astonishing revelation. Unbeknown to the people present on the *marae* or to the press, some of Sir Graham's relatives had taken the independent decision to provide their leader with an additional secret ring of protectors. During the investiture ceremony Sir Graham claimed that he had been 'surrounded by gang members carrying knives'. These armed gang members were inconspicuous, Latimer said, because they 'were wearing suits'. But, said Sir Graham:

> The protesters don't know how lucky they were – how near they came to death. There were gang members all around me. Several of my cousins' sons are leaders of the Headhunters ... They told me that they'd protect me, that they'd do the protesters in if I told them to. I said 'You boys keep out of this.' But they came anyway. 'Just give us the nod Uncle,' they said, 'Just give us the nod.' They [the protesters] wouldn't have got near me. The police came to me just before and were very worried. They wanted to cancel the investiture. They knew the plans of the protesters two weeks before I did ... They said the protesters were prepared to do anything to make their point.

Latimer added that his 'whole tribe' was also attending the investiture. 'They would have wrung their necks,' he said, if he had given them the authority. Sir Graham explained that this 'mandate for leadership' had been bestowed upon him through his grandfather, who had married a 'Maori princess' – a woman of a senior *rangatira* family. 'It's for this reason, and no other, that I am recognised.' As their leader he embodied the integrity of the tribe, he said, and he had always had their loyalty. On another occasion some of his people had wanted to 'put a *tapu* [curse] upon the protesters, to drive them mad':

> They were prepared to do anything for me. I told them to leave them alone. But the protesters don't know how near they courted death that day – and it wouldn't have been from the *Pakeha*!

Other Maori who were present at the investiture ceremony admitted no knowledge of the gang presence. There was also no indication that Latimer had related this information to the police, or that the authorities had prior knowledge of it from their own sources. In any case, the police appeared to have quite sufficient cause to be nervous about the situation developing into what they called 'a blood bath'. Police protection for the official party, comprising the Prime Minister, the Governor-General, ministers, and their wives, would have been pretext enough for imposing a restraining presence at the investitures. Had the police known of this additional danger, however, it would certainly have explained their desire to remove the protesters from the scene as quickly as possible. However, not only were the Maori gang members mysteriously unobserved by other Maori, the story never reached the ears of the press. Nor did it emerge as an issue in Maori debates over the next ten months. The secret protectors were a secret indeed.

To some extent this extraordinary twist to the story of the Waitangi investiture seems out of character with the conservative image which Latimer projects. It is possible that Sir Graham, in relating this information to an independent observer who was known to talk with his opponents, had purposefully exaggerated in the hope of discouraging further violence. (Latimer claimed he had been receiving threatening phone calls since the investiture.)

But in the context of the strong cross-currents within Maoridom, Latimer's story is not difficult to believe. Just as he was prevailed upon by his people to accept an imperial honour on their behalf, they were equally capable and sufficiently wilful to act to protect tribal and regional interests embodied in his person. The resentment generated within Northern Maori against the protesters could easily have spiralled outwards to the ears of their urban cousins and nephews – relatives of Sir Graham's, well versed in the arts of personal and territorial protection.

The past failure of the urban activists to effectively politicise Auckland gangs, and to recruit them to their cause, suggests that such potential alliances were undermined in part by political apathy, but also possibly by the remnants of kinship obligation which some Maori gang members felt towards rural Maori communities. Tribal politics were still more akin to gang concepts of territoriality than to the class-based Marxist philosophies pursued by the protesters. Nor could it be imagined that gang members would be enticed by the prospect of surrendering their autonomy and identity to soldier in the ranks for a radical intelligentsia.

Maori leaders are never assured of the unquestioned obedience of their supporters – just as they do not always do the will of

their people. Pleasing most of the people most of the time tends
to guarantee continuing political respectability and authority.
This century the bond between rural and urban has become fundamental to the continuity and maintenance of Maori ethnicity.
In 1981 Latimer's reputation hung in delicate balance between his
conflicting obligation toward his tribal elders and his district
council, the wishes of his relatives, his political connections in
high places of government, and his commitment to wider Maori
interests as president of the New Zealand Maori Council. Every
political move he made could draw tight his strings of commitment to another quarter. It would certainly draw public comment
and would be scrutinised by his ever-vigilant liberal and radical
opponents. Yet, perhaps, the worst that could happen would be
for a violent confrontation to have occurred between the body of
his rural supporters and the unruly and impassioned urban protesters.

Such a schism would have resonated throughout the Maori
world. If the urban radicals were to encounter anyone it was better that they encounter persons from their own turf and age
group, namely urban gang members, than the rural Maori. Better
still, it was perhaps a lesser calamity that they should encounter
an instrument of the state, which could conveniently be con-
strued as maintaining the oppression of their people, even as it
protected them from themselves.

Postscript

Those who have lived through the last decade of momentous
change in New Zealand will sense that this has been a story about
a world which in many respects has been transformed. So rapid
were the changes of policy, tone and mood brought about under
seven years of Labour government from 1984 that by the late
1980s the extreme radicalism of the beginning of the decade was
dated and largely discredited. The Waitangi Tribunal, empowered since 1985 to examine all Maori grievances in the context of
the treaty, has provided a powerful forum in which a new cadre
of Maori lawyers, accountants, academics and other professionals has operated to great effect. There has been a resurgence of
tribal consciousness, an emphasis on the *iwi* (tribe) as a cultural,
economic, and political entity. Maori identity and influence are so

far enhanced, the treaty so much a part of the texture of contemporary government and law, that a repetition of the protest rhetoric and symbolism of 1981 would now be more antiquarian than authentic. Throughout all the changes since 1981 there have been two constants: the presence and *mana* of Sir Graham Latimer and Dame Whina Cooper.

Bibliography

Banton, M., *West African City*, London: Oxford University Press, for the International African Institute, 1957
_____, *The Social Anthropology of Complex Societies*, (1st edn 1954), London: Tavistock, 1966
Bhagabati, A.C., *Social Relations in a Northland Maori Community*, Auckland: doctoral thesis, University of Auckland, Department of Anthropology, 1967
Firth, R., *Elements of Social Organisation*, New York: Philosophical Library, 1951
Fleras, A.J., *A Descriptive Analysis of Maori Wardens in the Historical and Contemporary Context of New Zealand Society*, Wellington: doctoral thesis, Victoria University, Department of Maori Studies, 1980
_____, 'The Politics of Maori Lobbying: The Case of the New Zealand Maori Council', *Political Science*, vol.38, no.1, July 1986, pp.27–43
Gluckman, M., *Analysis of a Social Situation in Modern Zululand*, Manchester: Rhodes Livingstone Institute, 1958
Hazlehurst, K.M., 'Maori Self-Government 1945–1981: The New Zealand Maori Council', *British Review of New Zealand Studies*, no.1, July 1988a, pp.64–100
_____, *Racial Conflict and Resolution in New Zealand: The Haka Party Incident and its Aftermath 1979–1980*, Canberra: Peace Research Centre, Research School of Pacific Studies, Australian National University, 1988b
_____, *Political Expression and Ethnicity: Statecraft and Mobilisation in the Maori World*, New York: Praeger, 1993
Kapferer, B., 'Norms and the Manipulation of Relationships in a Work Context', in *Social Networks in Urban Situations*, J.C. Mitchell (ed.), Manchester: Manchester University Press, 1969
Kawharu, I.H. (ed.), *Conflict and Compromise*, Wellington: A.H. and A.W. Reed, 1975
Kernot B., 'Maori–European Relationships and the Role of Mediators', *Polynesian Society Journal*, Wellington: The Polynesian Society, vol.73, 1964, pp.171–8

_____, 'Maori Strategies: Ethnic Politics in New Zealand', in *New Zealand Politics: A Reader*, S. Levine (ed.), Melbourne: Cheshire, 1975

Leinhardt, S. (ed.), *Social Networks: A Developing Paradigm*, New York: Academic Press, 1977

Little, K.L., 'The Role of Voluntary Associations in West African Urbanization', *America Anthropologist*, vol.59, 1957, pp.579–96

Lopata, H.Z., 'The Function of Voluntary Associations in an Ethnic Community: "Polonia:"', in *Urban Sociology*, E.W. Burgess and D.J. Bogne (eds), Chicago/London: University of Chicago Press/Phoenix Books, 1964

Mayer, P., 'Migrancy and the Study of Africans in Town', *American Anthropologist*, vol.64, 1962, pp.576–92

Metge, J., *A New Maori Migration: Rural and Urban Relations in Northern New Zealand*, London School of Economics, Monographs on Social Anthropology no.27, Melbourne: Athlone Press/Melbourne University Press, 1964

_____, *The Maoris of New Zealand: Rautahi*, London: Routledge and Kegan Paul, 1967

Mitchell, J.C., *The Kalela Dance: Aspects of Social Relationships Among Urban Africans in Northern Rhodesia*, Rhodes-Livingstone Papers, no.27, Manchester: Manchester University Press, 1956

_____ (ed.), *Social Networks in Urban Situations: Analyses of Personal Relationships in Central African Towns*, Manchester: Manchester University Press, 1969

_____, 'Tribe and Social Change in South Central Africa: A Situational Approach', *Journal of Asian and African Studies*, vol.5, nos 1-2, 1970, pp.83-101

_____, *Cities, Society, and Social Perception: A Central African Perspective*, Oxford: Oxford University Press, 1987

Ngata, H., 'Land Grievances and the Treaty', *Te Maori*, July/August, 1971

Orange, C., *The Treaty of Waitangi*, Wellington: Allen and Unwin/Port Nicholson Press, 1987

Sinclair, K., *A Destiny Apart: New Zealand's Search for National Identity*, Wellington: Unwin Paperbacks/Port Nicholson Press, 1986

Schwimmer, E.G. (ed.), *The Maori People in the Nineteen-Sixties: A Symposium,*. Auckland: Longman Paul, 1968

Walker, R.J., 'Korero', *New Zealand Listener*, 16 March 1974

_____, *The Social Adjustment of the Maori to Urban Living in Auckland*, Auckland: PhD thesis, Department of Anthropology, University of Auckland, 1970

_____, 'The Politics of Voluntary Association', in *Conflict and Compromise*, I.H. Kawharu (ed.), Wellington: A.H. and A.W. Reed, 1975

_____, *Nga Tau Tohetohe: Years of Anger*, Auckland: Penguin Books, 1987

_____, *Ka Whawhai Tonu Matou: Struggle Without End*, Auckland: Penguin Books (NZ), 1990

Wheeldon, P.D., 'The Operation of Voluntary Associations and Personal Networks in the Political Process of an Inter-ethnic Community', in *Social Networks in Urban Situations*, J.C. Mitchell (ed.), Manchester: Manchester University Press, 1969

Winiata, M., *The Changing Role of the Leader in Maori Society: A Study in Social Change and Race Relations*, Merran Fraenkel (ed.), Auckland: Blackwood and Janet Paul, 1967

Chapter 4

Cinco de Mayo and 15 January: Contrasting Situations in a Mixed Ethnic Neighbourhood

Alisdair Rogers

In *The Kalela Dance* Mitchell (1956) presents the reader with a paradox. The dance is clearly ethnic (or 'tribal', as Mitchell then described it), by virtue of the regional origins of the performers and the self-laudatory content of the songs. Yet the dancers adopt European-style clothing and use a lingua franca to express their comments on urban life, ethnic diversity and their own ethnic identity. In order to resolve this paradox, Mitchell unpacks the meanings of class, status and 'tribalism' within the context of the urban areas of the Copperbelt. He argues that these categories interact in a situational manner, their relative significance varying from occasion to occasion. In the case of the *kalela* dance, its location within a colonial town is highly significant. Here, ethnicity is less the communal expression of a geographically isolated group (the identification of like) and more a categorical distinction among sub-groups (the identification of unlikes). This is necessitated by the spatial proximity of individuals from a large number of backgrounds in the town, which requires some categorisation of others on the part of any individual as the basis for ordering social behaviour. The 'tribalism' of the dancers in this situation is therefore fixed externally by relation to others, rather than internally by relation to selves.

In this account Mitchell stresses the analytical significance of setting and situation, including place, for the interpretation of social behaviour. He demonstrates how abstract categories such as class, status and ethnicity are implicated in practice, where they are conditioned by the actors' own definitions of the

117

situation. Mitchell's view of ethnicity as a cognitive response to urban conditions is one which gives prominence to the importance of social geography, understood as both the spatial mixing of social groups and the significance of place or physical setting.

In this chapter it is intended to employ some of the insights from *The Kalela Dance* in the analysis of two contrasting situations in another continent and in a somewhat different context.[1] Both took place in a mixed ethnic neighbourhood in central Los Angeles, in which African-Americans and Latinos formed the majority of the resident population. The area will be referred to as Adams-Vermont, after a major intersection. The first event was a Cinco de Mayo Parade, an annual event which celebrates one of the most important dates in modern Mexican history. The second was the dedication ceremony of a city park in honour of Rev. Martin Luther King Jr, which occurred on his birthday (now also a national holiday), 15 January. Together these two events represent contrasting responses to the many changes which have brought together two ethnic groups in common space.

These two situations will be described briefly, identifying the significant elements. They are then interpreted in the light of a fuller consideration of their setting, demonstrating how features of the wider society impinge upon social behaviour and contribute to the social construction of its meaning. Finally, in the wake of the 1992 riots which devastated the neighbourhood, the account addresses some of the prevailing conceptions of ethnicity and territory in multi-ethnic cities.

The Cinco de Mayo Parade

Cinco de Mayo (5 May) is a major event in Mexican history. On this date in 1862 the French army of occupation was defeated at Puebla by Mexican forces under Benito Juarez and General Zaragoza. Indios and Mexicanos fought together against the French, so that the battle symbolises an anti-imperialist struggle as well as national solidarity. Although the French were not

1. The research on which this chapter is based was undertaken as part of a doctoral thesis (Rogers, 1988). It involved residence in the area described during the period 1983–4, together with occasional visits thereafter.

driven out for another five years, the battle marked the beginning of the anti-colonial struggle and the ascendancy of the future president, Juarez. The day is not widely celebrated in Mexico itself, but has become a major focus for Mexican and Mexican-American communities in the United States. It may be compared with similar festivals, parades and carnivals revived by other ethnic groups in American cities, such as the St Patrick's Day Parade or the West Indian Carnival in New York.

In 1980 Los Angeles had a Mexican-origin population of 1.65 million. Cinco de Mayo was conventionally celebrated by a grand festival in East Los Angeles, which is the main barrio. There was another parade which took place outside the barrio in neighbourhoods only recently settled by Mexicans and other Latinos from Central and South America. It was much smaller and received far less publicity than the main festivities. It was organised chiefly by the Adams-Vermont Community Centre Inc. (AVCC), a community association headed by a long-time Chicano resident of the city, Carlos Holguin. AVCC began as a neighbourhood watch group in 1972 and went on to provide advice on social and welfare matters to the local Latino population. It also acted as an institutional basis for Holguin's influence on local affairs. His stated motive for holding another parade was to provide a celebration of Cinco de Mayo free from the commercialisation of the eastside event. In 1984 the 'Family Fiesta' held in Highland Park, part of East Los Angeles, was sponsored by the brewing company Coors. Holguin was doubly opposed to this sponsorship, because it maintained the association of Mexicans with drinking alcohol. There was therefore a certain degree of geographical chauvinism involved. In 1984 there were also two co-organisers, the southwest division of the Los Angeles Police Department and the local city councilman, Robert Farrell.

The parade was first held in 1980 when fifty-five local groups and organisations participated. By 1984 there were almost one hundred associations represented in the official line-up. Of these, the largest component (44) and the majority of participants were provided by schools and youth bodies, including cadet corps.[2] Next in significance were various law enforcement

---

2. The classification of participants was made by the author, based on the official line-up as it appeared in the programme.

and military representatives (11) and folkloric or cultural bodies, such as dancers, bands and horsemen (10). There were eight politicians and other elected officials from state and city governments, including the Mexican vice-consul. Finally, four local businesses and five community organisations provided participants. The remainder included flag-bearers, beauty queens and others.

The composition of the parade was a reflection of the aims and interests of the organisers. The motto of AVCC is 'Working to Promote Law and Order Through Youth', and Holguin had stressed the participation of schools and organisations related to law enforcement and the armed forces. Given the high crime rates of the area, the aim was clearly to provide alternative models of, and avenues for, youth activity. There were some politicians and elected officials, but no political parties or trade unions. Furthermore, none of the participants represented the most powerful local institution, the University of Southern California. In fact, there were no distinctly Anglo-dominated organisations in the parade.

The event took place on a Saturday and consisted of two parts: the parade itself and a ceremony at the end. Between two and three thousand individuals took part, and there were a similar number of spectators along the streets. The route began in a car park on the campus of the University of Southern California, went north up a major thoroughfare lined by small shops and businesses, and doubled back to end outside a Baptist church where AVCC held its meetings. The parade began along a commercial strip off which were streets inhabited mainly by African-Americans, then moved into the narrower residential streets of a neighbourhood populated by Latinos. The composition of the spectators along the pavement reflected this ethnic division. There were few if any Anglo spectators, and the only Anglos present were students selling flags, horns and ices. The parade took three hours to pass by on a hot day.

The passing parade was obviously dominated by young people, but particularly African-American youths. The most spectacular elements were the school marching bands and drill teams, setting the tone of the parade by their showmanship. By contrast, the specifically Mexican displays were more static and subdued, often confined to floats or horseback. The sounds of march tunes and pre-recorded soul music, notably Michael Jackson songs,

overwhelmed the strains of the few *mariachi* bands. Although
there was a peculiar synthesis of visual and aural styles as the
parade went by, the most imposing sounds and impressions
were therefore linked to African-American performers. There
were few Mexican flags and little bunting along the route, and
only the occasional cry of 'viva Mexico' from on-lookers. As the
Virgen de Guadalupe – the dark-skinned Mexican Virgin Mary
and one of the key religious icons of the country – passed, one of
my Chicano companions commented sadly, 'She doesn't belong
here.'

When the Grand Marshals and the Parade Queen and her
court completed the course they established themselves on a
stage in the street outside the Baptist church in order to view and
judge the remaining participants. The last group was a break-
dance team called Members Only, which consisted of a number
of Latino youngsters performing to soul and hip-hop music. The
parade having finished, the remaining people entered the church
yard for a small fete and the awards ceremony. Most of the audience who stayed were Latinos, and, in contrast with the earlier
activities, the proceedings were conducted mainly in Spanish. A
raised platform was the stage for a series of speeches and presentations which emphasised the nationalistic meaning of the day.
The vice-consul spoke, as did the captain of the police division,
dressed in *caballero* style, and the local councilman, an African-
American male. Someone dressed as Sam *'El Aguila'* (The Eagle)
was on hand to promote the forthcoming Olympic Games which
were to be held later in the summer not far from the church. An
African-American female drill team won the prize for best act,
while some Michoacan dancers received an award for costume.
Several local businessmen were handed certificates for community service, and finally a *mariachi* band played six tunes while the
audience drifted away.

The paradox of the Cinco de Mayo parade was therefore that
an occasion of major importance in Mexican national pride
should, in its more public appearance, be so dominated by
African-American cultural styles and performers. The nationalistic element was confined to a small, more private ceremony, one
which took place in an African-American church. For one day an
event had combined the local African-American and Latino communities in a single celebration. The significance of this occasion
can be appreciated by contrasting it with a second situation.

The Martin Luther King Jr Park

Sixteen years after his assassination and in the year in which
Congress proclaimed a national holiday in his honour (1984), Los
Angeles's African-American community was finally able to com-
memorate Dr Martin Luther King Jr. The Santa Barbara
Elementary School and Santa Barbara Avenue were renamed
after him, and a small park was created and dedicated to his
memory. This last act took twelve years of planning and was
achieved despite the prevailing policy of the Parks Department
not to open any more 'vest-pocket' parks. They argued that such
spaces formed hang-outs for the non-respectable and 'deviant'
members of the community. There was also some opposition
from local residents to the park on these grounds. Commercial
businesses on the old Santa Barbara Avenue also protested
because of the costs incurred by the change of name. The original
idea of the local councilman had been for a library, but this was
dropped for lack of funds.

On the day of the dedication (the nearest Saturday to King's
birthday), a 10 km run was held in the morning along the
renamed street. That afternoon only 150 or so people gathered in
the school playground to attend the ceremony. It was organised
by the Southern Christian Leadership Conference, and I was told
that the similar occasions in previous years had attracted larger
audiences. The platform included a broad range of speakers
designed to address many questions of Civil Rights, 'minority'
interests, welfare, peace and justice. While a well-known Chicano
activist and academic and the African-American councilman
stressed the connections between King's ideals and those of other
communities, including Latinos, Asians, women and peace cam-
paigners, the audience itself was almost entirely African-
American. The councilman said in his address, 'for many of us
the mountaintop experience [referring to one of Dr King's
famous speeches] is not yet something we have really been able
to enjoy for ourselves, and say that I or my community has
arrived.'

In contrast to the Cinco de Mayo Parade then, the event was
more low-key, less optimistic and more explicitly political.
Despite the avowed aims of the organisers and the sentiments of
the speakers, the occasion was a largely African-American affair.
There were a few Anglos present – not selling ice creams this

time, but radical newspapers and pamphlets. The irony of the dedication ceremony was that, just as the street and landmarks were being rid of their Mexican names and receiving a new African-American identity, the population of the surrounding area was switching from African-American to Latino.

The Setting

Mitchell's analysis of the *kalela* dance depended upon an appreciation of its setting. Situational analysis, according to Mitchell (1983; 1987), requires the specification of relevant contextual parameters. For the two situations discussed here the context may be described under geographical, economic and political headings. Together they serve to demonstrate the significant coincidence of the ambiguous ethnic boundaries between African-Americans and Latinos and their increasing spatial juxtaposition in urban areas.

African-Americans and Latinos were once regional minorities with separate histories of incorporation into US society. What has happened, mostly in the years since the Second World War, is that the country's two largest ethnic groups have become increasingly concentrated in the largest metropolitan areas, where they are forming an ever-larger proportion of the population. African-Americans and Latinos are occupying common geographical ground for the first time and, in numerical terms at least, dominating the central spaces of some of the largest urban areas. In 1910 roughly 70 per cent of both groups were rural in residence, while half the Anglo population lived in urban areas. Subsequently, while Anglos experienced deconcentration from the cities, African-Americans and Latinos moved into them. In 1980 85 per cent of African-Americans and 90 per cent of Latinos were urbanised, compared with only 70 per cent of the Anglo population. Although Latinos are more urbanised, African-Americans are more concentrated in the central cities of metropolitan areas. Furthermore, both groups tend to be over-represented in the larger metropolitan areas: of the ten largest in the country, only Boston did not have a combined African-American and Latino population of over 100,000 persons and over 20 per cent in 1980. The New York metropolitan area, with almost 3.5 million African-Americans and Latinos combined, and the Los Angeles metropolitan area, with a little over 3 million, had the largest numbers of the two groups.

The demographic balance of these two groups is also gradually shifting. African-Americans were 12 per cent of the country's population in 1980, while Latinos, the fastest-growing minority in the country in the 1970s, were 7 per cent. Relatively high rates of natural increase, combined with large-scale immigration, indicate that at the national level Latinos possess a greater demographic momentum than African-Americans. Some projections suggest that by 2020 they will be the largest single minority group (assuming that Latinos are still officially recognised as a single category).

Within Los Angeles a geographical shift mirrors that of the nation as a whole. Latinos outnumber African-Americans roughly 2:1; 80 per cent of them are of Mexican origin, and about half are foreign-born. Just as in the country at large, immigration and natural increase give Latinos greater demographic momentum. The 'Latinisation' of Los Angeles, or more accurately perhaps, its 're-Latinisation', is transforming the city's social geography and its character (Rieff, 1992). Although there is still a distinct barrio on the eastside, Latinos have moved into every residential area except those of the highest status (Garcia, 1985; Massey and Mullan, 1984). This has meant that areas of predominantly African-American and Latino residence, distinct and separate for many decades, are merging. While there is no significant African-American movement into Latino areas, there is a clear Latinisation of the ghetto (Johnson and Oliver, 1989; Oliver and Johnson, 1984). Between 1970 and 1980 the African-American population of South Los Angeles, the ghetto, fell by 25,000 to 66 per cent of the area's residents. In the same period the Latino population rose from 87,000 to 184,000, almost 30 per cent of the area's population (Rogers, 1988). According to the conventional indices of residential segregation, there is an increasing spatial propinquity between the two groups.

Adams-Vermont lies in South Los Angeles, part of what urban ecologists often refer to as 'a zone of residential succession'. Between 1970 and 1980 the African-American population fell by a quarter while the number of Latinos more than doubled, many of them from Central America. This transition did not take the form of the total displacement of one ethnic group by another, as expected by the classical models of ethnic residential succession.

An analysis of exchanges in the housing market using surname as a surrogate for ethnicity shows that African-Americans continue to buy property and move into Adams-Vermont, albeit in steadily declining numbers (Rogers, 1988; see also Clark, 1989). The area is not ethnically mixed by default, therefore, but because individuals of both groups choose it for their residence.

The sharing of residential space is the first element of the context, and it may be appreciated more fully in relation to the restructuring of the urban economy (Soja, Morales and Wolff, 1983). Los Angeles's economic structure is one of considerable productivity and diversity, second only to New York as a concentration of employment, business, industry and finance. In common with many other 'World Cities', the industrial structure is shifting from goods to services production, but, within overall growth, there are both declining and expanding sectors (Sassen-Koob, 1984). In the 1960s the major cities were being described in terms of fiscal crisis, decline, unrest and social deprivation. Contemporary accounts now emphasise the recapitalisation or recomposition of urban economies around financial and business services, land speculation and gentrification (Logan and Molotch, 1987). The outcome of these processes is that the benefits of urban growth are uneven in their impact on local populations. In broad terms, African-Americans in Los Angeles are more closely associated with the public sector and personal services, while Latino labour has sustained the viability of manufacturing. Both are disproportionately concentrated in expanding low-wage sectors of the economy, including personal services and labour-intensive manufacturing. They both have higher levels of family and individual poverty and are more likely to be unemployed than the Anglo population (Rogers, 1988).

The Latinisation of the ghetto developed during a period of economic and social crisis for its African-American population. In 1984 a local civic body, the South Central Organising Committee, used the occasion of the Olympic Games being held in South Los Angeles to draw attention to the abandonment of the inner city. This report and others in the 1980s concluded that general social and economic conditions, levels of service provision in health, education and the like and rates of crime in the ghetto, had not substantially improved since the Watts Riot of 1965, and in some ways had deteriorated. Conditions did not improve by the time of the 1992 riots and, if anything, deteriorated. African-American workers were particularly badly hit by the haemorrhage of the inner urban manufacturing belt, once the largest of any US metropolis (Soja et al., 1983). Adams-Vermont lies at the intersection of, on the one hand, a vast stretch of urban space evacuated by capital, a reserve of cheap labour denuded of factories, businesses and shops, and on the other, an emerging internationalised zone of financial and corporate capital with its demands for commercial and residential space. Many of the incoming Latinos found low-wage work servicing the residents and employees of this centre. They moved into African-American neighbourhoods enduring chronic desuetude.

The third and final contextual element is political. Beginning in the 1970s and continuing in the 1980s there has been a trend of minority incorporation into urban regimes, which in many cases has brought minority politicians to power. In cities where African-Americans and Latinos form an increasing proportion of the population, the shape of local politics may be governed by the relations between them. Thus, in 1983 Harold Washington became Chicago's first African-American mayor while at the same time defeating the powerful Democratic machine, with the critical (though inconsistent) support of Latino voters.[3] In Miami, by contrast, the entry of Cuban-Americans into city politics has been regarded as detrimental to African-American aspirations. In New York, large minority communities were effectively disorganised and blocked from power by the political acumen of Mayor Koch and his coalition, until 1989, when David Dinkins was victorious (Falcón, 1988). These three cases suggest that the mere numerical presence of African-Americans and Latinos guarantees neither political incorporation nor co-operation.

In Los Angeles the political balance between the two minorities is shifting during a period of realignment. In the 1960s the national Democratic Party incorporated African-Americans politically through the provision of social programmes and the creation of bureaucracies to administer them. Given the lesser importance attached to the Latino vote by the party, African-Americans but not Latinos gained from this process in Los

3. Washington's sudden and untimely death in 1987 ended the African-American–Latino coalition, allowing the son of former mayor Daley to assume the mayor's office.

Angeles, causing some friction between them (Acuña, 1984). In 1973 Tom Bradley became the first African-American mayor of an Anglo-majority city, a position he was to hold for twenty years. His coalition of Jewish liberals, African-Americans, enlightened capital and some members of the Anglo middle classes included Latinos as a junior partner. The relative weakness of Latino politics was apparent in the fact that between 1963 and 1985 there were three African-Americans but no Latinos on the city council. By 1986, however, due in part to a court-ordered redistricting of council boundaries, two had been elected. One, Gloria Molina, went on to become the first Latino (and the first woman) to sit on the all-powerful Country Board of Supervisors in 1990. Their election coincided with a serious decline in Bradley's electoral base and a challenge to his position from a balanced-growth movement (Davis, 1987; Saltzstein and Sonenshein, 1991). In 1993 the coalition was to finally fail as a right-wing businessmen assumed the mayoralty, defeating the successor to Bradley's constituency. What is significant, however, is that in the mid-1980s the political relations between African-Americans and Latinos in Los Angeles were shifting, from a situation of African-American strength and Latino weakness to one in which Latino politicians were more able to realise the demographic strength of their constituency.

Adams-Vermont is in the northern part of one of the council districts held by an African-American, each of which has a significant Latino minority. Although Latinos are unlikely to challenge the incumbents, given low levels of citizenship and voter registration, there is a perception among some Latinos at least that African-Americans have too much power and use it for themselves (Oliver and Johnson, 1984). Denied access to City Hall through elected officials, the Latino community made use of prominent individuals and the city commission system of appointed citizens to voice their grievances. Holguin was one such individual, a broker between the Latino residents of the district and the city bureaucracy. He was certainly aware of the tensions between the two minorities over political representation. Given the social geography of Los Angeles, it is unavoidable that Latino aspirations for greater political power must be gained, in part at least, either at the expense of African-Americans or in co-operation with them.

Spatial Propinquity and Ambiguous Boundaries

Three contextual features have been outlined: geography, the urban economy and politics. From these, two themes emerge. Firstly, the significance of social geography as the context for the relations between African-Americans and Latinos. It not only affects the processes of ethnicity, but also influences political representation, community organisation and the provision of services. Falcón (1988) makes the same point in regard to New York City. In Adams-Vermont, for example, some African-American parents were attempting to withdraw their children from schools in which the number of Latino pupils was increasing. Secondly, the relative status of African-Americans and Latinos is not fixed, but is ambiguous. There is no clear relation of domination and subordination, but a tension between various aspects of social, political, cultural and economic life. In the case of social stratification, for example, African-Americans in Los Angeles have a higher aggregate level of education and occupation status, but lower levels of family income and higher rates of unemployment and dependence on entitlement programmes. African-Americans have more political power if it is measured by the number of elected officials, but the Latino voting population is growing more quickly. Their modes of ethnic political organisation may be said to differ (Falcón, 1988). Like New York, Latinos are organised at a more local level. Holguin, for example, acts as part of an alternative structure of influence and representation to the more institutionalised African-American political system which operates more within the framework of the city council. While African-Americans may be more 'American' in cultural and citizenship terms, Latinos rank higher in a social order conditioned by white supremacy. African-Americans are more residentially segregated than Latinos in Los Angeles, suggesting that Anglos prefer to place more distance between African-Americans and themselves than Latinos and themselves (Massey and Mullan, 1984). The experience of African-Americans in the USA is conditioned by racism, while all Latinos endure the nativism and exclusion that is directed against immigrants, legal and illegal. The ethnic boundary between the two groups is ambiguous, therefore, meaning that neither group is consistently ranked above the other, while both are subordinated within the class structure and socio-cultural order.

There is an implicit assumption in both academic and journalistic accounts that increased geographical proximity is associated with rising levels of ethnic antagonism and competition between African-Americans and Latinos (Johnson and Oliver, 1989; Oliver and Johnson, 1984). Johnson and Oliver describe a new type of inter-ethnic competition which contrasts with an earlier phase of racial conflict. They argue that it has come about because of immigration, the movement of immigrants into established African-American areas, and the ensuing competition for scarce resources. These concern jobs (particularly competition between young African-Americans and immigrants), housing (they argue that landlords perceive Latinos as better tenants), welfare and other services. The fact that this takes places in the context of economic deterioration accentuates the conflict. To this general background may be added a fact particular to Los Angeles, that power relations between the two groups may be about to switch as Latino political representation catches up with their demographic presence. Johnson and Oliver suggest that '[t]he emotional intensity of such intolerance serves to polarise the community, making interethnic minority conflict a likely outcome of a precipitating event,' (1989, p.456). The 1989 riots in Miami would seem to confirm their worst fears.

In this view, African-Americans and Latinos are locked into a spatially determined conflict. Antagonism follows from the process of residential succession. Rather less attention has been paid to the increased incidence of political and community co-operation that may also result from the same geographical changes. Church congregation-based organisations based on Alinskyite principles – the South Central Organising Committee (SCOC) in the ghetto and the United Neighbourhoods Organisation (UNO) in the barrio – demonstrated such alliances. Together they mobilised large numbers of people to campaign effectively for improved services, control over liquor stores, fairness in auto insurance rates, better policing, and similar matters.[4] Undoubtedly both conflict and co-operation occur, and the point is that the Latinisation of the ghetto is associated with a renegotiation of the ethnic boundaries between African-Americans and Latinos. Spatial change does not fully determine social situations.

4. Davis (1990) argues that, by 1990, UNO had withered, its membership falling off and its grass-roots radicalism being co-opted by professional organisers. In its targets, UNO (and, to an extent, SCOC) has moved away from social justice towards a concern for law and order.

It does, however, provide the necessary context in which social relations must be worked out. What happens in the streets and neighbourhoods is but one end of a hierarchy of situations and institutions which are arranged by scale; school districts, council districts, the city, the region, and even the country as a whole, are part of this hierarchy. These levels are not insulated from each other. What happens on the streets may have a bearing on what happens in the city council, and vice versa.

Expectations of competition or conflict based on ecological analyses must therefore be tempered by the consideration of alternative responses. One cannot generalise about a state of conflict or co-operation between two 'minority' groups, since these states are specific to situations and issues. Only a properly situational method of analysis can explore precisely what does happen. It was Mitchell's insight that ethnicity, rather than being a given fact of social behaviour, is situational. Whether, and how, it enters into actors' definition of any situation cannot be prescribed in advance.

Two Contrasting Situations

Having established the setting, it is possible to return to the situations and interpret them. This is done in two ways. Firstly, by examining the contrast between them as alternative responses to a common context: the social geography of Latinos and African-Americans. Secondly, by placing the situations in the context of ideals of the multiethnic city, adding a dimension of power.

Cohen (1985) has argued that as the structural and geographical bases of community boundaries are diminished by migration, urbanisation and so forth, so their assertion becomes renewed in symbolic terms. The *kalela* dance was one such occasion, and ethnic parades in urban areas also serve this purpose. The Cinco de Mayo Parade represented a partly deliberate and partly unavoidable accommodation between the two ethnic groups. It was unavoidable given the choice of youth and schools as the main participants. Local schools are not ethnically segregated. It was deliberate in the sense that it would not have been possible for the area's largest annual event to be identified too closely with one group or the other without creating some antagonism. In a mixed ethnic neighbourhood which, judging by the evidence from housing exchanges, both groups regard as their territory, what can be avoided in the routine activities of everyday life must be confronted in more public and symbolic occasions. Members of different ethnic groups may conduct the business of shopping, socialising, hanging out and so forth more or less without adjusting their behaviour with regard to others. A parade, however, by occupying public space exhaustively, rules out other activities. It is a public, as opposed to a private, statement which requires a response from local residents. Parades, as various authors have argued, exert claims of presence, ownership and/or exclusion in space (Jackson, 1988; 1992; Kasinitz and Freidenberg-Herbstein, 1987; Marston, 1989).

If the Cinco de Mayo had been a purely Mexican occasion, its meaning for the African-American community could have been exclusionary. As the 'junior partner' in Adams-Vermont (in contrast with the eastside barrio), Mexicans and other Latinos could not have fully justified their exclusive claim to territory. The organisers deliberately displaced potential conflict through the involvement of youth, confining the nationalistic element to a smaller, private ceremony. It was also mostly apolitical and non-commercial, and, as a largely symbolic action, was open to a wide range of possible interpretations by participants and observers. The significance of this point will become clear after considering the Martin Luther King Jr Park dedication ceremony.

The park ceremony shared the aim of bridging the divides between communities, but did so in a way which made this goal difficult to realise. The speakers emphasised the common objective interests of all disadvantaged groups, quoting King's words, but the occasion failed to embody these ideals. The goal of breaking down barriers conflicted with the aim of honouring and celebrating a great leader of an African-American cause. The civil rights movement in the 1960s did not manage to extend itself beyond African-Americans, and their white liberal allies, to the Chicanos of the Southwest. Despite some gestures of solidarity, the southern crusade and the western farmworkers' struggles were essentially separate movements. The benefits of the decade's social programmes flowed disproportionately to African-Americans, a source of some antagonism in Los Angeles itself (Acuña, 1984). In the 1980s Rev. Jesse Jackson also discovered the difficulty of reaching out to the Latino community on the basis of a progressive political project. Martin Luther King Jr was not perhaps an appropriate symbol for uniting the two communities, particularly when the range of possible interpretations which participants could make of the ceremony was limited. Although the speeches may have expressed a desire for a progressive and pluralistic politics, the nature of the occasion and the composition of the audience did not embody these ideals.

The event was therefore more exclusionary than the Cinco de Mayo Parade, and the ceremony was more expressive of the insecurity of the African-American community, locally and nationally, as the promises of the Civil Rights movement failed to materialise inside the ghetto. The councilman spoke of the community as having not yet 'arrived'. He had plans to make the newly renamed Martin Luther King Jr Boulevard a major business centre for the African-American community, reversing the flight of commercial capital. Yet the incoming Latino and Asian (mostly Korean) populations were already reviving small businesses by catering to ethnic clienteles, creating commercial strips whose vitality contrasted with those in African-American areas. The expanding commercial district of Koreatown lay a mile or so to the north of the renamed boulevard, and by 1984 there were already signs that it was creeping southwards via capital investment in property, malls and other businesses. The destruction wrought against Korean-owned stores during the 1992 riots expressed the resentment felt by many in the community. As a celebration of an African-American leader and an African-American cause, and as part of an attempt to create African-American economic prosperity, the park dedication and the other moves were perhaps at least a decade too late.

The contrast between the two situations is therefore one between inclusion and weakening ethnic boundaries and exclusion and maintaining them. Neither was an inevitable consequence of their shared setting. The Cinco de Mayo Parade may be exceptional, however. Other parades are usually more associated with one ethnic group. Marston (1989) discusses how, in the nineteenth-century US city, parades were collective displays of ethnic presence, often in the context of social antagonism and conflict. She shows how the St Patrick's Day Parades of Lowell, Massachusetts, were both an affirmation of the existing Yankee-dominated order, but also a challenge to it. Jackson (1992) details how Toronto's Caribana festival serves as a metaphor for wider social and political changes, including the criminalisation of the city's Afro-Caribbean youth. New York's Puerto Rican parade continues to act as an occasion for the assertion of a distinctive Puerto Rican voice in the city's streets (Kasinitz and Freidenberg-Herbstein, 1987). In each of these cases there were struggles over the meaning of the parade within the ethnic group itself, for example between assimilationists and radicals, and between those in favour of commercial and state support and those against.

The Cinco de Mayo Parade, smaller and less well-established as it is, differs from these others. It was neither commercial nor political. It was not confined to any single ethnic group. As long as it remained more inclusionary and symbolic rather than exclusionary and instrumental in its aims, its meaning could be interpreted in many different ways by the participants, without a conflict among them (Cohen, 1985). The geography of the parade assisted this plurality. It passed through both African-American and Latino neighbourhoods, its spectators were partially segregated along the way, and the nationalistic part of the event took place in more private surroundings. It was multi-referential, and so African-Americans and Latinos were free to construct their own meanings, such that it might be simultaneously a nationalistic celebration, a local event and a parade of youth.

If the participants were free to construct their own meanings then they were only able to do so within the constraints of the setting itself. Parades are short-lived but concentrated and potentially deeply significant rituals, their meanings shading off in time and space. Are there possibilities for the Cinco de Mayo Parade or similar situations to signify and create a more permanent negotiation between the two ethnic groups? If the event becomes as fully institutionalised as the others mentioned above, the range of possible interpretations may be reduced, leading to a greater possibility that they will contradict or exclude each other. This process may occur through its commercialisation, which the organisers deliberately sought to avoid, or its politicisation. Kasinitz (1987) notes the community resistance from West Indians in New York to the use of the Carnival by politicians running for office. Once instrumental goals are attached to a ritual, it may lose some of its inclusive capacity. But if the Cinco de Mayo Parade was to have any pay-off in terms of co-operating in local and citywide politics, then some sort of institutional linkages did need to be established.

The parade operated within the narrow confines of multi-referentiality on the one hand and an institutional embodiment of its aims and ambitions on the other. The park ceremony, by contrast, did not succeed in finding this balance.

Marston (1989) observes that the St Patrick's Day Parade had two audiences, the Irish themselves and the wider city. In both these cases the events were also outer-directed, towards a physically absent but none the less implied audience of the Anglo-dominated institutions of society. Adams-Vermont is not only overshadowed by the University of Southern California, but it is also subject to land speculation, development and gentrification. The hold of both groups on the area is tenuous, of which the organisers of both events were fully aware. The park ceremony claimed the right of residence for a community against those forces which are constantly uprooting and redistributing the urban poor. The parade announced the intention of two communities, subjugated and divided by the Anglo-dominated economic and political order, to refuse its terms. The negotiation of boundaries between African-Americans and Latinos occurs in settings not entirely of their own construction and choosing, but in conditions structured by the Anglo-dominated interests of the wider city. The full significance of both ceremony and parade can only be established by taking into account this wider context. Their meanings lie not just in the situations themselves, but also in their setting.

The Spaces of the Multi-ethnic City

Eight years after the events described above took place, these streets were the scene of rioting which followed the acquittal of four police officers accused of assaulting Rodney King. Vermont Avenue leads from the South Central ghetto into Koreatown, where much of the looting and violence occurred. Many observers noted the contrasts between these riots and the 1965 Watts uprising. The 1992 riots were more geographically diffuse; they could not be contained within a single compact curfew zone, but struck throughout the Los Angeles area (and beyond, to Atlanta, Las Vegas and other cities). The riots had no single centre, no single target. And, as Lynell George remarks in her eyewitness account of the events, the 1992 rebellion was not confined to the city's African-American community. She observed (1992, p.76):

an ironic twist on the multiethnic coalition that local community leaders have been talking about for years, but not successfully imple-
menting; black and Latino teenagers coming together to lift a sofa out
of a furniture store's showcase window, onto shoulders, then down
the sidewalk.

The riots were a perverse carnival, taking over the streets and
public spaces and overturning the social and political order. The
coalition that the Cinco de Mayo Parade had aspired to was
realised, though its affirmation of law and order through youth
was stood on its head.

The 1992 Los Angeles riots did mark a rejection of much of
what the parade stood for. Yet, at the same time, they point
towards both the significance of, and the necessity for, such public events. Contained within the Cinco de Mayo Parade, but not
the park ceremony, was an alternative to the dominant conceptions of the multi-ethnic city which still prevail in Los Angeles
and elsewhere. These conceptions and their alternative can be
understood through four models or ideals of the multi-ethnic
metropolis; the assimilated city, the city of division, the multicultural city and the city of difference.

The ideal of the assimilated city now perhaps belongs to the
past. The melting pot, in which all prior cultural differences and
particularisms become dissolved into a single homogeneous
community, is now an unrealisable, and indeed undesired,
dream. Its spatial expression, the city of no segregation, the diagonal on the Lorenz curve or the zero on indices of segregation, is
a normative benchmark rather than an achievable goal. Far closer
to reality is the city of division, built on inequality and the
defended encampments of homogeneous communities. Both
Davis (1990) and Rieff (1992) provide ample testimony to the
emergence of a 'Fortress LA', in which neighbourhoods are
mutually impenetrable. The proliferation of private security
forces, enclosed residential neighbourhoods, policed malls and
piazzas and the repression of movement by LA Police
Department barricades and curfew zones is gradually destroying
accessible public space. Davis describes how Los Angeles is
becoming a 'carceral city', in which social control is exercised by
the containment of 'threatening' populations and the restriction
on crossing the apartheid divides of rich and poor communities.

If this is 'the bad edge of postmodernity' (Davis's phrase), then
the city also encourages a more palatable version, the multicul-

tural city. The template for this city was the conversion of Los Angeles's historic centre into the Olvera Street Mexican market-place in 1930 (Parson, 1991). By removing many of the area's res-idents and restoring its buildings according to the theme of a *mercado*, Olvera Street became the forerunner for similar commer-cial-cum-tourist quaint spaces like Little Tokyo, Chinatown and Koreatown. The same ideal – each culture in its place to be sam-pled by the urban tourist – was expressed in the annual Los Angeles Street Scene Festival which once occupied the neutral territory of downtown in a celebration of the city's ethnic diversi-ty each September. Begun in 1978, it was closed down in 1986 after revellers clashed with police; carnival tipped over into riot (Davis, 1990). In 1990 it was revived in the guise of the LA Festival, a multicultural extravaganza of folkloric and traditional culture from around the Pacific Rim (strictly nothing European) held in sites all over the city, some free and open to all, others by ticket only (Martinez, 1992; Rieff, 1992). The multicultural city became an official ideal with the publication of the *LA 2000* report, which encouraged Angelenos to embrace the city's won-derful diversity (Los Angeles 2000 Committee, 1988).

The park ceremony can be viewed as a contribution to the ideal of the multicultural city. It claimed space for a community and named it, adding another tile to the city's ethnic mosaic. Yet there are profound problems with this ideal. Parson calls the transformation of Olvera Street a case of 'state-managed multi-vocality', a top-down exercise of control which sets the frame-work for permissible expressions of culture in terms of commercial possibilities and sanitised histories. Martinez is also uneasy. The LA Festival had a 'feel-good, uncritical atmosphere' (1992, p.128) in which all the class and race tensions of the city are covered up with 'a Disneylike It's a Small World After All theme' (p.129). The question is: who is to decide what fits into the multicultural mosaic, and what elements of ethnic culture are to be included? Is it to be the local state and its allies in the financial and commercial power bloc of Los Angeles, or the peo-ple themselves? Los Angeles's Latino community is fighting renewed attempts by the Recreation and Parks Department to convert Olvera Street into a multi-ethnic theme park by restoring its past Italian and Chinese presences (Parson, 1991). The usual clearances of existing uses will follow, including the sanitisation of La Reina de Los Angeles, the church which for years provided

assistance and a voice for refugees, immigrants and the home-
less (Martinez, 1992).

In the multicultural city, the commodification of 'ethnic culture' can be made compatible with the successful control of public space and the sustained accumulation of capital by
commercial enterprise. It depends upon a reduction of ethnicity
to an 'ethnic culture' which fails to escape from earlier and more
explicit processes of racial definition (Anderson, 1990). As
Kapferer (1988) has argued, multiculturalism can share the same
ontological presuppositions as inegalitarian or racially-inspired
ideologies. Each individual (and space) belongs to a single identifiable cultural group, and reproduces within him- or herself the
characteristics of the group as a whole. The groups are mutually
exclusive, and their sum exhausts the population as a whole; each
person to a group, each group in its place. The conception of ethnicity embodied in multiculturalism contrasts radically with
Mitchell's notion of ethnicity as situational and negotiable, and
also with the meaning of the Cinco de Mayo Parade.

The city of difference is partly an inversion of state-managed
pluralism, but it also attempts to transcend the commodification
and fixity of culture inscribed in the mosaic of ethnic spaces. Iris
Marion Young (1990, p.227) phrases this as yet unrealised social
ideal as one of 'openness to unassimilated others'. The ideals of
community as harmony, consensus, mutual understanding and
the transparency of subjects to one another avoids politics, is
wildly utopian and denies the realities of group difference
(pp.226–34). Young argues that it is necessarily exclusionary, as
community can only be valued by finding and excluding deviant
individuals and groups: '[c]ommitment to an ideal of community
tends to value and enforce homogeneity' (p.234). In its place,
Young advocates a normative ideal of city life as 'the being
together of strangers' (p.237). Groups, which are defined relation-
ally rather than essentially, and whose boundaries are fluid
and ambiguous rather than fixed and impermeable, overlap
and intermingle without becoming homogeneous.[5] The social
geography of this ideal city is already potentially present, though
unrealised: '[i]n the good city one crosses from one distinct
neighbourhood to another without knowing precisely where one

5. Young's description of group difference (1990, pp.156–225) is not incompatible with
Mitchell's own concept of ethnicity as situational.

ended and the other began' (p.239). The clear, marked boundaries of both the multicultural city and the city of division are dissolved. Further, the ideals are to be found in the multiple use of
public space, in its variety, unpredictability and sense of 'erotic
attraction' to difference. These public spaces should also be
spaces of political life, of meetings, demonstrations, arguments
and encounters, the politics of the streets and not the top-down
control of public expression and movement (Jackson, 1992).

If the park ceremony unwittingly realised the ideals of the
community-as-exclusion, then the Cinco de Mayo Parade was
perhaps closer to the city of difference. It was inclusive rather
than exclusive, directed towards a coalition-building which none
the less did not deny the differences between Mexicans and
African-Americans, and acted out in public space an alternative
to the vision of hermetically sealed and neatly labelled ethnic territories. The parade crossed the boundaries of turf and ethnicity.
Although its setting was shaped by the city's dominant political
and economic interests, it was not a determined outcome of the
social and spatial changes which brought about the 'being together of strangers' (Young, 1990, p.237).

Conclusion

The Cinco de Mayo Parade and the park dedication ceremony
represent contrasting situations in a common setting, a mixed
ethnic neighbourhood where Latino immigration, redevelopment
and gentrification presage social change. It was suggested that
the key themes among contextual features are ambiguous boundaries and spatial proximity. One situation was more inclusionary
than the other, suggesting that ecological context does not determine the character of boundary relations between two communities. Co-operation as well as conflict may occur, depending upon
the situation, the issue and the level of organisation.

In contrasting the two situations, therefore, questions were
raised about the possibilities of weakening ethnic boundaries.
What kinds of symbols, actions, issues and institutions can link
diverse social identities in the US urban context without reducing
this diversity? In part, the political questions for community
organisation and progressive projects are anthropological: how
are boundaries crossed? A small parade may not count for much

when contrasted with the explosive impact of the riots, an anarchic version of the city of difference. But it is a lesson that Young's ideal of city life is both a necessary condition for, and an unrealised possibility of, social justice.

Bibliography

Acuña, R., *A Community Under Siege: A Chronicle of Chicanos East of the Los Angeles River 1945–1975*, Monograph 11, Los Angeles: Chicano Studies Research Center, University of California, 1984

Anderson, K., 'Chinatown Re-oriented: A Critical Analysis of Recent Redevelopment Schemes in a Melbourne and Sydney Enclave', *Australian Geographical Studies*, vol.28, no.2, 1990, pp.137–54

Clark, W.A.V., 'Revealed Preferences and Neighborhood Transition in a Multiethnic Setting', *Urban Geography*, vol.10, no.5, 1989, pp. 434–48

Cohen, A.P., *The Symbolic Construction of Community*, London: Tavistock, 1985

Davis, M., 'Chinatown Part Two: The "Internationalization" of Downtown Los Angeles', *New Left Review*, vol.164, 1987, pp.65–86

_____, *City of Quartz: Excavating the Future in Los Angeles*, London: Verso, 1990

Falcón, A., 'Black and Latino Politics in New York City: Race and Ethnicity in a Changing Urban Context', *New Community*, vol.14, no.3, 1988, pp.370–84

Garcia, P., 'Immigration Issues in Urban Ecology: The Case of Los Angeles', in *Urban Ethnicity in the United States: New Immigrants and Old Minorities*, L. Maldonado and J. Moore (eds), Beverly Hills: Sage, 1985

George, L., 'Waiting for the Rainbow Sign', *New Left Review*, vol.193, 1992, pp.75–9

Jackson, P., 'Street Life: the Politics of Carnival', *Environment and Planning D: Society and Space*, vol.6, no.2, 1988, pp. 213–27

_____, 'The Politics of the Streets: a Geography of Caribana', *Political Geography*, vol.11, no.2, 1992, pp.130–51

Johnson Jr, J. and Oliver, M., 'Interethnic Minority Conflict in Urban America: The Effects of Economic and Social Dislocations', *Urban Geography*, vol.10, no.5, 1989, pp.449–63

Kapferer, B., *Legends of People, Myths of State: Violence, Intolerance and Political Culture in Sri Lanka and Australia*, Washington, DC: Smithsonian Press, 1988

Kasinitz, P., 'The Minority Within: The New Black Immigrants', *New York Affairs*, vol.10, no.1, 1987, pp.44–58

_____, and Freidenberg-Herbstein, J., 'The Puerto Rican Parade and West

Indian Carnival: Public Celebrations in New York City', in *Caribbean Life in New York City: Sociocultural Dimensions*, C.R. Sutton and E.M. Chaney (eds), New York: Center for Migration Studies, 1987

Logan, J. and Molotch, H., *Urban Fortunes: the Political Economy of Place*, Berkeley: University of California Press, 1987

Los Angeles 2000 Committee, *LA 2000: A City for the Future*, Los Angeles: Los Angeles 2000 Committee, 1988

Marston, S., 'Public Rituals and Community Power: St Patrick's Day Parades in Lowell, Massachusetts, 1841–1874', *Political Geography Quarterly*, vol.8, no 3, 1989, pp.255–69

Martinez, R., *The Other Side: Fault Lines, Guerrilla Saints and the True Heart of Rock 'n' Roll*, London: Verso, 1992

Massey, D. and Mullan, B., 'Processes of Hispanic and Black Spatial Assimilation', *American Journal of Sociology*, vol.89, no.4, 1984, pp. 836–73

Mitchell, J.C., *The Kalela Dance: Aspects of Social Relationships Among Urban Africans in Northern Rhodesia*, Rhodes-Livingstone Papers, no.27, Manchester: Manchester University Press, 1956

_____, 'Case Study and Situational Analysis', *Sociological Review (N.S.)*, vol.31, 1983, pp.187–211

_____, *Cities, Society and Social Perception: a Central African Perspective*, Oxford: Clarendon, 1987

Oliver, M. and Johnson Jr, J., 'Interethnic Conflict in an Urban Ghetto: The Case of Blacks and Latinos in Los Angeles', in *Research in Social Movements: Conflict and Change*, no.6, R. Ratcliff and L. Kriesberg (eds), Greenwich: JAI Press, 1984

Parson, D., 'Many Histories: Postmodern Politics in Los Angeles', *Science as Culture*, no.12, 1991, pp.411–25

Rieff, D., *Los Angeles: Capital of the Third World*, London: Jonathan Cape, 1992

Rogers, A., 'The Ghetto and the Barrio: A Social Geography of Blacks and Latinos in Los Angeles', Oxford: unpublished DPhil thesis, University of Oxford, 1988

Saltzstein, A. and Sonenshein, R., 'Los Angeles: Transformation of a Governing Coalition', in *Big City Politics*, H. Savitch and J. Thomas (eds), Newbury Park, CA: Sage, 1991

Sassen-Koob, S., 'The New Labour Demand in Global Cities', in *Cities in Transformation*, M.P. Smith (ed.), Beverly Hills: Sage, 1984

Soja, E., Morales, R. and Wolff, G., 'Urban Restructuring: An Analysis of Social and Spatial Change in Los Angeles', *Economic Geography*, vol.59, no.2, 1983, pp. 195–230

Young, I.M., *Justice and the Politics of Difference*, Princeton: Princeton University Press, 1990

Chapter 5

Where to Draw the Line: A Geography of Popular Festivity

Susan Smith

Introduction

The boundary is one of those core concepts of social science to which both geography and anthropology can usefully speak. 'What is Geography,' asks Gunnar Olssen (1992) in a recent and influential essay on the geographical landscape, 'if it is not the drawing and interpretation of lines?' (p.95). 'What is the boundary,' asks Dagmar Reichert (1992), if it is not 'this thin unstable line in which form and content meet in an affair called geography' (p.87). Boundaries may appear to be real – a line on a map, a wall, a customs office and so on – but social divides always have meaning as well as form. Anthropologists have argued that symbolic boundaries are as salient as any more tangible dividing line, and that public events like carnivals, fairs and fiestas are all boundary-marking exercises – mechanisms through which people might 'think themselves into difference' (Anthony Cohen, 1985; 1986). The significance of boundaries lies, in short, in both their symbolism and their physical extent. It is especially valuable, therefore, to look to the intersection of geography with anthropology – a position vigorously encouraged by J. Clyde Mitchell – in our attempt to analyse them.

The boundary is not, of course, a particularly popular concept in social science these days. We are much more interested in fluidity and flexibility, in transgressing the line between art and everyday life (Bonnett, 1992); in the globalisation of the economy and the move to pan-national labour markets; in a postmodern pluralism which recognises a multitude of social identities and

privileges none, and in a world shrunk by advanced communications technologies which divorce experience from location and
conflate 'here' with 'there' (Meyrowitz, 1985; Morley, 1991). The
dissolution of the boundary implied in these trends is, in my
view, very welcome. Our tendency to 'commit category', as
Campbell (1992) so aptly describes it, can be dangerous,
demeaning and counterproductive. It helps us assume that
'races' are real, that 'sex' has innate social significance, that intel-
ligence can be measured, that nations are natural, and so on. So,
if the postmodern world really were a world that transgressed
the boundary, I would be content, and this chapter would be
redundant.

But I have already argued that, notwithstanding the destructuring and restructuring of virtually everything, the boundary
is alive and well in the late twentieth century (Smith, 1993a). I
have pointed out that, despite (and, indeed, protected by) the
niceties of cultural pluralism, enduring inequalities predicated
on ideas about 'race', gender and 'normality' still provide the
ordering principles of late twentieth century social and economic life. Below, I shall take some further examples to illustrate the
symbolic ways in which boundary-building is maintained. I
shall argue that, while the process can be liberating and invigo-
rating, it is, simultaneously, problematic. Therefore, while it
may be impossible, even undesirable, to resist some of the
boundedness of social life, in embracing its inevitability, academics, policy-makers, practitioners and the public require
a much better sense of what underpins the idea of social differentiation, and a more informed idea of just where to draw the
line.

Symbolic boundaries are not always obvious or apparent, and
they are evident less in the routine of everyday life – though they
can certainly be found here (Smith, 1984) – than in the collective
behaviours that occur from time to time, both formally and spon-
taneously. These behaviours frequently occupy the much-contested but generally neglected public spaces of the streets (see
Goheen, 1993). Recognising the relevance of territoriality to the
structure of social life, and the significance of space to the organisation of social theory, this chapter explores the range of collective behaviours that have, in the past and more recently, been
performed by the public in an effort simultaneously to claim
space, make place and assert identity.

The Crowd and the Public

Collective behaviour has fascinated geographers, sociologists and anthropologists for years. Robert Park, in his doctoral dissertation, identified two kinds of collective behaviour – the crowd and the public – which he saw as the two basic categories of change-inducing behaviour operating outside the world of institutional change. The crowd, however, because of its tendency to emphasise members' similarities and suppress ingroup difference, might be seen as the most effective boundary-marking (or boundary-claiming) activity (Park, 1904).

Social theory has come a fair distance since Park wrote about the crowd. Perhaps the most impressive contribution has come from Mikhail Bakhtin. Bakhtin is commonly referred to as an authority on the carnivalisation of social life, but in practice he saw carnival as just one of a more general class of popular festive forms ranging from ritual ceremony (a serious and formalised pageantry designed to be observed rather than practised) to the carnivalesque (a public spectacle created by and for its participants) (see Bakhtin, 1984, p.7).

Ritual ceremony comprises 'serious, official, ecclesiastical, feudal, and political cultural forms'. It occupies public space in order to state and reiterate the claims made by a dominant majority to a position of authority, to define history and traditions, to link the past with the present and to assert a vision of the future. Carnival, consisting of 'forms of protocol and ritual based on laughter and consecrated by tradition', is more often read as a form of resistance to such assertions and is associated with the collective action of oppressed minorities seeking to change the status order, to establish a different view of the past and to open different paths to the future. Both festive forms, however, are linked in some way with the projects of domination, empowerment and with the assertion or subversion of identity. Both, moreover, use a struggle for space to symbolise wider social and political contests, and both use spatial strategies to establish cultural difference. Notwithstanding these similarities, and without denying that most public events involve a mixture of festive forms, I shall consider the two 'ideal' types in turn.

Spectacles of State

Spectacular ceremonial events require resources, organisation and co-ordination. They are normally, therefore, state, civic or (more recently) commercial ventures, engineered by and staged for a powerful elite. Explicitly or implicitly, they provide a link between culture and politics, using the emotional content of art forms as the vehicle through which societies define themselves and transform themselves to meet certain ideals. Strong (1984) discusses such art forms in the context of Italy in the fifteenth to seventeenth centuries. He shows how the Renaissance court fete acted as 'a ritual in which society affirmed its wisdom and asserted its control over the world and its destiny' (p.41). By the early seventeenth century, 'spectacle' had become part of the repertory of entertainment at virtually every European court, harnessing art and letters to the service of the state on the assumption that 'the court fete could express philosophy, politics and morals through a unique fusion of music, painting, poetry and dance' (Strong, 1984, p.6). Court fetes were, then, partly for enjoyment, but they were also meant to be read as a programme of political ideas.

The state spectacular of the Renaissance was preoccupied with visual display and acoustical brilliance (Cummings, 1992; Strong, 1984). These displays occupied a distinctive space in the urban landscape, and had an important place in securing public compliance with political projects. They achieved this by creating a sense of belonging to that project – a sense of incorporation within its boundary. This is most evident in the spectacles mounted in the seventeenth-century city state of Venice. On these festive occasions, 'the hero is not the Saint whose day is being celebrated, still less any individual venetian: it is Venice itself ... and care was taken to involve them [the populace] in such a way that they felt some stake in their Most Serene Republic' (Arnold, 1979, p.22). This sense of identity and compliance enabled the power-brokers of Venice to secure sufficient public support to resist the competing demands of Papacy and Empire, but it also facilitated the exercise of Venice's own political aggressions towards, for example, Padua and Verona.

The conduct and content of the state spectacle, in an era where images were the focus of a search for truth, were preserved in lavish and elaborately illustrated commemorative books designed 'to enable those who were not there to savour the transitory wonder and to grasp its import from afar' (Strong, 1984, p.21). The symbolic cultural landscape, every bit as much as the material world of painting and architecture, was thus harnessed to the task of creating an image of the monarch to draw people's allegience, and affirm their identity as subjects.

Cannadine (1983) identifies the renaissance spectacle as one of two 'great phases of royal ceremonial efflorescence' in Europe. Whereas the seventeenth-century events 'centred on absolutism in pre-industrial society', from the 1870s to the 1910s society enjoyed a period of 'invented, ceremonial splendour'. The former events were designed to affirm the status order through a massive display of wealth (even, perhaps especially, when those concerned were in financial difficulty); the latter were part of the Victorian 'invention' of tradition designed to 'give an impression of continuity, community and comfort, despite overwhelming contextual evidence to the contrary' (Cannadine, 1983, p.105). Both kinds of festivity were instrumental in securing a sense of social solidarity – of commonness, boundedness and exclusivity – as spectators were reminded of their common experience as 'subjects'.

Shils and Young's (1953) seminal article on the meaning of the Coronation argues that the state ceremonial provides people with an opportunity to 'reaffirm the rightness of the moral rules by which they feel they ought to live' (p.66). Coronation, from this perspective, is definitive of a society 'held together by its internal agreement as to the sacredness of certain fundamental moral standards ... [it is] ... a great act of national communion' (p.80). However, coronation is not only about the existential wellbeing of the general public; rather it has had an 'importance in legitimating the novelty of Empire and in giving an impression of stability at a time of international bewilderment', and 'in the post-war world it has provided a comfortable palliative to the loss of world-power status' (Cannadine 1983, p.157). In short, there is political gain to be made by elevating the status of royalty at a time of national decline by orientating people towards their sense of exclusivity.

In the last twenty years, while the state spectacular has remained important (in the UK, the Queen's Silver Jubilee and the wedding of the Prince and Princess of Wales, for instance, both prompted huge crowd events and street parties), the powers of capital and commerce often eclipse the significance of monarchy and polity in mobilising public spectacle. This is vividly illustrated by Ley and Olds (1988) in their interrogation of the World's Fairs. The fairs are produced by a business elite in conjunction with politicians, designers and artists, who are powerful enough to translate their own vision of the world into the landscapes of the fairs. A fair might, therefore, be seen as a symbol of social control, used to extend the authority of a country's corporate, political, and scientific leadership, (Rydell, 1984, pp.2–3, cited in Ley and Olds, 1988, p.198). It achieves success by emphasising fun, entertainment and education – a combination which people actively use to promote their own local identity even as they engage with the projects of a regional elite.

Similar spectacles arising from the power of fantasy to attract capital and the power of capital to promote fantasy are described by Zukin (1991). She shows how 'Disneyland' advances the ideals of a service sector society and has become 'a model for establishing both the economic value of cultural goods and the cultural value of consumer products' (p.231). It achieves this by creating a market-oriented landscape which, ironically, promotes a strong sense of place and a clear vision of US identity: Disneyland is an imaginary landscape which succeeds in securing public identification because it is able to manipulate the collective memory to its own (ultimately commercial, yet unquestionably socially stimulating) ends.

Spectacles of state and of capital link art to politics or commerce, to create a sense of local identity which secures compliance with political and economic projects which range from the erection of city states to the exercise of imperialism, and to the marketing of goods, services and, ultimately, places themselves. *En route* there is scope for the public to be awe-inspired, impressed, reassured of their place in the world, and to have fun. The essential ambiguity of the social construction of boundaries can hardly be better illustrated.

Carnival Culture

The distinction between carnival, state spectacle and, indeed, other forms of public life is one of degree rather than kind. As Harrison (1988) notes, a very broad range of crowd events – from political meetings to ceremonials and celebrations – are shot through with local antagonisms and politicised in complex ways. As a consequence the distinctions among popular festive forms are hard to maintain:

> Fine lines separate the quasi-ritual violence of elections, the quiet antipathy of ceremonials, the good-humoured co-mingling of public recreation and the physical violence of riot. (Harrison, 1988, p.266)

All these events reproduce and redefine traditions in an attempt collectively to map the past and project the future. Burke (1978) thus argues that carnival, just like spectacle, is partly a ritual of social incorporation as well as a mechanism of social control, providing 'the means for a community, a village or urban parish, to express its hostility to individuals who stepped out of line and so to discourage breaches of custom' (p.200).

Conceptually, however, there is a difference that can be read into carnival which is not apparent in spectacles of state and commerce: not only is one to be watched and the other to be engaged in (Bakhtin's point) but, whereas the spectacular is about the affirmation of power, carnival is more typically seen as a ritual of resistance. These oppositional qualities of carnival are apparent in virtually all accounts of the very diverse events that bear the label. It is through the practice of opposition that the carnivalesque negotiates its own social space and positions its own social boundaries.

Carnival is at one level simply opposed to the routines of everyday life. In early modern Europe, carnival was 'a time of waste precisely because the everyday was a time of careful saving' (Burke, 1978, p.178). It was an occasion which turned the world upside down to produce 'enclaved liminal moments of "ordered disorder"' to contrast with the tidiness and predictability of the daily round (Featherstone, 1991, p.136). Here the process of role-reversal – the rich changing places with the poor, men dressing as women – appears momentarily liberating, but it serves ultimately to emphasise what is 'normal' – a rigid social differentiation between classes and genders.

Carnival is also opposed to the prevailing economic order. This is best illustrated in E. LeRoy Ladurie's (1979) classic work on carnival in Romans which documents the tensions between the 'rich men's Carnival' which relied on display and hyperbole, and the 'lower group's' carnival which relied on caricature and

satire. Here again, there was never any danger of the power base
changing hands, but through collective opposition, the poor were
able to win at least some concessions from the rich. Carnival is
additionally a form of political protest. Marston's (1989) study of
the St Patrick's Day Parades in Lowell, Massachusetts in the late
nineteenth century shows that the celebrations were not simply a
passive display of Irish tradition and culture. They were enacted,
rather, as a demonstration of community power and solidarity,
and as a means of pressing for Irish participation in the republican USA. Likewise, Abner Cohen's (1982) study of the Notting
Hill Carnival and Jackson's (1992) account of Toronto's Caribana
show how carnival can be opposed to processes of racial categorisation, and to the hierarchies enacted on this principle.

As a ritual of resistance, carnival can be a vehicle by which
oppressed minorities challenge the existing order in an attempt
to claim a space and make a place in the prevailing political economy. Such events aim to undermine, unsettle and reposition
existing social boundaries, though they do so with variable success. The implicit (and generally unattainable) endpoint, however, is to replace one type of boundary with another. This means
that, while inequality might effectively be challenged, the fact of
having a boundary – signifying simultaneously the facts of
belonging and exclusion, entitlement and disenfranchisement –
goes unquestioned, with all the practically and theoretically
problematic consequences that Penrose (1994) documents.

Places on the Margin: The Scottish Borders

Notwithstanding the boundary-building of the past, it is fashionable to assume today that the advent of postmodernism has
either effaced the social boundary altogether or, at least, rendered
it too flexible and permeable to contain, constrain or exclude anyone. Postmodernism puts an end to fixity, denies conformity and
has no need to preserve the past. It marks the aestheticism of
experience, and erodes all distinction between culture as art and
culture as a way of life. We have entered, some would argue, a
world where style is a substitute for meaning, difference is celebrated rather than subsumed or resisted, and the aesthetic turn in
public life is no longer exclusive to the festive form. It seems
appropriate to wonder how the dominating and oppositional

events enacted in ceremony and carnival fare in these fluid new times; to consider whether their significance is undermined by a sense that boundaries no longer matter, and to assess just how negotiable the social worlds of postmodernism might be.

To date, studies of festival and carnival have generally focused on projects which draw on a version of the past and a vision of the future to either propagate or challenge 'core' cultures. Pageantry affirms a dominant urban status quo; carnival is a challenge to that dominance which is mounted most often in the heart of the city. Shields (1991), however, argues that the significance of the 'postmodern turn' to the organisation of social life can best be grasped by concentrating on what happens at the periphery rather than the core. It is here, in spaces at the lagging edge of postmodernisation, that we might best discover the meaning of popular festivity in a restructured world. Today, as a signifier of everything which 'centres' deny or repress, 'marginality' has become a central theme.

In the remainder of this chapter, I shall take an example of collective behaviour in the borderlands of Scotland to examine the tenacity and meaning of boundary building at the edge of a national territory and from the margins of a national way of life. The Borders, as indicated on Figure 5.1, have an ambiguous position relative to the rest of Scotland. On the one hand, they are signifiers of all that is Scottish, since they mark the much-contested point of differentiation with England; on the other hand, they are on the edge of Scottish space and are marginal both to a Scottish political economy which centres on the cities of the central belt, and to a Scottish cultural heritage which draws its core imagery from the rural Highlands of the north.

The Borders are not lacking in the ritual crowd events that Anthony Cohen (1986) sees as such crucial symbolic boundary-markers, and there is no indication that the postmodern turn has undermined their rationale. Indeed, their sustained popularity, accumulating momentum and continuous elaboration testifies to the increasing significance of what Johnston (1991) calls the cult of the anniversary in late twentieth-century life. Annually, between May and July a group of towns scattered across the Borders celebrate summer in style by performing a variety of rituals associated with the annual Common Ridings. The most significant of these within what is now the Borders Region are shown in Figure 5.2. Table 5.1 summarises the character of the main festivals.

Figure 5.1 The Regions of Scotland

Figure 5.2 Borders Region, Showing Peeblesshire (Now Tweeddale)

The peculiarities and particularities of the different Borders town events confirms, at one level, McCrone's (1992) observation that the hallmark of 'Scottish culture' is its variety and eclecticism. However, even at a superficial level there are a number of common themes: opposition to the English, protection of locality (through the ridings), solemnity and ceremony (usually surrounding the 'bussing' of the burgh flag), competition and the carnivalesque. The various common elements include having fun, nurturing civic pride, and celebrating locality. This all hangs around three premises. First, that there is a clear difference between local selves and proximate others: the Braw Lad is not the same as the West Linton Whipman; the Cleikum Ceremony has a different role and rationale to the civic events at Coldstream, and all the local festivals are organised around

Table 5.1 Annual Festivals and Fairs in the Borders of Scotland

Location	Date of origin	Key elements
Coldstream Civic Week	1952	Investiture of the Coldstreamer Ride to commemorate the dead of 1513; torchlight procession/fireworks; horse racing and fancy dress
Duns Summer Festival	1949	The Reiver leads mounted followers to Duns Law, where Charles I was resisted; Married men v. bachelors in handball; riding the parish bounds; fancy dress parade
Eyemouth Herring Queen Festival	1939	Queen leads flotilla – St Abb's Head to Eyemouth; sports; competition; commemoration of 1881 fishing disaster
Galashiels Braw Lads Gathering	1930	Brad Lad leads riders to Raid Stone, where English raiders killed by Gala Lads in 1337; riding and sports; ceremony of Sod And Stone (Sasines)
Hawick Common Riding	1703	Cornet leads male supporters on rideouts; chase to commemorate routing of English plunderers in 1514; horse racing and games
Jedburgh Callants Festival	1947	Ceremonial rides to places of historic interest; ceremony at tree from the ancient Jed Forest; games (dating from 1853)
Lauder Common Riding	1910	Sports, parades, dances, concerts; Cornet leads riding to the boundary stone; games and horse events
Kelso Civic Week	1937	Kelso Laddie receives Standard, is installed as Whipman and leads followers to the Trusting Tree; rideouts to neighbouring villages; fancy dress parade and games
Melrose Festival Week	1938	Gymkhana, rideouts, fancy dress parade; Installation of the Melrosian in the Abbey (ruin); Crowning the Queen; procession around places of historic interest; sports
Peebles Beltane	1897	Riding; crowning; sports (see pp.153–61)
St Ronan's Games, Innerleithen	1817	Cleikum Ceremony (to familiarise the youth with local tradition); torchlight procession and masonic ceremonies; Flower Parade; games; bonfire to burn effigy of the Devil
Selkirk Common Riding	c400BP	Riding of Marches; professional games, horse racing and gymkhana
West Linton Whipman	1803	Whipman leads mounted procession; sports; play; competition and bonfire

distinctive local histories and unique symbolic spaces. Second, that notwithstanding the commonalities between the English and Scottish borderlands, there is a clear distinction to be drawn between Scottish and English traditions, with the more favoured traditions lying north of the border (often, key ceremonies refer to moments at which local Scots defeated English invaders). Finally, that the hallmarks of tradition lie in the preservation of historical continuity, including continuities in the differentiation of gender roles and in the reproduction of particular forms of masculinity and femininity. The festivities are thus simultaneously about promoting a local status quo, *and* about resisting the imposition of alternative world views, either from England to the south, or from the Scottish mainstream to the north.

Most of the anniversary celebrations which take place in the Borders towns symbolise a search for local identity, rooted in local traditions, which are preserved by anchoring festivity to territory while, amongst other things, having fun. To this end, the celebrations combine elements of civic spectacle with the carnivalesque, and they are all exercises in social and spatial boundary-building. Civic spectacles mobilise the 'official' commentary on locality, while the carnivalesque elements defend this view against less marginalised versions of Scottish and UK lifestyles. Below, I take one example from these festivities to show how, even in the open-ended and mobile societies of the 1990s, and even when enacted in a setting which cannot be described as mainstream, the ostensibly innocent celebration of self is inextricably bound to the implicit subjugation of other. My point is not that this is something that can easily be changed, but rather that, precisely because it is a facet of social experience which is enduring, it is a project which needs to be engaged with more critically and, where appropriate, sculpted more sensitively.

The Peebles Beltane Festival

The Peebles Beltane Festival occurs annually in June. It runs from Sunday to Saturday, spanning seven days, each one of them rekindling the flame of local history in a distinctive way (Brown and Lawson, 1990). Its origins are supposedly lodged in antiquity, 'in the ceremonial observances of the original British people, who lighted fires on the tops of hills and other places in honour of their deity Baal; hence Beltane or Beltien, signifying the fire of Baal' (Chambers, cited in Lang and Lang, 1913). Although the modern form of the festival often refers to these pagan origins (usually in order to note its subsequent 'Christianisation'), today's celebration is largely a Victorian revival, dating from 1897.

The festivities comprising the Beltane provide local people with a link to the past, a defense of the present and a sense of self. A link to the past is secured at the beginning of the week by locating the opening ceremonies in the 700-year-old ruin of the Cross Kirk. The kirk survived the English invasion of 1548–9 and is a symbol of resistance as well as endurance. The element of defence is symbolised in the March Ridings, which take place a few days later, when modern riders re-enact the ancient practice of inspecting the burgh boundaries to prevent outsiders annexing the common lands. Celebration of self is secured at the culmination of the week with the proclamation of the Beltane Fair and the crowning of the Beltane Queen (see Smith, 1993b for more detail).

In Peebles, as in several of the other larger Borders towns, the ridings occupy a special place in the week's events. Long after their practical function ceased, they continued in commemoration of local legend, history and tradition. They have now become the key part of a ritual asserting the burgh's place within the Borders, and part of the symbolic preservation and protection of local identity. To these ends, the ridings are enacted partly to keep outsiders at a distance, but also to secure a distinctive position for Peebles within the cluster of Borders towns. As William Cleland reminded Peebleans during his address at Neidpath Castle in 1936, 'the day is not very far removed when Peebles was relegated to a position of being considered as in but not of the Borders' (Peebles March Riding Committee, 1949, p.35). The appointment of a Cornet – a young man designated to lead the riding and represent the burgh at key events throughout the year – thus not only signifies Peebleans' readiness to defend their own traditions but also allows Peebles to participate in the ritual exchange of hospitality with the other festival towns. The ridings are therefore a spatial strategy which are simultaneously exclusive and integrative. They enable the Beltane to testify to the unique history, identity and integrity of Peebles, while confirming the social status and geographical position of the town within a borderland setting.

This positioning is reinforced when the riding breaks its journey to enable the Cornet and his supporters to attend a short ceremony at Neidpath Castle, which stands just outside the burgh boundary. The castle is the gateway to Peebles, and occupies a key defensive site. However (not least because Peebles apparently once had another more centrally located castle), reference to Neidpath symbolises the wider defensive service that the Borders have traditionally provided for Scotland against the English: 'In an English invasion, whether the invader came by the east route or the west route, Neidpath was a menace to his flanks,' (Lord Tweedsmuir, cited in Peebles March Riding Committee, 1949, p.32). The castle, reflected William Crichton in 1938, 'comes to us from a time when men were fighting in the battles for Scottish independence' (Peebles March Riding Committee, 1949, p.38), and it was one of a series of beacon points used to warn the capital of invasions from the south.

In short, the riding ceremony, which takes place in the middle of Beltane Week, symbolises local identity in three ways. First, it marks out the territorial extent of the locality; second, it protects local identity against usurpation by outsiders, and finally, it sets the locality into a specific position within Scotland and the Scottish Borders. The ridings show that the essence of the festival is a discourse about what Peebles is, where it ends, and who belongs. It is good-natured, good fun, unashamedly sentimental and uncompromisingly introspective, and it is essentially an event promoted by local people to emphasise the commonalities among local people. Tourists and onlookers are welcome, but the event is performed for its participants, not for the tourist's gaze. 'Townsfolk United in Glorious Tradition' blazed the headline of the *Peeblesshire News* above pictures of the 1993 riding (*Peeblesshire News*, 25 June 1993, p.5). 'The Beltane,' affirmed the new Warden of the Cross Kirk when opening the week's events, 'is our annual opportunity to recognise the value of the way of life we enjoy here' (p.6). Not much has changed since Sir Robert Scott (as Warden of Neidpath Castle) observed twenty years ago that the traditions of the Beltane 'help to give the Royal Burgh of Peebles its distinctive personality' (Peebles March Riding and Beltane Queen Festival Committee, 1974, p.4). There is, then, no hint of placelessness, and no tendency to substitute style for meaning, in the conduct of the (post)modern Beltane, which continues to help define local identity and secure its distinctive position in Scottish space.

However, the vehicle so instrumental in nurturing commonality is also, by definition, a marker of difference. The form of the festival assumes and affirms the existence of many boundaries, the most significant of which is that which divides 'Gutterbluids' (those born within the burgh boundaries) and outsiders or 'Stoorifeet'. 'The Beltane,' noted John Gray in his address to the annual dinner of the Peebles Callants Club, is a particularly special celebration among true Gutterbluids, 'only you have that in-depth feeling of tradition that must never be removed' (*Peeblesshire News*, 25 June 1993, p.9). The Beltane Festival is, therefore, about the celebration of self – and in this it is remarkably successful and thoroughly enjoyable. But the ingredients of this celebration suggest that it is also about the identification and, I shall argue, on occasion, the exclusion and subjugation of others. This is because, in emphasising the importance of locality, heritage and tradition in particular ways, the Beltane not only invokes the niceties of local history and the pleasantries of spatialisation, but it also harnesses the more problematic legacies of the racialised and gendered society in which that history unfolded and in which local geographies are set. The implications of these legacies for the kinds of boundaries enacted through festivities like the Beltane are considered in turn.

Shields (1991) argues that society has become a formation in which 'social divisions are often spatialised, that is expressed using spatial metaphors or descriptive spatial divisions' (p.29). The Beltane ceremony is consistent with this generalisation, since it is an event in which 'people treat the spatial as charged with emotional content, mythical meanings, community, symbolism and historical significance' (p.57). The performance of the Beltane attaches social significance to birthplace, and most discussion and debate around the Beltane Week hinges on the distinctiveness, uniqueness and importance of locality. 'We are celebrating ... year by year ... a living spirit that breathes round us' observed Walter Buchan as Warden of Neidpath Castle in 1933 (Peebles March Riding Committee, 1949, p.29).

For Shields (1991), the significance of this attachment of community to place – of this process of spatialisation – lies in the imaginary geographies which allow particular sites to 'become associated with particular values, historical events and feelings' (p.29). Interrogating these imaginary geographies within Peebles we find, on the one hand, a festival which exemplifies the life of a quintessentially Scottish town, signalling agreement with McCrone (1992) that the 'real' Scotland is essentially rural. On the other hand, the festival signals a sense of the particularity of the Borders, with Peebles itself playing a key part in a unique corner of Scotland, whose identity is separate and distinct from that of the Scottish Highlands or the urban cultures of the central belt (which is perhaps why the Scottish National Party has never gained much support here).

This distinct identity is not, however, one looking back to the trappings of Kailyardism. The picture is not one of rural quaintness and nostalgia shot through with domesticity, rusticity, humour and piety. It is, rather, an identity shaped by an acute awareness of the economic and demographic crises of rural Scotland. The de-industrialisation of the Borders has been completed with the recent closure of the woollen mills, and Peebles has acquired both a commuter and a retirement community. Locals are not only aware of their consequent socio-economic marginality but have developed forms of resistance to it, challenging processes which are perceived to undermine the spatial and social integrity of the burgh, and adapting to change in a variety of imaginative ways. For instance, the Callants Club which, in many towns, is open only to those (men) born within the town's boundaries is, in Peebles, open also to men who have lived within the town for more than fifteen years. Thus the locality has adapted in some measure to the demographic challenge, although there is strong resistance to building more homes to cater to Edinburgh commuters.

Likewise, there has been a political challenge to local identity mounted through the local government reorganisations of 1974 and the proposed changes for late 1990s. The first of these simply substituted the name Tweeddale for Peeblesshire. Nevertheless, the 1974 Beltane was the last to be held in conjunction with a traditional burgh council and as the provost of the day observed, '[t]here are many who are saddened by the thought that the Royal Burgh may lose some of its individuality as a result of the change.' However, he went on, 'because we believe that sentiment is deep rooted we are convinced that the Beltane will go on and remain an important annual event' (Robert Kirkpatrick, cited in Peebles March Riding and Beltane Queen Festival Committee, 1974, p.1). Locals are determined to meet the next set of reorganisations with the same spirit. 'I wonder what our reaction would have been in 1855,' asked the speaker at the 1993 Callants Club dinner 'if someone said that Peebles would have no railway by 1962, or if, in the '60s and '70s, you would not have a town council. These are changes brought about by political intervention and, with more local government reform looming, they must never be allowed to encroach on traditions' (John Gray, cited in *Peeblesshire News*, 25 June 1993, p.9). He went on to charge the local Callants to act as watchdogs to 'monitor the new legislation and ensure your great week is protected for time immemorial'. In fact, it seems that Tweeddale will be absorbed into a much larger local government body and a redefined and enlarged parliamentary constituency by the end of 1994. The *Peeblesshire News* has already run a page one protest under the headline 'Tweeddale's identity crisis' (9 July 1993), and protesters are planning a campaign to keep Peebles in the Borders.

Finally, Peebleans have made a spirited response to the economic challenge to their local distinctiveness and traditional way of life. This response is a theme running through successive speeches of the wardens of Neidpath Castle, who have lamented the loss of industry, and the emigration of the youth, and finally, welcomed the advent of the tourist age. Jim Forsyth, warden in 1993, thus centred his speech on the importance of promoting tourism to replace the traditional industrial base.

The emphasis on locality, and on the anchoring of individuals by birth or long-term residence to a territorially circumscribed history – the process of spatialisation – helps kindle a sense of history and community solidarity. It offers a source of local resistance against the pressures of politics and economy. However, at the same time, this focus on local geography also informs those aspects of the Beltane ceremony which are implicitly racialised. The Borders are part of a Scotland that saw itself as a nation of empire-builders. Lord Tweedmuir's address as Warden of Neidpath Castle observed with pride that '[i]t was a Tweedside man, a Murray of Elibank, who conquered with Wolfe on the Plains of Abraham, and was the first British Governor of Canada,' (Peebles March Riding Committee, 1949, pp.31–2) . This colonial legacy is still alluded to in the Beltane celebrations. The regalia and paraphernalia of the ceremonies link participants to an empire with Peebles at its centre. The Coronation Chair was a gift from South Africa in 1922, and there are a casket from Canada, robes from New Zealand and a bell from the USA. The festival also includes an Indian carpet from Darjeeling, a Maharajah's shield and a procession of children dressed in a variety of national costumes.

Precisely because a key rationale for the Beltane is to preserve local tradition against the bland and homogenising forces of political and economic 'progress', its execution appears uncritically to reproduce many of the the trappings of colonialism and imperialism. As Lord Tweedsmuir put it in 1935:

> All is not well with Scotland. We are losing many of our old institutions, and there is a danger of a general decline in idiom and distinctive quality in our Scottish life. The only way to counteract this peril is to preserve jealously all these older things which are bone of our bone and flesh of our flesh. (cited in Peebles March Riding and Beltane Queen Festival Committee, 1974, p.31)

The problematic implications of this kind of exhortation became all too apparent in the conduct of the 1991 Beltane. These events are discussed at length in Smith (1993b). The key points are as follows. In the lead-up to the 1991 celebrations, an outsider (resident in Edinburgh) noted that part of the children's parade included golliwog costumes – demeaning racial stereotypes which are a legacy of the same colonial era that generated the 'Coon Songs' of the American South, with their 'cute picanniny' and 'Ol' Mammy' images (see Schafer and Riedel, 1973). Because the children's parade is organised by local schools, and the costumes did indeed violate the spirit of guidelines on multiracial education, they were withdrawn. However, because this withdrawal had been prompted by an outsider and did, in theory, require making a change to the time-honoured tradition of the Beltane ceremony, there was considerable local resistance, partly orchestrated by the local press and culminating in a bid to retain the golliwog costumes. When this failed, locals responded by flooding the annual fancy dress parade with golliwog images. Although this was initiated and generally experienced as a light-hearted protest, adding to the fun and revelry of the informal part of the Beltane Festival, it can also be read as an astonishing display of 'commonsense' or taken-for-granted racism which was reported on by national (UK) television and by the national newspapers. I have argued that there was much more to this protest than crude popular racism – that it was as much about the resistance of rural Scotland to the images of urban England, and about the differentiation of the Borders from a more mainstream version of Scottishness, as it was about the reproduction of racism. The protest does, however, illustrate the extent to which a seemingly innocent celebration of self can, where that self is part of a white colonial core, depict the 'other' as not only different but also inferior simply because of the extent to which this notion of difference is locked into a history of inequality.

In the same way that an appeal to tradition can awaken the problems of colonial history even as it nurtures the qualities of local heritage, so this appeal silences questions relating to gender role assumptions, with the result that the festival is not only racialised but also gendered and patriarchal. Notably, among adults it is the men who take the lead role – a role which involves both defending and representing the burgh. The Cornet is supported by 'his' 'lass', but she is a minor actor in the ceremony. It is the Cornet who carries and keeps the burgh standard, it is he who leads the riding and receives an address from the Warden of Neidpath Castle. The Beltane thus reproduces a particular form of masculinity – emphasising bravery, defence, protection and representation – as well as a particular complementary form of femininity, emphasising support, care, service and faithfulness.

This gendering is often apparent in the addresses of the wardens of Neidpath Castle (who have, on all but two occasions, been men). In 1935 Lord Tweedsmuir argued: 'I do not believe that you can exaggerate the importance of the preservations of old ways and customs and all those little things that bind a man to his native place,' (cited in Peebles March Riding Committee, 1949, p.32). The following year, William Cleland reflected on the 'glorious heritage' in which 'from this very courtyard, men have ridden forth and given of their all in the fight for freedom and right' (cited in Peebles March Riding Committee, 1949, p.34). William Crichton identified the castle itself as 'a strong tower into which men have resorted in all ages', and the pre-eminence of the masculine role is apparent in all the discourse of the festival. The Beltane song itself contrasts 'Huntsmen gallant and shepherd grey' with 'lassies blooming fresh and fair', and while there is an important place for the female presence – the Crowning Lady, the Virgin Queen, the Cornet's Lass – the male and females roles are clearly differentiated, and this form of differentiation is seen as part of the essential identity of the burgh. The gendering of the Beltane is consistent with McCrone's (1992) observation that women are marginalised in all the key images of Scottish identity – Kailyardism, tartanry and Clydesidism. Although I have argued that the claims on tradition associated with the Beltane do not reproduce these cultural stereotypes, it is hard to avoid the conclusion that they do reproduce gender stereotypes.

The Beltane and festivals like it are popular events, which are taken seriously by participants, enjoyed by everyone, and form an integral part of local biography. Their vibrancy has not been compromised by the advent of globalism and the homogenising forces of the world economy; but neither has the boundedness of the social and spatial identities they foster been undermined by the postmodern turn. Without such festivals a valuable dimension of local life and a key ingredient of local culture would be lost. In their present form, however, they risk preserving a sense of community and locality at the expense of fostering more universal goals associated with equality, rights and justice.

Conclusion

I have used the example of the anniversary celebrations in rural Scotland to argue that, despite claims to the contrary, boundary-building is alive and well, and that the localities and selves which these boundaries enclose are neither a mirage, destined to be engulfed in the shimmering sands of postmodernism, nor phenomena that can be thought of as natural or immutable. However, while boundaries are constructions which celebrate difference, in doing so they often signal inequality. Boundaries define who belongs, and they set the terms for that belonging. They say something not only about who we are, but also about who we might (and might not) be eligible to become.

A world without the kind of boundaries I've discussed is hard to envisage, and is probably undesirable; but a world with them requires a better understanding of the construction, dissolution and re-positioning of boundaries. Understanding the boundary is still one of the key challenges for social science, and whether we regard the boundary as a line on a map, an enduring spatial metaphor, or a powerful system of symbols, its interrogation is central to the projects of both geography and anthropology. The question of which boundaries to regard as salient, when, and

why – the issue of just where to draw the line – is surely fundamental to our analytical task, to our sense of social justice, and to
the basis of our participation in everyday life.

Author's Note:

The ideas in this paper formed part of my inaugural lecture delivered in the Department of Geography at the University of
Edinburgh on Thursday 15 October 1992. In the lecture I
acknowledged an intellectual and personal debt to J. Clyde
Mitchell, who introduced me and many other geographers to
some of anthropology's most exciting themes. In this paper I
have elaborated some of my arguments and examples in an
attempt to illustrate more explicitly the interplay of our two disciplines. The original text of the inaugural lecture, 'Where to Draw
the Line', relies too heavily on slides, sound and video to merit
separate publication, but copies of the complete manuscript have
been lodged in the university library. Other sections of the inaugural lecture are published as Smith (1993b), and as 'Immigration
and Nation-building in Canada and the UK', in Jackson and
Penrose (1993).

Bibliography

Arnold, D., *Giovanni Gabrieli and the Music of the Venetian High
    Renaissance*, Oxford: Oxford University Press, 1979
Bakhtin, M., *Rabelais and His World* (trans. H. Iswolsky), Cambridge,
    Mass.: MIT Press, 1984
Bonnett, A., 'Art, Ideology and Everyday Space: Subversive Tendencies
    from Dada to Postmodernism', *Environment and Planning D: Society
    and Space*, vol.10, 1992, pp.69–86
Brown, J.L. and Lawson, I.C., *History of Peebles 1850–1990*, Edinburgh:
    Mainstream, 1990
Burke, P., *Popular Culture in Early Modern Europe*, London: Temple Smith,
    1978
Campbell, A., '"Thou Shalt Not Commit Category" Ethnicity and
    Ethnocentricity: Imagined Communities and Imagined Selves',
    Edinburgh: unpublished paper, Department of Anthropology,
    University of Edinburgh, 1992
Cannadine, D., 'The Context, Performance and Meaning of Ritual: The
    British Monarchy and the 'Invention of Tradition', c. 1820–1977', in

The Invention of Tradition, E. Hobsbawm and T. Ranger (eds), Cambridge: Cambridge University Press, 1983

Cohen, Abner, 'A Polyethnic London Carnival as a Contested Cultural Performance', *Ethnic and Racial Studies*, vol.5, 1982, pp.23–41

Cohen, Anthony, *The Symbolic Construction of Communities*, London: Tavistock, 1985

_____ (ed.), *Symbolising Boundaries*, Manchester: Manchester University Press, 1986

Cummings, A.M., *The Politicized Muse: Music for Medici Festivals 1512–1537*, Princeton: Princeton University Press, 1992

Featherstone, M., *Consumer Culture and Postmodernism*, London: Sage, 1991

Goheen, P., 'The Ritual of the Streets in Mid-19th-century Toronto', *Environment and Planning D: Society and Space*, vol.11, 1993, pp.127–45.

Harrison, M., *Crowds and History: Mass Phenomena in English Towns, 1790–1835*, Cambridge: Cambridge University Press, 1988

Jackson, P., 'The Politics of the Streets: A Geography of Caribana', *Political Geography*, vol.11, 1992, pp.130–51

Jackson, P. and Penrose, J. (eds), *Social Constructions of 'Race', Place and Nation*, London: UCL Press, 1993

Johnston, W.M., *Celebrations: The Cult of Anniversaries in Europe and the United States Today*, New Brunswick, NJ: Transactions, 1991

Lang, A. and Lang, D., *Highways and Byways in the Borders*, Basingstoke: Macmillan, 1913 (edited and reprinted as *Border Life in Days Gone By*, Newton Grange: Lang Syne Publishers, 1976)

Ladurie, E. LeRoy, *Carnival: A People's Uprising at Romans 1579–1580*, London: Scolar, 1979

Ley, D. and Olds, K., 'Landscape as Spectacle: World's Fairs and the Culture of Heroic Consumption', *Evironment and Planning D: Society and Space*, vol.6, 1988, pp.191–212

McCrone, D., *Understanding Scotland*, London: Routledge, 1992

Marston, S., 'Public Rituals and Community Power: St. Patrick's Day Parades in Lowell, Massachusetts, 1841–1874', *Political Geography Quarterly*, vol.8, 1989, pp.255–69

Meyrowitz, J., 'The Generalised Elsewhere', *Critical Studies in Mass Communications*, vol.6, 1985, p.330

Morley, D., 'Where the Global Meets the Local: Notes From the Sitting Room', *Screen*, vol.22, 1991, pp.1–15

Olssen, G., 'Lines of Power', in *Writing Worlds*, T.J. Barnes and J.S. Duncan (eds), London: Routledge, 1992

Park, R., *Masse und Publikum*, Lack and Grunau, Bern, 1904 (reprinted as 'The Crowd and the Public', in *The Crowd and the Public and Other Essays* (trans. C. Elsner), H. Elsner Jr (ed.), Chicago: University of Chicago Press, 1972)

Peebles March Riding and Beltane Queen Festival Commitee, *Peebles*

March Riding and Beltane Queen Festival 1989–1974, Hawick News: Hawick, 1974

Peebles March Riding Committee, *Peebles Beltane Festival Jubilee Book 1899–1949*, Peebles: J.A. Kerr, 1949

Penrose, J., '*Mon Pays N'est Pas un Pays*', *Political Geography*, vol.13, no.2, 1994, pp.161–81

Reichert, D., 'On Boundaries', *Environment and Planning D: Society and Space*, vol.10, 1992, pp.87–98

Rydell, R., *All the World's a Fair*, Chicago: University of Chicago Press, 1984

Schafer, W.J. and Riedel, J., *The Art of Ragtime*, Baton Rouge: Louisiana State University Press, 1973

Shields, R., *Places on the Margin: Alternative Geographies of Modernity*, London: Routledge, 1991

Shils, E. and Young, M., 'The Meaning of the Coronation', *Sociological Review*, vol.1, 1953, pp. 63–81

Smith, S.J., 'Negotiating Ethnicity in an Uncertain Environment', *Ethnic and Racial Studies* , vol.7, 1984, pp.360–73

_____,'Social Landscapes: Continuity and Change', in *A Changing World: A Changing Discipline?*, R.J. Johnston (ed.), Oxford: Basil Blackwell, 1993a

_____,'Bounding the Borders: Claiming Space and Making Place in Rural Scotland', *Transactions, Institute of British Geographers (NS)*, vol.18, 1993b, pp291–308

Strong, R., *Art and Power: Renaissance Festivals 1450–1650*, Suffolk: Boydell Press, 1984

Zukin, S., *Landscapes of Power: From Detroit to Disneyland*, Berkeley: University of California Press, 1991

Chapter 6

Manufacturing Meaning: Culture, Capital and Urban Change

Peter Jackson

> Culture has become as necessary an adornment and advertisement for a city today as pavements or bank-clearances. It's Culture, in theatres and art-galleries and so on, that brings thousands of visitors to New York every year and, to be frank, for all our splendid attainments we haven't got the Culture of a New York or Chicago or Boston – or at least we don't get credit for it. The thing to do then, as a live bunch of go-getters, is to *capitalize Culture*: to go right out and grab it.
>
> Sinclair Lewis, *Babbitt*

Introduction

This chapter is about alternative ways of theorising the role of culture in urban change. Conventionally, 'culture' has been thought of in narrow terms, as in the references to theatres and art-galleries in Sinclair Lewis's fictional account of Chum Frink's address to the Zenith Rotary Club, quoted above. Many things have changed since Lewis wrote this passage. But a growing sophistication in charting the contours of an increasingly post-Fordist economy has not generally been accompanied by a similar sensitivity in ways of thinking about the role of culture in urban change. Since the late 1960s, urban municipalities have been faced with a declining tax base as industries and middle-class residents fled to the suburbs or abandoned the older metropolitan centres altogether. In searching for an alternative *raison d'être*, they began to capitalise on whatever resources were available. All too often this resulted in an unseemly rush to 'capitalize Culture', to convert historical buildings into heritage sites, to

transform industrial warehouses into chic residential lofts, des-
perately trying to project a new image of the city based on sanitised representations of their urban past. In criticising the kind of
redevelopments that have resulted from this process, I wish to
challenge our existing understanding of the role of culture in
urban change.

Here, as elsewhere (Jackson, 1989), I am concerned to advance
a broader conception of culture as the process through which the
material environment is invested with meaning. These meanings
are inherently unstable, actively forged and continually revised
by different groups of people. Meanings are never simply
'received'; they are always, to varying degrees in different times
and places, negotiated and contested. While much has been written about the 'heritage industry' and its relation to economic and
political decline (Hewison, 1987; Lowenthal, 1985; Wright, 1985),
the connections between 'the cultural' and 'the economic' have
been rather poorly articulated. Similarly, in much of the current
literature on gentrification and neighbourhood change (e.g.
Anderson, 1987; London and Palen, 1984; Smith and Williams,
1986), complex processes are all too readily reduced to glib discussions of yuppies, yuffies and DINKS (Short, 1989), to heroic
conceptions of 'pioneering in the urban wilderness' (Stratton,
1977) or to (largely illusory) mass migrations 'back to the city'
(Laska and Spain, 1980). The debate has degenerated into a form
of trench warfare between the proponents of 'culture' and 'capital' as alternative explanations for urban neighbourhood change
(e.g. Ley, 1986; Smith, 1982). Rather than continuing what has
become an increasingly sterile debate, this chapter seeks to articulate an alternative way of conceptualising 'the cultural' and 'the
economic'. It asks why an apparently economic process (like
urban reinvestment) has been culturally encoded (via the arts or
urban heritage), and it considers where we might turn for a more
adequate conceptualisation of the process – to Bourdieu's (1984)
notion of cultural capital, to Harvey's (1989) discussion of the
postmodern condition, or to Zukin's (1988) more grounded theorisations of the relationship between culture and capital in urban
change?[1]

This chapter cannot provide definitive answers to such questions. Instead, it has the more modest goal of providing some

1. These theoretical ideas are also reviewed in Jackson (1991).

empirical evidence of urban reinvestment in two [
which the claims of rival theorisations can
Specifically, I aim to investigate the process of [
vestment, warehouse conversion and historic preservativ
SoHo district of New York (based on three months' fieldwork in
1982) and in the warehouse districts of Minneapolis-Saint Paul
(based on five months' fieldwork in 1987).[2] This chapter considers each case study in turn, before bringing them together in a
comparative context that allows certain broader conclusions to be
reached.

Loft Conversion in New York

The industrial warehouse district of SoHo (south of Houston
Street in Lower Manhattan) was condemned as 'an industrial
slum with no buildings worth saving' in 1962 (City Club of New
York, 1962). Little more than a decade later, it had become 'the
most exciting place to live in the city', according to the glossy
New York magazine (20 May 1974). What lies behind such a rapid
transformation from a near-derelict industrial slum to a thriving
artists' district and, later, a luxury real-estate market for fashionable loft-living? To summarise a complex argument, the city's
changing political economy provided an opportunity for reinvestment in the built environment, the exact form of which (arts-
related reinvestment in the loft district of SoHo) was contingent
on particular local circumstances.[3] The virtual collapse of manufacturing employment in New York and the subsequent restructuring of the economy gave rise to high vacancy rates in
industrial areas such as SoHo, which encouraged the occupancy
of loft buildings by 'marginal' groups such as artists, who were
prepared to put up with poor services in exchange for low rents
and ample floor space.

Restructuring shaped the general form of redevelopment but

2. Fieldwork in New York was made possible by a grant from the British Academy
(July–September 1982) while the author was a Visiting Scholar in the Department of
Sociology at New York University. Fieldwork in Minneapolis-Saint Paul (August–December
1987) was carried out while the author was a Visiting Professor at the University of Minnesota
in Minneapolis and at Macalaster College in Saint Paul, funded in part by a grant from the
Fulbright Commission.
3. The process is explained in detail elsewhere (Jackson, 1985; Simpson, 1981; Zukin,
1988).

did not determine its precise contours, which were dependent on the presence in New York of a large population of (economically marginal) artists. Their marginality was further increased when some of the artists took up residence in their studio-lofts, which was technically illegal in terms of building codes, fire regulations and zoning laws. They were tolerated by the authorities, however, because they were relatively inconspicuous, and because there was, initially at least, little competition from more 'legitimate' tenants for this apparently redundant space.

The redevelopment of SoHo had been postponed throughout the 1960s because of the prolonged uncertainty over the construction of the Lower Manhattan Expressway which was projected to dissect the area along Broome Street. (It was the prospect of securing Title 1 funds for urban renewal that had led the City Club of New York to commission their 1962 report which declared SoHo an 'industrial slum'.) Uncertainty over when or if the proposed Expressway would be built also deterred major private investment. The threat of the Expressway encouraged SoHo's resident artist population to adopt a higher profile, drawing greater public attention to their plight through the organisation of Artists Against the Expressway, founded in 1969. (They had previously won a series of minor concessions from the city authorities, including the approval of an artist-in-residence scheme in 1963, through an organisation called the Artists' Tenants Association.) Following further pressure from the SoHo Artists' Association, formed in 1968 to argue that artists comprised a legitimate business use, SoHo was declared an Artists' District in 1971, extending the right of legal residence in lofts of less than 3,600 square feet to those who could demonstrate their legitimate professional status as artists through registration with the Department of Cultural Affairs.

In 1973, the whole 26-block area of SoHo was designated the first Historic District in New York under the city's Landmarks Preservation Law. The designation was intended to preserve the distinct cast-iron architectural façades of many of the district's loft buildings, a form of construction that was briefly popular in the early decades of this century, immediately after the introduction of steel-reinforced concrete that made the construction of skyscrapers possible (Gayle and Gillon, 1974). Ironically, in retrospect, the artists joined other preservation groups in supporting the historic designation which eventually led to their displacement from the area as rents began to soar and the gentrification of SoHo proceeded apace.

As loft-living began to increase in popularity, several uptown art galleries opened premises in SoHo, capitalising on the growing market for the work of avant-garde artists, many of whom now lived in Lower Manhattan. Smart restaurants, bars and boutiques were also attracted to the area as it began to attract tourists and other visitors. Finally, large-scale real estate firms began to invest in SoHo and surrounding areas. They were encouraged by the availability of generous tax incentives (under New York's J-51 programme, originally intended to encourage the upgrading of cold-water flats). These incentives had not been utilised by the artists as they were only available for 'legal' conversions, and the artists did not possess sufficient capital to buy their buildings or bring them up to code.

A classic process of displacement followed, bitterly contested by the Lower Manhattan Loft Tenants' Association, who claimed that the City Planning Commission had been too slow to intervene and was only belatedly attempting to 'balance the equities' among residential tenants, manufacturers and luxury real estate interests (New York City Planning Commission, 1981). The Planning Commission had discovered in 1977 that less than 10 per cent of New York's residential lofts had a legal Certificate of Occupancy. The Mayor's Office formulated an action plan which stressed enforcement. The subsequent re-zoning of Lower Manhattan was accompanied by the creation of a Business Relocation Assistance Corporation and an Industrial Advisory Board under the direction of the Mayor's Office of Loft Enforcement (Figure 6.1). These measures were resented by the artist-tenants, who felt that they had taken the initial risks (albeit illegally), and that the remaining industrial tenants, their landlords and the larger real estate interest were likely to reap the benefits.

Clearly, the city authorities were not neutral in the loft conversion process. Given New York's virtual bankruptcy in the mid-1970s it is not surprising that they seized the opportunity to bolster the dwindling tax base by encouraging large-scale reinvestment in the SoHo area. While the initiatives of small-scale artist-tenants had created favourable conditions for large-scale investors, the artists' illegality meant that they were not well

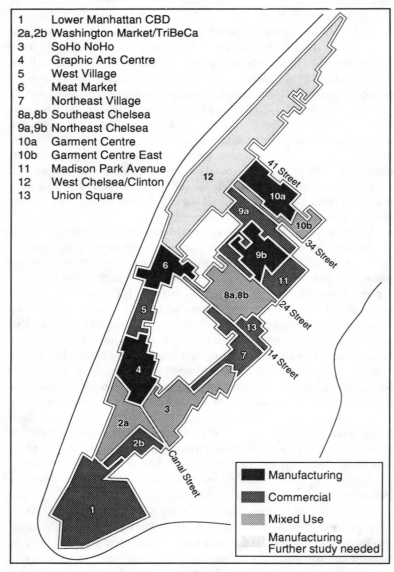

1   Lower Manhattan CBD
2a,2b   Washington Market/TriBeCa
3   SoHo NoHo
4   Graphic Arts Centre
5   West Village
6   Meat Market
7   Northeast Village
8a,8b   Southeast Chelsea
9a,9b   Northeast Chelsea
10a   Garment Centre
10b   Garment Centre East
11   Madison Park Avenue
12   West Chelsea/Clinton
13   Union Square

■ Manufacturing
■ Commercial
▨ Mixed Use
▨ Manufacturing
   Further study needed

Figure 6.1 Re-zoning of Lower Manhattan, April 1981

placed to benefit from the city's manipulation of the market through fiscal changes and revisions to the zoning map.

This case study has attempted to trace the economic and political contours of SoHo's redevelopment and to explore the variety of ways in which meanings are constructed, negotiated and resisted within the built environment. Old loft buildings were first devalued then revalued. Tastes for historic preservation grew, paralleled by a growing market for chic restaurants, upscale boutiques and other specialist stores. The popular association of artistic production with 'bohemian' lifestyles attracted a new group of wealthy residents, who could enjoy the aura of artistic production from the comfort and security of their luxury condominium.

Sharon Zukin (1985) has described the process of revalorisation as a 'historic compromise' which occurred as the investment climate began to favour gradual rehabilitation rather than comprehensive redevelopment. Others have doubted whether changing investment behaviour can be seen in such strategic terms (Whitt, 1987). But one cannot doubt that the state helped create the conditions that favoured one of investment over another. And it is equally clear that the reinvestment process was *culturally encoded* through shifting attitudes towards the arts and historic preservation. It might be argued, though, that such processes are unique to New York, both in terms of its extremely tight housing market and its unique role in the international art market. A parallel case study of urban reinvestment in the Twin Cities of Minneapolis-Saint Paul provides an opportunity to see how far this is so.

Historic Preservation and Warehouse Conversion in Minneapolis-Saint Paul

The architectural history of the Twin Cities is unusually well-documented. Besides standard sources such as Gebhard and Martinson's *A Guide to the Architecture of Minnesota* (1977), there are a number of well-informed accounts of the preservation of particular buildings in Minneapolis-Saint Paul (e.g. Borchert, Gebhart, Lanegran and Martin, 1983; Lanegran, 1986; Martin, 1985). From a wealth of possibilities I have selected four cases to illustrate my argument (locations shown in Figure 6.2).

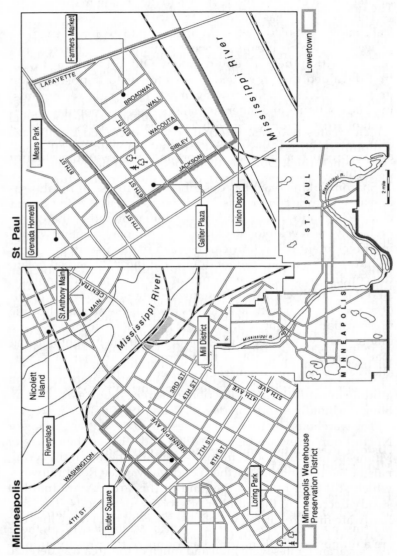

Figure 6.2 The Warehouse Districts of Minneapolis-Saint Paul

Butler Square, Minneapolis

The first major warehouse conversion project in the Twin Cities
was undertaken in two phases at Butler Square. The original
500,000 square foot Butler Brothers warehouse was the work of
the Minneapolis architect Harry Jones, in 1906. Its conversion to a
'mixed-use circus' combining retail and office space (Anon., 1981)
was undertaken by two different architectural firms, Miller,
Hanson and Westerbeck (1974) and Arvid Elness (1981). Two features dominate its design: a glass atrium at eighth-floor level
which creates two vast internal spaces, occupied by life-size
sculptures such as George Segal's 'Flying Acrobats', and the massive 24-inch-thick Douglas fir timbers which have been sand-
blasted and retained as part of the interior structure. Both
features have since been widely copied in conversion projects
elsewhere in the Twin Cities.

The firm of Arvid Elness specialises in warehouse conversions,
applying a formula which consists of finding suitable buildings
in historic districts and utilising tax incentives to make something distinctive that will attract the public (Elness, quoted in
King, 1985, p.39). The tax advantages, introduced in 1981, derive
from a building's 'historic' designation, which provides incentives for renovation. The Butler building benefits from such
advantages, having an independent historic designation as well
as being located in the Minneapolis Warehouse Preservation
District. Although Butler Square won architectural awards for
'historic preservation', Elness himself has a much more irreverent
attitude towards the past, describing the renovation as 'disassem-
bling the building from top down', (King, 1985, p.38).

The warehouse district, sometimes called the Butler Quarter or
North Loop, grew up between 1900 and 1920 as the centre of
Minneapolis's dry-goods industry, situated between the termi-
nals of the Burlington Northern and Milwaukee Road railways,
which still own much of the land in this area. A gradual but
steady decrease in the number of grocery, dry-goods, drug and
hardware firms requiring warehouse space in the Twin Cities can
be traced from the 1930s (Vaile and Nordstrom, 1932). By the
1960s, vacancy rates were high and much of the area was derelict.
Following years of neglect, the developer John Stielow was able
to acquire Butler Square and several neighbouring buildings,
amounting to 4 million square feet, at very low cost. As the price
of office space in downtown Minneapolis rose, the surrounding

area became increasingly attractive. This area now includes
Loring Park and the Mill District, as well as the Butler Quarter or
North Loop, all currently undergoing redevelopment.

Despite the efforts of its chamber of commerce, the First
Avenue North (FAN) club, Butler Square has suffered high
turnover rates among its restaurants and shops, customers being
deterred from crossing Hennepin Avenue from downtown
because of its reputation for street crime, drug-dealing and pros-
titution. Not surprisingly, there are now plans to demolish what
has become a notorious 'porn row' (Block E) which will presum-
ably encourage further development throughout the warehouse
district by increasing its accessibility to a wider public. The warehouse district in Minneapolis has attracted a substantial population of resident artists, though on a smaller scale than New York.
Significantly, it is this constituency that most vigorously opposes
the demolition of Block E (Weber, 1987), fearing that it will lead
to their displacement as rents and land prices rise
('Redevelopment Drives Out Artists', *Minneapolis Star and
Tribune*, 16 Aug. 1987).

Two other current developments are also likely to improve the
future viability of Butler Square: the completion of Interstate 394,
which will enter downtown Minneapolis on North Third
Avenue, with parking for 6,000 cars adjacent to Butler Square;
and the profusion of 'new wave' bars and restaurants that have
sprung up on the margins of Butler Square. Such places ensure
the area's continued vitality long after downtown office workers
have gone home. The biggest negative influence on Butler
Square's continued growth is competition from another redevelopment across the Mississippi at Riverplace which has, in turn,
outstripped its predecessor and near-neighbour, St Anthony
Main.

St Anthony Main, Minneapolis

One of the first warehouse projects in the Twin Cities, dating
from the mid-1970s, St Anthony Main developed from the renovation of a row of brick warehouses and their conversion to retail
use. The conversion was carried out to a high standard, the latter
stages being undertaken by Benjamin Thompson (well known for
his previous work at Faneuil Hall and Quincy Market in Boston).
Individual façades (such as the 1890s Pracna Building on Main
Street) were carefully preserved, while other 'historic' features

such as gas lamps and cobble stones were introduced. In other cases, developers eschewed conventional 'preservation' measures, gutting buildings and installing contemporary interiors. St Anthony Main was redeveloped in three phases, beginning in 1976 and comprising over 100,000 square feet of retail space with sand-blasted interior walls, exposed wood beams and a second-floor glass atrium. The shops are arranged around a series of narrow passageways, intended to give the development a human scale and to encourage pedestrians to wander throughout the building. The project started to break even financially in 1981. Its continued success encouraged its developers, Louis Zelle, to join with Upton Associates in 1985 to add a fourth phase, increasing the retail space by a further 90,000 square feet. The last phase incorporated several nineteenth-century buildings, such as the Upton Building, the Union Iron Works and the Martin and Morrison Building, each of which required substantial structural work before conversion to their current retail and restaurant uses.

St Anthony Main takes full advantage of its waterfront location. Its name derives from its location on the original site of the city of Minneapolis at St Anthony Falls. There are constant symbolic reminders of these historical associations from pumping machines which now double as outdoor sculpture to the wave-like design of the development's logo. The development's success can also be traced to more material forces, such as the relocation of the Pillsbury Company's research facility adjacent to St Anthony Main. In order to prevent the company from moving out to the suburbs, the city council offered Pillsbury a range of incentives including the construction of new sewer, water and road systems, also making additional land available for the company's future expansion (for details, see Kostouros, 1982). As a result, Pillsbury stayed in the area providing appropriate local clientele to ensure the redevelopment's viability.

Riverplace, Minneapolis

Following the success of St Anthony Main in the 1970s, a mixed-use redevelopment similar to Butler Square was undertaken next door at Riverplace, opening to the public in 1984. The project has been described in extravagant terms as a mixture of 'Tuscan hill-town dwellings, glittering interior shopping streets, brick-faced grain elevators, Victorian Crystal Palace façades [and] ultra-chic

apartment towers' (Anon., 1981). Just across the river from downtown Minneapolis and linked to it via a turn-of-the-century iron
bridge (moved downstream from Broadway), Riverplace comprises a 27-storey, 165-unit apartment tower (The Pinnacle) and a
26-storey condominium building (La Rive). Next to The Pinnacle,
in a 19-storey stepped tower, is an 80-unit condominium building
(The Falls) and a variety of retail units. Other buildings include a
retail complex, One Main, with a barrel-vaulted glass roof, and
Exposition Hall, a converted brick warehouse.

Located within the St Anthony Falls Historic District, the
developers (East Bank Riverfront Partners) were obliged to nego-
tiate with the Minnesota Heritage Preservation Commission and
with   the   land-owners,   the   Minneapolis   Community
Development Agency. The end result is a predictable compromise between 'historic preservation', and 'festive retailing' (introduced   by   the   Baltimore   firm,   D.I.   Design).   The   oldest
continuously-used church in Minneapolis, Our Lady of Lourdes
(built in 1857), occupies a central part of the site on Prince Street.
The Brown-Ryan Livery Stables, dating from the 1880s, has also
been retained, although its 'preservation' involved moving the
building 200 yards eastwards into the heart of the retail area and
re-orienting it 90 degrees towards Lourdes Square on 'Historic
Main Street'. Exposition Hall was also 'preserved', but with a hol-
lowed-out atrium, new cast-iron stairs and exposed elevator
cages. The main architects for the project (Miller, Hanson,
Westerbeck, Bell) were also employed on Phase 1 of the Butler
Square redevelopment. The principal developer, Robert Boisclair,
went on to develop Galtier Plaza, a $100 million mixed-use devel-
opment in Saint Paul. Both projects have suffered financial difficulties.

Galtier Plaza, Saint Paul

Galtier Plaza takes its name from Father Lucian Galtier, who built
the first Roman Catholic church in the city in 1841 and convinced
the early settlers to rename their community in honour of Saint
Paul. Situated in the warehouse district of Lowertown, the location of Galtier Plaza is one of its main assets. Facing Mears Park,
originally laid out in 1849, and close to the long-established
Farmers' Market, Galtier Plaza is also near Saint Paul's Lower
Landing, where paddle steamers used to moor to load or unload
their cargoes of lumber and grain. After decades of neglecting its

waterfront, Saint Paul's Mayor, George Latimer, began to talk
enthusiastically of 'returning to the river' (Latimer, 1984), giving
added impetus to the redevelopment of the entire Lowertown
district.

Approximately fourteen blocks (comprising thirty-eight individual buildings) in Lowertown were placed on the National
Register of Historic Places in 1983, rendering them eligible for
federal tax credits of up to 25 per cent of the first-year renovation
costs (*St Paul Pioneer Press*, 5 Aug. 1983). The designation recognised both the historical significance of Lowertown as the city's
original wholesale and manufacturing district, and the contribution of distinguished Saint Paul architects, such as Cass Gilbert
(who later designed the Woolworth Building in New York and
the US Supreme Court in Washington, DC). Given this historic
context, Galtier Plaza was obliged to make a number of concessions to its architectural surroundings, including dismantling,
storing and re-assembling two warehouse façades on Sibley
Street (the Sperry and Aslesen Buildings), and the 're-modelling'
of the 1890s McColl Building to create new office space.

Earlier plans to redevelop the warehouse district faltered in
1974 with the death of Norman Mears, a prominent local industri-
alist who had begun the process of clearance, land assembly and
reinvestment in the area. When George Latimer was elected
mayor in 1977 the process began again. Galtier Plaza emerged as
the major component in the planned redevelopment of
Lowertown, a 180-acre site on the eastern edge of downtown Saint
Paul. Other projects included the conversion of the Union Depot
Railway Station, construction of the Embassy Suites Hotel, and
conversion of several warehouse buildings for upmarket retail
use. Following the New York model, some of the warehouses, like
Lowertown Lofts and the Master Framers' Building on East 4th
Street, were redeveloped to provide studio living space for artists.
Conversion was financed by a complicated package of public and
private investment, including tax-exempt revenue bonds, grants
from the Dayton-Hudson and Bush Foundations, and a variety of
low-interest loans from the city's neighbourhood redevelopment
and rehabilitation programmes. Plans are also under way to convert the Jax Building into forty units of artists' housing, with at
least 25 per cent of the rehabilitation costs coming from the City of
Saint Paul via a federal Community Development Block Grant
(*Saint Paul Area Downtowner*, 30 Sept. 1987).

As part of its Riverfront Initiative, the Mayor's Office established a Downtown Riverfront Commission, which introduced a number of fiscal measures including a Tax Increment Financing District along the riverfront.[4] The Saint Paul City Council was also empowered by the State of Minnesota to designate a Riverfront Enterprise Zone, which aims to co-ordinate public expenditure. Private investment will also be encouraged through a package of tax incentives based on a $4.5 million allocation from state taxes over a period of seven years. As well as profiting indirectly from its location in the Enterprise Zone, Galtier Plaza has also benefited directly from the initiatives of the Lowertown Redevelopment Corporation (LRC), a private, non-profit organisation which works in public–private partnership with the City of Saint Paul and with other agencies such as the Port Authority of Saint Paul, which has helped finance more than a dozen projects worth over $75 million in the Lowertown area.

Despite its relatively modest working capital, LRC has established close links with Saint Paul's political and financial establishment. Besides the mayor, the city's two largest bankers and the president of the Burlington Northern Railroad were founder members of the LRC's board of directors. They were instrumental in gaining financial support from the McKnight Foundation and in attracting subsequent private investment. The LRC administers a revolving investment fund to provide 'gap financing' between private firms and government grants. It offers low-interest (i.e. below market rate) loans, and provides loan guarantees and other fiscal incentives to approved developments. Backed by the McKnight Foundation with a commitment of $10 million in 'program-related investment', LRC has made loans of over $7 million to thirty-five different projects in its first ten years of operation, claiming a private:public leverage ratio of more than 20:1.[5]

Galtier Plaza epitomises the kind of complex public–private partnerships that LRC seeks to co-ordinate. Besides investments of around $27 million from the Port Authority of Saint Paul in the form of industrial development bonds, Galtier's initial funding

4. Tax increment financing is a process by which cities can anticipate the increment of property tax revenues generated by new development to pay for public improvements and other costs incurred by the city supporting such a development.
5. 'Program-related investments' allow a foundation to advance money for capital investments for the same charitable ends for which the foundation normally makes grants, without losing its tax-exempt status.

included a federal Urban Development Grant (UDAG), contributions from the Saint Paul Housing Authority (including Section 8 financing for rental units), and developer equity of around $6 million. It benefited from tax-exempt financing because of the area's historic landmark status and a low-interest loan of around $2 million from LRC itself. This financial package was sufficient to attract the Boisclair Corporation as the developers of Galtier Plaza, even while Riverplace had still not proved itself financially.

Galtier Plaza is a classic mixed-use redevelopment, incorporating two massive 46- and 32-storey residential towers with 350 apartments and 150 luxury condominiums, a gymnasium and YMCA (with swimming pool, tennis court and outdoor running track), several cinemas, over 100,000 square feet of retail space, 60,000 square feet of offices, and underground parking for 800 cars (Lanegran, 1986; Mack, 1986). The development attempts to create an 'urban village' while retaining its links, at ground level and via the elevated pedestrian 'skyway' system, with downtown Saint Paul. The mixed-use formula allowed the developers to alter the balance of retail, office and residential space even while the building was under construction. Despite some last-minute changes in the balance between rental housing and office space, it has proved difficult to find tenants for all of Galtier's retail and office units. It became known locally as a 'beautiful building, with an echo', and the developers grew defensive about its current financial status. A new management team was appointed in September 1987 ('Texans to Give Galtier New Direction', *Saint Paul Area Downtowner*, 30 Sept. 1987). New York's Chemical Bank assumed responsibility for the retail, office, condominium and parking sectors of the building, and – through its subsidiary, the Mears Park Holding Company – appointed James D. Stout & Associates of Texas to improve the building's financial viability.

The project's difficulties stem from a number of competing demands: to achieve high-density mixed use on a single city lot without sacrificing architectural standards, and to meet the tight schedule imposed by UDAG funding while remaining sympathetic to the area's historical character. The growing recession and some costly delays in construction exacerbated the building's problems. The entire project was re-financed in September 1986 while neighbouring developments such as Riverplace were going through a period of retrenchment and the amount of office space was outstripping demand throughout the Twin Cities.

Architecturally, the development is a considerable success, its seventh-storey atrium and gabled roof effectively integrating the two halves of the building. D.I. Designs of Baltimore, who designed the interiors at Riverplace, designed the Palm Court and retail space at Galtier Plaza, introducing some novel theatrical effects as well as the inevitable exposed elevator cages. Financially, problems remain, while some observers have grown more optimistic ('St Paul's Urban Village Turns Another Corner', *Saint Paul Area Downtowner*, 30 Sept. 1987).

Comparison

Superficially at least, there is much in common between the developments described here in New York and the Twin Cities. The designation of historic districts in both cities was a turning point in the transition to new commercial and residential uses, providing the financial rationale for reinvestment. Similarly, in both cities a community of resident artists has played a vital role in the conversion process, shaping the residential re-use of former industrial buildings and attempting to resist the gentrification trend which threatens to displace them ('Where Have All the Artists Gone?', *Twin Cities Reader*, 28 Oct. 1987). While Minneapolis-Saint Paul has nothing to rival the vociferous and highly articulate protestations of the Lower Manhattan Loft Tenants' Association, redevelopment in the Twin Cities has not been without its critics. For example, the Minneapolis-based non-profit corporation Artspace Projects Inc. claims to have received more than 3,000 requests from artists having problems finding affordable living and working quarters. In response, the Minneapolis Community Development Agency hired an economic development specialist, though he is more concerned with the business potential of the arts than with the housing needs of indigent artists.

Despite these similarities, New York's unique role in the international art market has lead to certain clear differences, giving SoHo an early start in the reinvestment cycle. SoHo also experienced particular pressures from its location in downtown Manhattan, hemmed in on all sides by the Financial District and

City Hall to the south, Little Italy and the Lower East Side to the east, Greenwich Village and New York University to the north and the Hudson River to the west. The rapid expansion of Chinatown across Canal Street to the south has also increased pressure on space. Such circumstances helped offset the blighting effect of the proposed Expressway and kept up demand for commercial and residential property, even as industrial uses went into decline.

The relative strengths of the preservationist lobbies in New York and Minneapolis-Saint Paul are also rather different. While New York passed its Landmark Preservation Law in 1965, it has not developed a strong tradition of preservation. In the Twin Cities – especially in Saint Paul, where the Landmarks Commission was established in 1976 – a vigorous preservationist lobby has emerged with strong support from the mayor and city council. Historic District designations are now in force on Ramsey Hill and along Summit Avenue, with historic designations for specific downtown buildings such as Landmark Centre on Rice Park. Historic preservation also had a direct bearing on the process of warehouse conversion in Saint Paul. One indication of this was the appointment of Weiming Lu as Executive Director of the Lowertown Redevelopment Corporation, given his previous experience in the development of the Minnesota Heritage Preservation Commission.

Besides these specific comparisons, several general lessons can be drawn from the two case studies about the role of the arts and historic preservation in the process of urban regeneration. First, we can begin to trace how the economic logic of reinvestment came to be *culturally encoded* through its association with artistic production, via the aura of historic architecture and by connection with an area's industrial heritage. In each case, the process was mediated by a range of (sometimes competing) interest groups, responding to changing fiscal opportunities (tax breaks and other financial incentives) and shaped by various agencies of the state.

For example, the reinvestment and conversion process in SoHo was clearly mediated by the artists' professional status and occupational role. They were no ordinary tenant group, but a highly-educated and articulate group who were able to employ top-class lawyers to fight rent increases and eviction orders. Moreover, as Charles Simpson argues in *SoHo: The Artist in the City* (1981), artistic production has taken on almost sacred associations in a seemingly profane urban world. Small-scale investment in converting their own loft space by individual artist-tenants paved the way for larger-scale real estate development. Fascination with the bohemian world they created helped attract new investment from both residential and commercial uses. SoHo's subsequent gentrification turned an area of artistic production into one of stylised consumption (Simpson, 1981) – a 'disneyland of the aesthete' (Ratcliffe, 1978).

SoHo's resident artists were also able to generate more public support than other groups who were in dispute with private landlords and city planners. Support was not confined to a few 'patrician' families such as the Rockefellers or the Kennedys, though their support was instrumental, as both Zukin (1988) and Whitt (1987) have shown. It extended also to less exalted levels of the political establishment, who stood to gain from demonstrating their public support for the arts. In the early 1960s, for example, the artists successfully lobbied Ed Koch (then a congressman, later Mayor of New York), capitalising on his need to gain the support of liberal Democrats in Greenwich Village and SoHo. They won further support from Mayor Lindsay, who had embraced the Liberal Party and the Reform Democrats after his defeat in the 1969 Republican primary. These political alliances lay behind some of the early concessions that the artists were able to force from city government before the reinvestment wave began to overwhelm them.

A second lesson to be drawn from these case studies is the *essentially political* nature of neighbourhood change, not only in the sense that gentrification benefits some groups more than others, but also in the sense that it involves a variety of conflicting ideologies. When Laska and Spain observe that 'most Americans believe the renovation trend should be encouraged at every opportunity, regardless of the problems that accompany it' (1980, p.xvi) or when Federal Housing and Urban Development official Howard Sumka (writing here in a private capacity) maintains that gentrification is 'in the public interest' (Sumka, 1979), one is entitled to be sceptical. From his perspective, it becomes 'un-American' to oppose gentrification, and easier to ignore the problems of those who are displaced by this apparently benign process. While Sumka maintains that reinvestment is a fragile process with which the state should not seek to meddle, others argue just as strongly that US gentrification has been actively

planned and publicly funded (Smith, 1979) through a variety of
tax credits and similar inducements. Both the SoHo and Twin
Cities case studies reveal the extent to which 'market forces' were
actively moulded by agencies of the state through the J-51 law,
through changes to the zoning map, through the selective
enforcement of building codes and fire regulations, and through
a range of planning and policy instruments.

A third comparison concerns the *complex and contradictory*
nature of historic preservation: what is considered to be worth
saving and how it is 'preserved'. Historic preservation is
inevitably a selective process, reflecting and appealing to a limited spectrum of respectable, middle-class tastes. In the interests of
'preservation', factory buildings and industrial warehouses are
stripped of any associations they may have with a strife-torn,
conflict-ridden history. They are then re-presented as a sanitised
version of the urban past, suppressing unacceptable working-
class connotations. Thus, in Minneapolis, there is no public commemoration of the 1934 Teamsters' strike on First Avenue North,
despite its significance in US labour history. In Saint Paul, industrial buildings like the Jax Building (named after an industrial
product) have been renamed to honour their original architects
(in this case, the Michaud Building). Furniture and shoe factories
are 'creatively recycled' by firms such as the Philadelphia-based
Historic Landmarks for Living, but they are renamed to avoid
making these associations too directly. The renaming process has
also occurred in New York, where the South Houston Industrial
District was transformed into the SoHo Historic District (celebrating its cast-iron architectural façades), while neighbouring
districts also took on new identities and similar acronyms.[6]

Conclusion

Many discussions of the role of culture and the arts in urban
regeneration adopt the perspective of the potential investor and
consider how best to tempt him or her to choose one place rather
than the other. A new market has emerged in which places compete with each other for limited investment resources. As several

6. Examples include NoHo (North of Houston Street), TriBeCa (the Triangle Below Canal
Street) and DUMBO (Down Under the Manhattan Bridge Overpass).

observers (e.g. Burgess, 1982; Watson, 1991) have noted, advertising is designed with the explicit aim of 'selling places'. But what alternative ways exist of theorising the relationship between the 'cultural' and the 'economic', of thinking about the role of culture *and* capital in urban change without subordinating one element to the other?

In this conclusion I intend to move from a narrow definition of culture (as the artistic product of an elite) towards a more expansive definition (as 'maps of meaning' or 'whole ways of life').[7] As early as 1964, the art critic and historian Harold Rosenberg described the evolution of New York's artistic community in terms of a geography of modern art, where 'choosing a place to live has become for the American artist a problem of the first order' (Rosenberg, 1973, p.100). Where, in the United States, he continued, could one 'live like an artist?', residential choices apparently reflecting one's whole conception of what it meant to be an 'artist'. Rosenberg goes on to trace the logic of this 'geography of modern art': as one artistic movement declines, it is replaced by the next wave of the avant-garde, which distinguishes itself from its predecessor as much by choice of location as by purely aesthetic concerns. Rosenberg's analysis of the artists' self-location was combined with a more hard-nosed concern for New York's changing real estate market. In New York's Tenth Street, for example, '[a]rt ... is perched in an interstice of time – it became possible only because the block had reached a condition in which no one is prepared either to do anything with it or to do away with it. Once its history begins again, artists and bums will have to get out' (p.109).

The parallel with SoHo need not be laboured. Its relevance in the context of Minneapolis-Saint Paul is perhaps more muted. There, it was a richly ambiguous idea of historic preservation that mediated the cold logic of the market. If tradition can be reinvented, as Hobsbawm and Ranger (1983) suggest, then the past can just as easily be manufactured, as when turn-of-the-century lamp-posts were installed at Galtier Plaza in 1983. 'Historic' signs and other anachronistic paraphernalia have been added to this and other (re)developments in an essentially decorative manner, with railway lines carefully 'preserved' amid the cobble stones of Riverplace, but leading nowhere.

7. These definitions derive from the work of the cultural theorists Raymond Williams and Stuart Hall. They are described more fully in Jackson (1989).

This kind of playful quotation, or 'dual coding', has been taken as a definitive feature of postmodern architecture (Jencks, 1981). But the element of playfulness should not be allowed to obscure its political significance. David Harvey writes unequivocally of the residential conversion of industrial buildings as an appropriation of working-class history, whether the history in question is in London's Docklands or in Baltimore's Harborplace (Harvey, 1987). In each case, he claims, cities now rely on a kind of 'voodoo economics' to replace their declining industrial base.

While for some authors postmodern architecture can be reduced to the cultural logic of late capitalism (Jameson, 1984), others suggest a more complex relationship. Charles Jencks's interpretation of warehouse conversion in San Francisco is a good example. He describes the redevelopment as 'twee but alive, clean but rugged, phoney but authentic history', its transformation 'robs it of its guts, but supplies it with cash-flow, a worthwhile mephistophelian deal' (Jencks, 1981, p.103). Sharon Zukin's discussion of the politics of urban neighbourhood change is closer to Harvey or Jameson than to Jencks. She argues that the rebuilding of the inner city in a theatrical image of the urban past, 'demands both a reduction and a romanticizing of the city's industrial work force' (Zukin, 1988, p.202).

This may be 'politically correct', but it suggests a rather flat and one-dimensional interpretation of recent urban history. Rather than conceiving of the present as a pitched battle between different histories – between developers who are hell-bent on transforming the built environment, wilfully obliterating all traces of its previous occupants, and a working class, heroically resisting the developers – this chapter has sought to tease out some of the more complex intersections between 'culture and capital in urban change' (to use Zukin's phrase). As recent work in London also confirms, the battle-lines are rarely so clearly drawn. Developers have begun to anticipate the demands of the conservation lobby, incorporating local references and neo-vernacular elements into their designs. Likewise, conservationists have begun to strike deals with developers to win a more lucrative 'planning gain' package, while community activists can be shown to be defending a very selective reading of the urban past.[8]

8. I am drawing here on the work of Jane M. Jacobs. Her thesis, entitled 'The Politics of the Past' (University of London, 1990), draws on parallel case studies in the City of London and Spitalfields.

As these examples show, the complexities of urban change defy easy generalisation. Rather than debating the issues in an empirical vacuum, this chapter has sought to provide case study material from recent fieldwork in the United States. It has examined the way that meanings are 'manufactured' in the process of neighbourhood change, arguing that the cultural and the economic are fundamentally inseparable, and exploring the variety of ways that economic processes (such as investment in the built environment) are culturally encoded.

Acknowledgements

An earlier version of this chapter was presented at a meeting of the Informal Club of Saint Paul at the invitation of David A. Lanegran (Saint Paul Planning Commission). Discussions were also held with Kelly Lindquist (Artspace Projects Inc., Minneapolis), Weiming Lu (Lowertown Redevelopment Corporation, Saint Paul), Judith A. Martin (Center for Urban and Regional Affairs, University of Minnesota) and James R. Miller (Rollin & Associates Inc., Commercial Real Estate, Minneapolis).

Bibliography

Anderson, K., 'Spiffing Up on the Urban Heritage', *Time Magazine*, 23 November 1987, pp.72–83

Anonymous, 'Possibly the Greatest Show on Earth', *Architecture Minnesota*, vol.11, no.2, 1981, pp.68–9

Borchert, J., Gebhart, D., Lanegran, D. and Martin, J., *Legacy of Minneapolis Amid Preservation and Change*, Bloomington, Minn.: Voyageur, 1983

Bourdieu, P., *Distinction: A Social Critique of the Judgement of Taste*, London: Routledge & Kegan Paul, 1984

Burgess, J.A., 'Selling Places: Environmental Images for the Executive', *Regional Studies*, vol.16, 1982, pp.1–17

City Club of New York, *Wastelands of New York City*, New York, 1962

Gayle, M. and Gillon, E.V., *Cast-Iron Architecture in New York*, New York: Dover, 1974

Gebhart, D. and Martinson, T., *A Guide to the Architecture of Minnesota*, Minneapolis: University of Minnesota Press, 1977

Harvey, D., 'Flexible Accumulation Through Urbanisation: Reflections on "Post-modernism" and the City', *Antipode*, vol.19, 1987, pp. 260–86

——, *The Condition of Postmodernity*, Oxford: Basil Blackwell, 1989

Hewison, R., *The Heritage Industry*, London: Methuen, 1987

Hobsbawm, E. and Ranger, T. (eds), *The Invention of Tradition*, Cambridge: Cambridge University Press, 1983

Jackson, P., 'Neighbourhood Change in New York: The Loft Conversion Process', *Tijdschrift voor Economische en Sociale Geografie*, vol.76, 1985, pp.205–15

_____, *Maps of Meaning: an Introduction to Cultural Geography*, London: Unwin Hyman, 1989

_____, 'Mapping Meanings: A Cultural Critique of Locality Studies', *Environment and Planning A*, vol.23, 1991, pp.215–28

Jameson, F., 'Postmodernism, Or the Cultural Logic of Late Capitalism', *New Left Review*, vol.146, 1984, pp.53–92

Jencks, C., *The Language of Post-Modern Architecture*, New York: Rizzoli, 1981

King, S., 'Arvid Elness Architects', *Architecture Minnesota*, vol.11, no.1, 1985, pp.38–41

Kostouros, J., 'St Anthony Main', *Architecture Minnesota*, vol.8, no.3, 1982, pp.61–3

Lanegran, D.A., 'Public–Private Cooperation in Major Twin Cities Redevelopment Projects', in *AAG '86 Twin Cities Field Trip Guide*, Washington, DC: Association of American Geographers, 1986, pp.95–106

Laska, S.B. and Spain, D.M. (eds), *Back to the City*, New York: Pergamon, 1980

Latimer, G., 'Returning to the River', *Architecture Minnesota*, vol.10, no.2, 1984, pp.38–9

Ley, D. 'Alternative Explanations for Inner-City Gentrification', *Annals, American Association of Geographers*, vol.76, 1986, pp.521–36

London, B. and Palen, J. (eds), *Gentrification, Displacement and Neighborhood Revitalization*, Albany: State University of New York Press, 1984

Lowenthal, D., *The Past is a Foreign Country*, Cambridge: Cambridge University Press, 1985

Mack, L., 'The Rise of Galtier Plaza', *Architecture Minnesota*, vol.12, no.6, 1986, pp.52–62

Martin, J.A., 'Beyond the Malling of America: The Rise of Twin Cities Festival Markets', *CURA Reporter*, Minneapolis: University of Minnesota, vol.15, no.2, 1985, pp.1–6

New York City Planning Commission, *Lofts: Balancing the Equities*, New York: City Planning Commission, 1981

Ratcliffe, C., 'SoHo: Disneyland of the aesthete?', *New York Affairs*, vol.4, 1978, pp.64–72

Rosenberg, H., 'Tenth Street: A Geography of Modern Art', in *Discovering the Present*, H. Rosenberg (ed.), Chicago: University of Chicago Press, 1973

Short, J.R., 'Yuppies, Yuffies and the New Urban Order', *Transactions, Institute of British Geographers*, vol.14, 1989, pp.173–88

Simpson, C.R., *SoHo: The Artist and the City*, Chicago: University of Chicago Press, 1981

Smith, N., 'Gentrification and Capital: Theory, Practice and Ideology in Society Hill', *Antipode*, vol.11, 1979, pp.24–35

_____, 'Gentrification and Uneven Development', *Economic Geography*, vol.58, 1982, pp.139–55

_____ and Williams, P. (eds), *Gentrification of the City*, London: Allen & Unwin, 1986

Stratton, J., *Pioneering in the Urban Wilderness*, New York: Urizen, 1977

Sumka, H.J., 'Neighborhood Revitalization and Displacement: A Review of the Evidence', *Journal of the American Planning Association*, vol.45, 1979, pp.480–7

Vaile, R.S. and Nordstrom, A.L., *Public Merchandise Warehousing in the Twin Cities*, Minneapolis: University of Minnesota Press, 1932

Watson, S., 'Gilding the Smokestacks: The New Symbolic Representations of Deindustrialised Regions', *Environment and Planning D: Society and Space*, vol.9, 1991, pp.59–70

Weber, L., 'Surviving Block E', *Artpaper* (Minneapolis), vol.7, no.3, 1987, p.6

Whitt, J.A., 'Mozart in the Metropolis: The Arts Coalition and the Urban Growth Machine', *Urban Affairs Quarterly*, vol.23, 1987, pp.15–36

Wright, P., *On Living in an Old Country*, London: Verso, 1985

Zukin, S., 'Loft Living as "Historic Compromise" in the Urban Core: The New York Experience', *International Journal of Urban and Regional Research*, vol.6, 1985, pp.256–67

_____, *Loft Living: Culture and Capital in Urban Change*, 2nd edn, London: Radius, 1988

Chapter 7

Transported Lives: Urban Social Networks and Labour Circulation

Margaret Grieco

Introduction

The analysis and approach adopted in this chapter represent an extension and development of two areas of research initiated and elaborated by J. Clyde Mitchell in the African context. Mitchell's work on labour migration on the African continent (1961; 1970) and his analytic work on the potentialities and patternings of social networks (1969) indicate the need for a more sensitive approach to the social organisation of labour and migration within the UK. The most important of the range of ideas and concepts developed by Mitchell are, for the purposes of this chapter, those of labour circulation and the rate and incidence of migration. These concepts direct attention to the mechanisms by which social networks are reinforced, renewed and, to borrow a phrase from Bourdieu and Passeron (1977), reproduced. Whereas migration has been understood by many as destroying social ties (Goldthorpe, Lockwood, Bechhofer and Platt, 1968a; 1968b; 1969), Mitchell's work points the way to understanding the role of social ties in the organising of migration.

It is therefore important to understand the dependence of individuals on their social networks for accomplishing migration. The network approach highlights the significance of social relations as a mode of resourcing (Whipp and Grieco, 1989). The resource model is of great utility in the understanding of labour migration; simple decision models – a tool all too frequently used to analyse labour migration – cannot explain how community is so systematically and frequently reproduced.

The methods I adopt here are not those of Mitchell. It is the intuition, concepts and understandings rather than the computational analyses that I make use of. The aim of this chapter is to reveal the informal organising capabilities of labour which all too frequently go unnoticed in the literature, both within orthodox industrial sociology and within the labour process debate.

Social Networks and Labour History: A Time for Re-examination

The research upon which this analysis is based concerns the patterns of labour circulation between the East End of London and the hop-fields of southern England. Throughout the nineteenth century and until the mid-twentieth century, there was an annual out-migration from urban London to rural employment of considerable proportion. Those analyses of urbanism and urbanisation which concentrate solely upon the single and inevitable direction of rural-to-urban migration may be better viewed as caricatures than accurate and scientific accounts.

This chapter seeks to critique the existing characterisation of the development of urban social relations. It does so by drawing attention to the historical practices of labour circulation within the UK, which depended upon and compounded the cohesiveness of social relations within kinship and neighbourhood structures. I argue that employment relations in modern society frequently harness and depend upon existing patterns of social relations, or social networks, in their recruitment dynamic, whilst social networks frequently come to 'own' sets of clusters of employment vacancies, i.e. occupational property (Grieco, 1987). Where kinship, friendship or neighbourhood status are important in obtaining access to employment, employment relations may serve to reinforce and strengthen social boundaries rather than weaken them. The interaction between urban social network membership and access to rural sources of employment for East London labour provides but one example of such a dynamic, but it is not unique. Similar patterns of urban–rural labour circulation exist for other cities and for other activities (Grieco, forthcoming; Hareven, 1982).

The second objective of this chapter is to demonstrate the strength of the informal organising process of labour in the past, and by so doing to question the orthodox characterisation of working-class behaviour as hedonistic and poorly planned. This criticism of working-class competence is addressed at both a theoretical and empirical level. This is done by discussing the ways in which families and neighbourhoods built seasonal sources of employment into their annual budgeting. The return of family labour to the same source of employment on an annual basis – labour circulation – cannot be explained within the terms of conventional accounts of the working class's inability to form strategies or plan.

The standard characterisations of working-class budgetary and organising abilities are challenged by the empirical evidence of the historical complexity of their occupational repertoires and portfolios of income sources. Revealing the extent to which the stereotype of the working class as poor managers of resources is faulty also demonstrates that there are major problems in standard characterisations of the urbanisation process and urbanism. The conventional view of the urban environment may also be called into question. Furthermore, the evidence on the transportation of networks of social relations on an annual basis from city to countryside is at odds with approaches to urbanisation which focus on the cutting of ties, and with categorisations of occupational skills in terms of a clear division between urban and rural. It is significant that the labour circulation discussed here was anchored on an urban location, but the seasonal migration was to a rural source of employment. It is a pattern not easily encompassed by existing frameworks.

In addition to these critiques of the development of urban social relations and the ability of the working-class household to make strategies and budget, a critique is offered of the orthodox literature which regards power in the household as resting unambiguously with the male. It is argued, from both the case material and theory, that the negotiation of power within the household is more complex than previous historical accounts have suggested. Women's seasonal role as wage-earners has been seriously underestimated, both within the official records and within historical interpretations (Roberts, 1988; Yans-MacLaughlin, 1971). Hop-picking relied heavily upon female and child labour from the urban household, yet the record of this employment history is largely absent from the literature.

On a more positive note, this chapter suggests that the network approach has considerable utility for the understanding of urban social relations in general, that considerable management skills were contained within the working-class household, and that models which have been developed in Third World contexts are applicable to the First World if patterns of social relations are unpacked in a more thorough and detailed way. Understanding the relationship between social networks and the structuring of employment opportunity is crucial both to labour history and modern industrial studies (Grieco, 1987; Rees, 1966). Social networks are both traditional and modern forms; they operate in both developed and developing worlds (Okpala, 1977). Traditional/modern dichotomies in sociological and anthropological analysis have served to conceal the obvious: social network membership is as crucial to modern urban social practice as it is to rural existence.

In summary, the chapter uses case study materials, in particular the documentation of the role of urban social networks in agricultural labour, to illustrate the extent and consequences of misunderstandings in conventional literature. Its primary purpose is to call for a re-examination and re-formulation of the strategic capabilities of the working-class household. This chapter is not intended as an exercise in women's studies or in oral history, but rather these perspectives are brought to bear in a more general and fundamental analysis of the social organisation of employment. The objective of this chapter is to address the ability of the least formally empowered to plan their behaviour strategically. It thus lies within the 'contested terrain' approach to industrial studies (Edwards, 1979) and recognises that labour itself is gendered and engendering (Lee and Loveridge, 1987). The conclusion, based on the evidence presented here, is that the existing simple dichotomy between urban and rural existence cannot encompass the repeated incorporation by urban social networks of rural employment chances in occupational repertoires and survival strategies.

Data Collection

The material upon which this chapter is based is derived from a number of distinct and separate sources. The analysis provided results from a marriage of retrospective oral histories, contemporary press reports, Church and charity organisation documentation, biographical materials, a small but growing local history literature and occasional references in the secondary literature on the history of the urban poor. The general materials held by the Bethnal Green local history collection were used as a tool for initial familiarisation with the field and, subsequently, to support the data generated through oral history accounts.

The oral histories were collected from two separate social networks, access to one of which was obtained by tracking through recently published memoirs, and the other of which was given by personal contacts.[1] The first network provided eight interviewees and the second provided twelve. In addition to these accounts, interviews were also conducted with over twenty other persons who were involved in hopping, and who were unconnected to one another when they were participants in this activity.

Oral history accounts are a particularly important source of materials for this research because the casual character of the work resulted in weak practices of formal documentation. Collecting oral history by means of a social network methodology provides one mechanism for overcoming some of the difficulties posed by the missing records, not least because it provides a way of cross-checking materials and re-stimulating memories of times past. A more detailed summary of the materials and sources used is provided in Grieco (forthcoming).

The Scale of the Migration

What then was the scale of the annual resort from urban East London to rural employment? The 1970 Kent Museum exhibition gives us a rough guide. It states that between 1880 and 1940 up to 250,000 'strangers' would descend on Kent every year from the East End to join local labour in the hop-fields. *The Weekly Illustrated* (4 Sept. 1937) gave figures for labour going to the hop-fields of around 50,000 in total, of which 20,000 went to Kent. Bignall (1977) states that in the last decade of the nineteenth century the annual influx of migrant hop-pickers to Kent was of the order of 250,000, of which 70,000 to 80,000 were drawn from East

1. Subsequent to writing this chapter, an oral history of hopping has been published by Gilda O'Neill (1990) which provides further confirmation of the descriptions of hopping generated by the interviewees discussed here.

London. It seems probable that Bignall's figures are the most accurate; the Kent Museum document's source is unreferenced. Even if we take the lowest set of these figures, an annual migration of 50,000 East Londoners to the hop-fields of southern England is still a substantial reversal of the presumed one-directional rural–urban migration path.

The scale and the regularity of the migration was reflected in the provision by the railway companies of special services to accommodate this seasonal shift of residence. Commencing from London Bridge and Waterloo, these services, termed the 'Hopper Specials' departed in the night. No doubt this night-time movement is best explained by considerations of the scheduling of rolling stock. That this social group was required to journey outside of normal user hours, however, is consistent with the prevailing characterisation of its manner and its values as rough. Both time and cost mechanisms (the night-time scheduling of services and the concessionary fare arrangements) served to separate hoppers from the regular users or passengers on these lines. Thus, despite the mass character of the movement it had a low visibility. The Kent Museum Hopping Exhibition brochure (1979) says: 'whole families of pickers came by Hopper specials provided by the South Eastern Railway; others came in carts and wagons, by boat to Gravesend or they walked.'

Rural Skills in the Urban Occupational Repertoire: A Critique of the Urbanist Orthodoxy

The understanding of the separation of urban and rural lives as a set feature of modern industrial society is long-founded and deep-rooted. Although there has been a wealth of research in the areas of social and labour history (Hareven, 1982) and in migration studies (Arensberg and Kimball, 1940) which documents repeated patterns of rural–urban–rural linkage in industrial society, this literature remains fragmented and has not been harnessed to critique the existing characterisation either of the development of urban society or the patterning of historical and present urban social relations. The suggestion here is that, because the way in which urban society developed has itself been misconstrued (as the escape of individuals from traditional, constraining society to modern self-determining society), there has been a consequent misunderstanding of the nature of urban social relations in general.

The concentration of interest has been on rural–urban drift and assumed patterns of social network severance. On reaching their urban destinations, migrants are assumed to sever their connections with their kin and neighbourhood networks in their areas of origin. But analysing migratory behaviour in any depth reveals strong patterns of continued interaction and its importance for the resourcing of migration (Arensberg and Kimball, 1940; Brooks and Singh, 1979; Grieco, 1982; 1987). By focusing attention on the micro-processes of social network construction, maintenance and restoration in urban social life, the over-general analysis of urban society as simply anomic and atomising is called into question. The argument here is not that there is no structural division between urban and rural life in contemporary society, but that such a division has come into being at a much later date than is generally supposed, and by mechanisms which are not based in the attempt of the individual to flee his or her social environment. The implication is that we should look more closely at contemporary urban social relations in terms of their social network properties in seeking to understand urban behaviour (Pahl, 1988).

The annual practice of recruiting urban labour from the East End of London to the hop-fields of southern England persisted until the middle of the twentieth century (*Stepney Ahoy*, Mar. 1964). The journeying into, and sojourning in, rural territory was a regular feature of the urban calendar. The *Weekly Illustrated* (4 Sept. 1937), talking of one particular East End neighbourhood – Devon's Road in Bromley by Bow – described a situation where whole streets annually migrate to the country for three or four weeks of hop-picking: '[f]or the Cockney goes off the hopping as regularly as sportsmen to their grouse moors for the 12th.' The *Morning Post* (2 Sept. 1932) provides a similar vision of urban exodus. Under the headline 'When Limehouse camps in Arcady', it gives a set of vivid descriptions of the cohesiveness of this labour migration:

> Now they have become streets and neighbourhoods lifted out of riverside London and dumped for three weeks in the whispering folds of Kent. Shut your eyes for a moment, you can imagine yourself in Silvertown or Stepney or Limehouse.

Thus, in opposition to the conventional portrayal of rural–urban separation and severance, the cameo provide here through contemporary eyes is one of the replication of urban social relations and, moreover, urban neighbourhoods in the heart of rural existence itself. Urban social relations, or sets of social ties, are being transported wholesale into rural space each year, albeit on a seasonal basis. At the very least, it is clear that we have identified a strong and persistent pattern of labour circulation in a modern industrial society. The scale and cohesiveness of the migration requires us to define it as a communal practice. The rest of this chapter investigates the social organisation of this complex and communal migratory movement.

The Role of Urban Social Networks in the Organisation of Rural Employment

Even the most superficial investigation of the way in which this replication of urban neighbourhood in rural space took place reveals the extent to which kinship and neighbourhood linkages played a pivotal role in the organising of this mass migration. Whilst many of the contemporary analyses portrayed hoppers as undisciplined and indolent social individuals – and indeed some of the recent local history literature reproduces such images uncritically (Bignall, 1977) – both our oral history evidence and documentary materials demonstrate the active and disciplined role played by East London labour in the organising of its rural employment chance. Although in other periods different recruitment arrangements had held, in the twentieth century the onus was upon the workforce to make the contact with the hop farmer to arrange employment for the season. Typically, the matriarch of the family wrote to the farmer with whom last season's employment had been found, requesting work for the season to come (letter from W.H. Brownlow to the *Hackney Gazette*, 23 Dec. 1977). Where family work groups were looking to change employer, this was accomplished by a relative, friend or neighbour negotiating on their behalf with their own employer: reputation, references and sponsorship were essential features of the recruitment process. Social connectedness was important to employment chance in a situation which appeared to the external world as the loosest and most chaotic of labour arrangements. The oral history evidence collected in the course of this research indicates that the matriarch of one family would frequently arrange the employment of four or five related or neighbouring families (Grieco, forthcoming).

Obtaining hopping employment happened, contrary to the contemporary images of social disruption and chaos, within a tight sponsorship system. Patron–client relationships were, it should be noted, as important within the hopping workforce as they were between it and the employers. Viewed from the perspective of a labour process, the workforce was unavoidably involved in the control and supervision of its own activity in the interest of the employer. Urban social networks were the crucial instrument, ensuring both the recruitment and the supervision of the large, skilled, temporary labour force necessary for the hopping harvest. It is precisely the urban nature of the workforce which provides the social stability and network density necessary for skill transmission and workplace performance and reliability.

If attention is paid to the demands of hop farmers for reliable labour and to the various processes which resulted in the matching of the farmers' demands and labour's survival needs by the repeated recruitment of the same workers, then doubt must be cast upon both the view of such people as dangerous classes or indolent workers and upon those analyses which fail to recognise the active role taken by labour in the organising of its employment chances. The repeated hiring of the same labour provides the best conditions for the reconstruction of the urban neighbourhood in its temporary rural location, because it offers the necessary social space for employment patronage and sponsorship. The repeated character of this social exchange consolidates and intensifies social cohesiveness. Migration is serving to strengthen social linkages, rather than weaken them.

Some oral history sources and other materials indicate that those families which went hopping were those in which the head of household did not enjoy a reliable and permanent source of employment. There was a stigma attached to hopping within the urban community. The suggestion is that not only families but whole streets were stigmatised. Indeed, the moral crusader literature often expressly talks of this labour as having been drawn from the worst slum areas of the East End (*The Sign*, Sept. 1917) and frequently argues that the poor working and accommodation conditions this labour enjoyed were congruent with its values and behaviour. Whatever the deficiencies of the crusaders' analyses of the moral environment of London's migrant labour, they were correct in their identification of its origin: it was certainly drawn from riverside locations. It was dockland labour (Phillips and Whiteside, 1985). Different farms drew their labour from different parts of East London. The Whitbread house magazine of 1935 identifies its catchment areas as Bermondsey, Shadwell and Rotherhithe, as well as East London.

The evidence indicates that the social hierarchy of the urban neighbourhood was replicated in the rural setting. Families from 'better' areas obtained employment in 'better' hop gardens (Grieco, forthcoming). The social gradations, as measured by types of accommodation, bedding and employment conditions, are highly differentiated, and social position in the hopping environment closely reflects social position in the urban neighbourhood environment. A distinction is conventionally drawn between the 'rough' and 'respectable' working class, but this collapses into one category those markers of social difference which are crucial in the understanding of employment behaviour. Families worked their way up the social hierarchy of the hopping farm system in the attempt to improve both their living conditions and wage levels. 'Rough' and 'respectable' distinctions operated at and within every social level (Ross, 1985) and provided an effective mechanism for the disciplining and control of labour. Images of 'roughness' served to legitimise the accommodation of migrant labour in the same facilities used for the wintering of animals.

Organising the Household Finances: The Contribution of Rural Wages to Urban Household Budgeting

A particularly significant feature of this pattern of labour circulation is its gender base (*East London Advertiser*, 22 Mar. 1974). The migrant East London hop-pickers were primarily married women and school-age children.[2] Employed men remained in London, the male labour requirement being met by those men in

2. Children's presence on the hop-field during school term times can be discussed as 'survival truancy'. Oral history evidence indicates that general practitioners frequently furnished children with sickness certificates in order to cover their absence from school in the knowledge that the children were going hopping, and in the belief that such an excursion would be beneficial for their health.

casual employment, such as docking labour (*Greater London and Essex Newspapers*, 28 Dec. 1979). Employed males visited the hop gardens each weekend. On Saturday nights relatives would arrive from London by lorries, and 'we would all go to the cook-house and have a good drink' (*East London Advertiser*, 22 Mar. 1974). The organisation of the male visitors to the hop-fields mirrored the social organisation of the employment itself. Because families from the same streets and neighbourhoods typically worked for the same or neighbouring farmers, transport arrangements were simplified. Lorries were arranged on a neighbourhood basis by the workforce itself. Likewise, the movement of female workers was not accomplished by the railway companies alone, but rather by the neighbourhood matriarchs (*Hackney Gazette*, 23 Dec. 1977); transport arrangements were quite simply in the hands of women. They were responsible for making the arrangements with the haulier for the movement of goods to and from the hop-fields and for the weekly transport of menfolk. Interestingly, Chinn (1988) finds a similar relationship between transport organisation and the women of the urban poor in Birmingham. Payment was typically made at the end of the season: reputation and reliability were of extreme importance in such circumstances. The need for co-ordination amongst groups of households was also of great importance: the hiring of a lorry was outside the financial capabilities of any one family, so combining and co-ordinating employment destinations under such circumstances was a matter of great necessity.

In order to obtain access to this important rural source of employment and income, the East End working-class family was involved in a complex set of transport arrangements which necessarily took a communal or neighbourhood form. Membership of a social network was an important pre-condition for access to certain sources of employment, especially the relatively highly-paid. The importance of these complex arrangements is best understood from the perspective of family survival strategies. In the absence of secure and adequate urban employment opportunities, the East End working-class family generated the necessary transport infrastructure to gain access to rural employment as a means of raising the income needed for its survival.

In discussing the contribution of women and children to the household budget, it is important to recognise that this contribution is frequently unrecorded in official statistics and official accounts of household organisation. Such under-recording has received wider recognition within the New American Labour History literature, where similar practices of female seasonal migration have been identified (Yans-MacLaughlin, 1971). The casual or seasonal character of this employment results in its exorcism from the official account, yet its repeated nature makes it an important aspect of household budgeting. The material collected demonstrates the importance of women in the social organisation of employment. There is considerable evidence of women being responsible for determining the particular destination of the family group, which members should go and which should stay behind, and for organising transport and accommodation. There are therefore links between gender and the general area of brokerage which, as yet, have received minimal attention within a literature that views women as simply passive and powerless (although see Ross, 1985).

In terms of wage employment strategies, it is important to recognise that hop earnings were largely controlled by women. Within the oral histories collected, and from a variety of press materials, it is clear that this seasonal earning was an important part of the annual budgeting. Many accounts of working-class life suggest that it has short-term budgeting and accounting horizons; typically the focus is on the absence of savings habits and so forth. Paying attention to the seasonality of the various sources of earning and employment leads to an understanding of the complexity of organising work and earnings over the course of the year (Stedman Jones, 1971). Within the popular information sources there are many references to the dependence of households on this money for winter clothing and shoes. It was money which could be depended upon once the initial contact with the employer was made and represented an important component in an organised and scheduled annual budget (Grieco, forthcoming).

Although the concern here is primarily with the hop-picking harvest and its associated labour migration, East London labour also harnessed other sources of rural employment in its occupational portfolio. The families involved in hop-picking were also often employed in pea-picking. Whereas hop-picking happened in the autumn, pea-picking took place in spring. Migration to the pea fields of Essex was on a daily basis. Whereas hop-picking employment was provided for the season, pea-picking employment was made available by the day. Hop-pickers had a guarantee of work from the farmer before their arrival at their destination, while pea-pickers were hired at the farm gate. Undertaking the journey to a farm was no guarantee of work. Transport to pea-picking was arranged by the same individuals who organised hopping transport. The organiser determined the composition of the workforce. Labour itself played a role in determining the composition of the workforce as a consequence of the hiring methods of the employer and its own active role in the provision of transport. Another source of rural employment for East London labour was apple-picking. The apple harvest followed the hop harvest, and there was an overlap between the areas in which the two crops were grown. Hoppers often stayed on in the hut accommodation provided on the hopping farm and helped with the apple harvest. The evidence is that women of London's urban poor combined a complex set of casual sources of rural employment as a routine part of household earning and budgetary practice.

Following the recent developments in the literature on the distribution of power within the household, it is important to recognise the contribution that hopping as an annual earning opportunity gave women to organise household budgeting. It provided a source of income which could be relied upon, independent of the economic activities of the males. Although this form of work was not permanent and would conventionally be classified as casual and transitory, it should be noted that, despite the conventional assumptions, casual employment is not necessarily a spot market. Where seasonal employment occurs on the basis of a set of customary obligations it can be reliably incorporated into the household budget. It is not the permanence of employment which is different in this case, but rather its annual repeated nature – its predictability – which permits this social group to organise its finances even outside the specific period of employment – to borrow against the season's wages. It is only by examining the detail of hiring arrangements that this 'casual' form of employment can be revealed as a highly structured and strategised activity.

The assumption that 'casual and transitory' employment have limited impact on the organisation of power within the household requires more scrutiny. The burden of this chapter is that the social organisation of employment is frequently and typically complex, even at the 'bottom end' of the labour market. One consequence of the understanding adopted here is likely to be a recasting of existing materials so that the absence of formal power would no longer automatically be taken as evidence of the absence of informal power. The analysis presented here does not intend to challenge the general analysis of patriarchy, but rather sets out to identify areas of informal or interstitial power. It is part of a general analysis being developed around issues of the conflicts present in the simultaneous serving of gender and kin interests (Grieco and Whipp, 1986).

A Festival for Labour: Redressing the Damage of Urban Living

The annual resort to the hop-fields of Kent was important not only as an income strategy, but also as a means of remedying the dietary deficiencies of urban living. It was also viewed as a health strategy for recuperating from the various hazards of city life. It seems important from the evidence collected to pay heed to the holidaying and festive aspects of the migrations.

The form and location of employment provided access to quantities and qualities of food not easily obtainable in town. The geographical separation of the community of men and the community of women thereby generated a radically changed and improved diet for those family members conventionally disadvantaged in the allocation of food. Nor was the impact of rural employment on diet confined to the duration of the harvest, for these urban dwellers returned to the city with farm products which could be stored and preserved for future use. For instance, on their return from the hop-fields, hoppers frequently brought with them part of the apple harvest. The fruit was interestingly termed 'hopping apples'. It was a gift from the farmer at the end of the season, and could be carried back to London to be stored in outhouses for use through the winter.

Social Networks and the Transmission of Occupational Skills

It was argued above that the occupational repertoire of the East End family was significantly wider in its base, incorporating both industrial and agricultural skills, than the existing literature would lead us to suppose. It is important to discuss the mechanisms by which skill is achieved and transmitted. Among labour historians there has developed recently an important and vital critique around the social construction of skill. There is now a substantial literature which discusses the concept of tacit skill and recognises that training processes are often conducted at the workplace by the social networks of new employees (Grieco, 1987; Manwaring, 1982). Many tasks previously viewed as unskilled are now seen in terms of the informal organisation of training. The distinction is between informal and formal training, rather than between unskilled and skilled.

Within the employment context of East London, much work was casual, seasonal and intermittent. As a consequence, individuals and families required a wide-ranging occupational repertoire in order to survive. The recorded mobility between these various sources of employment gives rise to a description of the tasks involved as being 'unskilled'. However, this type of analysis fails to take account of the recurrent nature of the various tasks. It is in this context that we should understand the annual migration to the hop-fields, for farmers repeatedly recruited the same families. Family was the training agency, and repeated annual recruitment resulted in the retaining of skills within the work groups. Where skill is held within connected social groups rather than by unconnected individuals, the loss of relevant skill information because of periods of interruption or non-use by the individual is corrected. The existence of a collective skill memory is important to annual seasonal work performance. Cohesive groups rather than random individuals create the better performance, which is in the interest of the employer. Here then we have some understanding of why urban workers should come to possess and maintain rural skills.

An examination of the involvement of East London labour in hop-picking requires us to revise the orthodox literature on the possession and transmission of skills. High levels of mobility between types of employment should not be taken as evidence of the low skill content of the various types of work. Indeed, the evidence suggests that the opposite is true: that it may be the sign of a highly skilled and flexible workforce.

The Reproduction of the Urban Neighbourhood in a Rural Setting: The Commercial Dimension

An important dimension of this labour migration is that it was accompanied by many of the local commercial services. Newspaper accounts draw attention to the presence of small East End traders carrying on their usual business, but within the hopping camps (*Morning Post*, 2 Sept. 1932). To provide a highly graphic illustration, the local whelk-sellers followed their clients into Kent for the season. The movement of community over distance was reinforced by the propensity of customary traders to join in with the move.

The first grounds for accounting for the presence of traders can best be explained by the large-scale flight of their major customers to rural pastures. This is most particularly the case in respect of consumer goods. As the hop-picking labour was primarily female, it was the household managers – the very group responsible for ordering and buying food – who had left the neighbourhood. Since her children accompanied her, it meant that the greater part of the household transferred to the hop-fields. As this movement also typically involved whole streets, the major source of neighbourhood custom departed for the season. The social organisation of hopping thus provided the very basis for the transfer of commerce to the fields. With women and children absent from the neighbourhood, shop-keepers either had to rely on the reduced and fickle custom of men, or transfer along with their local customers. Strongly developed gender roles in the East End household meant that cooking and the kitchen were strictly the business of women. For traders, reliance on males was a poor prospect. The move to the fields rarely meant a permanent departure for the whole season on the part of traders; rather it took the form of a regular servicing of the steady urban business whilst it was in the hop-fields. It is the neighbourhood element of the hopping labour migration which best explains the commercial migration.

In order to have access to their normal volume of custom, traders had to operate across two sites. The willingness to do this was no doubt aided by the ties of debt which bound the hopping customers to their local traders – debt and credit ties operated to guarantee traders a certain source of custom at the other end of their journey. Arrival in the hopping area was, however, more than a guarantee of the routine volume of custom, for hopping provided earnings in a form and fashion which permitted the financing of a festival. This festival element shaped the memories of children, who viewed hopping as a time of plenty and of pleasure. It was also a boost for the trader. That the earnings were in the hands of women meant that the traders' share, as opposed to the publicans' share, was likely to be all the greater. Whereas conflicts in the household were usually resolved in favour of men, women's control over hopping wages ensured a greater volume of trade for the grocer than would have been the case in the city, even without the element of festival luxuries and frivolity. The festival of hopping was a consumer festival for women and children, just as it was a sales festival for the trader. It was also a period which was accompanied by the opportunity to clear or reduce the existing levels of debt.

The provision of urban facilities in rural space was not left to the discretion of urban traders alone. Employers also made camp-based provisions for their workforces. Hop-owners often operated, or arranged for the presence of, a shop on their premises. Such shops provided a range of general goods, including clothing. There is much evidence to the effect that local rural traders were not welcoming of hopper custom, a factor which no doubt provided some of the necessary commercial space for urban traders and hop farmers themselves to enter this rural niche.

Strengthening the 'Dangerous Classes' Stereotype: The Role of Religious Missions

The Church also followed the workers of East London into the hop-fields of Kent, but its intention was to reform the customs and practices of the East Enders, not to renew or support them. Missions from the Universities of Oxford and Cambridge, staffed by the young men of Christ Church and Clare College, extended their urban reforming activities into the Kent countryside in the cause of temperance and the moral reform of the 'dangerous classes' (*Stepney Ahoy*, Oct. 1955). The weekend holidaying of East London in the hop-fields, with its social life based around the pub and the cookhouse, was viewed by these educated outsiders as moral disorder (*The Sign*, Sept. 1917).

This regular activity provided the missions with a point of purchase for their activities in the urban areas for the rest of the year. The removal of neighbourhoods to the hop-fields rendered them more approachable. There are a number of issues which are of importance here. To begin with, the removal of substantial parts of the urban community to a rural context reduced the scale of the community and made it more encompassable, which alone facilitated the prospect of successful missions. The removal also created a degree of structural isolation from those elements of the wider environment which normally constituted barriers to entry, and thus made the population more accessible. The element of structural isolation was further enhanced by the composition of the workforce; approachability was enhanced by the age and gender composition of the field labour.

The missions offered many practical services to the hopping community in this annual window of rural activity, such as tea-carts, baths, medical services, forms of child-care and educational services. The provision of such services when the hoppers were separated from other means of obtaining them increased the missionaries' access. Not only were the services generally welcomed, but the absence of males meant that many of the normal barriers to acceptance of these services were removed. Strong gender roles meant the receipt of charity and other forms of financial aid, including borrowing, were socially forbidden to men and frequently became the province of women. Women could more easily accept assistance in general, and this was further enhanced by the absence of men.

From the many oral accounts it is clear that both the providers of the services and the recipients of them understood that spiritual instruction was part of the price for the service. It is equally apparent that the degree of compliance with the full price was always less than complete. The extent to which the religious form was parodied rather than simply accepted should be considered. Providing the appearance of conformity in order to obtain some desired resource while maintaining the original values and views was an important skill. 'Posturing', and shaping the appearance to that desired by those with resources, was a significant capacity of the poor. Impression management was important in a situation where respectability was enforced as a condition of allocation.

When considering the relationship between the visibility of the urban poor and the intensity of the missions, it is important to recognise that the transition to the fields rendered its distinctive characteristics more immediate and visible by the differences perceived and existing between this labour and that surrounding it. This intensified the perceived urgency of the problems of redemption. The rules which forbade stealing from one's own did not necessarily operate in respect of others. Difference changed the rules which were in play. Removal to the fields expanded the space for social crime. At this distance it is not possible to ascertain the facts, but what is clear is that there was a large volume of complaint about such practices, and this legitimised the presence of the missions on the hop-fields and their role as reformers.

The reformers did not confine their activity to the behaviour of the hopping community, but also attempted to reform the environment in which they operated. The equation between poor physical conditions and wrongful behaviour was strong enough to lead to assumptions that improvements in physical environment would change the parameters of behaviour. Reformers were not merely trying to redress the behaviour of the hopping community when in the fields, but were also trying to correct their general behaviour back in the city. It was possible to get a greater purchase on the community when it was removed from the more embedded and readily defensible urban space. Entering the environment of the hop-fields put reformers at a lesser risk of exposure and hostility than in London.

The main argument of this section has been that the cohesiveness of neighbourhoods made connection more difficult for missions in the urban setting. It is the easier rural access to urban souls, and the opportunity to more readily transform their social behaviour, which explains the following by the missions of the neighbourhood to the fields.

The Employers' Perspective: Securing a Reliable Source of Labour

Approaching the migration from a different perspective, how did the hop farmers of Kent organise the recruitment of the seasonal labour necessary for the harvest? The recruitment of labour had taken a variety of forms in the past. Early nineteenth century accounts are of labour casually organising employment by presenting itself at the farm gates. This produced a number of problems, the most severe of which was that the scale of the influx was typically in excess of the labour requirements of the season (Bignall, 1977). This arrangement was superseded in the late nineteenth century by the use of hiring agents and the supply of a form of documentation known as a Hopper's Letter, which placed hiring on a more organised basis. Precisely when this system broke down is not clear from the literature, but, from historical accounts we have collected, this system had already disappeared by the end of the First World War. By this time the annual recruitment of labour from the East End was customary, and arrangements for employees were made by letter. Neighbourhood and family members acted as brokers but with no formally instituted hiring agent being involved. The function of the hiring agent became located within the labour force itself. To summarise, a form of ganging system developed; hopping labour was not disorganised or politically unorganised, rather it was informally organised.

Wages were paid in full at the end of the season, but money could be borrowed against the tallied earnings of the family work group during the season. This was referred to as 'subbing' (*East London Advertiser*, 22 Mar. 1974). Rules, however, applied as to how much could be borrowed, and the amount subbed was never allowed to reach more than a set proportion of the weekly wages earned. In this way the migrant workforce remained tied to a particular employer for the season. Within the existing literature the implications of different forms of wage payment systems for employers' control over their workforces have received little attention, yet the material presented here would suggest that such an analysis is important to the discussion of industrial relations.

East End workers were not the only source of labour on the hop-fields. Three other distinct categories of labour were involved; home dwellers or pickers, that is permanent rural employees, gypsies and travellers, and urban workers from areas other than London. The different types of labour were housed separately and worked on different parts of the hop-field. Within London labour, Irish workers were of great importance. Although so far no statistical material has been found, references to this source of labour are plentiful, and the oral history accounts are replete with information. Irish names appear in hopping songs, for example in the well-known chorus:

> When you go a-'oppin',
> 'oppin' dahn in Kent,
> See ol' Muvver Riley,
> Livin' in a tent,[3]
> Wiv an eio, eio, ei-eio

3. In the late nineteenth century much of the accommodation provided for hoppers was in tent form. Photographs of hopping tents set out in military style in the fields of Kent are held in the Bethnal Green History Collection.

The general point about the hiring strategy of the employer is that, from the materials collected, it does seem as if they attempted to recruit and maintain social and cultural divisions within the labour force so as not to be over-dependent on any one source. It also seems, however, that employers, despite clear evidence of the existence of divide-and-rule strategies, were highly dependent upon London labour. To provide an example, one hop farm (Whitbread's at Beltring in Kent) recruited 4,000 workers each year as late as the 1930s. From the oral histories it appears that these various social divisions within the hopping workforce were important from the perspective of strike organisation. Homedwellers or local pickers were constrained from joining such events by their situation of tied accommodation. On the other hand, East London labour, recruited on a neighbourhood basis, was more solidaristic on such occasions. The consequence of strike-breaking in Kent would accompany any erring party back to the city. The presence of the social network in both locations was a strong norm-enforcement mechanism.

A number of accounts speak of the social distances between local and migrant hop labour. Local images of crime, chaos, swearing and fighting as the identifiable characteristics of this urban labour source were highly stereotyped. East London labour was viewed as ethnically distinct, and was labelled 'foreign'. Indeed, the work organisation arrangements made by the various hop-field owners served to reinforce rather than eradicate such differences. Labour drawn from different types of area and community lived and worked in different parts of the hop-fields. Detectable differences consequently remained. Local perceptions of the moral character of the annual influx mirrored those of the charity agencies and Christian missions.

There is, of course, a contradiction between such stereotypes and the annual recruitment of the same labour by farmers. Perhaps an important part of the explanation is that the work discipline which was imposed upon the field was strong. It was imposed both by family, which was earning on a piecework rather than an hourly or weekly basis, and by the farmer, through a supervisory system which measured output through the day and which set definite picking standards and targets. Time-keeping discipline was imposed by the employer through the hiring of parties responsible for waking up the various families in their huts and turning them out onto the fields by six o'clock. Children

were taken to the field and, with the exception of babies and
infants, were required to share the workload. There were particular tasks allocated to the very young, such as bine rolling. Older
children joined in with the picking of the crop, with the family
frequently setting such children to the picking of a set family
quota in the earlier part of the day.

No formal controls were held over absenteeism other than the
general waking up procedures, and families could substitute their
various members into hop employment provided the quotas set
for each were met. Families would lend members to neighbours
on occasions, but the earnings of the borrowed team member
would be attributed to his or her own family. This exchange of
labour between families in the rural setting provides yet another
rationale for the organising of migration on a kinship and neighbourhood basis. It connected migration with a safety net against
the chance loss or injury of a work group member. This exchange
had the consequence of strengthening ties and generating co-ordi-
nated work rhythms or synchronisation between families.

Journey's End

Whereas the moral crusaders of the period saw loose living in the
annual migration to the hop-fields, employers saw a reliable and
trained labour force. As analysts we can identify labour as
remaining within, and organised by, its moral community
throughout the migration. Hopping may have been an annual
escape from the urban environment, but it was a communal and
not an individual escape. The contemporary portrayal is a useful
starting point for investigating the incidence of hopping migration, and an oral history approach which has a social network
focus is the relevant tool with which to research it. The tools and
concepts provided by Mitchell (1961; 1969; 1970) clearly have a
useful and important role to play in understanding the character
of urban social relations and their interaction with employment
chance and organisation in the industrial UK. This is therefore a
rich field for the analysis of the role of social networks in organising urban existence in general. Its special feature, of course, is the
annual and repeated transportation of urban linkages, practices
and lifestyles into the heart of the rural environment – a moveable feast, a moveable community, transported lives.

Bibliography

Arensberg, C.M. and Kimball, S.T., *Family and Community in Ireland*, Cambridge, Mass.: Harvard University Press, 1940

Bignall, A., *Hopping Down in Kent*, London: Blake, 1977

Bourdieu, P. and Passeron, J., *Reproduction in Education, Society and Culture*, London: Sage, 1977

Brooks, D. and Singh, K., 'Pivots and Presents: Asian Brokers in British Foundries', in *Ethnicity at Work*, S. Wallman (ed.), London: Macmillan, 1979

Chinn, C., *They Worked All Their Lives: Women of the Urban Poor in England, 1880–1939*, Manchester: Manchester University Press, 1988

Edwards, R., *Contested Terrain: The Transformation of the Workplace in the Twentieth Century*, London: Heinemann, 1979

Goldthorpe, J., Lockwood, D., Bechhofer, F. and Platt, J., *The Affluent Worker: Political Attitudes and Behaviour*, Cambridge: Cambridge University Press, 1968a

_____, *The Affluent Worker: Industrial Attitudes and Behaviour*, Cambridge: Cambridge University Press, 1968b

_____, *The Affluent Worker in the Class Structure*, Cambridge: Cambridge University Press, 1969

Grieco, M.S., 'Family Structure and Industrial Employment: The Role of Information and Migration', *Journal of Marriage and the Family*, vol.44, 1982, pp.701–11

_____, *Keeping it in the Family: Social Networks and Employment Chance*, London: Tavistock, 1987

_____, *Workers' Dilemmas: Recruitment, Reliability and Repeated Exchange*, London: Routledge, forthcoming

_____ and Whipp, R., 'Women and the Workplace: Gender and Control in the Labour Process', in *Studies in Gender and Technology in the Labour Process*, D. Knight and H. Wilmott (eds), Aldershot: Gower, 1986

Hareven, T., *Family Time and Industrial Time: The Relationship Between Family and Work in a New England Industrial Community*, Cambridge: Cambridge University Press, 1982

Humphries, S., *Hooligans or Rebels?*, Oxford: Basil Blackwell, 1981

Lee, G. and Loveridge, R., *The Manufacture of Disadvantage*, Milton Keynes: Open University Press, 1987

Manwaring, T., *The Extended Internal Labour Market*, Berlin: IIM, 1982

Mitchell, J.C., 'Wage Labour and African Population Movements in Central Africa', in *Essays on African Population*, K.M. Barbour and R.M. Prothero (eds), London: Routledge & Kegan Paul, 1961

_____, 'The Concept and Use of Social Networks', in *Social Networks in Urban Situations*. J.C. Mitchell (ed.), Manchester: Manchester University Press, 1969

_____, 'The Causes of Labour Migration', in *Black Africa*, J. Middleton (ed.), London: Macmillan, 1970

Okpala, D.C.I., 'Received Concepts and Theories in African Studies and Urban Management Strategies: A Critique', *Urban Studies*, vol.24, no.2, 1977, pp.137–50

O'Neill, G., *Pull No More Bines*, London: Women's Press, 1990

Pahl, R., 'Some Remarks on Informal Work, Social Polarisation and the Social Structure', *International Journal of Urban and Regional Research*, vol.12, 1988, pp.247–67

Phillips, G. and Whiteside, N., *Casual Labour: The Unemployment Question in the Port Transport Industry, 1870-1970*, Oxford: Clarendon, 1985

Rees, A., 'Information Networks in Labour Markets', *American Economic Review*, vol.56, no.2, 1966, pp.559–66

Roberts, E., *Women's Work, 1840–1940*, London: Macmillan, 1988

Ross, E., 'Not the Sort Who Would Sit on the Doorstep: Respectability in Pre-World War I London Neighbourhoods', *Journal of International Labour and Working Class History*, no.27, 1985, pp.35–59

Stedman Jones, G., *Outcast London: A Study in the Relationship Between Classes in Victorian Society*, Oxford: Clarendon, 1971

Tebbut, M., *Making Ends Meet: Pawnbroking and Working Class Credit*, Leicester: Leicester University Press, 1983

Whipp, R. and Grieco, M.S., 'Time, Task and Travel: Budgeting for Interdependencies', in *Gender, Transport and Employment*, M.S. Grieco, L. Pickup and R. Whipp (eds), Aldershot: Avebury

Yans-MacLaughlin, V., 'Patterns of Work and Family Organisation: Buffalo's Italians', *Journal of Interdisciplinary History*, vol.2, 1971, pp.229–314

Chapter 8

From Commodities to Gifts: Pakistani Migrant Workers in Manchester

Pnina Werbner

Introduction

The anthropological literature on labour migration is premised on notions of continuing obligation. Despite their physical absence, labour migrants' earnings remain subject to claims by rural kin and dependants. Young 'target' migrants often convert their entire earnings into gifts for their return home (see Gregory, 1982). Within the city, 'home boys' pool their resources in burial or friendly societies, thus supporting one another during crises and emergencies. In addition to these institutional arrangements for sharing earnings, labour migrants often pool their wages in joint consumption – for instance the sharing of food, drink and accommodation (Jacobson, 1973; Mayer, 1961). These are all familiar urban phenomena which highlight the moral dimensions of labour migration – regarded both in terms of the moral pressure to which migrants are subject and the moral bonds generated between them.

There is a common thread running through the different modes of sharing: in all, earnings gained within the commodity market are converted into 'gifts', incorporated into a currently prevalent system of gifting. For our purposes here, the fundamental distinction between gifting and commodities relates to the different relationship set up by the transaction. A gift, whether in the form of a good or a service, is essentially inalienable. It implies permanent debt and, reciprocally, permanent trust. Gifts thus reflect the long-term and durable nature of social bonds.

Pakistani labour migrants in the UK, both men and women,

often appear to develop vast networks of acquaintances over time. They also evolve some very close friendships. As migrants find themselves in novel contexts, they extend their relationships beyond primary village and kin networks. The expansion is generated by current experiences and common interests. It is articulated culturally within the idiomatic framework of an elaborate gift economy. Hence, the expansion of friendship networks is associated with a conversion of relations often initiated within a context of the commodity economy into relations defined in terms of an indigenous gift economy (see also Werbner, 1987).

The fact that gifts objectify valued social relationships needs to be taken into account in the analytic construction of social networks. Urban networks constructed on the basis of utilitarian economic models necessarily obscure the contrast between gifts and commodities. A more valid way of constructing a social network is to base it on the exchange of gifts as these are ranked within a specific culture. Since the ranking of gifts and services objectifies the ranking of valued relationships, this mode of network construction incorporates actors' own views of where their most valued relationships are to be found.

The 'Strength' of Friendship

Among Pakistani factory workers in the UK it is often men who dominate the choice of close family friends, and it is important, therefore, to examine the nature of friendship between men. Factory work side-by-side provides an important context in which close friendships are built up. The work experience is so fundamental to men's world view and sense of identity, and the time spent at work – many work twelve-hour shifts – so extensive, that work together becomes a powerful basis for trust and friendship. As men move, they make new friends, whilst retaining prior close friends. Ritual and ceremonial occasions serve to preserve and renew past, currently 'inactive' friendships. Friends and kin are scattered throughout the UK; in Manchester alone, although friends no longer share a workplace or neighbourhood and may see each other less, they nevertheless continue to regard each other as friends.

Pakistani migrants hold strong views regarding the duties of friendship, and distinguish clearly between close or true friends and more distant friends and acquaintances. Cultural standards of what constitutes the behaviour of a true friend are strictly defined. It follows that the granting of loans follows certain basic rules, although the details vary from person to person. Pakistanis often rely on personal loans for start-up capital, factory workers tending to rely more heavily on personal loans, traders on rotating credit associations. I was given several accounts of the rules governing the extension of loans by migrants who at the time were still factory workers. Several of them have since become businessmen in the garment industry. The loans are commonly extended on the basis of a verbal agreement and are rarely witnessed. The following account of loans between Pakistanis was given to me by an informant named Iftahar. At the time he was a factory worker, although he later became a successful manufacturer. (His account is similar to those given to Dahya (1974) by his informants in Bradford and Birmingham.) Iftahar explained:

> If a Pakistani needs money he can go to a relative or friend and asks him for £200 or £300 and he cannot be refused. Even if the friend has to borrow money in order to lend to him. Say he wanted to open a business. Only the time would be fixed – at one year. The lender would not go to him and ask for his money. It is up to the debtor to go to the creditor. The money is interest free [because this is our religion]. If a friend needs money he gives warning in advance that he will need some money some time in the future for some purpose. [According to Iftahar there is a limit to the sum a man will agree to lend.] A man can tell his friends frankly that he can't afford a thousand pounds, only three hundred pounds. It could be someone a man has worked with side-by-side for a number of years. It is a matter of trust. If a man dies his debt will be repaid by his son.

Loans are generally restricted in purpose: they are granted only for capital investment in a house or business, and for emergencies. They are not given for conspicuous consumption – for items such as furniture, electrical goods or cars (unless these are needed for business purposes). Traders sometimes grant each other short-term loans. By convention, however, loans are of one year's duration, but some migrants specify the time while others do not. Creditors usually wish to have the loan returned in a lump sum rather than in instalments which they may be tempted to spend. Borrowers prefer to obtain loans from friends rather than relatives. They give a number of reasons for this preference. First, it is easier to specify the time limit with a friend, and it is also less embarrassing to be refused. If a brother refuses to lend money, they say, it is much worse than if a friend refuses. Clearly, the contractual basis of a loan is acceptable among friends (and by implication, it is also easier to break off relations with a friend if he does not fulfil his obligations). Money causes friction between brothers. Secondly, although wives are usually consulted before loans are granted, they tend to be less involved when the loans are between friends, while loans given by relatives may get entangled in other family disputes and be raised by wives in the course of settling other accounts. Borrowing is thus kept separate from other transactional relations between kin. Thirdly, I was told, there is sometimes competition between close kin, and in such cases people do not like to provide them with too much information about their financial situation. Close friends can be trusted to be discreet and, indeed, it seems that the size of the loan, if not its purpose, is kept extremely private. Friendship between men is often valued above kin relations. The expectations of performance made of kinsmen are so high, and this, compounded by the density and complexity of affinal ties among Pakistanis, often leads to bitter quarrels. The case of Tariq demonstrates this.

Tariq came to the UK a few years after his younger brother. When he first arrived he lived as a lodger in his younger brother's house, and the latter had also found him a job in a large food manufacturing factory. Tariq had spent many years in the army and had travelled widely before coming to the UK. He began to explore the UK way of life independently of his brother. He struck up a friendship with Yassir, who had earlier been a lodger of his brother, before buying a house of his own. Yassir 'taught' Tariq to save, as he told me, and persuaded him to invest in his own house. He also took him to drink and play cards with other Pakistani men. Tariq's brother disapproved of what he regarded as this dissipated behaviour, and wrote back to Pakistan, where it greatly upset Tariq's wife. He also mobilised the brother of Tariq's wife, living in the UK, on his side. A family quarrel ensued. Tariq complained that he, as the older brother, had the authority to make decisions, and that his younger brother should apologise to him. At about this time, the wives and families of both Tariq and his brother arrived in the UK. Tariq's wife sided with her husband, despite the rumours about his behaviour, but she did not immediately quarrel with her sister-in-law. At first, the two women worked together in the same factory. Relations between them were strained, however, and eventually the two women did quarrel; Tariq's wife also argued with her brother, who had sided with Tariq's brother.

During the whole period, Tariq and Yassir and their wives remained very close friends, lent each other large sums of money and worked together as market traders when their factory closed down. Yassir had had a serious quarrel with Tariq's brother even before Tariq arrived in the UK. Indeed, when Tariq first came to Manchester, Yassir refused to talk to him. Tariq had approached Yassir, denying that he and his brother should be treated as one and the same. The friendship between the two men prospered, as the relations between Tariq and his brother cooled.

In one sense, loans between migrant may be seen to represent a type of restricted exchange *par excellence* – a dyadic contract between two parties based on strict reciprocity. Each loan may, however, generate further loans in a chain reaction, for in many cases the granting of a loan involves the lender in borrowing money from a third party, again on a long-term, interest-free basis. The consequent circulation of borrowed money establishes a complex system of credit and debt, founded upon the paramount moral obligation to lend. The perpetuation of the system depends on the complete trust that the loan will be returned, and I heard of no cases of defaulting.

This system of loans appears to take place among 'pools' of migrants, each pool constituting a field of potential friendships. The limits of the pool are the limits of acquaintance, based on three major contexts of recruitment: the factory, the neighbourhood and shared area of origin. Pakistani factory workers, like Pakistani neighbours and migrants from a single sub-district, tend to know one another, at least as casual acquaintances. This is demonstrated in both Iftahar's networks presented below, in which the network of acquaintances can be seen to be extremely dense and compact. It is the high density and reachability of Pakistani labour migrants' networks which generates the renewal and extension of an indigenously defined gift economy, as it evolved locally (see Chapter 9).

Properly speaking, loans cannot be regarded as 'gifts' since they constitute part of the infrastructure of economic relations between migrants, rather than the superstructure of symbolic exchanges of substance. What loaning does very importantly, however, is to convert individual commodity earnings into a 'pool' of circulating shared earnings. In other words, discrete individual workers are transformed through the mediation of the system of loans into a corporate 'brotherhood' with residual rights in each other's earnings. The ceremonial exchange system parallels the system of loans, reflecting this corporate sharing through exchanges of substance.

Alternatively, it may be argued that, although loans are extended in cash and assume the 'appearance' of commodities, they operate as gifts: they are personalised, based on the obligation to give, carry no interest and are part of a total set of prestations. They are extended without any signed contract or witnesses, and thus hinge on ongoing relations of mutual trust. Because they constitute the objective economic interdependency between migrants, men not surprisingly regard them as superior to ceremonial gifting as indices of friendship and loyalty.

Gift Exchange in an Urban Industrial Setting

Urban relations in modern industrial cities are characteristically segmental, and thus fundamentally incompatible with a gift economy and its 'totalising' features. Gifts are at the same time 'legal, economic, religious, aesthetic, morphological and so on': they thus 'embrace a large number of institutions' (Mauss, 1966, pp.76–7). They objectify relations between groups, not individuals. 'The persons represented in the contract are moral persons – clans, tribes and families,' (p.3). They are part of a 'system of exchange' not confined to a single context or event (p.6) and include a whole range of items (pp.11–12). Within this system the principle of like-for-like is a pervasive one. It circumscribes the apparent 'diffuseness' of obligations between kinsmen and friends. At the same time, however, the existence of one kind of reciprocal relationship implies the existence of other reciprocities as well: those who exchange women also trade with one another: friends who exchange dinners on certain key occasions also help one another in emergencies and attend each other's ceremonies. Ceremonial gifts, to use an alternative formulation, are thus diacritical objectifications or 'pivotal attributes' (Nadel, 1957, pp.32–3), implying a cluster of role attributes.

What persons give to, and receive from, each other is historically and culturally determined, in relation to their mutual roles and positions within society. Some transactions, and in particular ceremonial prestations, only exist as part of wider systems of exchange. Gifting is thus not simply personalised: it denotes social distance, juniority or seniority, dependence, trust and long-term or short-term obligation. A gift economy is not constituted by isolated or idiosyncratic exchanges between particular individuals, but through a set of expectations, a customary 'system of exchange' in Mauss's terms (1966, p.3).

In urban society, gift economies are encapsulated within a broader economy. Yet their significance should not be underestimated: gift economies may dominate familial and communal activities, setting apart urban sub-groups, and generating multiplex relationships and dense social network clusters. In its ceremonial form, the Pakistani gift economy is closely associated, as Gregory (1982) has argued, with social reproduction. Marriage, birth, *haqiqa* (a male rite of passage) and circumcision are thus pivotal occasions for the initiation and exchange of gifts. Weddings, in particular, are associated not only with a transfer of persons, but also with a vast and complex transfer of valuables and prestations which I describe more fully elsewhere (Werbner, 1987).

The explicit application of exchange theory to network analysis has hitherto been based on neo-classical economic models, with an associated stress on maximisation and individual strategy. The most thorough application has been by Kapferer (1972; also 1969; 1973) who provides a meticulously detailed network analysis of individual strategies and transactions in the more restricted context of an African factory. A less rigorous application has been that of Boissevain (1974), who discusses networks of friends in Malta. Although both scholars have shifted their approaches since, it is perhaps worth examining the limitations of neo-classical model application to network analysis. The most problematic feature of both Kapferer's and Boissevain's accounts relates to the assumption that all transactions are, by definition, equivalent and interchangeable. Individualist approaches obscure the cultural basis of social relationships, grounded in agreed definitions of exchangeable goods, ranked values, and resulting from flows of goods. They thus obviate the possibility of outlining 'cultures of exchange', seen as historically evolving systems.

Boissevain's account provides an instance of a valued service – intercession with bureaucrats and officialdom – which may be regarded as a key 'gift' in Malta, generating a society highly

dependent on social patronage and patron–client relationships.
The system of occupational favouritism appears, like the distribution of economic resources, to be self-perpetuating: those in
more highly valued and strategically placed occupational positions are able to dispense new positions of this kind to kin and
close friends. The perpetuation of class divisions is confirmed by
the continuous class basis of such factions for over a hundred
years. Yet this somewhat stagnant political-economic picture is
obscured by the use of a neo-classical model which focuses on
individuals and their strategies. In Kapferer's account the reader
is provided with few clues about the rank values ascribed by
workers to specific gifts or services, and about the resultant flow
of goods either within or outside the shop floor. For example, it
would be illuminating to know whether assistance with factory
tasks is regarded as a debt-generating 'gift', and thus part of a
'total' set of prestations extending beyond the factory boundaries
and encompassing other domains (ritual, kinship, political, etc.).
Because the cultural systematics of exchange remain obscure, network changes can only be assessed strategically: they have no
cultural or historical dimension.

With this in mind, I have attempted to utilise an alternative
application of exchange theory to network analysis. Among
Pakistanis in the UK, relationships between friends and kin are
objectified through elaborated transactions: the obligations and
expectations entailed by these roles are therefore complex and
explicit. Even 'acquaintances' – neighbours, workmates and business associates – are caught up in the gift exchange system in
specified ways. The elaboration of relationships is objectified by
flows of distinct kinds of goods, which constitute their 'pivotal
attributes'. It is possible to place these flows of goods and services along a hierarchy of valued services and transactions.
Before turning to a general discussion of this hierarchy, it is useful to examine in detail the social network of Iftahar, who was a
factory worker at the time the network was constructed.

Iftahar's Network: The Greeting Friends

The families in Iftahar's network were amongst the later arrivals
to Manchester, and the majority came from Jhelum district, with
a few coming from Mirpur and Gujar Khan. Most of the men in

these households had immigrated to the UK in the early 1960s.[1]
Some had moved to Manchester in search of work from other,
smaller towns in Yorkshire and Lancashire, leaving behind relatives in these places. They had come to the UK alone, as single or
recently married young men, often from the same area of origin
or with prior links with it. In the late 1960s and early 1970s, following changes in the immigration laws, they began to bring
their wives and families over to the UK and, at the beginning of
the research period in 1975, many of the families were recent
arrivals. Some young men had not yet married and, during the
following two years, were returning to Pakistan in order to
marry.

Compared to other Pakistani migrants in Manchester, most of
these migrants, and especially the wives and children, were newcomers to the city. Moreover, they came from relatively underdeveloped *barani* (rainfed agriculture) areas of the Punjab,
especially by comparison to East Punjab, the Canal Colonies and
the cities whence most other Pakistanis in Manchester originate.
The land in their districts (until the recent introduction of tube
wells) was unirrigated and infertile. The majority originated from
little villages of smallholders with a long tradition of service in
the army and the police. Even Jhelum city has, until very recently, remained underdeveloped and village-like in the eyes of
Punjabis from further south.

The families in Iftahar's network led a distinctive lifestyle,
recalling that of Pakistani migrants in Bradford and Rochdale
(Anwar, 1979; Dahya, 1974; Saifullah Khan, 1975). The genesis of
the present lifestyle of these migrants, and the type of networks
associated with it, lies in the relationships developed between
men, most often before the arrival of their wives. Wives have, on
the whole, continued to depend on the social networks formed
and managed by their husbands. This is the central, generative
aspect of their lifestyle. At the start of the research none of
Iftahar's friends had children of marriageable age, and this itself
was a crucial lifestyle determinant. They had not yet faced the
need to organise large-scale ceremonies, and most lived as

---

1. The network discussed here, which I knew well, was comprised mainly of migrants
from Jhelum sub-division in Pakistan. However, less extensive knowledge of families from
Mirpur and Gujar Khan sub-divisions suggests that they shared a similar lifestyle, depending
also upon whether they lived in the central residential cluster and how long their wives had
been in Manchester.

nuclear families in single households, sometimes with a resident cousin or nephew.

Migrants in Iftahar's network tend to share, or to have shared in the past, a number of contexts of association. From Network 1 (Figure 8.1) the overlap between area of origin, work and neighbourhood for members of his network can be inferred. In particular, close friends in the network appear to share or to have shared at least two of the three salient contexts of association with each other, unless they are kinsmen – in which case they are regarded as intimates even if they do not share these characteristics.

Friends shared in common were sometimes described as *dostan da kihale* (literally 'how are the friends?'). I therefore call these circles of male migrants 'greeting' friends. The friends referred to are those sharing mutual acquaintances and drawn from the dense acquaintance network of overlapping pools generated in specific associational contexts. The same expression is applied in Pakistan, I am told, to a peer group of young men who spend much of their leisure time together.

Network 1, based on the program NTVA, shows that of fifteen close friendships in Iftahar's network, eleven shared at least two contexts of association.[2] Of the four that shared only one context, all are kin. The observation can be made in diagrammatic form (Figure 8.2). Not all migrants who share more than one context of association become close friends, but this appears to be a prerequisite for the formation of close friendships – the development of a high degree of trust – between non-kin.

The reason for the overlap of acquaintances drawn from different contexts has to do with a number of factors. First, migrants from the same area of origin often buy houses near each other. Hence, when some migrants among Iftahar's friends (numbers 3–9, Network 2, Figure 8.3) left the central cluster, they chose to buy houses in a single area of east Longsight relatively close to one another. Several migrants from Jhelum district thus live in the neighbourhood which has a relatively small Asian population. Secondly, neighbours and acquaintances from the same area of origin vouch for each other at work. In the case of Iftahar's friends, many worked together in a single factory making artificial fibres. A job in this factory was much sought after, since the work was considered clean and easy, the hours convenient and

---

2. NTVA, NTAU and NDIS are programs devised by J. Clyde Mitchell.

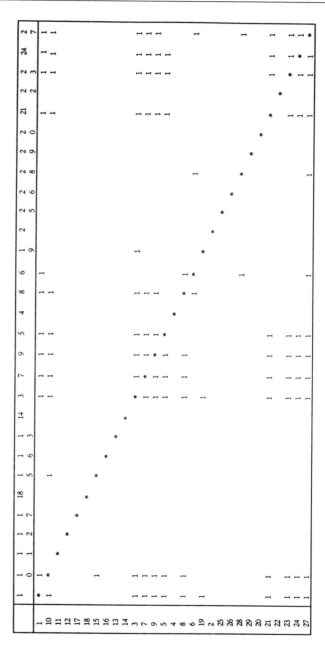

Figure 8.1 Network 1: Iftahar's Network – Multiplicity of Associations

(a) Worked Together in the UK or Pakistan

Note: For identity of case numbers (1 – 28) see Figure 8.3

(b) Neighbours in the UK (Past or Present)

Note: For identity of case numbers (1 – 28) see Figure 8.3

(c) Area of Origin

Note: For identity of case numbers (1 – 28) see Figure 8.3

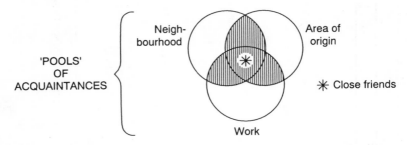

Figure 8.2 Pools of Acquaintances

the pay relatively high. Some workers had worked together previously in a food-processing factory which had a large Pakistani
workforce. Many of the men in the fibre factory came from
Jhelum district, although the man who first 'discovered' the factory, Moh, came from Faislabad (number 27, Network 2). He
vouched for his friend, Naim (number 10), who later brought
Iftahar, with the mediation of Choudry (number 19) and a mutual friend in Bolton. Iftahar had worked with Yassir (number 3) in
a factory in Jhelum where Choudry had been foreman. Yassir
was at the time a close friend of Tariq's brother (number 7) and
vouched for him, and later Tariq himself (number 5) was brought
in.

Usually the close friends of close friends – that is those in the
secondary zone of a person's close friendship network – are
known, but are regarded as distant friends or acquaintances; the
friends of acquaintances are usually, however, totally unknown,
unless they are members of a pool, who thus share the same context of association. It was striking that Iftahar's involvement in
the affairs of the wider community was extremely limited. This
was so even though it is possible in theory to trace indirect connections of two or three steps from him to some of the more
prominent members of the community (via number 27's business
partner to the professionals, via Choudry (number 19) to a similar
range of community leaders). While he seemed quite well
informed about public events surrounding the mosque, he and
his wife appeared to be virtually unaware of, and were rarely

Row labels (network members):

8. 7' wife
6. 5's wife
4. 3's wife
3. Yassir
5. Tariq
7. Tariq's bro.
9. Friend
24. Friend
23. Friend
19. Choudri
29. Friend
25. Rafiq
26. Rafiq's wife
28. Moh's wife
27. Moh
1. Iftahar
2. Iftahar's wife
17. Imtiaz
18. 17's wife
11. Naim's wife
14. 13's wife
15. 13's bro.
16. 15's wife
12. 10's neph.
13. 10's uncle
10. Naim
22. 21's wife
21. Friend
20. 19's wife

Measures for network	Including all links (1-9)	Including close friendship & marriage links only (8,9)
Index of Compactness	0.9811	0.4922
Overall Density	49.51	8.99
Maximum Finite Distance	3 steps	6 steps

Key: 9 = married; 8 = close friend (same sex); 7 = spouse of close friend; 6 = friend
5 = spouse of friend; 3 = former close friend with whom quarrel has occurred;
2 = uneasy friendship; 1 = acquaintance

Figure 8.3 Network 2: Iftahar's Network

invited to, the stream of weddings, *khatme quran* (domestic Koran readings), funerals and rotating credit societies which so preoccupied many of the migrants in the central cluster who lived nearby. This was true of most of his friends as well, especially those living outside the residential cluster.

The network matrix of Network 2, based on a NTAU program, shows the whole of Iftahar's social network, with the type of relationships indicated by a number, as indicated by the key to Figure 8.3 (there is no 4 value). The relationships are all treated as reciprocal, i.e. if Iftahar is a close friend of Yassir, Yassir is also a close friend of Iftahar. This means that the matrix above the diagonal is a mirror image of the matrix below the diagonal. The matrix below the diagonal has been marked to show the approximate boundaries of blocks of acquaintances and cliques.[3] The major block (A) is that of the acquaintances who live, or used to live, in the central residential cluster in West Longsight. A smaller block (B) is that of migrants currently living in East Longsight. Some of these form a clique around the two siblings who have quarrelled – Tariq and his brother. There is also a clique of migrants from East Africa (C). Within the larger set of acquaintances from the central cluster, there are two main cliques: of relatives (D), and of close friends on the road where Iftahar used to live (E). The meeting point of the two blocks (A) and (B) is a single factory where many of the migrants, including Iftahar, work or used to work. This is indicated in the rows marked F.

Program NTAU does not provide measures of density and compactness. These are given by program NDIS. According to NDIS, the density of Iftahar's network when all acquaintances, as well as friendships and marriages, are taken into account, is very high at 49.51. Compactness (reachability) is also high at 0.9811, while the maximum number of steps it takes for any one member of his network to reach another is low, being only three (8 is unknown to Iftahar). By contrast, the compactness of the network of close friends and spouses (i.e. when relations of lesser value are excluded) is much lower (0.4992), while density is also very low (8.99). This low density in the networks of close friends contrasts with the much higher density found amongst professionals.

3. A clique is a set of actors in which each is linked to the other completely, i.e. all possible links exist. By contrast, in a cluster some individuals may not be linked to others.

The only cliques of which Iftahar and his wife are members were formed during their residence in the central cluster. The cliques in the network are composed of either immediate neighbours (1,10,17 and 1,10,13 and their wives) or relatives (10,12,13,15 and their wives) (see Figure 8.4). Apart from the latter clique of kin, no clique is composed of more than three couples. The women's cliques are clearly a reflection of their husband's cliques, and in some situations conjugal pairs must therefore be regarded as forming a single clique. Among the Pakistani elite, cliques of close friends tend to be somewhat larger, given their more frequent participation in ceremonial events together.

Iftahar's current local network thus reflects 'layers' of his social involvement in different places and contexts in Manchester. Key events, such as life cycle celebrations, enable Pakistanis to renew links forged in these different contexts of association, and the transaction of gifts on such key occasions sustains the momentum of friendships over time. Although there are many types of gifts and services, the gift of sweets (*mithai*) is perhaps the most universal.

The Gift of Sweets

For Pakistanis, the gift of Asian sweetmeats is an important marker of transition. At weddings and *haqiqa* ceremonies, visiting between affines and between hosts and guests is marked by sweet-gifting, so that dozens of boxes are distributed during the

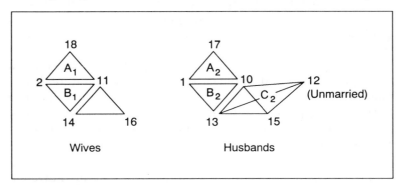

Figure 8.4 Cliques in Iftahar's Network

various ceremonials. The simplest offering consists of sweets or
fruit, and these may substitute for more elaborate offerings.
Hence, when a child completes reading the Koran for the first
time, usually at afternoon Koran lessons, sweets are distributed
by the child among the children present. Often on the festival of
Eid zoha, if people have not slaughtered an animal, they carry
boxes of sweets with them on their rounds of visiting instead.
When a woman finishes reading the Koran on her own, she celebrates by distributing sweets among the members of her family.
When a child is born, boxes of sweets are distributed by his or
her parents to all their friends living locally. The range of distribution is often the widest possible, and includes the proprietors
of shops where a person is a regular customer, workmates,
neighbours and other relatively distant acquaintances, as well as
close friends and relatives. By tradition, the sweets distributed
on this occasion were of a single round type known as *laddu*.
Some people still only send *laddu* at birth, explaining that it
allows them to discriminate between closer and more distant relatives and friends. Most Pakistanis in Manchester prefer to send
everyone a similar box containing a variety of different types of
sweets. This custom of sending *laddu* is celebrated by everyone –
even by those emigrants who perform few domestic rituals locally. Although the custom is supposed to be followed only for
newborn sons, in Manchester sweets are often sent when daughters are born, and especially in the case of a first child. The
costs incurred may be very high, but the recipients are usually
expected to reciprocate with a gift (usually cash) for the newborn
baby.

The custom of sending boxes of Asian sweetmeats at the birth
of a child serves to re-establish past links in a symbolic way. An
examination of one such list of recipients reveals the temporal
'layers' of a migrant's social network, of both 'active' and 'dor-
mant' friendships. Yassir, one of the earliest of the Jhelum
migrants, arrived in the UK in 1960. His wife joined him about a
year later, which was unusually soon. Before she came he worked
in Rochdale for a year and was befriended there by a man from
Lyallpur (Faisalabad) who 'taught him everything about Britain'.
Yassir's relatives in Slough did not like the idea of his living on
his own where there were no men from Jhelum. They persuaded
him to join them in London. He did not like London, however,
and after a few months returned north and found a job in a small

Lancashire town. There he bought a house which he let to tenants. His wife joined him but after a year she went home, feeling isolated as the only woman among men. In 1972 she joined him a second time and , after several years, Yassir moved to Manchester where he had some relatives and neighbours from his village in Pakistan. They first lived in West Longsight (near some of their relatives) in the residential enclave, but later move to East Longsight. When his third son was born, Yassir sent sweets to the following people:

1 Iftahar, his close friend and co-worker in both Jhelum and Manchester.
2 Tariq, a very close friend whose brother had been Yassir's landlord in Manchester and whose village in Pakistan was only ten miles away from Yassir's. They were trying to start as market traders together.
3 Friends and lodgers in the small Lancashire town where Yassir had lived and owned a lodging house.
4 An Indian friend who was also a wholesaler and was helping Yassir get started as a market trader.
5 A former neighbour and female friend of Yassir's wife from West Longsight.
6 A former co-worker in a factory where he worked in 1965, who was also a neighbour in West Longsight and remained a close friend.
7 One close family of relatives from the same *biraderi* (extended kin-group) and village of origin. They lived in north Manchester but were not seen very often.
8 A close relative living in Yassir's former neighbourhood who was also from the same area in Pakistan.
9 Two brothers, one living in Whalley Range and the other in Charlton, both of whom were market traders.
10 Choudry, who had been the foreman in Yassir's factory in Jhelum and was a 'man of reputation'.
11 A current neighbour who served with Yassir in the army and came from the same area.
12 Someone Yassir described as his 'best friend' whose relatives lived in a village one mile from Yassir's and who was on good terms with his family back home. He ran a taxi rank and Yassir gave sweets to the other drivers as well.
13 The friend from Lyallpur (Faislabad). Yassir travelled to Rochdale to give him the sweets.

14 Three other single men with whom he had made friends in different factories in Manchester.
15 Two families in Yassir's village (though not from his *biraderi*) living in Longsight.
16 The English saleswoman in Yassir's shop.
17 The school friends of Yassir's children.

Yassir did not send sweets to his numerous relatives in London. This was because they lived too far away for the sweets to be delivered personally.

The time depth of migrant's networks extends as far back as the years in Pakistan before their immigration to the UK. Most migrants have a prior history of labour migration and have therefore usually spent time in a number of different areas and workplaces in Pakistan. Iftahar had spent many years in Faislabad and Jhelum working in factories, while Yassir had grown up partly as a refugee in Indian Kashmir and also in two villages in Gujrat and Mirpur. Mirpur, Jhelum and Gujrat are adjacent districts. Many migrants had relatives in more than one district. Moreover, the dialect spoken is very similar in all of them. However, while Iftahar may be considered an 'honorary' member of the Jhelum 'pool' of migrants, he lacks the density of links held by those migrants who were born and brought up in the small villages around Jhelum town, where they still maintain active ties. This makes his position within a network of Jhelum men less straightforward than that of Yassir or Tariq, for example.

The Hierarchy of Exchange

Social networks are implicitly constructed upon a 'concentric circles' view of friendship (Boissevain, 1974; Epstein, 1969a; 1969b; Kapferer, 1972). This view posits that an individual's acquaintances and friends – all those who belong in the primary zone of the social network – may be classed according to the 'closeness' of their relationship with ego. The attempt is to define the variable 'strength' of network ties (Granovetter, 1973), and closeness is defined by different operational measures, most commonly by the frequency of interaction between network members or the 'multiplex' relations they manage in different contexts of association (Mitchell, 1969; sometimes multiplex relations are defined as relations combining 'instrumental' and 'emotional' or 'associational' ties).

A 'concentric' network metaphor is a means of representing social relations on a scale of relative value, a scale often implicit in the people's own classifications and taxonomies. For Pakistanis the gift economy is modelled, in Manchester as in Pakistan, on relations between kin and the services associated with close kinship. In the context of migration these have been extended to embrace a wide range of non-kin; new acquaintances class one another and identify themselves during early encounters as 'home' people, kin, workmates, neighbours, potentially close friends or mere acquaintances, and future behaviour is anticipated and judged accordingly.

The expectations from acquaintances – whether neighbours, co-workers or business associates – differ from those obtaining between friends and kin in their degree of *elaboration*, the relative *value* of obligations incurred and the *deferment* of reciprocation allowed.[4] Like friends, however, acquaintances also tend to have intrinsically multiplex relations. Because they help with minor economic transactions and participate in rituals (mainly funerals), their support may be enlisted in political and factional disputes. They also tend to meet rather frequently on a casual basis, at work or in the neighbourhood. Multiplexity or frequency of interaction are thus inadequate indices of social distance. Value, as Gregory (1982) stresses, is ordinally rather than quantitatively determined.

The gift economy focuses around key rituals and ceremonials in which social distance is publicly proclaimed. Because of the common kinship model they share, the symbolic significance of services and gifts extended during such events is widely understood and shared. They form the basis of a value ranking system. Close friendship, whether forged in the workplace or the neighbourhood, is not determined by its recruitment base, for it stems from relationships developed in a variety of contexts. It transcends the roles of neighbours and workmates and subsumes the expectations surrounding 'friendship'. If the relationship between neighbours or workmates changes to friendship, the complexity of expectations and the scale of social exchanges inevitably increases. Kinsmen may also increase the value and

---

4. Bloch (1973) discusses the implications of long-term and short-term obligations. He assumes, however, that each type of obligation is associated with a distinct kind of relationship. This is only partially correct, since those who incur long-term obligations also tend to incur short-term ones – usually involving the transaction of different goods. A refusal to discharge these short-term obligations may also damage the continuity of the relationship.

scale of their mutual social interaction and come to regard themselves as 'close kinsmen'. This involves an increase both in levels of exchange, and in the degree of recognition and acceptance of joint responsibility. As Vatuk (1972) has noted, in towns distant kinsmen living nearby are regarded as close, while kin networks beyond the city contract.

The most highly valued transactions only occur within an inner circle of close kin, who also engage in less valued transactions open to a wider and less select class of persons. Similarly, the network 'role' of friends, while being less elaborate than that of close kin, is still relatively elaborated and encompasses some of the less valued expectations and customary transactions characteristic of relations between neighbours and workmates.[5] This hierarchy of exchanges has evolved in Manchester in response to current circumstances and currently scarce resources, but the diacritical goods and services objectifying relationships are often ceremonial gifts and other acts which have been transferred from Pakistan and derive their meaning partly from the way these acts are performed there. The level of performance expresses the nature of the relationship as it is currently perceived ('he is like a brother to me').

While most of ego's relationships may be placed on a ranked continuum, relations within the three-generational family are qualitatively demarcated from the rest: they hold joint property, are jointly responsible for elders and minors, hold ritual events together and share a joint reputation. For Manchester Pakistanis, the immediate family, the 'house' (*ghar*) is, in Mauss's terms, the moral group which is represented in ceremonial or gift exchanges. There are thus important distinctions to be made within the kindred itself, while kin and friends overlap in respect of the types of exchange they conduct with one another, and the level of performance.

Finally, it is important to stress that the transaction of gifts amongst Pakistani workers takes place in the sight of, or within the context of, pools of acquaintances. Levi-Strauss has stressed the brittle nature of dyadic exchanges (1969, pp.441–8). High-density networks allow for indirect communication and the pooling or sharing of information and resources. Most gift transactions take place in public, in the context of communal

5. Nadel comments that it is 'doubtful if such descriptions as 'friend' ... refer to roles proper, at least in societies where these positions are not conventionalized and in some degree "elaborated"', (1957, p.27). I argue that among Pakistanis such roles are indeed conventionalised.

feasting; alternatively, they precipitate chain transactions. Moreover, the form and context of gift exchanges is generated by specific cultural or inter-subjective understandings. It extends to strangers and newcomers, enabling their incorporation into local sets of friends and kin.

Conclusion

Pakistani factory workers in Manchester are commodity producers, individual wage-earners within a capitalist economy. Yet they conceive of these earnings as in some senses open to claims by morally recognised fellow workers. Through the transaction of valued gifts and services they convert contractual relationships into morally binding ones. In doing so, they follow culturally specific and mutually recognised forms of exchange. The services they exchange are ranked in value in response to current requirements, yet the idiom of gift exchanges is a development of the customary Punjabi Muslim exchange system.

Gifting 'totalises' relationships. One type of exchange implies others as well. Through gifting, migrants transform persons who are strangers into lifelong friends. Through such exchanges not only men, but whole households and entire extended families, are linked, and exchanges initiated on the shop floor extend into the domestic and inter-domestic domain.

Bibliography

Anwar, M., *The Myth of Return: Pakistanis in Britain*, London: Heinemann, 1979

Bloch, M., 'The Long Term and the Short Term: The Economic and Political Significance of the Morality of Kinship', in *The Character of Kinship*, J. Goody (ed.), Cambridge: Cambridge University Press, 1973

Boissevain, J., *Friends of Friends: Manipulators and Coalitions*, Oxford: Basil Blackwell, 1974

Dahya, B., 'The Nature of Pakistani Ethnicity in Industrial Cities in Britain', in *Urban Ethnicity*, ASA Monographs no.12, A. Cohen (ed.), London: Tavistock, 1974

Epstein, A.L., 'The Network and Urban Social Organisation', in *Social Networks in Urban Situations*, J.C. Mitchell (ed.), Manchester: Manchester University Press, 1969a

_____, 'Gossip, Norms and Social Networks', in *Social Networks in Urban Situations*, J.C. Mitchell (ed.), Manchester: Manchester University Press, 1969b

Granovetter, M.S., 'The Strength of Weak Ties', *American Journal of Sociology*, vol.78, no.6, 1973, pp.1360–80

Gregory, C.A., *Gifts and Commodities*, London: Academic Press, 1982

Jacobson, D., *Itinerant Townsmen: Friendship and Social Order in Urban Uganda*, Menlo Park, Ca.: Cummings, 1973

Kapferer, B., 'Norms and the Manipulation of Relationships in the Work Context', in *Social Networks in Urban Situations*, J.C. Mitchell (ed.), Manchester: Manchester University Press, 1969

_____, *Strategy and Transaction in an African Factory*, Manchester: Manchester University Press, 1972

_____, 'Social Network and Conjugal Roles in Urban Zambia: Towards a Reformulation of the Bott Hypothesis', in *Network Analysis: Studies in Human Interaction*, J. Boissevain and J.C. Mitchell (eds), The Hague: Mouton, 1973

Levi-Strauss, C., *The Elementary Structures of Kinship*, revised edn, London: Social Science paperbacks in association with Eyre and Spottiswoode, 1969

Mauss, M., *The Gift*, London: Cohen & West, 1966

Mayer, P., *Townsmen and Tribesmen*, Cape Town: Oxford University Press, 1961

Mitchell, J.C., 'Introduction', in *Social Networks in Urban Situations*, J.C. Mitchell (ed.), Manchester: Manchester University Press, 1969

Nadel, S.F., *The Theory of Social Structure*, London: Cohen & West, 1957

O'Flaherty, W.D., *Women, Androgynes and Other Mythical Beasts*, Chicago: Chicago University Press, 1980

Saifullah Khan, V., 'Asian Women in Britain: Strategies of Adjustment of Indian and Pakistani Migrants', in *Women in Contemporary India*, A. de Souza (ed.), New Delhi: Manohar, 1975

Vatuk, S., *Kinship and Urbanization: White Collar Migrants in North India*, Berkeley: University of California Press, 1972

Werbner, P. 'Business on Trust: Pakistani Entrepreneurship in the Manchester Garment Trade', in *Ethnic Communities in Business: Strategies for Economic Survival*, R. Ward and R. Jenkins (eds), Cambridge: Cambridge University Press, 1984

_____, 'Enclave Economies and Family Firms: the Case of Manchester Pakistanis', in *Migration, Labour and Social Order*, ASA Monographs no.25, J.S. Eades (ed.), London: Tavistock, 1987

Chapter 9

Social Networks of Pakistanis in the UK: A Re-evaluation

Muhammad Anwar

Since the publication of a study of Pakistani social networks in *The Myth of Return: Pakistanis in Britain* (Anwar, 1979), several developments have taken place in relation to Pakistanis in the UK. First, I will take a brief look at some of these developments. Second, I will concentrate on Pakistanis in Rochdale, the site of the original study, and examine how their networks have changed over a decade. I follow the same methods and techniques in 1985, when the cases were restudied, as for the earlier work in the mid-1970s.

Migration and Settlement

The migration of Pakistanis to the UK can be explained in terms of colonial links, political freedom of movement and an economic 'push' and 'pull' which slowly developed into a 'chain migration'. The immigrants left Pakistan in order to return home with money to buy land and build better houses and to raise their economic and social status. The only exceptions were some professionals, for example doctors, who first came to the UK to improve their qualifications, but settled here. Therefore, for most Pakistanis the economic incentive to migrate was clearly the major one.

Information about better wages and job opportunities was transmitted through relatives and friends. There were also necessary and sufficient conditions to start the chain migration process. Pioneer migrants decisively influenced those who followed, by their letters, visits and remittances home, demonstrating the economic opportunities. One of the characteristics of the Pakistani mass migration was that these following migrants were given financial assistance by way of sponsorship to help pay the fare when necessary. They were also given hospitality on arrival, in terms of accommodation, meals and help in looking for a job, by the established migrants. This means that a majority of Pakistanis came to the UK using their kinship-friendship networks before the immigration restrictions, and even after the Commonwealth Act of 1962 (Anwar, 1979).

The settlement patterns of Pakistanis in different towns, or on a smaller scale within towns, on the basis of their home origins came about as a result of the kin-friend chain migration. The importance of kinship-friendship networks becomes clear when analysing the persistence of ethnic values and norms among the Pakistanis in the UK. It appears that Pakistani settlement has reached a stage where their communities are structurally, socially and culturally distinctive. The Pakistani chain migration process has contributed to the building up of interconnected communities. The role of social networks of sponsorship and patronage in the formation of Pakistani communities in the UK and the process involved therefore form an important part of the study of Pakistani ethnicity.

Most of the ethnic facilities and services provided by Pakistanis are generally found in the areas of their concentration. Within a typical area, in Rochdale for example, there are streets which are predominantly Pakistani. This provides opportunities to interact with each other on a daily basis. The lifestyle in some areas is similar to a village in Pakistan, except that there are more modern amenities in the UK. Visits to each other's houses are quite frequent. By living in a 'Pakistani' area they all know each other at least by name, and people exchange greetings and often stop and talk to each other in the streets. In addition to a strong kinship-friendship and neighbourhood base, Pakistanis share a religious and cultural background. These characteristics lead to a sense of community among Pakistanis in the UK. Mutual aid and physical and emotional support in times of need seem to be part of the way of life. Regular meeting places include Pakistani shops, mosques, supplementary schools and ordinary schools with a significant number of Pakistani children. The situation as a whole leads to multiplex relations and a close-knit community in such areas. Among many, it is not felt necessary to deal with the indigenous people due to the availability of ethnic facilities. This may be reinforced by a perception of external hostility which Pakistanis face, particularly as a result of reactions to developments such as the Rushdie Affair. These facilities and feelings clearly have an impact on the ethnicity of Pakistanis, lead to internal cohesion, and reduce the chances of interpersonal relations across ethnic boundaries.

Social Networks

The kinship networks are a major element in the operation of the Pakistani community. In Pakistani society the extended family is very significant. The extra-familial networks are also very important. These types of relationships are known as *biraderi* in Pakistani society, and they affect the whole flow of goods and services.

Relationships of Pakistanis in the UK tend to be multiplex, within kin-based 'clusters', and they encapsulate them from non-kin and the wider society (Anwar, 1979). These may not be face-to-face relationships. Mitchell (1969) refers to such relationships as intense links, with people at home maintained by migrants, in which both sides continue to honour obligations. He argues that frequency of contact is not a significant criterion for the durability and intensity of such relationships. The continuing ties with people in Pakistan are important to consider in describing the migrants' total relations.

Regardless of where Pakistanis live or how the immediate residential group is composed, the structural rules for the Pakistani family are: (1) joint and extended-type family; (2) patrilineal group; (3) patrilocal residential rule; (4) patriarchal authority and respect related to age and sex; and (5) preferential marriage patterns which lead to kinship networks in the wider sense. The questions arises, what structural and functional changes have taken place in Pakistani families in the UK?

In order to understand Pakistani social networks it is necessary to study the complete pattern of kinship networks, and not simply the relationships within the elementary family itself. In the Pakistani kinship system, the type of relationships and levels of contact, obligation and behaviour towards kin determine the flow of services. The social networks involving kin are found to be multi-stranded. From the point of view of choice of residence, job selection, reciprocal services and other related matters in Pakistani families, the *biraderi* networks play an important role. In fact, the whole way of life of Pakistanis is directly or indirectly related to this institution. It is the function of *biraderi* as a kinship and friendship ground which is relevant to the UK context: how it helps the individual Pakistani in the process of migration and settlement through mutual support, and how it forces them together as part of Pakistani communities. *Biraderi* plays an important role in the mobilisation of Pakistanis in the UK.

Major activities related to *biraderi* consist of members giving each other financial aid and goods of value, and a wide range of services at specific times and under certain conditions (see Chapter 8). Kinship networks assist with the settlement, the achievement of status and the occupational advance of member families and individual members. However, some services are provided by the *biraderi* on specific occasions – including births, circumcisions, weddings, deaths, accidents, disasters and personal troubles. A sense of moral obligation to give services or acknowledge one's kin in a manner appropriate to the occasion exists among Pakistanis in the UK. Turning to *biraderi* when in trouble before using other agencies established for such purposes is the rule rather than the exception in Pakistani families. Frequent visits, messages and letters keep the *biraderi* members in contact and up-to-date. Sometimes hundreds and, in the case of Pakistanis in the UK, even thousands of miles are travelled to attend ritual functions of the close members of the *biraderi*. *Biraderi* networks are also used to find jobs and in starting and running businesses.

Friendship ties tend to rest on free choice and affection, neighbourhood ties on face-to-face contacts, and kinship networks on relatively permanent relations. There is no reason why all these primary groups could not overlap – friends may be neighbours and kin members at the same time. As kin are considered more reliable than mere friends, close friends are generally sought inside the *biraderi*. This seems to be the pattern among Pakistanis in the UK. There is a high degree of cohesion within the group which contains these overlapping networks. The relationships tend to be diffuse, the same individuals who are related to one another by one set of interests are also related to numbers of others.

One system which extends to all these relationships in Pakistani society is the mechanism of gift exchange known as *vartan bhanji*, which is widely practised in the Punjab. The term means 'an exchange of gifts', and also refers to the gifts so exchanged: it denotes the relationship between people established through this exchange (Eglar, 1961).

The ties which UK Pakistanis maintain with their kin group can broadly be grouped as, firstly, obligations which the migrants should fulfil towards their relatives in Pakistan, and secondly, the migrants' economic ties with Pakistan through property they own and which is mainly looked after by their relatives in Pakistan. The obligations of kinship in Pakistan extend beyond the man's wife and children, and include his parents, in some cases grandparents, siblings and even cousins, uncles and aunts. The migrant is expected to earn, save and send money back to Pakistan to support his family and invest there. The majority of Pakistanis covered in my study supported their joint/extended families back home and had also invested in Pakistan – bought or built houses, purchased land and in some cases, started small business, usually power-looms or towel-making industries (Anwar, 1979).

It is clear from my studies of Pakistanis in the UK that migration does not necessarily detach the migrant from kin ties and obligations to them in Pakistan. Therefore, to understand the relationship and behaviour of Pakistanis in the UK it is important that the Pakistani end is not forgotten. The obligations which migrants are supposed to fulfil, and the regular contacts they keep with relatives in Pakistan through letters, messages and visits, are a reminder of what their relatives expect of them. There is no discontinuity of relationships with Pakistan. However, the nature and frequency of these relationships is certainly changing with the passage of time.

The National Demographic and Social Picture

The present number of Pakistanis in the UK is 475,800 (OPCS, 1992a). The primary immigration has now completely stopped and only the reunification of families (i.e. dependants' entry) is being allowed. Therefore, the increase in numbers in the past two decades is mainly due to this secondary migration and also due to those children who are born in the UK to Pakistani parents already settled here. Pakistanis are still concentrated in certain parts of the country. The 1991 census shows that 31 per cent of them live in London and the South East, and nearly two-thirds live in the conurbations of the West Midlands (22 per cent), Yorkshire and Humberside (19.9 per cent), and the North West (16.5 per cent). There is also a concentrated Pakistani community in the Central Clydeside conurbation (4 per cent), mainly in Glasgow. The settlement pattern of Pakistanis in different towns, or on a smaller scale within towns, on the basis of their home origin is not a chance phenomenon. It came about as a result of the kin-friend chain migration as explained above.

As evidenced in earlier years, there is still a relatively high ratio of men to women. In 1961, 82 per cent of the Pakistani population was male, falling to 58 per cent in 1982, which was nevertheless still above the level of the general population, at 48 per cent (Brown, 1984). According to the 1990 *Labour Force Survey* there were 52 per cent males and 48 per cent females among Pakistanis (OPCS, 1992b). Clearly, one important reason for this change in recent years is the arrival of wives and children of those settled here.

The Pakistani population is much younger than the indigenous population. It is estimated that a little over 40 per cent of Pakistanis are under sixteen years old, compared with 22 per cent of the general population. For those aged under twenty-five, Pakistanis account for over 50 per cent compared with 35 per cent for the general population. At the same time, there are relatively few elderly people among Pakistanis. It is worth noting that almost half of UK Pakistanis are born in this country. This is clearly changing the needs and priorities of the community, with more emphasis on the second-generation Pakistanis.

The employment patterns of Pakistanis since 1979 generally have not changed all that much in relation to their concentrations in certain industrial sections. As far as job levels of Pakistanis are concerned, the 1982 survey referred to above showed that only 10 per cent were in the professional (employers and management) category, compared to 19 per cent of whites. Apart from 8 per cent in other non-manual categories (23 per cent for whites) other Pakistanis were in manual categories, mostly unskilled or semi-skilled. A vast majority of Pakistanis are still employed on shift work. They also work in 'ethnic work groups' in a few mills in some locations, as they have done in the last thirty years. But the number of self-employed Pakistanis is growing.

However, due to the general economic recession, unemployment among Pakistanis has increased recently. This is also following the general trend that ethnic minorities suffer disproportionately from unemployment. Most Pakistanis still work in the manufacturing sections of industry, and, as these are particularly hard-hit by the recession, the effect on Pakistanis is greater when compared with white workers. The textile industry is a good example of this point. In the early 1970s over 20 per cent of Pakistanis were working in textiles, compared with only 2 per cent of the general population. There is also the fact of racial discrimination which Pakistanis, like other ethnic minorities, face in employment, leading to higher unemployment rates. Pakistani school-leavers in particular are finding it difficult, like other ethnic minority youth, to find jobs (Anwar, 1982). Their unemployment rate is normally double that of white young people.

Most Pakistanis are now UK citizens. Their participation in the civic life of the UK has increased. The registration of Pakistanis on the electoral register has increased in the last decade, as have their rates of turn-out; these are now higher than for white voters (Anwar, 1986). The number of Pakistanis standing for parliamentary and local elections for the main political parties has also increased in the last fifteen years, as has the number of elected councillors. At least four of them have become mayors in recent years.

Several developments have taken place in the last few years regarding activities within the Pakistani community. Some new local, regional and national social and welfare Pakistani organisations have been formed. There are also several organisations now serving exclusively people who come from Azad Kashmir. For religious facilities many new purpose-built mosques have been completed in Birmingham, Bradford, Glasgow, London, Watford and Kingston, to mention a few. New community centres and supplementary schools have been started in some areas to meet the religio-cultural needs of the community. The emphasis is now very much to facilitate the religio-cultural education of second-generation Pakistanis in addition to their formal schooling.

The Rochdale Scene

The national developments mentioned above equally apply to Pakistanis in Rochdale. However, I would like to mention some significant demographic changes to put the subsequent discussion in its proper context. According to the 1981 census, 5.2 per cent of Rochdale's population lived in households where the head of household was born in the New Commonwealth and Pakistan (details are given in Table 9.1). The majority of those born in India (as shown in Table 9.1) are in fact Pakistanis who migrated to Pakistan in 1947 (see Anwar, 1974). It is clear from these data that there are still a greater number of Pakistani men than women, contrary to the trend for the general population.

Like the findings in the 1970s, the Pakistani population is still concentrated in five wards. Wardleworth and Smallbridge and Central and Falinge wards have the highest number of Pakistani residents (see Table 9.2). Pakistanis are concentrated in a small

Table 9.1 Ethnic Groups in Rochdale, 1981, Based on Country of Birth

	Total	Male	Female
All countries of birth	206,331	100,680	105,651
United Kingdom	192,920	93,438	99,472
Irish Republic	3,299	1,628	1,671
Old Commonwealth	281	144	137
New Commonwealth	2,780	1,649	1,131
East Africa	459	224	235
Rest of Africa	90	60	30
Caribbean	226	150	76
India	1,050	634	416
Bangladesh	545	369	176
Far East	205	100	105
Mediterranean	151	81	70
Remainder	54	31	23
Pakistan	4,058	2,315	1,743
New Commonwealth & Pakistan	6,838	3,964	2,874

Note: The majority of those born in India are in fact Pakistanis who migrated to Pakistan in 1947 (see Anwar, 1974)
Source: 1981 Census of Population, County Report, Greater Manchester; usually resident population by country of birth and sex (100% sample)

Table 9.2 Wards in Rochdale with Above-average NCWP Population, 1981

	NCWP (%)
Brimod & Deepfish	12.2
Central & Falinge	26.4
Newbold	14.8
Smallbridge & Wardleworth	21.9
Spotland	5.9

Note: NCWP = New Commonwealth & Pakistan Population

number of areas in Rochdale, and this facilitates their social networks. The 1991 census, which included an ethnic question (Anwar, 1990), shows that 7.9 per cent of Rochdale's population belonged to all ethnic minorities, and 5.5 per cent were Pakistanis. This indicates that just over 11,000 Pakistanis lived in Rochdale in 1991 (see Table 9.3 for details).

The housing tenure patterns for Pakistanis have not changed much since the 1970s, and owner-occupation is still very high compared with the general population. For example, in Central and Falinge wards, almost 80 per cent of Pakistani dwellings

Table 9.3 Ethnic Group Composition of Rochdale, 1991

OPCS ethnic group	Population (× 1000)	Percentage of total	Percentage of minorities
White	186.2	92.1	–
All minorities	15.9	7.9	100.0
Black – Caribbean	0.4	0.2	2.5
Black – African	0.2	0.1	1.3
Black – Other	0.4	0.2	2.5
Indian	0.8	0.4	5.0
Pakistani	11.1	5.5	69.8
Bangladeshi	1.6	0.8	10.1
Chinese	0.4	0.2	2.5
Other – Asian	0.4	0.2	2.5
Other – Other	0.6	0.3	3.8
Total population	202.2	100.0	

Source: 1991 Census Monitor for Greater Manchester

were owner-occupied, compared with 44 per cent for the general population (Table 9.4). In Smallbridge and Wardleworth wards the level of Pakistani owner-occupation was almost 85 per cent, contrasted with the general population, of which only 46.8 per cent were in this tenure category (Table 9.5).

The situation in employment has deteriorated for Pakistanis since the 1970s survey. A local Community Relations Council employment survey in 1983–4 found that unemployment among Asian males (mainly Pakistanis) was 43 per cent, compared with 18 per cent for the general population. Unemployment among young people was especially high. Another survey conducted in

Table 9.4 Ethnic Group Housing Tenure in Central & Falinge Ward, Rochdale, 1981

	General population (% households)	NCWP population (% households)
Owner-occupied	44.0	77.9
Council	43.8	13.2
Housing association	2.0	0.5
Rented	10.2	8.4

Note: NCWP = New Commonwealth and Pakistan Population (in Rochdale, mostly Pakistanis)
Source: Small Area Statistics, 1981 census; special tables prepared for the Commission for Racial Equality

Table 9.5 Ethnic Group Housing Tenure in Smallbridge & Wardleworth Ward, Rochdale, 1981

	General population (% households)	NCWP population (% households)
Owner-occupied	46.8	82.9
Council	45.0	10.4
Housing association	1.2	1.4
Rented	7.0	5.3

Note: NCWP = New Commonwealth and Pakistan population (mostly Pakistanis in Rochdale)
Source: Small Area Statistics, 1981 census; special tables prepared for the Commission for Racial Equality

the autumn of 1986 showed that 51.7 per cent of Asian males (mainly Pakistani) were unemployed, compared with 12.8 per cent of non-Asians (Penn, Scattergood and Martin, 1990). The survey also found low levels of training and low levels of educational qualifications among Pakistanis. There is also persistent direct and indirect discrimination which affects the employment training prospects of Pakistanis.

On top of this, the large fall in employment in textiles between 1973 and 1985 and the reduction of night-shift work has made the employment situation of Pakistanis worse. The largest employer in town, Rochdale Borough Council, employs very few Pakistanis. This situation forced some Pakistanis to move out of Rochdale to search for other opportunities, and, as a consequence, several of them used their social networks to move to other towns and cities, including some in Scotland.

Pakistani organisations continued to play an important role in elections (Anwar, 1985), but they did not manage a breakthrough in terms of electoral representation. At the time of writing there was only one Pakistani councillor representing the Labour Party. *Biraderi* and kinship-friendship networks continued to play an important role in politics and other spheres of life.

Social Networks of Pakistanis in Rochdale

Since my study of Pakistanis in Rochdale in the early 1970s I have kept in touch with the community generally, and in particular with the twenty 'cases' studied in depth. In 1985 I went back to examine how their networks had changed. By 1985 at least four cases had moved out of Rochdale, and therefore sixteen cases were restudied. Since I did not live in the area in 1985 the fieldwork was completed over a three-month period.

It appears from the analyses, both ethnographic and statistical, that *biraderi* and *vartan bhanji* still played a significant role in the lives of Pakistanis (Anwar, 1985). Intensity of a Pakistani network with kin-*biraderi* members is likely to be greater than that with another Pakistani who is not *biraderi* but lives in the same street and comes from the same area of Pakistan. This is partly due to the obligations attached to the kin-*biraderi* members in Rochdale, in other parts of the UK and in Pakistan.

It was also confirmed again that face-to-face interaction is not a

necessary condition for Pakistanis to honour the obligations
attached to their *biraderi* or *vartan bhanji* relationships. It was clear
in 1985 that the use of the telephone and regular visits, including
visits to Pakistan, had increased to honour these obligations. The
kinship-friendship networks were dominant in almost all fields
of the Pakistanis' social interaction, which cuts across the occupational groupings. This brings us to the most important interactional aspect of the links in a network, which concerns the
meanings which persons in the network attribute to their relationships. The links between an individual and the people with
whom he or she interacts come into being for some purposes or
because of some interest which either or both of the parties recognise (Mitchell, 1969). This may be *biraderi*, economic assistance,
vartan bhanji, religious or political co-operation, friendship, ethnic
or neighbourhood ties.

Numerical Analysis

It is worth reminding the reader that the original twenty research
cases were chosen from five different occupational groups (four
cases from each group), using the 'snowball' technique of taking
one person from each group as a starter. The occupational groups
included: night-shift workers, day-shift workers, public transport
workers, professionals and self-employed Pakistanis. By 1985 one
night-shift worker, one day-shift worker, one public transport
worker and one professional person had moved out of Rochdale,
therefore the numerical analysis covers the remaining sixteen
cases. At the time of the fieldwork, two were unemployed and
two had changed their shifts.

As mentioned above, the kinship-friendship networks are
dominant in almost all fields of Pakistani social interaction,
which often cuts across the occupational groupings. A pattern of
social relationships by matrix manipulation (see Table 9.6) is produced about the degree to which there appears to be a 'cluster' or
'clique' in the collectivity, and to what extent every individual is
linked to every other individual in the collectivity.

To measure the hierarchy of cliques, Hubbell's procedure was
used (Hubbell, 1969); this means coding from closeness to distance as 3, 2, 1 and 0 consecutively. The results give an idea of the
structure of cliques in the group, as shown in Figure 9.1. Like the

Table 9.6 Input Matrix: 1985

Cases	1	2	3	4	5	6	7	8	9	10	11	12	13	14	15	16
1	*	3	3	3	3	2	3	2	3	2	2	2	1	1	2	3
2	3	*	3	3	3	3	3	3	2	3	3	1	2	3	2	2
3	3	3	*	2	3	3	2	3	3	1	3	1	2	3	1	2
4	3	3	2	*	3	3	3	3	2	3	3	3	3	2	2	1
5	3	3	3	3	*	3	1	3	3	2	2	3	2	3	0	2
6	3	3	3	3	3	*	3	3	3	3	3	2	1	3	2	1
7	3	3	3	2	2	3	*	2	2	2	3	2	2	3	2	2
8	3	3	3	2	2	2	3	*	3	3	2	3	3	3	3	2
9	2	2	2	3	3	3	1	3	*	3	3	2	3	2	3	1
10	3	3	2	3	2	2	3	3	2	*	3	1	0	2	3	2
11	2	2	2	3	3	3	1	2	2	3	*	3	3	3	2	1
12	3	2	2	2	3	2	2	3	3	2	3	*	3	2	3	3
13	3	3	1	3	3	3	2	3	3	3	3	2	*	2	2	2
14	3	2	3	3	2	3	2	3	2	1	3	3	3	*	3	3
15	3	3	2	3	1	3	3	3	3	1	3	3	3	3	*	3
16	3	3	2	2	2	3	2	3	2	2	1	3	3	3	2	*

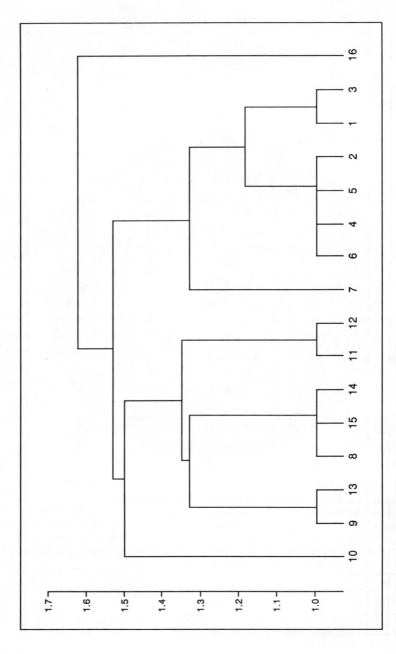

Figure 9.1 Clustering of 1985 Rochdale Data by Cell Value 3

1970s analysis (Anwar, 1979) these clusters are based on *biraderi* of origin and *biraderi* of participation.[1] The former related to the full extended kinship-based *biraderi* found in Pakistan, while the latter describes the *biraderi* in which an individual is actively involved in the UK, which may include some non-kin. Figure 9.2

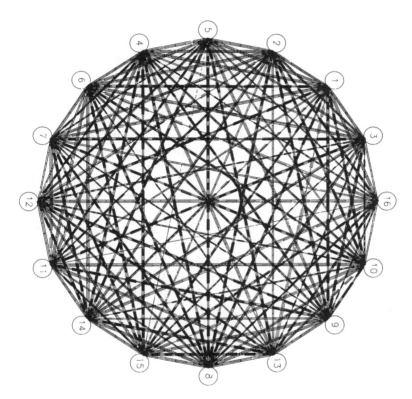

Figure 9.2 Social Networks of Rochdale Pakistanis, 1985
Note: The thickness of the lines in this diagram is proportional to the perceived closeness of the relationship between the elements in the set, the closer relationships being represented by thicker lines, and less close by proportionately thinner lines. The relationships are not necessarily symmetrical in terms of their closeness.

1. For a comparison with the 1970s numerical analyses, see Chapter 5 of Anwar (1979). For a more complete account of the differences between *biraderi* of origin and *biraderi* of participation, also see Anwar (1979).

shows the total network of the collectivity, the links, and the direction of the relationships in the network. It is clear that the relationships have become more close in 1985 and this is because of the new relationships established by wives and children of research cases, which have become family relationships.

However, as far as the direction of relationships was concerned, this had changed in 1985. For example, in 1973 some working-class people claimed their close relationships with the people in the professional and self-employed groups, but this was not reciprocated. In 1985 there was some change, and there was more acknowledgement from professional people that they had relationships with working-class people (see Figure 9.2). There could be three explanations for this change: the length of stay; relationships through children, and relationships through the activities of Pakistani organisations. However, informal relationships were still more intense than formal relationships. Nevertheless, identification with those in a position of authority still seemed a characteristic of the group, as it was in early 1973.

Now we present the morphological characteristics of the Pakistani networks, which refer to the patternings of relationships in the network in respect of one another. The characteristics are 'anchorage', 'density', 'reachability' and 'range', but we will be concerned only with measures which are relevant to the analysis. For example, if a large proportion of Pakistanis in the network can be contacted in a relatively small number of steps then the network is compact in comparison with one in which a smaller proportion may be reached in the same number of steps. Mitchell explains such reachability thus: 'the degree to which a person's behaviour is influenced by his relationships with others turns on the extent to which he can use these relationships to contact people who are important to him or, alternatively, the extent to which people who are important to him can contact him through these relationships' (1969, p.16).

It appears that the maximum finite distance for the Pakistani network is two steps (Table 9.7). This is certainly a change from the earlier analysis which showed that the maximum finite distance for the group studied was four steps. Similarly, the compactness – i.e. the measure which reflects the extent to which people in the network can contact one another – has changed from 0.9526 to 0.9714 (Index of Compactness). This is a very high degree of compactness, as the index value of complete compactness is 1.0.

Table 9.7 Distance Matrix on the Basis of Cell Value 3

Cases	1	2	3	4	5	6	7	8	9	10	11	12	13	14	15	16
1	*	1	1	1	1	2	1	2	1	2	2	2	2	2	2	1
2	1	*	1	1	1	1	1	1	2	1	1	2	2	1	2	2
3	1	1	*	1	1	2	1	1	2	2	1	2	2	1	2	2
4	1	1	2	*	1	1	1	1	2	1	1	1	1	2	2	2
5	1	1	1	1	*	1	2	1	1	2	2	1	2	1	2	2
6	2	1	2	1	1	*	1	1	1	1	1	2	2	1	2	2
7	1	1	1	1	2	1	*	2	2	2	1	2	2	1	2	2
8	2	1	1	2	2	2	1	*	1	1	2	1	1	1	1	2
9	1	2	2	2	1	1	2	1	*	1	1	2	1	2	1	2
10	2	1	2	1	2	2	1	1	1	*	1	2	2	2	1	2
11	2	1	2	1	1	1	2	2	2	1	*	1	1	1	2	2
12	2	2	2	2	1	2	2	1	2	2	1	*	1	2	1	1
13	2	1	2	1	1	2	2	1	1	1	1	2	*	2	2	1
14	2	2	1	1	2	1	2	1	1	2	1	1	1	*	1	1
15	2	1	2	1	2	1	1	1	2	2	1	1	2	1	*	1
16	1	2	2	2	2	1	2	2	1	2	2	1	1	1	2	*

The significance of the notions of reachability as measured by median steps and compactness lies in the way in which the links in a person's networks may be used to transmit information, exert social pressure and mobilise support within the network. These notions also provide us with a measure of whether the network is close-knit or loose-knit. The numerical and ethnographic data about Pakistanis in Rochdale clearly show that they have close-knit networks. One other way to look at these networks is to analyse their density, or the degree to which all possible links in the network among persons actually exist. The 'primary' or first-order 'star', as Barnes (1969) calls it, denotes the number of people ego has direct contact with, i.e. the number of people put into the first category. Table 9.8 shows the star sizes of all sixteen individuals in the network. The overall density of the group is 57.08 per cent, which is high (it was 31.84 per cent in 1973). However, it is even higher if we look at the individuals' network zone density in Table 9.8.[2] The 'span', or the proportion of links captured by

Table 9.8 The Morphological Characteristics of Sixteen Persons Using Order 1

Cases	Star size	Zone density	De-rooted zone-density	Span	Median steps
1	7	58.93	47.62	24.09	1.06
2	10	68.18	64.44	54.74	0.75
3	8	72.22	67.86	37.96	0.94
4	10	61.82	56.67	49.64	0.75
5	9	71.11	66.67	46.72	0.83
6	11	65.91	61.82	63.50	0.68
7	6	78.57	80.00	24.09	1.17
8	9	54.44	45.83	35.77	0.83
9	9	65.56	62.50	43.07	0.83
10	6	61.90	56.67	18.98	1.17
11	7	64.29	54.76	26.28	1.06
12	9	58.89	54.17	38.69	0.83
13	7	67.86	64.29	27.74	1.06
14	11	60.61	56.36	58.39	0.68
15	11	59.09	57.27	56.93	0.68
16	7	62.50	59.52	25.55	1.06

2. Zone density is calculated inclusive of ego, while derooted zone density excludes ego from the calculation.

ego in his first-order zone, is also presented in Table 9.8. It shows that cases 6, 14 and 15 are centrally placed, whereas cases 7 and 10 are weakly placed. This means that, in terms of influence, flow of information and mobilisation of support in the group, cases 6, 14 and 15 are in a better position. This finding is consistent with the observations made in the ethnography. 'Median steps' in Table 9.8 refer to the number of theoretical steps each person must take to reach half the people in the network. In the 1970s the lowest value was 0.79, and all nineteen other cases scored above 1.0. In the present network the three well-connected cases score 0.68, and only six of the remaining thirteen have values of over 1.0. This no doubt helps the flow of information and services, and in mobilising support in different intra-ethnic and inter-ethnic situations. Therefore those who are better placed in terms of median steps have an advantage over others in terms of using the network, as was confirmed by observations.

Conclusion

It is clear from the above analysis that overall social networks of first-generation Pakistanis in Rochdale are still close-knit and multiplex, reinforced by kinship and friendship ties. However, it will be interesting to see how these relationships develop with the second-generation Pakistanis. Observations indicate that, in the short term, the children of Pakistanis are in fact helping the networks of first-generation Pakistanis to become more dense. Whether they would carry on this trend as individual adults depends on their kin-friend obligations, educational achievements, residential patterns, and so on.

Looking at the UK Pakistani context, it appears that the first generation have not detached themselves from their kin ties and obligations to them in Pakistan. Their ties are mainly through their obligations towards their relatives in Pakistan and their economic ties through their property in Pakistan. The research cases mostly fulfilled their obligations to their relatives and kept in touch through telephone calls, messages, letters and visits to Pakistan. However, the frequency of contacts and number of visits were not as regular as found in 1973. One change which had taken place in the mid-1980s was that more relatives from Pakistan were now coming to visit their relatives in the UK, something which was rare in the early 1970s. This trend is continuing. Finally, it appears that the myth of return, which was widespread in the 1970s, is slowly diminishing as children of the first-generation Pakistanis are settling down after going through the educational system in the UK. Their priorities as UK citizens are very different compared to their parents. They would like to compete and succeed in the UK and not in Pakistan, despite the difficulty they face because of their race and colour. At the same time, most of them would like to follow their religion and culture and fulfil their kin obligations.

Acknowledgements

I am grateful to Professor J. Clyde Mitchell for his help in the analysis of social network data.

Bibliography

Anwar, M., 'Pakistanis and Indians in the 1971 Census: Some Ambiguities', *New Community*, vol.3, no.4, 1974, pp. 394–6
_____, *The Myth of Return: Pakistanis in The UK*, London: Heinemann, 1979
_____, *Young People and the Job Market*, London: Commission for Racial Equality, 1982
_____, *Pakistanis in The UK*, London: New Century, 1985
_____, *Race and Politics*, London: Tavistock, 1986
_____, 'Ethnic Classifications, Ethnic Monitoring and the 1991 Census', *New Community*, vol.16, no.4, 1990, pp.607–15
Barnes, J.A., 'Network and Political Process', in *Social Networks in Urban Situations*, J.C. Mitchell (ed.), Manchester: Manchester University Press, 1969
Brown, C., *Black and White The UK*, London: Policy Studies Institute, 1984
Eglar, A., *A Punjabi Village in Pakistan*, New York: Columbia University Press, 1961
Hubbell, C.H., 'An Input-Output Approach to Clique Identification', *Sociometry*, no.28, 1969, pp.377–99
Mitchell, J.C., 'The Concept and Use of Social Networks', in *Social Networks in Urban Situations*, J.C. Mitchell (ed.), Manchester: Manchester University Press, 1969
OPCS, *1991 Census Monitors* (National and Greater Manchester), London: Office of Population Censuses and Surveys, 1992a

_____, *Labour Force Survey 1990*, (unpublished data), 1992b

Penn, R.D., Scattergood, H. and Martin, A., 'The Dialectics of Ethnic Incorporation and Exclusion: Employment Trajectories of Asian Migrants in Rochdale', *New Community*, vol.16, no.2, 1990, pp.175–98

Chapter 10

Gentrification, Class and Community: A Social Network Approach

Gary Bridge

The Study of Gentrification

This chapter describes the usefulness of social network analysis, both theoretically and empirically, for an understanding of social and spatial change commonly known as 'gentrification'. It draws on fieldwork carried out in a part of London in the 1980s.[1] As a result of these observations the potential for an expanded use of social network analysis in social geography and urban sociology is outlined.

Gentrification is commonly understood as the 'rehabilitation of working-class or derelict housing and the consequent transformation of an area into a middle-class neighbourhood' (Smith and Williams, 1986, p.1). The defining quality of the process is thus the change in class composition within a residential neighbourhood.

Both materialist and liberal analyses of gentrification couch the discussion of social change in terms of class transition in residential neighbourhoods (for example Smith and Williams, 1986). More recent contributions point to the importance of gender relations as a central feature of the process (for example Bondi, 1991; Warde, 1991). In all of these discussions, structures of class or patriarchy are read onto the motivations and behaviour of individuals in those neighbourhoods undergoing change. This theoretical transposition to a lower level of abstraction is both jus-

---

1. The research findings discussed in this chapter formed part of a doctoral thesis supported by a competition award from the Economic and Social Research Council. A full account of the area of research, Sands End in Fulham, and the methodology of the questionnaire and network analysis can be found in Bridge (1990).

tified and problematical. It is justified because structures of class and patriarchy do impinge crucially on the perceptions and motivations of the working-class and middle-class residents of gentrifying neighbourhoods. What cannot be assumed, however, is that individuals will react in perfect consonance with the assumptions derived from the more abstract analysis; the fact that they do not in any clear way (as this chapter will indicate) can either be investigated or ignored. It might be ignored from the point of view that the attitudes and behaviour of individuals have no bearing on the more abstract claims. This can be seen in materialist analysis in the distinction between abstract (objective) and individual consciousness. These two types of consciousness might only be united at times of particular struggle or revolutionary transformation. The more common disjuncture between them may be understood as false consciousness.

The claim of this chapter is that individual experience cannot be read off social or spatial change, but that the nature of individuals' perceptions and behaviour is necessary for a complete understanding of social change and the particularities of social transformations. Any difference between individual experience and structural expectation leads one to hypothesise the role of other factors in social change. In the case of gentrification, the more abstract analysis (both liberal and materialist) led observers to assume that social residential change would lead to class resistance, or class antagonism at the very least. The empirically observed absence of such antagonism leads one to question the abstract analysis. This chapter proceeds from the assumption that materialist and liberal analysis is imbued with a spatial formalism that ties social change to residential spaces and solidary groups (classes or communities). The intellectual traditions and the constraints of this approach are dealt with elsewhere (Bridge, 1994).

One way of overcoming this formalism is through the use of social network analysis. A social network is 'a specific set of linkages among a defined set of persons, with the additional property that the characteristics of these linkages as a whole may be used to interpret the social behaviour of the persons involved' (Mitchell, 1969, p.2). Network analysis can deal with networks as wholes, and the linkages can be treated formally through the use of, for example, graph theory. Networks may also be oriented on individuals to avoid any shortcomings of institutional or structural functional analysis. Personal networks can be studied from the 'outside in' to assess the effect network structure has on individual behaviour. This approach is often used in 'family studies' – for example Bott on network structure and conjugal roles (Bott, 1971) – and is linked to interaction theory and interpretative sociology. Personal networks can also be viewed from the 'inside out' by observing individuals' manipulations of their networks for their own purposes (political networks). This relates to exchange theory and can be operationalised though rational choice theory. The operation of political networks can be seen most clearly in Granovetter's (1973) concept of 'the strength of weak ties', where loose-knit networks are argued to have greater resource-gathering potential for the individual (ego) than close-knit networks, because the members of dense networks are shaken down more quickly, and the reach to other potential sources of support is more circumscribed. Weak ties, on the other hand, are often bridges into other social realms and potential sources of support.

Social Networks and Gentrification

In the study discussed here, network analysis was used to interrogate personal networks from the 'outside in', in the sense that the attitudes of residents interviewed in the gentrifying neighbourhood were taken as reflecting the structure of their networks as well as other potential influences such as community, class or gender. Personal networks might have been investigated from the 'inside out', but this approach is best served over an extended period of time, allowing a longitudinal analysis or the construction of life histories. Both these approaches were beyond the scope of the present research. An approach based on network structure and content and its influence on social attitudes was the most manageable in terms of time and money constraints. One pertinent indicator of structure was deemed to be the geographical distribution of ego's network. This was proposed because the assumption of class antagonism derived from the literature on gentrification can be re-written, in network terms, to the effect that the claim for dense, geographically proximate nature of the social networks of working-class residents (working-class community) is inevitably disrupted by the influx of middle-class residents (displacement or lack of replacement of working-class residents in the neighbourhood), which will lead to class antagonism. Thus network analysis provides a practical means of investigating the *de facto* links between residents, rather than asserting such links from traditional notions of social and spatial solidary groups. Investigation of such links may indeed support the contentions of the spatial formalist literature. For example in her study of twenty urban families Bott (1971) sums up her empirical resultant as 'families with close-knit networks are likely to be working class ... [b]ut not all working-class families will have close-knit networks' (Bott, 1971, p.112). She continues:

> It is only in the working class that one is likely to find a combination of factors all operating together to produce a high degree of connectedness [density]: concentration of people of the same or similar occupations in the local area; jobs and homes in the same local area; low population turnover and continuity of relationships; at least occasional opportunities for relatives and friends to help one another to get jobs; little demand for physical mobility; little opportunity for social mobility. (p.121)

This view puts emphasis on the geographical localisation of networks, an argument supported by the work of Laumann (1973), who asserts that increasing length of residence in a neighbourhood and being working-class resulted in denser, more spatially constrained social networks. This density can be conceptualised in terms of a number of partial networks (of co-workers, kin, neighbours, friends) intersecting on the same people and/or in the same place. Thus Klein (1965) noted a high degree of neighbourliness in Bethnal Green, but only because neighbours were kin. In their classic work on the same area, Young and Wilmott (1957) observed that kin, neighbours and work associates were all the same people, i.e. that the sectors of partial networks were overlapping to give a high-density network.

Bott contrasts the typical working-class network with the middle-class experience:

> In contrast, the structure of professions is such that this pattern of forces almost never occurs. Homogeneous local areas of a single profession are very rare; a man's place of work and his home are usually in different local areas; professional training leads him to make relationships with people who do not know his family, school friends, and neighbours; in most cases getting a job depends on skill and training rather than on the influence of friends and relatives; many professional careers require physical mobility. (1971, p.113)

These observations are consistent with arguments from the urbanisation literature which deals with the sociological effects of urban living. Melvin Webber (1964), for example, makes a distinction between middle-class professionals (cosmopolites) – highly mobile, members of far-flung but interactionally intimate non-place communities – and working-class residents (localites), who are less mobile and who have more place-bound ties. Janowitz (1967) argues that middle-class cosmopolites do have place-related roles (as parents, members of residents' associations, etc.) but their wider networks mean that their neighbourhood of residence is for them a 'community of limited liability'. Discussion of the significance of the separation of home and work emerges later in the privatism thesis (Lockwood, 1966), part of which claims that the separation of work and home reduces working-class solidarity and encourages privatism, involving the pursuit of private goals in the home.

It is clear from the arguments above that geography is critical to conceptions of the crucial distinctions between the network structures typical of the working class and the middle class. Working-class networks are usually geographically localised and dense; middle-class networks are less geographically localised and sparse. Indeed, the emphasis that Bott gives to the influence of space on networks is evident from her explanation for the less common loose-knit working-class networks:

> Because a man has a manual occupation he will not automatically have a close-knit network. He may be living in a relatively heterogeneous area, for not all manual occupations are localized. He may live in one place and work in another. He may move from one area to another. Similarly his friends and relatives may move or make new relationships with people he does not know. A high degree of connectedness may be found in association with manual occupations, but the association is not necessary and inevitable. (p.113)

The development of the city may mean that working-class networks become more like middle-class networks. Thus Cubitt (1973) notes:

> As these [working-class] families become more mobile and as they move into new working environments, their networks take on the characteristics of the middle-class network, the sectors become separate and the density of the network decreases. (p.70)

Other network researchers have questioned the relationship between density, spatially constrained networks and social support. The usefulness of density as an indicator of social support depends on the quality of the ties. Local ties need not be superior ties. Thus Claude Fischer (1982) has argued that distant friends are no less intimate than local ones, and in fact might be more intimate, which is why they are maintained, despite being distant. Fischer does concede, however, that it is harder for working-class residents to pay the 'freight of distance' that maintaining distant relationships involves, 'proximity is important to the extent that distance is an unsupportable cost, which it tends to be for the poor, the elderly, burdened mothers, and the like' (p.175). Proximate contacts do have their uses, however: 'nearby associates are preferred when nearness is critical. When proximity is less critical – and these are often situations involving most intimacy, sacrifice and faith – there is little or no preference for those nearby'. (p.175)

Wellman (1979) deals with the claim of spatially constrained networks in his assessment of the community question in a Toronto neighbourhood. Wellman asserts that increasing levels of personal mobility and telephone ownership render outdated the assumption that neighbourhood intersects with community, even for working-class people. He characterises the debate as being between arguments for 'Community Lost', 'Community Saved' and 'Community Liberated'. Wellman asked questions on the intimate networks of a random sample of 845 adult residents of East York, Toronto. East York is a British-Canadian upper working-class/lower middle-class district with a reputation of solidarity. Eliciting information for up to six intimates for each respondent, Wellman found that primary ties 'tend to form sparsely knit, spatially dispersed, ramifying structures, instead of a single, densely knit solidarity' (p.1,211). The great majority of East Yorkers' intimate networks were not organised into local solidarities. Few respondents had more than one intimate residing in the neighbourhood. Wellman observes that 'the metropolitan area thus bounds the field of interaction more than does the neighbourhood' (p.1,211). East York was neither a Gansian urban village nor a Webberian community without propinquity. Instead the findings give broad support to the 'Community Liberated' argument, where the spatial constraints on social networks are loosened. Furthermore, Wellman observes that 'proximity tends to be more important on the job than in the neighbourhood for the availability of help from intimates ... [t]he spatial range of assistance relationships has expanded to encompass the entire Metropolitan area' (p.1,222). However, local ties have not lost all their importance:

> While local ties are real and important, their importance comes from their being only a component of a diverse array of relationships. Intimate ties are into local solidarities even less often that they are into solidary kinship systems. Indeed the car, the telephone, and the airplane help maintain many kinship ties. Yet space is still a constraint; there are distances for each tie at which the cost of keeping in contact becomes too great for it to remain viable. (p.1,222)

Barnes's seminal paper (1954), in which he coined the term 'social network' to describe the intimate contacts of parishioners in Bremnes, proceeded on the basis that networks were not constrained by institutions or territory. This was confirmed by Bott's notion of 'the immediate social environment' of the twenty families in London. This immediate social environment consisted of the network of friends, neighbours and relations which mediated between the family and the total society. The present analysis is predicated on the assumption common to much network analysis, that personal network structure can influence individual attitudes and behaviour.

The claim made in this chapter is that the immediate social environment of individuals or families can help explain the poor correlation between individual attitudes to neighbourhood change in a gentrifying district (discussed below) and those one might anticipate on the basis of class analysis or social geographical analysis. Thus one can advance the immediate social environment of personal networks as an explanation for the lack of consistency with the non-personal structural attribute of class location. Numerous commentators would suggest that the immediate social environment of the personal network has grown in importance at the expense of class location. The basis of the assertion is clearly stated by Smith (1980): 'because work life no longer occupies a central role in satisfactorily defining personal identity for a large part of the workforce, [the] needs for a social identity structure are often satisfied in more intimate primary group relationships' (p.221). Smith suggests that 'it is precisely the structural separation of work from the rest of life that has driven many people inward in search of the meaning, unity, and integration that a fragmented social structure no longer adequately provides' (p.221).

According to this analysis, social networks might be an escape from competitiveness in the workplace. Changing work relations are particularly influential for certain fractions of the working class: 'the more superfluous the unskilled marginal classes are to the advanced capitalist mode of production and distribution, the greater is their need for the extended family and kinship networks that provide them with mutual aid' (Smith, 1980, p.174).

Even within this view of the declining importance of work there does seem to be some confusion about the size of networks that people retreat into. The privatism literature (beginning with Lockwood, 1966) puts emphasis on the retreat from work to home and into the small network of the nuclear family. This process suggests a withering of social networks (based on work) and is seen to be aided by the spatial separation of work and home (for an excellent critique see Pratt and Hanson, 1988). Sennett and Cobb, on the other hand, put the emphasis on the larger network of primary ties in neighbourhood. They point to the example of white ethnics in working-class enclaves who privilege friendship networks over promotion at work (Sennett and Cobb, 1972). The logical inference of this argument is that primary ties in neighbourhood will persist, rather than wither away as Wirth (1938) had predicted.

On the other hand, work and workplace can be seen as a source of personal network development. This was certainly the conclusion of the study of working-class networks in Bedminster, Bristol, conducted by Franklin (1989). He argued that 'the arrival of new industries and labour processes, together with new leisure industries and necessary or preferred housing moves outside crowded natal localities created a local working class with new social expectations and the social skills to achieve them' (p.93). In sum, he proposed that working-class sociability increased over time.

Two important points emerge from this discussion. First, do personal social networks relate in any way to notions of community? Secondly, do personal social networks have any bearing on class analysis?

Social Networks and Community

Definitions of community are multifarious (for a thorough review see Bell and Newby, 1971). In the sense of the term pursued here, the most useful definition comes from Elias (1974):

> A community ... is a group of households situated in the same locality and linked to each other by functional interdependencies which are closer than interdependencies of the same kind with other groups of people within the wider social field to which a community belongs. (p.xix)

This definition combines the ideas of close ties and geographical proximity. One objection that might be raised is that the network members included in the present study (discussed below) were all intimates of ego ('close friends'), and that networks based on ties between intimates are not strictly measures of community ties: that is, the networks depicted represent the inner circle of networks, or first-order zone to use Barnes's idea (Barnes, 1969), and that a full description of community might warrant inclusion of alters other than the respondents' six closest friends. In this sense it is arguable that spatially-based community reaction to social and residential change might be prompted regardless of the attributes of intimate networks. While this difficulty is acknowledged, the reply is that such intimates are anchors for wider network development, and therefore the class location and geographical location of these alters is some indication of wider network membership – membership on a scale that can be argued to constitute community. It is also links with close friends that are most likely to initiate action by ego.

Social Networks and Class

The second point is how networks relate to class. The question might be raised of why appeal to the immediate social environment of personal networks and the perceptions based thereon, if class location is a non-personal structural attribute? There are two possible responses. The first is that personal networks do not relate to larger structural attributes, and indeed may help explain the lack of consistency between individual perceptions and social change. Given one line of argument (discussed on p.266), personal networks (of whatever scale) may be a retreat from class and from the workplace and the structural relations there that crucially define class location. In a less extreme sense, class attitudes may reside within personal networks, but the structure of those networks may affect each individual's perception of class difference. This comes about because of the intermediate influence of the 'immediate social environment' that the personal social network represents. Following Bott (1971);

> A family does not live directly in the total society, or even, in many cases, in the local community. The effective social environment of a family is its network of friends, neighbours, relatives and particular social institutions. This is the primary social world. (p.159)

However, 'this does not mean that families have no ideas about their society as a whole or about families in general' (p.159). It is simply that they have widely different views based on varying social expectations and personal needs. These different views also include views of class. Again citing Bott:

> Although a finisher in Bermondsey and an account executive in Chelsea are both members of the larger British society, they live in different worlds; they have different jobs, different friends, different neighbours, and different family trees. Each bases his ideas of class on his own experience, so that it is hardly surprising that each has a different conception of the class structure as a whole. In these circumstances it would be naive to assume that peoples' ideas about class will be a valid representation of the 'real' or 'objective' class structure of the society as a whole. (p.159)

At this level, Bott sees classes as 'constructed reference groups' which are 'used by individuals to structure their social world and to make comparisons and evaluations of their own behaviour and that of other people ... [a]lthough these concepts may not be objectively real, they are psychologically real, in the sense that they affect the behaviour of the individual' (p.168). Thus the immediate social environment of the personal network can give individuals an idea of class that does not match 'real' class divisions. The variation in perceptions of class might be advanced as a reason for the lack of consistency of reaction to neighbourhood change: people do not rally around class, because they have personal networks that give them support and help shape their image of class, i.e. there is no consistent class alignment in the first place.

As an alternative to conceptions that see personal networks as an escape from, or filter between, the individual and the class structure, a second major possibility is that social class is one of the factors structuring personal social networks. This would be demonstrated most powerfully if co-workers of the same class were represented prominently in the network. Some degree of class consistency between ego and friends (little class spread or range – see below) would indicate a class effect. The claim here is that such structuring attributes as class and patriarchy condition the contexts in which networks are constructed. Kin are not chosen, although their membership or absence from intimate networks certainly is. Friends are chosen. Neighbours are part given and part chosen from those available. The arenas in which contacts are made may be influenced strongly by class location, gender or ethnicity as these structural attributes limit the range of people that it is normally possible for ego to meet (class-homogeneous work situations or residential neighbourhoods, for example). Lack of class-consistent reactions to gentrification may not represent a retreat from class or emerge from diffuse notions of class as much as a more complex geography of class relations. It is these competing notions that the social network analysis on a sample of residents in a gentrifying north London neighbourhood was used to investigate.

Social Networks in Sands End

Sands End is a district comprising 3,300 households in the London Borough of Hammersmith and Fulham. It separated from the rest of Fulham by the New King's Road and King's Road to the north, Wandsworth Bridge Road to the west, the River Thames to the south and Stanford Brook to the east (where it meets the boundary with Kensington and Chelsea). As well as this physical separation, the distinctiveness of the neighbourhood arises from the fact that the Victorian terraces consist of smaller houses and flats than the rest of Fulham. Unusually for Fulham, Sands End was also (up to the 1970s) a major employment site, comprising the industrial installations along the riverside (Fulham Power Station, North Thames Gas Works, an oil storage depot, etc.). This had given the area a reputation for working-class solidarity, with people living and working in the same neighbourhood. At the time of the research in the late 1980s, Sands End was experiencing the gentrification of the Victorian terraces by incoming professionals and small local building firms, as well as the wholesale transformation of the industrial riverside into a luxury residential and commercial zone (becoming Chelsea Harbour and Sands Wharf).

The social network research was part of an in-depth, semi-structured questionnaire administered to fifty households (both working-class and middle-class) in Sands End over the summer of 1988. The network exercise consisted of a network diagram for up to six intimates, with a series of questions about the nature of the ties and attributes of the contacts named on the diagram and their relations with each other (see Figure 10.1 for an example). Other questions on the interview schedule concerned the occupation and household characteristics of the respondent, as well as their experience of, and attitudes to, Sands End as a place to live.

Network Measures

The measures used to indicate network structure consisted of volume; density; class spread (range); and geographical spread. The details of personal networks were gained by asking the respondents for up to six close friends. The names were then inserted in the boxes (Figure 10.1) and additional details on alters (occupation, frequency of contact, place of residence, nature of relationship) were inserted into the boxes. Density was established through the links between boxes, which were drawn either by the interviewer or the respondents themselves. This visual representation of network was readily understandable to the majority of respondents.

Volume – Volume refers to the number of contacts named in the network (between 0 and 6 for the interview schedule used in the present study). According to Burt (1983, p.177), 'the number of actors directly connected to an individual is an index of the extent to which the individual is involved in many different relationships', and is therefore an indicator of the potential resource-gathering capabilities of that person, whether these resources be emotional, practical or convivial.

Density – Density is defined as the number of links existing between ego's alters, expressed as a percentage of the total possible number of links. This definition is normally limited to the

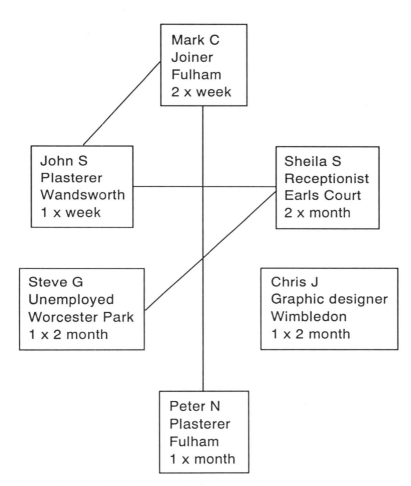

Figure 10.1 Sands End Network: An Example

first-order zone of contacts, i.e. ego's contacts but not the contacts of contacts who are unknown to ego. The measure of density used in the present research varied between 0 and 1 (if 0, none of ego's alters knew each other; if 1, all ego's alters knew each other). If ego's contacts are highly inter-connected, and especially if they live in close proximity, it does suggest some form of local solidary grouping. The problem of density as a measure of social circumscription is the status of alters: are they what ego says they are? This requires some form of verification, usually achieved by contacting alters. This also helps establish whether the relationship is reciprocated, and helps confirm the quality of the tie (a dense network with ties of poor quality may not be particularly supportive or influential). The problem of verification of alters is that it is costly and time-consuming. It was certainly beyond the limits of the research reported here. Egos' accounts of their networks were taken at face value. Another weakness of the density measure is that it can be a numerical artefact: the number of potential links increases at a much higher rate than the number of network members; thus the larger the network the lower the measure of density is likely to be, all other things being equal. In the present research the size of the network was limited to six alters (six 'close friends'), and so the problem of size is to some extent avoided. A third conceptual problem with density is that dense clusters may occupy loose-knit networks. Furthermore, density may not be the best measure of network structure when the analyst is considering how network structure influences individual behaviour. Mitchell (1969) argues that reachability has more relevance here. Reachability 'implies that every specified person can be contacted within a stated number of steps from any given starting point' (p.15). He goes on to explain: 'if a large proportion of the people in a network can be contacted within a relatively small number of steps then the network is compact in comparison with one in which a smaller proportion may be reached in the same number of steps' (p.15).

The usefulness of reachability is that it is a more direct measure than density of the degree to which a person's behaviour is influenced by his or her relationships with others in that it is able to capture the extent to which he or she can use the relationships to contact people who are important to him or her, or alternatively, the extent to which people who are important to him or her can contact him or her through these relationships. Reachability involves a more comprehensive recording of the alters in a personal network, and one that was beyond the scope of the present study. Density thus offered a practicable, if indicative, measure of the inter-connectedness of the personal networks observed. Its usefulness for the present study came in combination with the measure of the geography of the personal networks, or geographical range.

Geographical Range – Respondents were asked to state where their close friends lived. Any friends living in areas outside the borough in which the neighbourhood was situated scored 1 point. Thus if a respondent had a social network comprising six close friends all of whom lived outside Fulham then the geographical range measure would be 6. This measure might have been weighted to give more points to zones of increasing distance from the locality, but, since the point was to establish the degree to which intimate contacts were local, the more simple measure sufficed.

Class Spread – The fourth network measure used in the study was class spread, which is the number of social classes other than ego's represented by his contacts. This is similar to Wheeldon's (1969) concept of range, which, for her, is the number of people in direct contact with ego combined with the social heterogeneity of the individuals concerned. This measure offered some indication of the degree to which class location structured ego's network by the degree to which ego's contact were in the same social class.

There are several qualifications of the method used to gain network information that must be stated. The first is that the network questions in the survey asked for up to six close friends (following Fischer's approach). Much of the general sociological and network literature points to the importance of kin, particularly for working-class respondents, i.e. the most significant network members may be relatives rather than friends. This problem was dealt with in a number of ways. First, respondents were told that members of their family or relatives could be included as close friends. If kin were mentioned they were included in the network diagram. Second, two later questions on the interview schedule asked for emotional and practical ties with alters who may or may not have been mentioned on the network diagram.

The second qualification is that respondents were asked to name up to six *close* friends. This presents the problem of what 'close' actually means. Close is self-defined by respondents, and therefore, it can be argued, is non-comparable. However, a number of network researchers, for example Claude Fischer, have argued that closeness self-defined by respondents is the most efficient way to elicit significant relationships. The alternative is to put a number of hypothetical situations to the respondents (for example 'Who would you turn to if you needed to borrow a large sum of money?'; 'Who would you ask to help you put up a garden shed?') as a means of revealing relationships of varying intimacy.

Network Measures: The Results

Semi-structured questionnaires were administered to fifty individuals in Sands End. Respondents were selected randomly, and only eighteen-year-olds or younger were excluded.

Density – In the Sands End study, most density values clustered in the middle of the range: twelve of the thirty-one values obtained in the survey were concentrated between 0.51 and 0.7. Below this were a further eight respondents, and there were eleven respondents who had network densities above 0.7. When these simple network measures were cross-tabulated with social class, cell counts were obviously low, and no clear trend was discernible. The only respondent in social class I (professional/managerial) described a six-person network that had a density of 0 (i.e. totally unconnected alters). This accords with the assumptions in the literature concerning lower network densities for professionals who have far-flung interest groups as cosmopolites. Eight of the eleven respondents in social class II (intermediate) also described 6-person networks; one of the eleven had a 4-person network and two individuals gave volumes of 3 and 2 persons respectively. In the skilled non-manual category (IIINM) there was a steady decline from a maximum of 4 (out of 11) persons giving a 6-person network, three respondents naming 5 alters, two naming 4 and two naming 3-person networks. Moving to the manual classes, of the nine respondents in the skilled manual category, five cited 6-person networks, one a 5-person network, two a network of 2 close friends, and one had a network volume of 1. The sole semi-skilled worker appearing in the cross-tabulation had a network volume of 4, the one unskilled respondent a volume of 3. The lambda statistic[2] for the cross-tabulation of social class with network volume was very low, showing little

2. The lambda statistic is a non-parametric test that has the advantage over its better-known counterpart (the contingency coefficient) of not being a chi-square-based test. For chi-square-based measures, if more than 20 per cent of the cells in the cross-tabulation matrix have expected frequencies of less than 5, then the measure is unreliable. Lambda is based on the idea of proportional reduction in error, introduced by Goodman and Kruskal (1954), and is not subject to the restriction that applies to chi-square-based measures. In the cross-tabulations of the present research, significant numbers of cell counts could easily be less than 5, so the lambda statistic was chosen. These measures are all essentially ratios of a measure of error in predicting the values of one variable, based on knowledge of that variable alone, and the same measure of error applied to predictions based on knowledge of an additional variable. Lambda always ranges between 0 and 1. A value of 0 means that the independent variable is of no help in predicting the dependent variable; a value of 1 means that the independent variable perfectly specifies the categories of the dependent variable.

statistical association. It must be borne in mind, however that out of an interview sample of fifty there were thirty-eight completed network diagrams (a small sample for statistical analysis), and that cell counts on all cross-tabulations were low. Lambda was also low for the cross-tabulation of social class with network density (0.17), showing little association. Although these results are tentative, given the size of the sample of interview respondents, they call into question Bott's original claim that working-class people have denser networks.

Class Spread – Class spread is the number of social classes other than ego's represented by his or her contacts. Here the results were less indicative. The class categories are those of the Registrar General (RG) Classification of Occupations. In the present study this meant six categories ranging from professional/managerial through to unskilled manual. Respondents' contacts scored 1 point if they were in any social class category other than that of the respondent. Of the twenty-four respondents for which class and network information was reliable, eleven had networks with at least one member of the network in a different social class to ego. Seven respondents had social networks in which two other social classes were represented. Three respondents had networks containing three social classes other than their own. There were also three respondents who had networks in which no social class other than their own was represented. Obviously, absolute numbers are small (twenty-four) and do not bear sub-division; suffice to say that the class spread revealed by the raw figures also occurred across the manual/non-manual divide. These preliminary observations suggest that further empirical research is necessary. It is possible that Cubitt's assertion that, with the development of cities and increasing levels of personal mobility, working-class networks become more like middle-class networks might be correct. Alternatively, class spread might reveal different social destinations from similar social origins, or reflect social mobility of the respondent. In several cases it arose from the personal networks of women in routine non-manual work (e.g. clerical) who had a spouse in a manual occupation and friends in both manual and non-manual locations. Certainly the use of the RG classification, whilst pragmatic, given the limits of the research, presented logical difficulties given the Marxist approach adopted in the research. In this sense the class schema developed by Wright

(1985) would have been more consistent with the theoretical approach adopted. Unfortunately, the interview schedule required to elicit class location was too unwieldy given the other elements of investigation pursued in this research.

Geographical Range – The final network measure which has significance for the present study is that of geographical range. Respondents were asked to state where their close friends lived. All locations outside Fulham scored 1 point. The spatial divisions are crude, and so is the measure, but it does indicate the broad geographical range of ego's network. The cross-tabulation of social class with geographical range revealed a very low lambda statistic (0.09). This suggests little association between social class of respondents and their geographical range of contacts.

Conclusions drawn from the cross-tabulations are necessarily tentative, but the trends indicated – no greater density or neighbourhood-boundedness of social contacts for working-class compared to middle-class residents – are given greater credence by the case studies that emerge from the household interviews. These case studies are illustrative, in the sense that they provide contextual richness to the analysis. They are also analytical (Mitchell gives an excellent explanation of analytical case studies – Mitchell, 1983) in that they demonstrate a range of reactions to neighbourhood change which is logically consistent with the idea underlying the investigation that the experience of neighbourhood change need not be class-consistent. They also provide a conceptual route out of the seeming impasse of the inability of class analysis to cut into individual experience of neighbourhood change, by revealing the variation of network structure for respondents in the same social class and showing that the immediate social environment is not consonant with the immediate spatial environment for working-class and middle-class residents, except for those persons at specific stages in the lifecycle (young mothers, elderly long-term residents). The case studies of several working-class residents of Sands End are given in the next section.

'*Steve*' – Steve[3] was born in Sands End and had lived there all his life (he was twenty-four). Given the conventional assumptions of the literature, we would expect him to have a blue-collar occupa-

3. Fictitious names are used to preserve the anonymity of respondents.

tion and working-class friends. However, Steve worked as a designer in Surrey, 10 miles south west of Fulham, and travelled to work by car. He lived in his parents' four-bedroom owner-occupied house in Sands End, which they had converted from two maisonettes. Steve was single and had no children. Although he had been born in the neighbourhood and had lived there all his life, he said that he had no feeling of community. In fact he was about to leave Sands End, having bought a home of his own in Worcester Park, which is 5 miles south west of Fulham on the border between Greater London and Surrey. Worcester Park was a favourite destination for original Fulhamites.

Steve's lack of interest in his neighbourhood of birth is shown not just in his arrangements to leave, but in the nature of his social network. As well as being diverse in terms of social class it also scored high on the geographical range measure: 4 out of a maximum of 6. However, part of this network owed its existence to Sands End. Peter, Edmund and Felix were brothers and child-hood friends of Steve. Edmund and Felix still lived in the same street as he did. Peter, a childhood friend and now a sales engi-neer, had moved to Croydon; he and Steve met once a month. Another friend, Chris, was an engineer who lived in Carshalton (6 miles south of Fulham). He and Steve met every two weeks in each others' homes. Steve's girlfriend Debbie was a receptionist who lived in Fulham, and they met every day. Steve saw the two brothers still living in his street 'all the time'. Felix worked as a waiter, and Edmund was still at school. The only isolate in the network was David, a process engineer who lived across the river in Barnes. In a personal crisis, Steve said he would turn to his brother who lived in Lower Morden, Surrey (just up the railway line from Worcester Park) and whom he saw on average every ten days at the family home in Sands End. Steve would turn to Chris, the friend in Carshalton, for practical help.

Steve had 'occasional chats' with his neighbours, and he was a member of the Surrey Porsche Club and the caravan-owners' club in Fulham. In response to the closed questions, he thought that it was important that the government allowed people to get ahead on their own, suggesting an orientation to the Conservative Party. It was clear from the interview that Steve saw getting away from Sands End as part of 'getting on', or of being successful. Two of his successful friends, Chris and Peter, had moved to outer suburbia, and a similar move on his part was enabling him to buy his own home; he said he couldn't afford the prices in Fulham. He was typical of the children of working-class parents, born in Fulham, who were being effectively displaced from the neighbourhood of birth by rising house prices. He was moving to a location that was typical of such outmovers. However, what was also clear from Steve's case was that, although he had to move further out from central London to be able to buy property, that move itself was seen positively, in that it was a move to the pleasant suburbs and away from the cramped Victorian terraces of Sands End.

'*Vicky*' – Vicky was in her early twenties with young children, but her network was extensive (volume = 6, with two friends living outside the neighbourhood) with medium density (0.53). She lived on the eighth (top) floor of a council block of flats built in the 1970s. Her kitchen window had a commanding view of the river and the scaffolding and glass domes of the luxury Chelsea Harbour development. Vicky's husband, a self-employed builder, was actually working on the site: 'it's very long hours but good money', she said. She had two children, aged two and six, the eldest of whom went to the local primary school. Vicky had lived most of her life in Sands End, having moved with her parents from West Kensington nineteen years before. Many members of her extended family lived in Sands End (including her parents, mother-in-law, sister-in-law and brother-in-law).

Vicky named six close friends, four of whom lived in Sands End. Ella lived a few doors down the corridor in the same council block and she and Vicky met every day in each others' homes and at the local toddlers' club. Diane lived in one of the Victorian terraced streets of Sands End, and she and Vicky met three times a week. Annette lived in an adjacent council block and met with Vicky every day in each others' homes and at the toddlers' club. Vicky and Sally, who lived in another council block in the neighbourhood, met on average once a week in Sally's home. Vicky met her friends who lived outside Sands End less frequently. She met Debbie, who lived 2 miles to the north in West Kensington, once a month in a restaurant on the North End Road in Fulham. Sara, who lived in Shepherd's Bush (one mile north) came to Vicky's house once every three months, on average. Vicky considered Ella, who lived just down the corridor, to be her best friend. In a time of personal crisis and when needing practical help in the home Vicky said she would go to her mum who lived

100 yards away in an adjoining street. Vicky and her mother met at Vicky's home on average four times a week.

The advantages of Sands End as a place to live, according to Vicky, were that it had a 'nice park' (just next to where she lived) and the toddlers' club. The disadvantage was the pond that the council was constructing in the middle of the park, which she considered to be dangerous for the children and a waste of money. Not surprisingly, Vicky's sense of community in Sands End was strong: 'I've lived here all my life and know everyone.' In conversation, she did not seem to be perturbed by the social and physical changes going on in the neighbourhood. The Chelsea Harbour development was at that moment providing her husband with plentiful and lucrative work. Her family and friends were close to her, and there was no prospect of them leaving. In one sense, living in a block of flats on a council estate, she was not directly affected by the gentrification which was occurring in the Victorian terraces below her home.

'*Lucy*' – Lucy had lived in Sands End since the First World War. She was typical of many of the older Sands End residents, in that she had a small social network (involving two close friends). The network had a density of 1 (both friends knew each other). Both lived outside the neighbourhood, one in White City (two miles north) and the other in Manchester (a geographical range of 2). Lucy had moved with her parents from Kensington to Sands End in 1918. She had moved from the street they first lived in into her present ground-floor council flat in a Victorian terraced street in 1934. Lucy had worked in domestic service in Chelsea, travelling there by bus. She was now retired and was also a widow. Her husband had been a bricklayer, who later in life became a full-time union official. Lucy had two children aged fifty-five and forty-eight. One was a sheet-metal worker who lived in Basildon, Essex (30 miles east of London), the other a mechanic at Heathrow airport, living in Teddington (6 miles south west of Sands End). In a personal crisis Lucy said she would turn to the son who lived in Teddington. She went to his house every Sunday, and he also called at her home on Saturdays, 'if Chelsea [Football Club] are playing at home'. Lucy commented that 'lots of yuppies have moved in', and her son-in-law wished he had bought a house in Sands End: 'he would like to move back to Sands End but can't afford it.' She said that a taxi driver-turned-builder, up the road, had just sold his home for £250,000. Like

Steve, Lucy's son is representative of children of Sands End residents effectively displaced from the neighbourhood by rising house prices. She did not say much about her other son: they did not get on, 'because of my daughter-in-law', she said.

According to Lucy, the advantages of Sands End were its good bus service and the fact that it was near the shops; she could think of no disadvantages. Nevertheless, she had limited interaction with others in the area. She said she hardly knew her neighbours, and added 'I don't want to.' When asked whether she had a sense of community living in Sands End, she said she had some sense, but wasn't interested: 'It's there if you want it, I don't.' Her lack of interest in other residents in Sands End was reflected in her social network, which, although small, was drawn from outside the neighbourhood. Freda lived in White City, and they spoke on the telephone twice a week and met four or five times a year in different locations. Helen lived in Manchester, and they met twice a year at a concert, but otherwise spoke on the telephone about once a month.

Although she was not interested in her relations with neighbours, Lucy regretted that her son had not been able to buy into Sands End. This is typical of the feelings of a number of people interviewed who expressed resentment or regret that their children could not buy, or had not bought into, Sands End. Nevertheless, her own interest in Sands End as a resource for social contacts was negligible. It is unclear whether this was a defensive response to the social changes that had occurred in the neighbourhood, or whether it was an outcome of Lucy's personal introversion.

A Summary of the Social Network Analysis

The three examples of Steve, Vicky and Lucy indicate the range of involvement in the neighbourhood for several long-term residents with working-class origins. These were the very people one would expect to be affected most by the gentrification process. There were some more general conclusions that emerged from the network information for all the respondents included in the survey (see also Bridge, 1990)

1 The influence of social class on networks was slight. Most social ties existed with intimates outside the neighbourhood, for all social classes. For those respondents of all social classes

who were in employment, social networks were metropolitan-wide, and co-workers were a significant part of network membership. Class spread, network density and network volume for all networks showed no correlation with social class of respondent.

2 The influence of a person's stage in their lifecycle was significant. Attitudes to neighbourhood change and the state of personal social networks were bound up with the respondents' stage in the lifecycle. Greater dependency and involvement in the neighbourhood was evident for women with young children (such as Vicky) and older, long-term residents (whose networks were contracting because other network members were dying). The research revealed the importance of time and stage in the lifecycle for an appreciation of the experience of gentrification. In this sense, neighbourhood and residence can be seen as a process. Residence is as much a temporal process as a spatial condition.

3 Network analysis was used to assess the degree of interaction within a geographical neighbourhood. It was concluded that social segregation can be maintained despite spatial proximity (revealed in disparate social networks) – as in the case of Lucy, for example. Limited interaction in Sands End was not because of the proximity of different social classes, but the fact that different individuals of both classes had already extant networks that extended beyond the neighbourhood.

The Uses of Networks and Their Future Possibilities

In general, social network analysis had two important uses in the present study. There was a practical use of social network analysis as a way of revealing *de facto* active networks rather than *a priori* assumptions of community solidarity. Secondly, network analysis played a conceptual role in providing a potential explanation for the lack of consistency of reaction to neighbourhood change assumed in the gentrification literature. The immediate social environment of the network helped explain different attitudes to the social changes, and the geographical extent of most networks provided an explanation for the fact that social change in neighbourhood was not the critical site of social interaction or social solidarity. This explained the lack of defence of neighbourhood by working-class residents: their immediate social environment did not intersect with their immediate spatial environment. In this sense, social network analysis forces us to raise our stare from the residential neighbourhood, and from residence itself, and gaze across the whole city, including its workplaces, for a complete understanding of the experience of the social change known as gentrification by the residents living in those neighbourhoods that the process is assumed to affect. Not only will this give us leads to link the contextual consciousness with larger, objective interests but it will also give us a more relevant and finessed social geography of the city.

Based on the experience of the use of social network analysis in the research, there are a number of suggestions for greater use of such analysis in social geography and urban studies.

1 – The spatiality of social networks: a common assumption in the sociological literature is that social networks are aspatial (given increasing levels of personal mobility and telephone ownership). The contention here is that space is still a crucial element of the structure of networks because of three factors. To begin with, face-to-face contact rejuvenates a relationship, which tends to 'sag' with extended separation. Secondly, it would be very difficult to sustain a network where all intimates were distant, because of the freight of distance (time/money costs) that maintaining such a network would demand. Finally, the different needs of ego can only be met by an array of spatial relationships, some of which must be relatively close in geographical terms (help in an emergency, for example). Further investigations of the spatiality of social networks might help us understand how people experience the city rather than relying on the spatial block/ social block assumptions of traditional social geographical analysis.

2 – Following from this, the geographical range measure should have a greater role in social network analysis. In the research discussed here, this was formulated in a relatively crude manner of local/non-local ties. Depending on the investigation at hand, the measure could be weighted to take account of linear distance, or territory (to take in boundary effects, for example).

3 – Discussions of the spatiality of social networks have a good deal in common with some of the concerns of time-geography (Hägerstrand, 1975). The daily space-time rhythms of social life are subject to 'coupling constraints' which equate with opportu-

nities for social contact. Time-geography was adapted by Giddens (1984) to serve his arguments over time-space distanciation (the stretching of social relationships and influences of power over time and space). Social network analysis could be used to help reveal the details of distanciation and the efforts of individuals through social integration (face-to-face overcoming of time-space distanciation in a time and place) interrogated through the analysis of personal social networks, or system integration (institutional integration across time and space) through the use of organisational network analysis. The potential use of social network analysis in empirically tracing time-space distanciation becomes of greater theoretical interest when linked to Giddens's notion of social relations in modernity (1991). He argues that one of the defining characteristics of modernity is the 'disembedding' of social relationships, and the attempts to overcome this and re-embed the self. Social network analysis provides a potential means of empirically testing at least part of this proposition by investigating the nature of social networks, although a pre-modern comparator is clearly not possible.

4 – Social network analysis also has the potential for greater use in class analysis. Wright (1985) realised this in his snippet of social network analysis used to construct class biography variables to establish the links between class structure and class consciousness. He constructed a 'working-class networks' variable, in part composed of a measure of working-class density of the respondent's social networks, based on data concerning the class location of friends (up to three friends or relatives the respondent felt closest to). This approach could be expanded for a fuller investigation of class consciousness. There are numerous other potential applications in class analysis; for example it might be possible to explore the extent to which social mobility changes social networks alongside possible changes in attitudes, politics and consciousness.

5 – Social network analysis offers the possibility of further investigation of the structure/agency debate (see, for example, Giddens, 1984). The social consistency of network membership (or otherwise) indicates the structures that impinge on individuals – structures not as limits to action, but circumscription of the social field (again linked to time-geography and class analysis). Network analysis also offers potential insight into the possibilities for resistance to such determinants, in that analysis of the

content of ties indicates the potential resource-gathering capabilities of the individual. This might be investigated from a Marxist perspective which assumes that society does not consist of individuals, but expresses the sum of interrelations, the relations within which individuals stand. This is a model of networks, relationships and social processes rather than an emphasis on the extremes of either voluntarism or determinism. The use of network analysis to assess the circumscription of the social field could be set in the context of a longitudinal study as a way of unearthing socialisation. Thus network analysis has longitudinal as well as spatial use.

6 – The individual manipulation of social networks (from the 'inside out') has links to exchange theory. Thus social networks approached in this way can be tied to game theory and rational choice theory, and the development and use of social networks can be seen as a rational choice problem, subject to all the methods of analysis associated with this approach.

The pioneering work of Mitchell on the investigation of social networks in urban situations in the 1950s and 1960s, and his dedication to the importance of the social network approach, was an inspiration to the present study (as it has been to numerous network researchers and the literature they have produced). The hope is that the description of the use of social network analysis in the study of gentrification and the indication of some of its other potential uses in sociological analysis will help to re-affirm the importance of an approach that demands direct engagement with social relationships which, in some theoretical schemes, are merely the material of assertion. Social network analysis requires us to swallow our theoretical pride and confront social relationships (in all their inconsistency) in order to abstract some structure to those relationships so that we may develop greater theoretical and practical understanding of the nature of social relations in the modern (or even postmodern?) urban situation.

Bibliography

Barnes, J.A., 'Class and Committees in a Norwegian Island Parish', *Human Relations*, vol.7, 1954, pp.29–58

_____,'Networks and Political Process', in *Social Networks in Urban Situations*, J.C. Mitchell (ed.), Manchester: Manchester University Press, 1969

Bell, C. and Newby, H., *Community Studies*, London: Allen and Unwin, 1971

Bondi, L., 'Gender Divisions and Gentrification: A Critique', *Transactions of the Institute of British Geographers*, vol.16, 1991, pp.190–8

Bott, E., *Family and Social Network: Roles, Norms, and External Relationships in Ordinary Urban Families*, 2nd edn, London: Tavistock, 1971

Bridge, G.H., 'Gentrification, Class and Community', Oxford: unpublished DPhil thesis, University of Oxford, 1990

_____,'Gentrification, Class and Residence: a Re-appraisal', *Environment and Planning D: Society and Space*, vol.12, no.1, 1994, pp.31–51

Burt, R.S., 'Range', in *Applied Network Analysis: A Methodological Introduction*, R.S. Burt and M. Minor (eds), London: Sage, 1983

Cubitt, T., 'Network Density Among Urban Families', in *Network Analysis: Studies in Human Interaction*, J. Boissevain and J.C. Mitchell (eds), The Hague: Mouton, 1973

Elias, N., 'Towards a Theory of Communities', in *The Sociology of Communities*, C. Bell and H. Newby (eds), London: Frank Cass, 1974

Fischer, C., *To Dwell Among Friends: Personal Networks in Town and City*, Chicago: University of Chicago Press, 1982

Franklin, A., 'Working-class Privatism: A Historical Case Study of Bedminster, Bristol', *Environment and Planning D: Society and Space*, vol.7, 1989, pp.93–113

Giddens, A., *The Constitution of Society: Outline of a Theory of Structuration*, Cambridge: Polity, 1984

_____, *Modernity and Self-Identity*, Cambridge: Polity, 1991

Goodman, L.A. and Kruskal, W.H., 'Measure of Association for Cross-Classification', *Journal of American Statistical Association*, vol.49, 1954, pp.732–64

Granovetter, M., 'The Strength of Weak Ties', *American Journal of Sociology*, vol.78, 1973, pp.1,360–80

Hägerstrand, T., 'Space, Time and Human Conditions', in *Dynamic Allocation of Urban Space*, G. Karlqvist, L. Lundqvist and F. Snickars (eds), Farnborough: Saxon House, 1975

Janowitz, M., *The Community Press in an Urban Setting*, Chicago: University of Chicago Press, 1967

Klein, J., *Samples From English Cultures*, London: Routledge & Kegan Paul, 1965

Laumann, E.O., *Bonds of Pluralism*, New York: John Wiley, 1973

Lockwood, D., 'Sources of Variation in Working-class Images of Society', *Sociological Review*, vol.14, 1966, pp.249–67

Mitchell, J.C., 'The Concept and Use of Social Networks', in *Social Networks in Urban Situations*, J.C. Mitchell (ed.), Manchester: Manchester University Press, 1969

_____, 'Case and Situational Analysis', *Sociological Review (N.S.)*, vol.31, 1983, pp.187–211

Pratt, G. and Hanson, S., 'Gender, Class and Space', *Environment and Planning D: Society and Space*, vol.6, 1988, pp.15–35

Sennett, R. and Cobb, J., *The Hidden Injuries of Class*, New York: Vintage, 1972

Smith, M.P., *The City and Social Theory*, Oxford: Basil Blackwell, 1980

Smith, N. and Williams, P. (eds), *Gentrification of the City*, Boston: Allen and Unwin, 1986

Warde, A., 'Gentrification as Consumption: Issues of Class and Gender', *Environment and Planning D: Society and Space*, vol.9, 1991, pp.223–32

Webber, M.M., 'Urban Place and Nonplace Urban Realm', in M.M. Webber, J.W. Dickman, D.L. Foley, A.Z. Guttenberg, W.L.C. Wheaton and C.B. Wurster (eds), *Explorations into Urban Structure*, Philadelphia: University of Pennsylvania Press, 1964

Wellman, B., 'The Community Question: The Intimate Networks of East Yorkers', *American Journal of Sociology*, vol.84, 1979, pp.1,201–31

Wheeldon, P.D., 'The Operation of Voluntary Associations and Personal Networks in the Political Process of an Inter-Ethnic Community', in *Social Networks in Urban Situations*, J.C. Mitchell (ed.), Manchester: Manchester University Press, 1969

Wirth, L., 'Urbanism as a Way of Life', *American Journal of Sociology*, vol.44, 1938, pp.1–24

Wright, E.O., *Classes*, London: Verso, 1985

Young, M. and Wilmott, P., *Family and Kinship in East London*, Harmondsworth: Penguin, 1957

Chapter 11

What's in a Name? The Social Prestige of Residential Areas in Malta as Perceived by Their Inhabitants

David Boswell

Introduction

The aim of this chapter is to combine the insights and methods of two schools of thought to a unique and interesting context. It draws on both the pioneering work of David Glass on the social grading of occupations in the UK (Glass, 1954) and the urban and anthropological research of J. Clyde Mitchell in Central Africa (Mitchell, 1987). Although I rely heavily on their work, the analysis below is also original: whereas many have investigated occupational prestige and deduced the status of residential areas from their patterns of settlement, occupancy, land values and the socio-economic status of their residents, no one has applied similar techniques to people's perceptions of each other by reference to the social prestige and social stereotypes of the areas in which they live, although Hourihan (1979) had a similar interest. For reasons that will be explained, Malta, effectively a city-state, offered an ideal opportunity for such research. This chapter will therefore provide both an indication of the fruitful influence of Clyde Mitchell's research ideas and analytical skills and an extension of these to a new, but closely related, field of investigation of urban social structure and interaction.

Malta – A Mediterranean City State

The islands of Malta lie at a strategic point in the central Mediterranean between Sicily and North Africa. But, unlike

Sicily, which has been ruled by almost every dominant European power in its time, Malta, from 1530 to its political independence in 1964, had only two rulers – the religious order of the Knights of St John, and from 1800 the British, who were invited to support the Maltese rebellion against the Napoleonic secularisation of the islands and, once victorious, stayed on to run the islands as a fortress-colony. Unlike many depopulated Mediterranean islands, modern Malta has sustained both extensive emigration and a high population concentration and density. About two-thirds of its 320,000 people lived, in the late 1970s, in about one-third of the main island's area, which in total only just exceeds 15 miles by 8 miles.

By reason of their language – which is certainly Semitic and basically Arabic – and their religion – which is unequivocally and enthusiastically Roman Catholic – the Maltese are very specifically identified as a distinct people on the borders of both Christendom and Islamic North Africa. The Maltese people as a whole, including most of the *professinoisti* (professionals), have a self-conscious identity which is neither Italian nor North African and a perception of Malta which sometimes resembles Laputa out of *Gulliver's Travels*, floating in its own ether a little apart from the surrounding world.

Reference to Malta as a city-state is based on more than demographic distribution. Throughout its many representative constitutions during and after UK colonial rule, the island has always had one central government without any second tier of local government. Since 1922, its system of proportional representation has been based on multi-member constituencies with one legislature. Only Gozo has at times had some form of separate administrative identity. But, despite their centralised government and administration, Maltese people are intensely parochial, loyal to their locality and often active in promoting its political, social and especially religious activities. The regular outward celebration of the Christian calendar, with great emphasis on particular local festas, claims not only the attention of local residents, but also the nostalgic opportunity for reidentification with one's roots by those who have married out or migrated internally or even abroad (Boissevain, 1965; 1969; 1984).

The Aims and Research Procedure of the Maltese Urban Mobility Survey

My secondment to the University of Malta in 1977 was directly associated with the development of a joint degree programme in Social Studies for full-time and part-time evening students. In Malta I was impressed by the extent to which people, including my students, made use of locality-based stereotypes in assessing the social status and likely occupation of other people. This was borne out in the answers to open-ended essay questions which helped to suggest the main lines of enquiry. This was designed to incorporate four different lines of questioning and, to some extent, to interrelate them. These were:

1 The residential migratory experiences of the householder and spouse, as well as their occupational histories and housing standards and amenities.
2 The social status accorded to a randomly presented set of occupations, whose selection was based on the results of a much larger but similar assessment of the students' own perceptions.
3 The social prestige accorded to a randomly selected set of Maltese residential areas, whose selection was based on criteria outlined in the following section.
4 The occupational, educational and residential characteristics of the parents, children and children-in-law of the householders and their spouses from which any pattern of social mobility might be investigated.

The stages of enquiry followed a pattern similar to that of Hall and Jones (1950) and Glass (1954), and the investigators were all students from the research methods course for whom up to ten interviews each formed an essential part of their practical experience.[1] The schedule of questions covering the four aspects of the enquiry was administered to a 10 per cent randomly selected sample of households in four urban areas, which were themselves carefully selected for their socio-economic characteristics in order to maximise the chance of differences of direct relevance

1. Aspects of the subsequent coding and analysis of the data were funded by small grants from the Nuffield Foundation and the Research Committees of the Open University.

to the investigation. The actual survey was conducted in the spring of 1979, a few years more than halfway between the previous census of 1967 and the much less extensive census of 1985. A total of 565 schedules were completed, and these form the database for analysis.[2]

The Perception of Social Class in Malta and the Social Status of Occupations

Malta is not only a small country with a vigorous outward expression of religion, but also a state with similarly articulated participation in party politics, organised through party branches and clubs in almost every locality. Initially a feature of the Malta Labour Party (MLP), through the 1970s these permanent political foci were developed by the Nationalist Party as well. The major difference was that the MLP came to power in conjunction with the General Workers' Union, essentially the trade union of Malta Drydocks workers, but greatly extended during Dom Mintoff's years in power, whereas probably only in opposition was there some coalition of interest between the Nationalists and most of the white-collar unions with whom the Labour government was in almost permanent dispute (Boswell, 1980; Kester, 1974; 1980).

Remarkably, despite sixteen years of virtual impotence because of the lack of alternative sources of employment and the effective demolition of apparently alternative pluralist pockets of power, the opposition vote had not been whittled away, nor had the position of the Labour government-sponsored trade union become a practical monopoly, as has often happened in other new states. Early retirement on medical grounds and careful supervision of promotion had, however, ensured a docile civil service, which, although a permanent career entered through examination, and the largest source of employment, lacked a professional administrative *esprit de corps*.

This is relevant to the ways in which social class is perceived in Malta. The population of this tiny state is a highly self-conscious society, deeply and evenly divided in political allegiance. It is in

2. In addition to J. Clyde Mitchell, much gratitude is owed to Caroline Hawkridge, who mastered the computer procedures, and to others who have been involved in various stages of the research, Chris Hamnett, Philip Sarre, Mary Clayton, Douglas Boomer, and to John Hunt for drawing the figures.

the localities that national power is won, and in which both political interests organise their competition alongside the established – but for sixteen years non-party political – pressure of the parochial Church.[3] It is significant that both this study of a wide sample of the Maltese population in four different localities in the conurbation, and that of Edward Zammit (1984), which was directed to different types of Malta Drydocks employees, should have received similar responses to questions concerning people's perception of social class, and that these different strata should have shared a broadly similar view of its structure.

From Table 11.1 it is apparent that, although the majority perceived their society in terms of three 'classes', a substantial minority did view it as dichotomous, especially in the localities with the most manual workers. In older places, however, more people also perceived society as a multi-tiered range of status positions. This dominant pattern of responses in terms of three or more social classes is not only an important indication of Maltese perceptions of their own social structure, but also of methodological importance, because it shows that the exercise in grading occupations was not mainly carried out to please the interviewers, but as an activity based on assumptions already observed and expressed by the subjects.

Although the ranking and grading of occupations is fully

Table 11.1 The Number of Social Classes in Malta as Perceived by Householders in the Four Sampled Localities

No. of classes	Senglea (%)	Fgura (%)	Sliema (%)	Attard (%)
1	0.8	0.0	0.5	—
2	27.1	22.1	19.3	18.8
3	54.9	68.6	66.3	60.9
4	11.3	5.7	9.9	13.0
5	3.8	2.1	2.5	4.3
6 or more	2.3	0.7	1.5	2.8
Total no.	133	144	202	69
No information	5	2	10	—

3. Bishop Gerada is credited with the agreement between Archbishop Gonzi and Dom Mintoff that led to the Church's withdrawal from active political campaigning prior to the 1970 general election and the MLP victory (Koster, 1984; Vassallo, 1979).

reported elsewhere (Boswell, 1982), it may be summarised by observing that householders in the same four sampled localities generally responded in ways consistent with their perception of social class. The loading of factors and patterns of clustering followed lines which may be summarised in the Multidimensional Scaling (MDS) plotting shown in Figure 11.1.[4] There was a single significantly strong dimension which represents a general estimate of occupational prestige within which types of occupations were meaningfully clustered and differentiated. The clusters delineated a high-status service category of professional, managerial and administrative occupations; a less clearly defined central set of categories comprising white-collar occupations, government functionaries and skilled manual workers, and a lower stratum of unskilled manual, petty self-employed and undesirable occupations. Not only was the overall pattern of responses consistent with a view of society in terms of three social classes or status groups, but the responses from each of the four sampled localities were similar, which indicated a high level of common social perception. The more detailed consideration of the social prestige accorded to Maltese residential areas, which is the subject of this chapter, should therefore be considered in this context, and not as a particular phenomenon on its own.

Maltese Patterns of Urbanisation and Perception of Locality Status

Although land values, accessibility and other contemporary phenomena must be associated with people's perceptions of the social prestige, or desirability, of residential areas, I was struck by the way in which the Maltese assessed one another by stereotypes explicitly associated with the reputations of different localities. For centuries this has taken a form not unlike provincial France or the UK, but with a much smaller frame of reference because Malta's settlements can never be more than a few miles apart, and often only a few hundred yards.

But, in addition to these almost proverbial reputations – such

4. Multidimensional Scaling is a method of isolating the theoretically significant relationships among a number of distances among items by removing dimensions while preserving the rank order of distances. The method therefore maintains the pattern in an ordinal form, while making it possible to represent it graphically in a three-dimensional form.

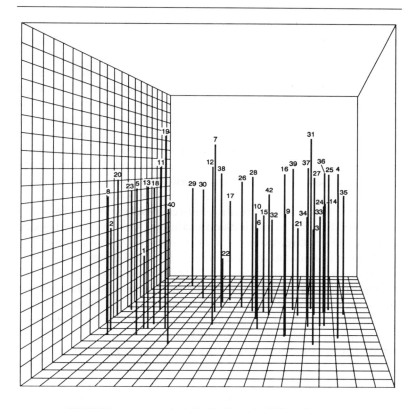

(MINISSA programme included in Coxon's MDS package)

Dimension	1	2	3
Sigma	0.8571	0.3784	0.3495

MAXMIN clusters

Figure 11.1 The Perception of Occupational Prestige by Householders of the Four Sampled Localities Analysed Within a Three-dimensional Social Space

as the meanness of Gozitans or the roughness of people from Mqabba – forms of broad categorisation were superimposed upon this more specific pattern. In their essays my students expressed the strongly felt distinctions that were drawn between the population of 'the other side' of the Grand Harbour in the

'Cottonera' cities of L'Isla, Birgu and Bormla, and the people on 'the Sliema side' whom the others call *'Tal Pepe'*, in reference to their snooty speech.

The social implications of this distinction could not have been more clearly demonstrated than in the two areas' powers of attraction and repulsion. In the 1970s, young people from the three cities would spend their Saturday evenings mingling with those from other parts of the island beside the ruined chalet or pier on Sliema's waterfront, whereas little could induce outsiders to set foot in the Cottonera towns, which they envisaged as a dangerous den of footpads, prostitutes and vicious political mountebanks – a source of much political posturing and legend. In many respects a person's place of residence was taken as indicative of a set of other assumed social factors and attitudes, not least their party political allegiance, which, in a large industrial country such as the UK, would tend to be associated with occupation.

The urban focus of the Maltese population is nothing new. Since the Order of St John was established in 1530, the bulk of the population have been sustained by external funds and the importation of basic resources. Although their activities changed after the eviction of the Knights by Napoleon in 1798, with the naval basis for UK supremacy in the Mediterranean from 1800 the urbanisation of the population proceeded fast (Blouet, 1967; Richardson, 1961). By the end of the 19th century only a minority were in full-time agriculture, and this fell to 10 per cent by 1967 (Malta Government, undated).

The new demographic characteristic was the dependence of the Maltese population on emigration to sustain their increased population without extensive internal economic development. The Mediterranean littoral, then the USA, Canada, and especially Australia after the Second World War, took the mainly unskilled emigrants, leaving Malta with a relatively stable population of just over 320,000 in the twenty years up to the closure of the UK defence base in 1979 (Bowen-Jones, Dewdney and Fisher, 1961; Price, 1954). During the same period there was a dramatic decline in the birth rate, only partly accounted for by the emigration of young adults in their childbearing years (Malta Government, 1986).

Whereas the Knights had built the fortified towns around the harbours, and relatively isolated villas elsewhere, UK enlargement of the dockyard and other defence activities in the early twentieth century was associated with an increased population in these old towns and the substantial construction of residential areas on the northern side of the harbours, which served as summer houses for some of the old city residents and property let to the British, who built their own large barracks there. This urban expansion continued after the Second World War with two major innovations; the first being the foundation of new towns, or rather garden suburbs, at Santa Lucia and San Gwann, and the second being the expansion and rebuilding of the larger village nuclei throughout the island (see Figure 11.2) (Harrison and Hubbard, 1945; Hughes, 1956; 1969; Zammit, 1928).

As people left Valletta or obtained certain sorts of job, so they settled on the Sliema side, whereas the repopulation of the Cottonera after the war is said to have introduced a poorer and socially more depressed working-class population than it had before its elite moved out. Mosta developed as a service area for the centre of the island and another major zone of UK rented accommodation and, after independence in 1964, retired UK settlers set the pattern for the first building boom of rural suburbs with detached villas, a fashion followed by those Maltese who could afford them, and echoed in the subsequent redevelopment of the villages by Maltese owner-occupiers. Meanwhile Floriana and Sliema have respectively adopted some of the institutions and characteristics of governmental and private business districts.

Probably because of its scale and available documentation, Maltese emigration and return migration later in life have received academic attention (Jones, 1973; King, 1979) denied to the recent phase of urban expansion and internal migration, the sources for which are either inaccurate (Malta Government, 1978) or, in the case of the 1967 census, unpublished.[5] Even the 1985 census failed to ask a specific question about place of previous residence, although the general patterns of growth and decline are clear enough. Fortunately the proofs of the 1967 census do provide an instructive table from which the patterns of internal migration over the previous decade have been mapped in Figure

5. The corrected proof of the population volume of this census was withdrawn from publication by order of the new prime minister in 1971, but a copy is now lodged with Melitensia at the university library.

Figure 11.2 Map of Localities in Malta

11.3, and about which three primary observations may be made. First, one notes the flow out of the older central areas to their hinterland on both sides of the harbours and the repopulation of the rebuilt Cottonera towns. Second, the population expansion in the central rural parts is apparent as well as in the south west around UK military and indigenous seaside developments. Third, the exodus of population from rural districts on the north, west and

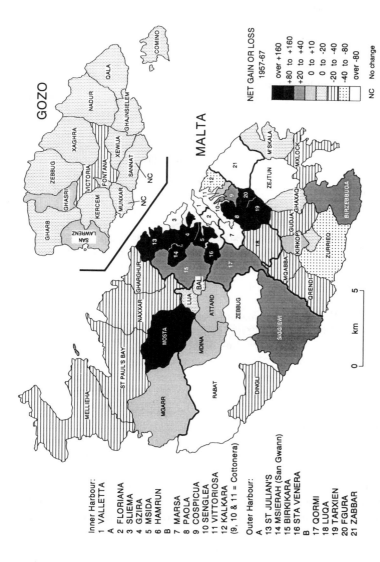

Figure 11.3 Net Inter-locality Flows of Heads of Household in Malta and Gozo, 1957–67
Notes: Data are drawn from Table 11.2. Valletta is treated separately as the capital city

south coasts of Malta continued, and these areas have only been revived by tourist and suburban development since 1967.

Internal migration within the Maltese conurbation, defined by the inner and outer harbour areas on either side of Valletta as shown in Table 11.2, showed a clear pattern of selective migration. Within the general flow from the central to peripheral areas, selective migration was directed to the higher-status, northern sides of the harbours. By contrast the inner-harbour localities on the dockyard side generally migrated out on that same side of the harbour, and the largest number received from the 'other side' of the outer harbour area came from an immediately adjacent district, Hamrun.

The residential expansion and specialisation of settlements has coincided with a substantial shift in the form and distribution of the Maltese economy. Although government employment has been maintained, UK defence establishments had been phased out by 1979, the civilianised dockyard required less skilled labour, and wholesale and retail trading has lost its prominence. Package-tourism has to a great extent replaced these, as well as a variety of a few large and many often short-lived manufacturing companies in new industrial estates on both sides of the Marsa, between Tarxien and Zeitun, in the valley below San Gwann, and on the Mosta plain (Grech, 1978; Malta Government, 1977; 1981; Metwally, 1977).

The effect of these internal migration patterns and the short and cheap journeys to work has been a centrifugal form of conurbation development. New jobs and a wider distribution of incomes has enabled a larger proportion of the population to enjoy the social and residential mobility characteristic of industrialised consumer-oriented societies. Owing to its external funding through the UK military base, the Maltese population indulged in such developments before the development of its own industrial base. Even the government, a late-comer to public housing on any scale except post-war reconstruction, had embarked on major building schemes in most localities by 1970 (Misfud, 1983). By the end of the decade, the sheer quantity of quite recent building – infilling, suburban construction, quasi-new town planning, and in Sliema demolition to provide more new hotels and holiday-flats for foreigners – warranted some sociological investigation. How did the Maltese people perceive their predominantly urban environment?

Table 11.2(a) Net Migratory Flow of Heads of Households Within the Maltese Conurbation, 1957–67

	1	A	2	3	4	5	6	B	7	8	9	10	11	12	C
1. Valletta	—	292	28	64	48	99	53	92	-4	55	26	11	5	-1	132
A. In. Harb. A	-292	—	-78	-91	115	145	-96	1	-42	44	16	5	-4	-18	428
2. Floriana	-28	73	—	24	6	25	18	11	3	10	3	1	-2	-4	37
3. Sliema	-64	91	-24	—	102	38	-25	-2	-6	5	9	-4	-3	-3	183
4. Gzira	-48	-115	-6	-102	—	2	-9	-10	-11	-3	5	-1	3	-3	-1
5. Msida	-99	-145	-25	-38	-2	—	-80	-16	-15	-1	-3	4	1	-2	-23
6. Hamrun	-53	96	-18	25	9	80	—	18	-13	33	2	5	-3	-6	186
B. In. Harb. B	-92	-1	-11	2	10	16	-18	—	-40	78	-33	25	-5	-25	43
7. Marsa	4	42	-3	6	11	15	13	40	—	26	6	4	5	-1	30
8. Paola	-55	-44	-10	-5	3	1	-33	-78	-26	—	-49	7	-9	-1	11
9. Cospicua	-26	-16	-3	-9	-5	3	-2	33	-6	49	—	3	5	-18	-11
10. Senglea	-11	-5	-1	4	1	-4	-5	-25	-4	-7	-3	—	-14	3	-1
11. Vittoriosa	-5	4	2	3	-3	-1	3	5	-5	9	-5	14	—	-8	6
12. Kalkara	1	18	4	3	3	2	6	25	1	1	18	-3	8	—	8
C. Out. Harb. A	-132	-428	-37	-183	1	-23	-186	-43	-30	-11	11	1	-6	-8	—
13. St Julian's	-18	-92	-3	-108	12	12	-5	-12	-1	-4	2	-1	-2	-6	15
14. San Gwann	-13	-88	-5	-53	-10	-9	-11	-10	-2	-4	-3	0	-1	0	-16
15. Birkikara	-60	-73	-18	-5	1	3	-54	14	-1	4	9	3	0	-1	47
16. Sta. Venera	-41	-175	-11	-17	-2	-29	-116	-35	-26	-7	-3	-1	-3	-1	-46
D. Out. Harb. B	-81	-128	-30	-10	-6	-11	-11	-149	-25	-89	5	-28	-6	-6	6
17. Qormi	-6	-33	-2	4	1	-5	-31	20	5	16	-7	2	5	-1	35
18. Luqa	0	3	0	1	-1	4	-1	6	0	7	0	-1	2	-2	5
19. Tarxien	-59	-71	-18	-83	-8	-5	-27	-115	-25	-41	-13	-24	-8	-4	-22
20. Fgura	-17	-27	-8	-9	0	-5	-10	-149	-8	-81	-32	-11	-14	-3	-13
21. Zabbar	1	0	-7	7	2	0	-2	89	3	10	57	6	9	4	1
Total house hold flow	-597	-265	123	-218	168	226	-318	-99	-141	77	25	14	-16	-58	609

Notes: Net flow to (positive); continues to Table 11.2(b)

Table 11.2(b) Net Migratory Flow of Heads of Household Within the Maltese Conurbation, 1957-67

	13	14	15	16	D	17	18	19	20	21	Total h'hold flow	Total heads h'hold (1967)	Total pop. (1967)	Total pop. (1977) (est.)
1. Valletta	18	13	60	41	81	6	0	59	17	-1	597	4,177	15,299	14,096
A. In. Harb. B	**92**	**88**	**73**	**175**	**128**	**33**	**-3**	**71**	**27**	**0**	**265**	**16,576**	**61,743**	**60,500**
2. Floriana	3	5	18	11	30	2	0	18	3	7	123	1,323	4,944	4,695
3. Sliema	108	53	5	17	10	-4	-1	13	9	-7	218	5,997	21,000	20,123
4. Gzira	-12	10	-1	21	6	-1	1	8	0	-2	168	2,634	9,575	9,884
5. Msida	-12	9	-3	29	1	5	-4	5	5	0	-226	2,959	11,437	12,051
6. Hamrun	5	11	54	116	71	31	1	27	10	2	318	3,663	14,787	13,747
B. In. Harb. B	**12**	**10**	**-14**	**35**	**149**	**-20**	**-6**	**115**	**149**	**-89**	**99**	**10,572**	**41,350**	**40,687**
7. Marsa	1	2	1	26	25	-5	0	25	8	-8	141	2,303	9,722	9,147
8. Paola	4	4	-4	7	89	-16	-7	41	81	-10	-77	3,112	11,794	11,789
9. Cospicua	-2	3	-9	-3	-8	7	0	13	32	-57	-25	2,309	9,123	9,208
10. Senglea	1	0	-3	1	28	-2	1	24	11	-6	-14	1,279	4,749	4,698
11. Vittoriosa	2	1	0	3	6	-5	-2	8	14	-9	16	1,076	4,017	3,956
12. Kalkara	6	0	1	1	6	1	2	4	3	-4	58	493	1,945	1,891
C. Out. Harb. A	**-15**	**16**	**-47**	**46**	**-6**	**-35**	**-5**	**22**	**13**	**-1**	**-609**	**8,229**	**32,863**	**34,900**
13. St Julian's	—	14	-1	2	8	-2	0	5	5	0	-99	2,073	7,394	8,043
14. San Gwann	-14	—	-3	1	-1	0	-1	1	0	-1	-128	508	2,122	4,213
15. Birkikara	1	3	—	43	0	-18	-3	14	6	1	-72	4,204	17,213	16,320
16. Sta. Venera	-2	-1	-43	—	-13	-15	-1	2	2	-1	-310	1,444	6,134	6,324
D. Out. Harb. B	**-8**	**1**	**0**	**13**	**—**	**-8**	**-17**	**3**	**89**	**-67**	**-352**	**9,350**	**41,704**	**42,195**
17. Qormi	2	0	18	15	8	—	-4	5	6	1	24	3,272	15,398	15,301
18. Luqa	0	1	3	1	17	4	—	4	6	3	-31	1,124	5,413	5,281
19. Tarxien	-5	-1	-14	-2	-3	-5	-4	—	21	-15	-270	1,943	7,989	6,776
20. Fgura	-5	0	-6	-2	-89	-6	-6	-21	—	-56	-295	700	2,737	4,697
21. Zabbar	0	1	-1	1	67	-1	-3	-15	56	—	158	2,411	10,167	10,104
Total household flow	99	128	72	310	352	-24	-31	270	295	-158	-	48,904	192,940	206,474

Notes: Continuation of Table 11.2(a); net flow to (positive)

The Socio-economic Characteristics of the Respondents in the Four Sampled Localities

The localities selected for the survey all typified characteristics of the urban settlement and internal pattern of Maltese migration. Although based on current observation and printed sources, some of the latter were twelve years old, so it is useful to review the results in terms of initial expectations. Senglea (L'Isla) is an old town built under the Order and developed by Maltese traders in the nineteenth century and later by the British as a dockyard, but the impact of the Second World War was dramatically apparent; 55 per cent of its dwellings had been reconstructed in the subsequent twenty years. By contrast, Sliema was built in the hundred years up to the war, with only 14 per cent built since then for Maltese domestic use. The retailing and hotel streets were omitted from the survey. Ninety per cent of Fgura has been newly built since 1945, and over 64 per cent since Maltese independence in 1964. This is only partly the case in Attard, which consisted of 54 per cent new villas built since 1964, often initially for UK settlers, and 28 per cent dating from before the First World War, often farmer's dwellings – a dichotomous pattern reflected in many other sets of responses from this urban village.

These different settlements and construction histories explain much of the different age distributions of the population of the four localities shown in Figure 11.4.[6] Both Senglea and Sliema had ageing populations, but the motivations for young emigrants differed. Many of those in Senglea wanted to move away even if accommodation was available. The offspring of Sliema could not afford the high land values in competition with commercial and tourist developments. By contrast, Fgura and Attard demonstrated the characteristics of settled immigrant populations of middle-aged couples with their children, although the average age in Attard was increased by the elderly villagers and suburban villa owners, as distinct from the first-time buyers and tenants of Fgura. Over a quarter of Senglea, Sliema and Attard residents had lived there for over twenty-five years, but about two-thirds of Attard's and three-quarters of Fgura's residents were relative newcomers.

The classic pattern of urban development and distribution of

---

6. The apparent absence of female infants from Senglea may result from recording errors.

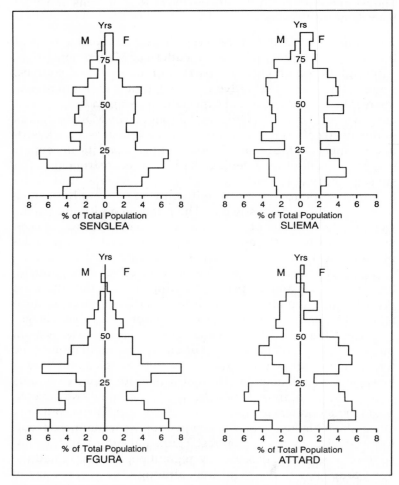

Figure 11.4 Age and Sex of the Total Population in the Households of the Four Sampled Localities

housing types and tenure were found in the Maltese conurbation, and are exemplified in the four sampled localities with a flow from more densely-built and rented inner-city areas to a sparser and privately-owned suburban fringe. Even public housing has increasingly favoured home-ownership schemes. Senglea was typified by private terraced houses and apartments over shops in tall, narrow houses with glazed balconies, almost all of which were let unfurnished at low rentals controlled by statute,[7] including the post-war government flats. But in Sliema, half were owner-occupied or decontrolled rented accommodation. By contrast three-quarters of Fgura and Attard residents lived in their own homes, although only 6 per cent of the former and nearly half the latter lived in detached or semi-detached villas. This again reflects their different positions in the housing market and the sectoral migration of the population from the two sides of the Grand Harbour.

This differentiation is based on the levels of income in the four localities, which were lowest in Senglea, highest in Sliema, and most concentrated within a narrow central band in Fgura. But it is also significant that, despite the remarkably low rentals paid in the controlled sectors of the older localities – half in Senglea and a quarter in Sliema paid less than Lm20 per year – so many residents wanted to own their own homes elsewhere. Attitudinal responses indicated a widespread desire to 'get on' by moving out, with places like Fgura as a stepping stone in the process. As overcrowding has been reduced, Senglea's average occupancy rate has fallen to those of Sliema and Attard, although the poorest and most overcrowded conditions could still be found there. The young families in Fgura, however, experienced the highest occupancy rates, despite the reduced birth rates in Malta since independence.

One would expect a strong relationship between income, occupation and education which combine to determine the types of housing and therefore residential localities within a household's reach. Malta is no exception. Less than a third of Senglean householders had completed more than primary education, and less than 7 per cent of their children had stayed beyond the minimum school leaving age. In the other three localities at least 11 per cent of householders had stayed at school, and in Attard almost half. Between a quarter and a half of their sons had stayed on to complete technical or A-level education, in governmental schools in Fgura, and through private fee-paying Church schools in Sliema and Attard. However, there was a significant difference in the

7. Dwellings built before 1956 were held at pre-1939 rent levels by statute, thereby virtually socialising the older privately rented sector. Although relaxed in 1980, the new controls were extended to cover most dwellings rented to Maltese citizens by specifying the permissible limits to rent increases and easing conversion of such property to home-ownership.

educational experience in Fgura. Whereas the other three tended to maintain their levels of education, Fgura's residents were socially as well as residentially mobile. But a much higher proportion of Fgura's children had failed to proceed beyond the minimum statutory leaving age, with the result that this locality will be a social sifting ground separating those who prosper and move out and those who do not. This potential use of Fgura as a social and residential staging post may explain the much higher proportion of householders who disliked their own locality than was found elsewhere.

The relative ages of each population, of course, determined the proportion in gainful employment and this was further affected by the reduction in UK defence establishments, which were finally closed at the time of the survey in March 1979. Government and Malta Drydocks remained the largest employers, with small-scale industry and commerce – particularly tourism – filling some of the gap. In this chapter it is sufficient to deal in broadly generalised categories, such as the Office of Population and Census Surveys (UK) manual and non-manual occupations, or the Hope and Goldthorpe (1974) classification into three occupational classes (also Goldthorpe, 1980). If householders who were housewives, most of them widows, are excluded, the patterns are very plain. In Table 11.3 the occupational divergence of the localities is obvious in the manual and non-manual or service categories. Only intermediate white-collar, sub-professional and supervisory occupations are relatively evenly spread between them. On both sides of the harbour, as people have migrated out so their participation in the economy has changed. Their children's experience has been rather different because, although the overall pattern is similar, many fewer daughters than sons were in employment, except in Attard, and those who were in work were more often in non-manual jobs than their brothers. It seems that this reflects the different opportunities offered by a more diversified labour market compared to their householder parents.

Fgura's overall position lay between Senglea on the one hand and Sliema and Attard on the other, sharing a wide range of occupations with these latter, but with less attainment of the most prestigious posts. Fgura had technicians and engineers, whereas Sliema and Attard had more professional and senior manager employees. Fgura's interstitial position is further exemplified by its many school teachers, who, like Attard, make up over 7 per

Table 11.3 General Types of Occupation of Householders in the Four
Sampled Localities

	Senglea (%)	Fgura (%)	Sliema (%)	Attard (%)
OPCS Classification				
Non-manual	18.5	48.9	57.7	67.2
Manual	48.3	38.2	23.0	18.5
Armed services not elsewhere included	8.0	3.5	3.8	1.4
Housewives without paid employment	16.5	6.2	14.2	4.3
Inadequately described	7.2	3.4	1.9	7.2
Hope/Goldthorpe Classification				
Service	9.4	33.6	33.5	46.4
Intermediate	28.1	23.3	34.4	29.0
Manual	38.8	33.6	16.0	13.0
Housewives, without paid employment	16.5	6.2	14.2	4.3
Inadequately described	7.2	3.4	1.9	7.2
Total Number	139	146	212	69

cent. Entry into teaching probably represented the most common opportunity for occupational mobility through the education system until the drastic rearrangement of higher education by the government in the late 1970s.[8]

From this brief socio-economic survey, it is apparent that there were considerable differences between the four sampled localities, and that these were consistent with the aims of the survey. With the exception of localities largely dependent on self-employed retailing, or with populations housed in public or private tenements, these four localities do represent Malta's urban types of community. Most importantly, they do represent broad differences in housing tenure, age, income, education and occupation, both in the generations of householders and their children. These differences should be recalled in subsequent sections, where cruder categorical terms may be used in describing these localities.

8. University degrees were abolished except for a restricted set of professions, the system and curricula of secondary education were repeatedly revised, and teacher training courses were considerably lengthened. For several years only about 50 per cent of teacher training places were taken up.

Mobility and People's Experience of Maltese Localities

Reference was made above to the ways in which Maltese people characterise localities, thereby implying a set of political, occupational and general socio-economic judgements. We have also seen how the localities of the survey respondents differed in these respects. From responses to the occupational prestige study it was apparent that the householders of these four localities shared similar perceptions of a local occupational hierarchy. Given the common use of residential stereotypes for a similar purpose, it seemed appropriate to study the social prestige of localities in the same way.

In due course I will argue that certain localities, like certain occupations or, in Mitchell's case, certain ethnic categories (Boswell, 1969; Mitchell, 1974), have the role of 'brand-leaders' for a cluster that are perceived similarly, like Hoovers for vacuum cleaners and Biros for ball-point pens. If this sort of associative labelling occurs, it is likely to operate differently for those within a cluster who 'know' the niceties of their differences, and between one such cluster and others with which members of the former may have less social, physical or other contact.

It is easy to see which localities are closest to each other topographically, and in the first section we have seen who moved where in Malta residentially between 1957 and 1967. Similar patterns were maintained by the householders of the four sample localities in 1979, the most common reasons being associated with marriage – the desire to live near the bride's family – or the necessity of moving out to find their own accommodation. But, even if these past associations are ignored, there are other reasons for close current associations with other localities.

Figures 11.5, 11.6 and 11.7 show the current level of close association between the householders of each of the sampled localities and other places, as evidenced in their place of work, the residences of those children who had left home, and the current residence of the living parents both of householders and their spouses. Most employed householders worked outside their place of residence, but only in Fgura did less than 10 per cent work in their home town; in Sliema this exceeded 17 per cent. This indicates not only the availability of jobs, but the type of work undertaken by the sort of people living in each locality. Householders form Sliema and Attard were twice or three times as likely to work in Valletta as those from Senglea or Fgura,

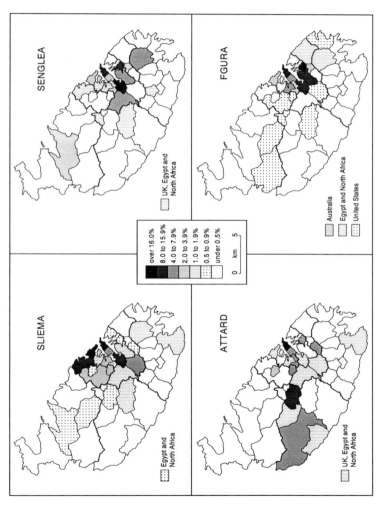

Figure 11.5 Current Workplace of the Householders in the Four Sampled Localities

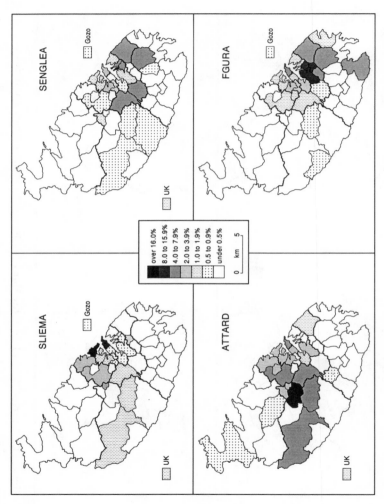

Figure 11.6 Current Residence of Parents of Householders in the Four Sampled Localities

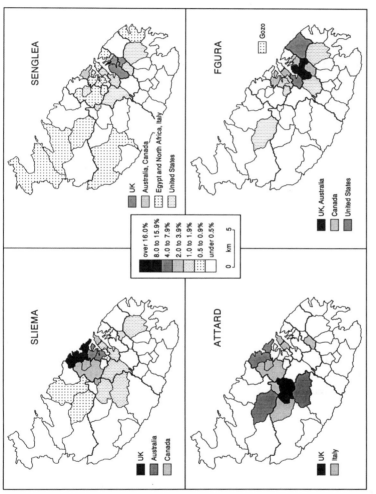

Figure 11.7 Current Residence of Children Living Away from Homes of Householders in the Four Sampled Localities

because the capital city was a centre of governmental, business and some professional work.

This zoning of predominant employment for different localities was even more obvious in the two inner harbour regions. Even after excluding home-town employment from the calculation, nearly half the householders from Senglea and Fgura worked on their own side of the harbour, with less than 10 per cent coming from Sliema and Attard. However, more than 12 per cent went from Senglea to Fgura to work on the other side, particularly in Floriana, another centre of government employment. Broadly speaking, occupational experience of other localities was restricted to the inner harbour regions and adjacent industrial estates, in the cases of Senglea and Fgura, but for Sliema extended to wider use of the outer harbour regions, including the airport. Attard's heterogeneous householders were divided between those working in rural areas as well as the older centres of Maltese government, industry and retailing. In addition to the usual influence of proximity to work, the patterns reflect the extent to which householders of each locality were differentially involved in manual labour and industry, management and government services, or in Attard, even in agriculturally-related work.

From Figure 11.6, different patterns in the distribution of living parents of householders from the four localities are apparent. Valletta, an old city reduced by emigration, was still the home of over 4 per cent, and Sliema housed 8 per cent of these parents. Only Senglea was less interlinked. Each locality except Fgura had a high proportion of second-generation residents, over 50 per cent in Senglea and Sliema, and 35 per cent in Attard – mainly local villagers. Many parents lived in adjacent localities. Indeed, these are the socially and regionally selective links that one associates with sectoral migratory flows, close contact between residents of certain localities, and a tendency to marry within quite circumscribed socio-geographical boundaries.

These patterns are broadly reflected in the distribution of householders' children living away from home (Figure 11.7). But, although only 16 per cent of them lived in the same locality as their parents, this only reached 40 per cent in Senglea and Attard, a reflection of the age structure and the cost and availability of housing in these localities. it was in emigration abroad that children differed from their grandparents. The UK has been a focus for short-term migration from the urban core of both 'working-class' and more educated young people. Only in Fgura was this equalled by the usually long-term migration to Australia, which was common from Maltese villages.

General Perceptions of the Social Prestige of Different Localities

The significance of these locality-specific patterns is that they may modify or reinforce any general status hierarchy of localities through personal experience. In order to assess this, twenty-four localities were selected from a potential Maltese total of about seventy. Most were in the inner harbour or outer harbour regions that form much of the Maltese conurbation, with another eight selected from older villages in other parts of the island, holiday resorts used by Maltese people, and areas with new villas. Householders were given a randomly-ordered set of place name cards and asked to group them in up to five categories (from very high to very low).

Figure 11.8 shows the mean status grading accorded to this set by each sampled locality. Although the overall hierarchy is fairly constant, some responses are locality-specific. With the notable exception of Sliema, Sengleans used a narrower range of the available scale, but the position – e.g. of Taxbiex – may change in grade but not in order. It is more important to seek explanations for more substantial differences in perception. Santa Lucia, a new town or garden suburb with a high proportion of rentable housing, had high prestige for Sengleans who aspired to move there, but was much more lowly placed by the other three localities. Senglea itself was only esteemed by Sengleans, and coupled with Cospicua at the bottom by everyone else. Gzira was probably elevated by Sengleans owing to its position on the other side of the harbour, but despised by the others because of its reputation as a red-light district.

The factor analysis of responses from the combined sample indicated a principal factor accounting for 20 per cent of the variance on which most of the localities were loaded, with the notable exception of the seven most affluent and prestigious localities in the set. By taking the Varimax rotation of the factor matrix, using the principal factor (with iterations), a wider spread of localities across the factors was obtained (see Table 11.4), which virtually reflects each type of urban settlement in Malta. Significantly loaded on the first factor were all the 'working-class' towns in the

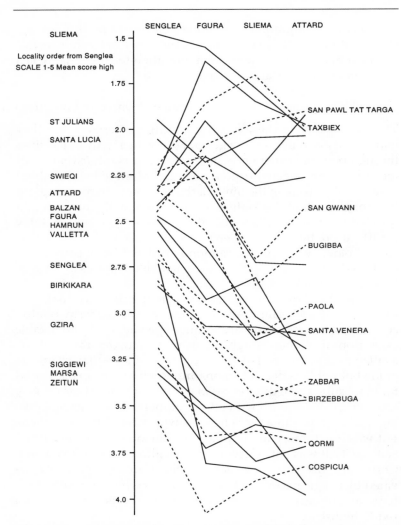

Figure 11.8 Mean Status Grading of Residential Localities in Malta as Perceived by the Householders of the Four Sampled Localities

set: those with the lowest educational and income levels in the 1967 census and the highest levels of manual, industrial employment. Gzira was the main red-light district surviving the departure of the warships. Zabbar and Zeitun were urban villages closely associated with manual labour in the dockyard, new industrial estates on their boundaries, with a reputation for a

Table 11.4 Factor Analysis of the Householders' Assessment of the Social Status of Localities in Malta: Varimax Rotation of the Factor Matrix (With Iterations) Restricted to Seven Factors

Factor 1	Factor 2	Factor 3	Factor 4	Factor 5	Factor 6	Factor 7
Cospicua 0.68	Santa Lucia 0.71	San Pawl-tan-Targa 0.72	Balzan 0.83	Sliema 0.66	Siggiewi 0.66	Santa Venera 0.47
Gzira 0.56	San Gwann 0.58	Swieqi 0.66	Attard 0.72	St Julians 0.57	Zabbar 0.48	
Senglea 0.50	Fgura 0.57	Taxbiex 0.51		Taxbiex 0.35	Zeitun 0.46	
Valletta 0.49	Paola 0.56			Valletta 0.31	Qormi 0.42	
Marsa 0.45	Bagibba 0.43					
Hamrun 0.41	Birzebbuga 0.38					
Qormi 0.38						
Zeitun 0.37						
Zabbar 0.31						

Note: Birkikara is omitted from any significant loading on any factor

rather riotous MLP organisation. Valletta has been a place of major emigration, and Hamrun is a densely-built thoroughfare, adjacent to some of the poorest localities in urban Malta.

Although much less variance is explained by subsequent factors, two questions may be asked. Is there any pattern in the localities loaded on any factor? Does the most heavily-loaded locality at the top of the list represent some form of model or ideal type for those loaded with it, such as one finds with occupational, ethnic and linguistic categories? In analysing ethnicity and social distance, Mitchell (1974) indicated how ethnic groups in town assessed one another according to broad categories associated with a dominant tribe in each group, as well as in terms of more specific sets of tribal hierarchies within each category. There may be some parallel with the levels of categorisation of places as similar which were adopted by Maltese people in assessing the social prestige of residential areas. Given their passionate identification with localities, some of these may act as lodestones for a cluster of similar places, and mention of them may trigger a set of responses and expectations. Cospicua performs such a role on factor 1. On factor 2 fall two new towns, two localities that have absorbed emigrants from the old dockyard towns and two rapidly-expanding seaside resorts used by the Maltese for second homes. Santa Lucia may be seen as a good model for them. Similarly San Pawl-tat-Targa is one of the three most prestigious new and old residential districts constructed by people with high business or professional incomes. And two of three similarly prestigious old villages in the centre of the island are loaded together on factor 4, the third, Lija, not being included in the survey set.

All the 'Sliema-side' harbour localities are loaded together on factor 5, including Taxbiex and Valletta for the second time, probably for different reasons. Taxbiex fitted into both its factor-groups for the same reason, whereas Valletta may have meant different things to different people – damp, dilapidation and overcrowded poverty to some, and the capital city, il-Belt, to others whose business premises and town houses were located there. Loaded on factor 6 are the four large urban villages included in the survey set, three of which had manual industrial populations, hence their loading on factor 1, with Siggiewi having a much higher proportion of its population engaged in full-time agriculture. The two localities that were isolated were Santa

Venera, a suburban infilling adjoining Hamrun and even more recent than Fgura, and Birkikara, which is one of the oldest large urban parishes in Malta, with a largely unskilled manual working population, artisans in small enterprises and a high density of old dwellings.

Irrespective of the statistical significance of their loading, there is some meaning in the resulting categories, which may be further analysed through the hierarchical linkages between the locality statuses, which are based upon their points in a social space. The pattern shown in Figure 11.9 was obtained using Ward's method.[9] It is not the same as the factor loadings, because factor analysis is based on the Euclidean distance on one dimension, whereas hierarchical linkages are based on all dimensions as an overall distance. The regional association between localities seems stronger but the overall pattern is similar to Table 11.4. Three core clusters break down into several smaller groups. Cluster A consists of all the most prestigious old and new localities outside the main towns corresponding with factors two and three. Cluster C links St Julian's and Sliema with the suburban expansion localities and holiday resorts in a consistent way, the older (C4) and new (C3) towns on the Sliema side being relatively distanced from the three on the dockyard side (C2) and the urban village and seaside resort on that side of the island (C1). There appear to be two criteria for association: urban type and regional position. Given the post-war pattern of sectoral migration from the inner harbour core and the social significance attached to residence either side of the harbours, one can see the social reputation of the latter extended to their areas of expansion.

Cluster B is less obviously explicable. B2 consists of the dockyard and other industrial, low-income towns. Siggiewi stands apart, as befits the only essentially agricultural village in the set, but it does not obviously link with Birkikara, which supported two MLP candidates as well as the leader of the Nationalist Party, and therefore lacked the unitary social structure of Siggiewi. B1 and B2 share a low socio-economic status and are clustered with a set of localities linked by their indeterminate status, to which I

9. Ward's method enables the analyst to create clusters by progressively amalgamating closest items, while checking at each step that the clustering could not have occurred by chance according to some predetermined level of significance. See Wishart (1978) for an explanation.

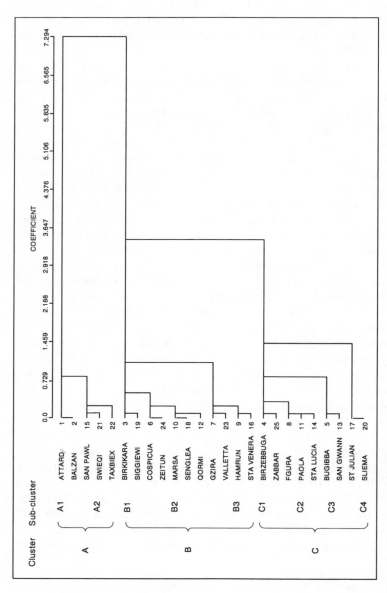

Figure 11.9 The Hierarchical Linkages of Locality Statuses as Perceived by the Householders of the Four Sampled Localities

have already referred. Taken overall, there is a pattern in the clustering of locality prestige according to socio-economic status, regional position and reputation, although there are areas of disputed, ambivalent or intermediate status needing more investigation.

Differential Desirability and Status Perception in the Sampled Localities

In the previous section, the responses of householders from the four localities were aggregated to present a general perception pattern. In the case of occupational prestige a highly significant correlation was found between the four sets of responses but, from Figure 11.8, it is apparent that there was less agreement in the case of locality status where residents were asked to rate their own against others. Responses to an open-ended question as to which localities the householders would most, or least, like to live in provides a useful introduction to the consideration of differences between the four status-linkage dendrograms.

From Tables 11.5 and 11.6 one can see that residents displayed a high degree of loyalty to their own locality. In the case of Sliema and Attard, this was consistent with the desirability of these localities to respondents in other places. But Sengleans were loyal to their own town, which others rejected, although they did reject their adjacent Cottonera towns of Cospicua and Vittoriosa just like everyone else, and selected as desirable localities on the dockyard side of the harbour, places outside the actual dockyard towns, in particular Paola, the oldest nearby expansion town.

Fgura residents, by contrast, preferred or rejected their own locality in equal numbers, which seems consistent with an aspiring and socially upwardly mobile population. Some were glad to have got there, but others were eager to get out. And whereas virtually no one in Attard or Sliema wished to live in the inner harbour around the dockyard, a substantial proportion of Fgura householders preferred the adjacent Paola, although they also rejected the Cottonera towns from which many of them had migrated.

There is a pattern in these variations. First, the residents on the two sides of the harbour did not present mirror-image responses. Local loyalties did not override the general preference for higher-status localities. Second, within each region some localities were more esteemed than others, but this differentiation was more obvious to local residents than people living further off, so that

Table 11.5 Localities Most Liked by Householders in the Four Sampled Localities

Most liked	Householder's Place of Residence			
	Senglea (%)	Fgura (%)	Sliema (%)	Attard (%)
Own locality	Senglea 15.5	Fgura 13.8	Sliema 47.0	Attard 23.0
Capital City	Valletta 1.9	Valletta 1.5	Valletta 3.0	Valletta 3.4
Inner	11.7	17.9	7.0	15.9
Harbour A	Sliema 7.9	Sliema 9.9	Gzira 3.0	Sliema 10.3
	Floriana 1.5	Floriana 1.9	Taxbiex 1.9	Swieqi 2.3
	Other 2.3	Other 4.2	Other 2.0	Other 3.3
Inner	14.8	20.0	1.0	1.1
Harbour B	Paola 6.4	Paola 14.2	Other 1.0	Other 1.1
	Marsa 2.3	Cospicua 2.3		
	Cospicua 2.3	Kalkara 1.9		
	Vittoriosa 1.5	Other 1.6		
	Kalkara 1.5			
	Other 0.8			
Outer	8.7	8.5	17.0	9.1
Harbour A	Hamrun 2.3	Hamrun 1.9	St. Julian's 8.0	Hamrun 2.3
	San Gwann 1.9	St. Julian's 1.9	Birkikara 3.0	San Gwann 2.3
	Birkikara 1.9	Birkikara 1.5	St.Andrew's 2.0	Birkikara 2.3
	Other 1.6	Other 3.2	Kappara 2.0	
	Other 2.0			
Outer	17.9	16.1	3.0	1.1
Harbour B	Fgura 7.2	Zabbar 10.7	Other 3.0	Other 1.1
	St. Lucia 4.6	St. Lucia 5.4		
	Zabbar 4.2			
	Other 1.9			
Region 3	6.9	6.2	3.0	0.0
(SE)	Birzebbuga 2.3	Marsascala 2.3	Other 3.0	
	Other 4.6	Birzebbuga 1.9		
	Other 2.0			
Region 4	10.3	11.8	15.0	27.4
(W)	Rabat 3.0	Rabat 3.0	Balzan 4.0	Balzan 10.3
	Attard 2.3	Attard 3.0	Rabat 3.0	Rabat 6.9
	Balzan 2.3	Balzan 1.9	Attard 3.0	Lija 4.6
	Other 2.8	Lija 1.5	Lija 3.0	Zebbug 2.3
		Other 2.4	Other 2.0	Other 3.3
Region 5	7.8	5.0	11.0	14.6
(N)	St. Paul's Bay 2.3	Other 5.0	Mosta 2.0	Mosta 4.6
	Mosta 1.5		Madliena 2.0	St. Paul's Bay 2.3
	Other 4.0		Other 7.0	Other 7.7
Gozo	0.8	0.0	1.0	1.1
Total no. of mentions	264	261	310	87

Table 11.6 Localities Least Liked by Householders in the Four Sampled Localities

Least liked locality	Senglea (%)	Fgura (%)	Sliema (%)	Attard
		Householder's Place of Residence		
Own locality	Senglea 3.5	Fgura 13.8	Sliema 0.0	Attard 0.0
Capital City	Valletta 9.5	Valletta 12.9	Valletta 20.0	Valletta 19.2
Inner	7.4	8.7	7.0	3.8
Harbour A	Sliema 3.9	Sliema 5.1	Gzira 2.0	Sliema 2.5
	Msida 1.3	Taxbiex 12.0	Msida 2.0	Msida 1.3
	Gzira 1.3	Other 2.4	Other 3.0	Other 0.0
	Other 0.9			
Inner	46.4	51.6	47.0	43.4
Harbour B	Vittoriosa 21.7	Cospicua 18.4	Cottonera 19.0	Cottonera 32.0
	Cospicua 19.9	Cottonera 12.1	Cospicua 13.0	Vittoriosa 3.8
	Marsa 2.2	Vottoriosa 11.3	Senglea 7.0	Marsa 3.8
	Kalkara 1.7	Senglea 8.6	Vittoriosa 4.0	Senglea 2.5
	Other 0.9	Marsa 1.2	Marsa 2.0	Cospicua 1.3
		Other 0.0	Other 2.0	Other 0.0
Outer	4.8	3.5	5.0	5.1
Harbour A	Hamrun 2.6	Hamrun 1.0	Hamrun 4.0	Birkikara 3.8
	Birkikara 1.3	Birkikara 1.5	Other 1.0	Hamrun 1.3
	Other 0.9	Other 0.4		Other 0.0
Outer	10.9	5.9	10.0	15.4
Harbour B	Paola 3.5	Qormi 2.7	Qormi 6.0	Qormi 10.3
	Qormi 3.0	Paola 1.6	Other 4.0	Fgura 2.5
	Zabbar 2.6	Zabbar 1.6		Paola 1.3
	Other 1.8	Other 0.0		Zabbar 1.3
				Other 0.0
Region 3	7.4	13.4	9.0	13.9
(SE)	Gudja 2.2	Zeitun 6.6	Zeitun 2.0	Zeutin 10.3
	Zeitun 1.7	Qrendi 1.6	Other 7.0	Mqabba 1.3
	Mqabba 1.3	Mqabba 1.6		Safi 1.3
	Qrendi 1.3	Zurrieq 1.6		Other 0.0
	Other 0.9	Gudja 1.6		
		Other 0.4		
Region 4	5.7	1.6	6.0	0.0
(W)	Zebbug 2.6	Other 1.6	Zebbug 2.0	Other 0.0
	Dingli 1.3		Other 4.0	
	Other 1.8			
Region 5	6.7	3.6	0.0	1.3
(N)	Mellieha 1.3	Mellieha 1.2	Other 5.0	Mellieha 1.3
	Other 5.4	Other 2.4		Other 0.0
Total no. of mentions	231	256	310	78

one observes broad categories of ascribed status within which lesser hierarchies of desirability, or prestige, were perceived by those acquainted with them. I am not only drawing a close parallel between those expressions of residential desirability and the perception of social prestige, but also between the reference-group patterning of ethnic or occupational categorisation.

Each of the four sets of hierarchical linkages, based on the householder's locality status assessments, were correlated to measure the extent to which one locality's set of responses could be predicted from those of another locality. The first canonical correlation of these different statuses is shown in Table 11.7, from which we infer that there was a significant level of correlation between the four, but that this was highest between Fgura and Sliema and lowest between Senglea and Attard. The old dockyard town residents shared fewer perceptions with the old villagers and their affluent suburban newcomers.

Although space requires a selective discussion, it is worth considering both the larger clusters (lettered in the left margins of Figures 11.10–13) as well as the sub-clusters which form them. Sengleans essentially linked all localities on 'the other side' of the harbours, where there had been extensive post-independence private villa development – in a broad category of high prestige. Birkikara was linked with its adjacent high-status villages, Attard and Balzan (A1), the resort and villa developments on 'the other side' (A2) and the two new towns (A3), of which only Santa Lucia was not on 'the other side'. A second cluster of older high-status and geographically associated localities forms cluster D. Clusters B and C repeat points already discussed above. Sengleans placed their town with those just beyond the Cottonera dockyard core,

Table 11.7 First Canonical Correlations of the Responses Given by Householders in the Four Sampled Localities in Their Assessment of the Social Status of Localities in Malta

	Senglea	Fgura	Sliema	Attard
Senglea	—	0.91166	0.88256	0.85613
Fgura	—	—	0.95189	0.91780
Sliema	—	—	—	0.88833
Attard	—	—	—	—

Note: All significant at 0.005 level

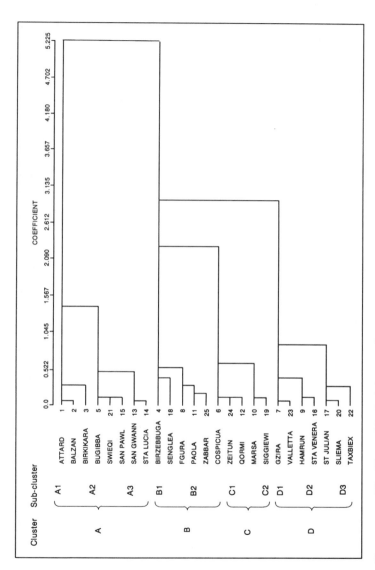

Figure 11.10 The Hierarchical Linkages of Locality Statuses as Perceived by the Householders in Senglea
Note: The diagram uses Ward's method for calculating inter-cluster distances

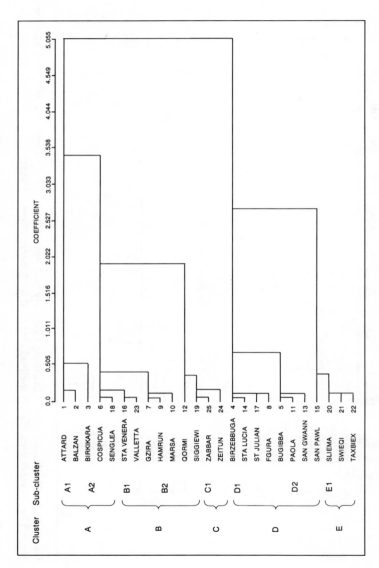

Figure 11.11 The Hierarchical Linkages of Locality Statuses as Perceived by the Householders in Attard
Note: The diagram uses Ward's method for calculating inter-cluster distances

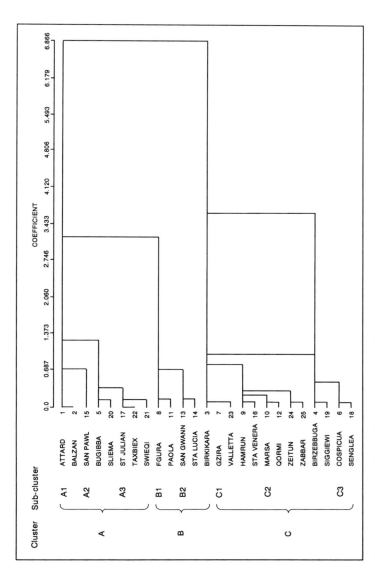

Figure 11.12 The Hierarchical Linkages of Locality Statuses as Perceived by the Householders in Fgura
Note: The diagram uses Ward's method for calculating inter-cluster distances

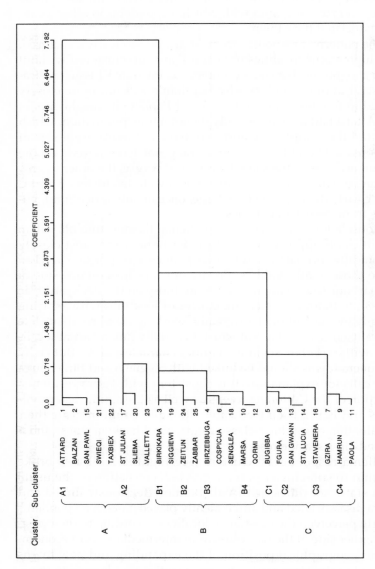

Figure 11.13 The Hierarchical Linkages of Locality Statuses as Perceived by the Householders in Sliema
Note: The diagram uses Ward's method for calculating inter-cluster distances

where they were most likely to migrate or have relatives, and distinguished Senglea from the other industrial and low-status urban and rural localities with which respondents in other localities associated their town.

The pattern of responses from Attard is less clearly structured. The high-status localities in D and E are sub-clustered without clear geographical or socio-economic distinction. E1 is an explicable set, but one wonders why St Julian's was not more closely linked to Bugibba and San Gwann, or Paola to its neighbours in D1. Attard had a small, socially dichotomous population, which affected the sample size and may have led to different sets of responses. The elderly villagers may not have perceived the urban localities in the same hierarchical way as the other townspeople, or simply knew the places less well. In clusters B and C they clearly distinguished the large, once or still agricultural, villages from the urban parishes.

Householders from Fgura and Sliema, the new and old urban localities on opposite sides of the harbour, were most closely canonically correlated, and Fgura's pattern of responses was closest to those of all localities. Prestigious localities on one side of the harbour (A1–3) are linked, as are those on the dockyard side (C1–3), with an intermediate cluster of localities with aspiring socially mobile but often originally 'working-class' residents like Fgura itself (B1–2). The sub-clusters usually link adjacent localities with similar socio-economic characteristics. But why Cottonera towns should be linked with Siggiewi and Birzebbuga (C3) calls for explanation. It is consistent with Fgura residents' rejection of the Cottonera towns as well as the south-eastern villages and Fgura itself (see Table 11.6) and could indicate their devaluation of working-class origins, rural backwardness and a second-class seaside resort.

Sliema respondents' clusters (see Figure 11.13) also broke down into sub-cluster pairs, e.g. A1–2, consisting of the usual high-status localities, with Valletta more tenuously linked and Gzira disassociated and ambivalently placed. Sliema respondents clearly perceived the prestige of localities according to their position either side of the harbours, or in intermediate socio-economic and geographical position of the expanding and new towns (C1–3) but discriminated between localities well-known to them, such as Gzira, which was commonly associated with the high-status localities by respondents on the Cottonera side.

The differences between the patterns of responses from each locality usually seem explicable from the context of their general perceptions and topographical location. Attard householders were fewer in number and drawn from a dichotomous population of peasants and bourgeoisie, which may explain their relative departure from the general pattern. However, it should be emphasised that, even in Attard, this response pattern was significantly correlated with those of each of the other sampled localities.

Plotting the Relationship Between Social Prestige of Localities in a Social Space

This broadly shared pattern of social perception combined with a locality-specific range of variation will affect the overall distribution of the prestige accorded to localities in a social space. This may be represented through the use of the multi-dimensional scaling programs, MDS(X), originated by Roskam and Lingoes, which is a modification of Guttman-Lingoes's smallest space analyses and is included in Coxon's MDS package.[10] We have already seen the patterns in locality loading on different factors and their hierarchical linkages. The final analysis is restricted to three dimensions in order to plot the whole perception pattern within a single perspective using Clyde Mitchell's program (Mitchell and Critchley, 1985). The result provides confirmation of the impression already built up through these other modes of analysis, although the dimensions are more restricted than those potentially available through factor analysis.

Figure 11.14 plots the relationship between locality statuses across pairs of dimensions, which are united in the perspective of Figure 11.15. Given the pattern of sub-clustering, often in pairs, and the subtly different ways in which householders of different localities assessed the same set of places, there is less emphasis on a single dominant dimension, or unilinear distribution, than in the case of occupational prestige. The sigma value of one dimension was much higher than the other two, 0.77 as opposed to 0.49 and 0.41, and indicates the general prestige determinant of the

---

10. J. Clyde Mitchell summarised the process as follows: Minissa Maxmin basically takes the lower triangle of the correlation matrix as its input and then finds space within which the points may be accommodated with the minimum amount of disturbance of the ordinal relationships between the original correlations.

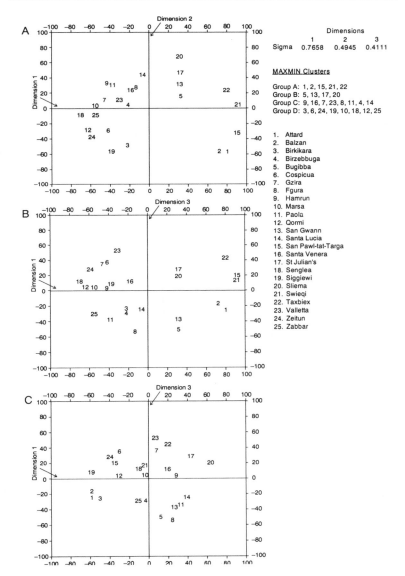

Figure 11.14 The Relationship Between the Statuses of Residential Localities Perceived by All Householders of the Four Sampled Localities
Note: Data analysed within a three-dimensional social space using MINISSA program included in Cox's MDS package

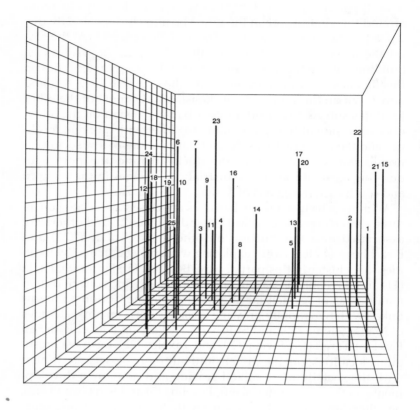

1. Attard	10. Marsa	19. Siggiewi
2. Balzan	11. Paola	20. Sliema
3. Birkikara	12. Qormi	21. Swieqi
4. Birzebbuga	13. San Gwann	22. Taxbiex
5. Bugibba	14. Santa Lucia	23. Valletta
6. Cospicua	15. San Pawl-tat-Targa	24. Zeitun
7. Gzira	16. Santa Venera	25. Zabbar
8. Fgura	17. St Julians's	
9. Hamrun	18. Senglea	

Figure 11.15 Three-dimensional Perspective Diagram of the Statuses of Localities Perceived by All Householders in the Sampled Localities Note: Data analysed within a three-dimensional social space using MINISSA program included in Coxon's MDS package

overall pattern. But the localities were more loosely clustered around this central core in the four Maxmin clusters already discussed in the previous section. The four clusters are: (A) the oldest and newest high-cost and socially select areas of private villa building outside the urban core; (B) the oldest urban localities on the Sliema side of the harbours with the new seaside resort and new town on the same side of the island; (C) most of the other localities subject to considerable urban expansion on the other, dockyard, side of the conurbation, together with adjacent localities and the resort on that side, and (D) localities of low socio-economic status built around the dockyard and the port with outlying agricultural and industrialised villages in the western and south eastern regions of Malta.

Within each cluster some localities are closely associated on all three dimensions, like Attard (1) and Balzan (2), and others are associated on some but not on others, like Valletta (23) and Birzebbuga (4). It is worth exploring what may be shared by localities that cluster in this partial way. Bugibba (5), Fgura (8), Paola (11) and Birzebbuga (4) form one example, in which one finds two major areas of residential migration from the Cottonera towns linked with two rapidly-growing seaside resorts on opposite sides of Malta. Sliema (20) and St Julian's (17) are on a level with San Pawl-tat-Targa (15), Swieqi (20) and Taxbiex (22), the most prestigious localities, on one dimension, but more closely associated with the socially more mixed seaside and new town developments on that side of the island, Bugibba (5) and San Gwann (13), on other dimensions. Dimension 3 with dimension 1, clearly separates the two sides of the harbour, with only Santa Lucia, the other new town, placed topographically between them, close to the dividing line. Birkikara is the only town 'misplaced' in this respect, but, as already described, this is often the case with this locality. Within the low-status sector, a quarter of the plot consists of all towns and villages with the lowest socio-economic status, as well as Valletta (23) and Gzira (7), about which respondents showed divided opinions, in a marginal position.

Conclusion

In his Central African work, Clyde Mitchell (1987) has demonstrated the value of factor and cluster analysis, as well as MDS plotting, in presenting and analysing occupational prestige and the use of selective marital, residential and attitudinal data for delineating both the perception and practice of ethnic differentiation. With his methodological help, in this chapter I have sought to use this range of techniques, supported by more elementary analysis or other relevant questions, to investigate the significance of, and the patterns in, the ways in which Maltese people accord social prestige to residential areas.

Malta is sufficiently large for people to resort to broad social categorisation as well as local specification. But the island is sufficiently small for respondents to be referring to the same localities with a shared knowledge of the places or their reputation. In principle the method could be applied elsewhere but might not offer much more than a reflection of occupational distribution. As I observed at the outset, Maltese people seem to have a sense of places that is so often and so pointedly expressed that residence could be seen as a social characteristic like ethnicity, and this is borne out in the results of this study.

By comparison with occupational prestige, there is not as high a level of commonality in the assessment of the status of residential areas by residents of different localities. But, as the sample was stratified by locality, one would expect this to have some impact on responses. More importantly, the pattern of their responses showed less emphasis on a single dimension, but rather the clustering of like localities in distinct groups. A broad distinction was drawn between localities on either side of the great social watershed that runs out of Valletta up the Hamrun road: the distinction between 'them' and 'us' on either side of the harbours. Another distinction was drawn between expanding urban residential areas, usually of mixed private and public housing, and older, built-up localities within the harbour regions. These latter criteria tended to be used to form clusters within the former mode of differentiation.

Where response patterns differed between the four localities, these reflected not only a general loyalty to one's home town (except in Fgura), but consistency with the householders' separate evaluations of the places in which they would most, or least, like to live. The differences did not alter the broad categorical status dimension, but the criteria respondents may have used for assessing what appear statistically as related clusters. In discussing what these may have been I have drawn on my knowledge of these localities and the socio-economic evidence in the 1957 and 1967 censuses.

Respondents were asked where they would most and least like to live, which streets or districts in their own localities carried highest or lowest status, and where in Malta they would be most likely to find most residents like themselves. This was intended to prepare them for questions with which this chapter has been primarily concerned, so they started from a common ground. Responses should not, therefore, have been haphazard, although they may have been more or less informed about the particular characteristics of certain places, which is an acceptable basis for differences. In discussing the locality clusters I have therefore assumed that the respondents were indeed assessing them according to some form of social grading, but also drawn on my own knowledge of the socio-economic characteristics of these localities. Of course, the respondents' actual experience of other localities, e.g. through internal migration, may have influenced their perception, as may their age, education, occupation and housing tenure status, and I have taken these factors into account in my discussion of the results, but this survey was stratified by locality, so it would be inappropriate to use these other variables for this purpose.

This chapter has been concerned with the general perception of the social prestige of localities by a population of householders living in significantly different types of locality within the Maltese conurbation. This perception took the form of a status hierarchy less unilinear than their assessment of occupational prestige, and characterised by distinct clusters of similar localities. In some cases one locality may have acted as an example with which others were then associated, such as Sliema or the Cottonera cities as ideal types for their respective sides of the harbour. Had I wished to classify Maltese localities by urban type, I could not, on the evidence available, have achieved anything more generally precise, nor as subtly variable, as the responses reported here. Given the fact that much of the 1967 census was never published, it cannot have predisposed their responses.

One may therefore conclude that Maltese people in general have very clear perceptions not only of their own locality and others near or like it, but also of the island as a whole. The perceptions closely accord with socio-economic characteristics verifiable from other sources. They have been found in a population known to have high, but often sectoral, patterns of internal migration and association with other localities, as well as a high level of participation in local festivals and a high electoral turnout. If this method of inquiry has proved reasonably effective in a situation were meaning could be attributed to statistical clusters by independent formation, it may be appropriate to consider its application to other countries where less is already known about their populations and socio-economic differentiation, and reputational assessments may provide a guide.

Bibliography

Blouet, B., *The Story of Malta*, London: Faber & Faber, 1967

Boissevain, J., *Saints and Fireworks: Religion and Politics in Rural Malta*, London: Athlone, 1965

_____, *Hal-Farrug: A Village in Malta*, New York: Holt, Reinhart and Winston, 1969

_____, 'Ritual escalation in Malta', in *Religion, Power and Protest in Local Communities*, E.R. Wolf (ed.), Amsterdam: Mouton, 1984

Boswell, D.M., 'Personal Crisis and the Mobilization of the Social Network', in *Social Networks in Urban Situations*, J.C. Mitchell (ed.), Manchester: Manchester University Press, 1969

_____, 'Patron–Client Relations in the Mediterranean With Special Reference to the Changing Political Situation in Malta', *Mediterranean Studies*, vol.2, no.1, 1980, pp.25–42

_____, 'Patterns of Occupational and Residential Area Prestige in the Maltese Conurbation', paper for the 10th World Congress of Sociology, Mexico City, 1982

Bowen-Jones, H., Dewdney, J.C. and Fisher, W.B., *Malta: Background for Development*, Durham: Durham University, Department of Geography, 1961

Glass, D.V. (ed.), *Social Mobility in Britain*, London: Routledge & Kegan Paul, 1954

Goldthorpe, J., Llewellyn, C. and Payne, C., *Social Mobility and Class Structure in Modern Britain*, Oxford: Clarendon, 1980

Grech, J., *Threads of Dependence*, Malta: University Press, 1978

Hall, J. and Jones, D.C., 'Social Grading of Occupations', *British Journal of Sociology*, vol.1, no.1, 1950, pp.31–55

Harrison, A. St B. and Hubbard, R.P.S., *Valletta: A Report to Accompany the Outline Plan for the Region of Valletta and the Three Cities*, Valletta: Maltese Government, 1945

Hope, K. and Goldthorpe, J., *The Social Grading of Occupations*, Oxford: Clarendon, 1974

Hourihan, K., 'The Evaluation of Urban Neighbourhoods 1: Perceptive' and '2: Preference', *Environment and Planning A*, 1979, pp.1,337–53 and 1,355–66

Hughes, J.Q., *The Building of Malta During the Period of the Knights of St. John of Jerusalem*, London: Tiranti, 1956

_____, *Fortress: Architecture and Military History in Malta*, London: Lund Humphries, 1969

Jones, H.R., 'Modern Emigration from Malta', *Transactions of the Institute of British Geographers*, no.60,1973, pp.101–19

Kester, G., *Workers' Participation in Malta: Issues and Opinions*, Malta: Department of Economics, 1974

_____, *Transition to Workers' Self-Management: Its Dynamics in the Decolonizing Economy of Malta*, The Hague: Institute of Social Studies, 1980

King, R., 'The Maltese Migration Cycle: An Archival Survey', *Area*, vol.11, no.3, 1979, pp.245–9

Koster, A., *Prelates and Politicians in Malta: Changing Power-Balances Between Church and State in a Mediterranean Island Fortress (1530–1976)*, Assen: Van Gorcum, 1984

Malta Government, *Malta Census 1967: Census of Population, Housing and Employment*, Valletta: Central Office of Statistics, undated

_____, *Annual Abstract of Statistics: 1976*, Valletta: Central Office of Statistics, 1977

_____, *Demographic Review of the Maltese Islands for the Year 1977*, Valletta: Central Office of Statistics, 1978

_____, *Malta: Guidelines for Progress: Development Plan 1981–1985*, Valletta: Office of the Prime Minister, 1981

_____, *Census '85: Volume 1: A Demographic Profile of Malta and Gozo*, Valletta: Central Office of Statistics, 1986

Metwally, M.M., *Structure and Performance of the Maltese Economy*, Malta: Aquilina, 1977

Mifsud, P.V., 'A Study of the History, Allocation, Social Composition and Role of Government Housing in Malta', unpublished PhD thesis, Valletta: University of Malta, 1983

Mitchell, J.C., 'Perceptions of Ethnicity and Ethnic Behaviour: An Empirical Exploration', in *Urban Ethnicity*, A. Cohen (ed.), London: Tavistock, 1974

_____, *Cities, Society and Social Perception: a Central African Perspective*, Oxford: Clarendon, 1987

_____ and Critchley, F., 'Configuration Similarity in Three Class Contexts in British Society', *Sociology*, vol.19, no.1, 1985, pp.72–92

Price, C.A., *Malta and the Maltese: A Study in Nineteenth Century Migration*, Melbourne: Georgian House, 1954

Richardson, M., 'Modern Malta – a Population and Migration', in *Malta: Background for Development*, H. Bowen-Jones, J.C. Dewdney and W.B.

Fisher (eds), Durham: Durham University, Department of Geography, 1961

Vassallo, M., *From Lordship to Stewardship: Religion and Social Change in Malta*, The Hague: Mouton, 1979

Wishart, D. *CLUSTAN: User Manual*, Inter-University Research Council Series Report no.47, Edinburgh: Program Library Unit, Edinburgh University, 1978

Zammit, E.L., *A Colonial Inheritance: Maltese Perceptions of Work, Power and Class Structure With Reference to the Labour Movement*, Malta: Malta University Press, 1984

Zammit, T., *Valletta: A Historical Sketch*, 3rd edn, Valletta: Empire Press, 1928

Afterword

J. Clyde Mitchell

It gave me considerable pleasure when Alisdair Rogers and Steve Vertovec asked me to write a conclusion to this book. They had both been students of mine when I was at Nuffield College, Oxford, before I retired, and I saw a good deal of them when they were writing their theses. I continued to have contact with them after they had duly completed the requirements of their doctorates. Many of the other contributors to this book were also students of mine at Oxford, although Kayleen Hazlehurst received her doctorate from Toronto. Bruce Kapferer and David Boswell date from my Central African days. Pnina Werbner and Muhammed Anwar, together with Bruce and David, are associates from my stay in Manchester before I moved to Oxford.

It is perhaps a characteristic of anthropological-type research that the contact a supervisor has with students who are engaged in participant observation is intense. One lives through the research experience of one's students as they are conducting their inquiries. This does not mean, of course, that one knows as much about the research material as the student does. That would be ridiculous, since the researchers in participant observation have personal (and usually intimate) experience with the events described in their reports. I kept in touch with those doing research in distant places by requiring them to write me a letter at least once a month, describing to me what they had been doing and what they felt about their activities. I tried to write back to them as soon as I had received their letters, commenting on their experiences and generally suggesting lines of enquiry which might be helpful in their research. I required them to write to me once a month even if they had little to report, because I know how lonely anthropological research can be when one is living as a stranger amongst people who may be one's hosts, but who may nevertheless feel a trifle distant to the stranger in their midst.

When it came to those who lived within easy distance of Oxford, I tried to see them as regularly as I could to give them an opportunity to 'get things off their chests' if they were having a difficult time.

It is obvious that the events which attracted their attention depended partly on what their undergraduate training had been, but, I submit, also upon ideas they had picked up in their association with me. Not all the contributors, I repeat, had been my doctoral students. Only they can describe the process whereby the parallels in what they were observing in the field with what they had either read or heard from me prior to getting there developed. In the event, four authors seem to have settled on ceremonial events in their field in which *The Kalela Dance* (Mitchell, 1956) appeared to provide hints on how to extract theoretical meaning from what they were observing.

The Kalela Dance Revisited

I shall start with Kapferer's account (Chapter 2) of the performance of a group of Aboriginal actors at a theatre in a northern Australian town. Tourists form an important element of this town's economy, and the theatre is one of the main attractions. The emphasis in the entertainment is on Aboriginal customary practices, and includes performances on the didgeridoo as well as mock battles and the like, all relating back to the common view of Australian Aboriginal culture. But Kapferer points out that the performance is not intended to be an accurate portrayal of this culture, but rather a statement of the identity of a group of Aborigines in a bureaucratic system dominated by white Australians. Many local Aborigines object to the theatre because they feel that the performances are not accurate reflections. Kapferer's point is simply that, in presenting their 'differentness' to predominantly white tourists – many of whom are white Australians – the local Aborigines are making a statement to the effect that they are different and have something of their own to distinguish themselves from other Australians. The main burden of what Kapferer has to say is that the statement of identity by the players is a consequence of the whole bureaucratic structure of the Australian administration. It cannot be understood without reference to this overarching context. In this respect, his analysis accords very well with that of *The Kalela Dance*.

The second chapter to draw inspiration from *The Kalela Dance* is that by Alisdair Rogers (Chapter 4). He describes two public performances in Los Angeles. The first is mainly associated with Latinos and celebrates 5 May, the day on which Mexican forces defeated the French army in 1862, and which therefore symbolises an anti-imperialist struggle as well as expressing national solidarity. The intriguing contradiction is that the event being celebrated refers to a completely different historical era and to a completely different national state. He elucidates this contradiction by drawing attention to the ethnic identity of Mexicans and other Spanish-speaking immigrants in the USA. The parade combined the participation of Latinos with that of others, while both traditional Mexican and modern African-American music filled the air; the local police chief, a white male, dressed as a *caballero*; the award ceremony at the end recognised the contributions both of groups in traditional costume and younger Latinos who had adopted African-American dance and musical styles. It is clear that the expression of identity in this parade refers not so much to Mexican identity *per se*, but to the identity of Mexicans as citizens of Los Angeles.

A second occasion which exhibited *kalela*-like characteristics was the day of dedication of a renamed street and small park in the same neighbourhood of Los Angeles. Santa Barbara Boulevard was renamed Martin Luther King Jr Boulevard. This occasion was more low-key than the Cinco de Mayo parade, but nevertheless provided the opportunity for the African-American population of Los Angeles to make a statement about their identity. Rogers points out the paradox of switching the names of urban features from Latino to African-American just as the surrounding streets are shifting from African-American to Latino.

Rogers develops the idea of competition between the two groups, which was not open, but latent. They occupied different positions in the local economy and polity, and also different residential areas, although Latinos were at that time beginning to move into African-American neighbourhoods in ever-larger numbers. He has thus used his observation of the two social situations to explore the nature of the relationships between two different ethnic groups in Los Angeles. In doing so he is able to show how complex the situation is, but also how the somewhat different situations may be used to make statements about the social position of disadvantaged ethnic immigrants on the one hand, and the mobilisation of ethnic sentiments without necessarily generating hostility on the other. This analysis shows how the prescient use of some of the ideas expressed in *The Kalela Dance* some thirty-six years ago may help us to understand a particularly complex situation in modern Los Angeles.

Kayleen Hazlehurst (Chapter 3) analyses the investiture of two Maori dignitaries in New Zealand which served to mobilise ethnic sentiments of the country. The investiture was held on a public holiday which marked the signing of the Treaty of Waitangi (1840) between the indigenous Maori and the invading UK colonists. From Hazlehurst's description it is apparent that the treaty, though originally intended to secure peaceful relationships between the two sides by securing Maori land rights, traditions and customs, has come to represent for many of the younger Maori an occasion which glorifies the white colonialists. The conflation of an honour decreed by a symbol of colonial power, the Queen, with a celebration of the treaty on a site normally reserved for Maori rites was clearly unacceptable to many present. On the night before the ceremony the matter had become the subject of heated debate, and in the early hours a resolution was passed that the people did not want the investiture to proceed. One of their number was delegated to put this point to the dignitaries the next day.

Hazlehurst then describes in some detail the course of events on the day itself. A police unit had been organised to keep the peace in case of trouble. The appearance of the symbol of control of the colonial power on these special premises was clearly considered to be insensitive by the protesters, and served to exacerbate the situation. During the ceremony a young militant leapt on to the dais where the investiture was taking place. Though his intention was not clear, he was thrown to the ground by the dignitaries' supporters, and the police moved in. Several young protesters were arrested and subsequently charged with rioting, although these charges were later dropped. The ceremony was quickly completed.

In analysing the events surrounding the investiture, Hazlehurst refers to Gluckman's 'Analysis of a Social Situation' and to *The Kalela Dance*. She remarks how these analyses emphasised how ceremonies reflected the wider social and political environments in which they took place. While this is undoubtedly true in the earlier two studies, the wider framework was implicit. The ceremonies assumed the framework, but did not directly attack it. The opposition was expressed symbolically and indirectly. In this respect Hazlehurst's account of the Waitangi Day incident differs substantially from the earlier studies; in the former, the protest was obviously more direct.

Susan Smith's Chapter 5, like *The Kalela Dance* and the chapters by Kapferer and Rogers, addresses an occasion of entertainment rather than serious political confrontation. She deals with an annual celebration which takes place in a small market town in the Borders of Scotland. The towns of this area lie between two powerful but different neighbours. The English were hostile conquerors in the past, and frequently dispatched armed forces through the Borders to attack Scottish forces further north. The northern Scots however, in the shape of the Highlands, provided much of the popular cultural imagery of Scotland. There was therefore a good deal of pressure on the people of Peebles to differentiate themselves publicly from their neighbours. For this they used an annual parade in the late spring or early summer, an occasion called Beltane by the locals. In its present form it seems to date from 1897. 'Beltane' in fact refers to a pre-Christian deity associated with Baal, whom the Border inhabitants propitiated for good crops and the welfare of their beasts every year. Smith does not here explain why the ceremony was revived in 1897, nor why it had fallen into abeyance. At the time of the events reported by Smith, the Beltane had incorporated a 'beating of the bounds' to emphasise the geographical identity of the town. She stresses that the occasion was one of fun, civic pride and local celebration, and that, although tourists may appear as spectators, they have no role in the proceedings themselves.

It would seem that, in the same way as the performance in the Tjakupai Theatre in northern Australia or the Cinco de Mayo parade in Los Angeles expressed the sentiments generated in a socially insecure situation by inhabitants who felt it necessary to re-emphasise their identity, the residents of Peebles achieved a good deal of satisfaction by making an annual public statement of who they were; along the way they also had fun. In this sense I feel that the Beltane has much in common with the *kalela* dance.

Social Network Analyses

Three chapters in this volume use ideas generated from the recent interest in social networks. Muhammed Anwar (Chapter 9), for example, uses data he collected among Pakistani migrants in Rochdale in 1973, and then again in 1985. He uses them to trace the changes in social relationships amongst his sample. Although only sixteen of the original twenty respondents were left by 1985, Anwar has been able to show that over time the relationships between the sixteen have become closer. He demonstrates this by using the formal methods of social network analysis. Anwar interprets these changes as being due to the effect of three things: the spreading of social relationships amongst those remaining over time; the relationships which have been generated through the contacts made by children, and finally through the activities of Pakistani organisations.

There seem to me to be some questions in this material which may be worth exploring. For example, would it be possible to identify characteristics of the patterns of social relationships of those who had moved out of Rochdale which might provide some insight into why these four rather than the other sixteen had chosen to move? Did they move for purely economic reasons? The fact is that network studies in general are notoriously synchronic. Analyses over time are still very rare, and when they appear one hopes that they will provide hints for further research into the dynamics of networks.

Pnina Werbner's analysis of Pakistani migrant workers in Manchester (Chapter 8) also has a temporal dimension to it. The central figure in her study had been in Manchester for many years, and the changes in his network over time are addressed in an earlier publication, *The Migration Process* (1990). In her essay in this volume she deals with the pattern of relationships among friends and colleagues in terms of the exchange of gifts. She is able to show how some migrants from a particular region of Pakistan have settled in Manchester but retained some of their original relationships. Using formal methods of network analysis, she analyses the links among fifteen of the close friends of Iftahar, demonstrating how the network reflects involvement with close friends in different places and different contexts. Werbner is able to make good use of the custom of making gifts of candy and other sweetmeats to friends on various occasions to show how the relationships with different friends vary. In doing this she relates the observations she has made back to the structure of the network links among the set of friends. In this way the whole matter of gift-giving is given a clear and unequivocal reference, and her analysis is a model of combining formal network analysis with ethnographic interpretation.

Gary Bridge's Chapter 10 provides the third example of the use of network ideas to illuminate a problem. The issue is the nature of personal links in relation to the pattern of local social structure during the process of gentrification in a London suburb. Bridge is a geographer, and as a result is particularly interested in the localisation of social networks. He concludes that geography is critical to the conceptions of the distinctions between network structures typical of the working class and the middle class. The former, he suggests, are usually presumed to be geographically localised and dense, while the latter are though of as less local and more sparse. Bridge uses only elementary network analysis, a restriction which stems from limitations of funds and time. Even so, from the data collected from fifty respondents and described by simple network measures, he demonstrates how these measures relate to social class and geographical dispersion. From the data he is able to cast doubts on the widely accepted generalisations about the 'closed' networks of working-class households and the relatively open networks of middle-class households. In this chapter Bridge opens up a number of consequential research topics which he had not been able to pursue at the time. The value of all good research is to throw up more research problems than those answered in the research.

Further Enquiries

There is more diversity among the four remaining chapters in the book. They take up very different research interests of mine in the past, and make their distinctive contributions to them. The most general and most philosophical is that by Chris Pickvance (Chapter 1), who explores the topics of comparative analysis, causality and case studies.

Pickvance raises important questions about the strategy of research, and argues that what is missing from J.S. Mill's discussion of the scientific method is the significance of the observer's theoretical approach in deciding what the significant causal features are in any set of events. It is only theoretical analysis which can isolate the essential from the non-essential causal features. He criticises my own discussion of the use of case studies in determining the causal linkages in observed phenomena on the grounds that a single case study may be analysed differently by observers with dissimilar theoretical perspectives. This, of course, is all too true. Much heat and little light has been generated from many discussions of this sort, and I am sure that the same will happen again. My own defence of the position I was arguing for in an article a decade ago is that the really telling case study is not just any case study in general, but the *strategic* case study, i.e. the case study so chosen as to illuminate alternative explanations. I do not for one moment consider that the use of strategic cases would resolve the issue, since analysts working within strongly-held theoretical positions will no doubt see in any case study, however strategic or otherwise, whatever they are predisposed to see. In the end, the interpretive position will be decided by the uncommitted academic community at large.

Peter Jackson (Chapter 6) handles a very different problem in sociological analysis. His study is based on the development of localities in New York and Minneapolis-Saint Paul. The problem that he addresses is the process whereby run-down urban areas become the focus for redevelopment and gentrification. In particular he concentrates on the buildings of the Twin Cities and the warehouse lofts of inner New York, which had fallen into disrepair with the passing of their original economic rationales. In the latter, artists who were looking for more spacious studios than were usually available to them in conventional apartment buildings opted to bear the state of disrepair and the absence of regular urban facilities in order to obtain cheap and appropriate working and living spaces. In due course the places became fashionable, and the warehouses were refurbished to cater to a wealthier class of residents. Jackson is able to show how similar processes occurred in different areas and cities, thereby uncovering both regularities and local specificities in the redevelopment process.

Margaret Grieco (Chapter 7) deals with a process not often reported in Western industrial societies, but familiar to those of us who have worked in colonial settings. I refer to what is frequently called 'labour migration' or perhaps more accurately, 'labour circulation'. This is a topic which was so much a part of colonial society in the part of Africa where I worked that I spent some time trying to clarify the social processes underlying it. The essential feature of this process is that workers leave their homes to seek wage-earning employment. Because the places where they can find this employment are situated at some distance from their places of residence, they migrate from their homes for a period. In Africa this was frequently a matter of some years, but in Kent it was only for a few weeks every year. In Grieco's example, the workers seeking employment were women and children, in contrast to Africa, where the migrants were almost entirely male. In Africa women cultivated the fields to support themselves with food, and children were kept back in the village until they reached a wage-earning age. In Kent the women and children repaired to the fields and left the men in their London homes, although in both Kent and Africa the spouses made short visits to their absent partners.

In the African context the period of absence was usually for two years or more, and frequently followed the birth of an infant. But in Kent the absence was shorter, and after three or so weeks women returned to resume their normal domestic duties. In spite of these differences there is a striking structural similarity in the two situations which, to her credit, Grieco has been able to highlight. By the device of spending temporary absences at places where waged employment is available, the family as a whole is able to not only sustain their existence, but also able to improve it by securing extra income. Grieco describes how the whole process of migration was organised. The workers usually returned to the same farmers year after year. It was usual for a matriarch in the community to arrange for transport. By contrast, in Africa the migration which I observed was usually an individual affair, sometimes achieved on foot, but most commonly by motor coach.

The organisation of the labour was facilitated by local kinship and neighbourhood ties, according to Grieco. The role of the local matriarch was crucial in obtaining employment and guaranteeing the farmer reliable labour at the critical time of harvest. It is in this sense that the idea of social networks plays an important part in Grieco's presentation. She admits, however, that she did not have the requisite network data to enable her to use formal analytical methods. Instead she uses the concepts in a general way to suggest the mechanism of the social arrangements of the type of labour circulation she describes.

Chapter 11, by David Boswell, picks up on a long-standing interest of mine, namely the formal quantitative procedures for revealing the patterns in social data. He chooses to analyse the prestige of occupations and residential areas in Malta, where he was engaged in teaching and research for several years. In this study he makes use of questionnaire data collected in interviews by students taking a research course at the university. A total of 565 schedules were completed, based on a 10 per cent random sample of households in four selected urban areas. He devised a questionnaire which asked questions both about the residents' perceptions of the social standing of a number of Maltese residential areas and about the prestige rating they accorded to a number of occupations. Methods have been developed to analyse data of this kind. Boswell was particularly interested in making the patterns of responses in these data apparent. For this purpose he makes use of a number of devices which have been developed for particular use on sociological data where measurement techniques imply that some measurement error is likely.

The main technique he uses is Multidimensional Scaling (MDS), which is a device to represent the relationships among the elements in the analysis effectively in as few dimensions as will not distort the relationships too severely. He uses this technique both to study the structure of the perceptions of occupational prestige as well as the perceptions of the prestige of places of residence. Boswell employs a dendrogram to depict the perceived prestige of occupations, and hence structure social status as perceived by the respondents. To analyse the perceived prestige of localities he makes use of three-dimensional diagrams. He elaborates his analysis by comparing the locality-prestige perception of respondents from several localities, some accorded general high prestige, others lower prestige. This analysis enables him to make some perceptive observations about the way in which the general prestige of localities varies with the locality within which the respondent happens to be living. One of his intriguing findings is that, regardless of the overall standing of a locality, the overall pattern of prestige does not differ too much.

In retrospect, it has been fascinating to me to see how my varied interests over a long research career have been picked up and developed by my students and associates in different ways. It would be difficult for me to say which particular research fields have provided me with most satisfaction. In the course of a varied research life one naturally moves from topic to topic, the topic at hand being dictated by the circumstances into which one is thrown by fate. What is interesting, however, is the way in which different students find ideas helpful to them and are able to seize upon them and take them to a new level. Long may it last.

Bibliography

Mitchell, J.C., *The Kalela Dance: Aspects of Social Relationships Among Urban Africans in Northern Rhodesia*, Rhodes-Livingstone Papers, no.27, Manchester: Manchester University Press, 1956

Werbner, P., *The Migration Process: Capital, Gifts and Offerings Among British Pakistanis*, Leamington Spa: Berg, 1990

Index

347